Y0-EMO-701

THE HARVARD CLASSICS

Registered Edition

Shakespeare and His Friends

From the painting in the Corcoran Gallery, Washington, D. C.

THE HARVARD CLASSICS
EDITED BY CHARLES W. ELIOT, LL.D.

Elizabethan Drama

Marlowe · Shakespeare

With Introductions and Notes

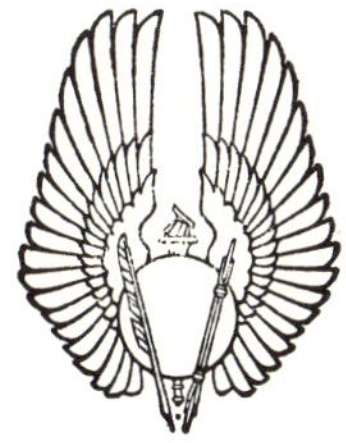

P. F. Collier & Son Corporation
NEW YORK

Manufactured in U. S. A.

CONTENTS

EDWARD THE SECOND

BY

CHRISTOPHER MARLOWE

INTRODUCTORY NOTE

A SKETCH of the life and work of Christopher Marlowe will be found prefixed to his play of "Doctor Faustus" in the volume of the Harvard Classics containing Goethe's "Faust."

The precise date of "Edward II" has not been determined, but it is generally and plausibly assigned to 1590–91. The historical basis for the plot Marlowe found in the Chronicles of Fabyan, Stow, and Holinshed, especially the last. In its treatment of the facts of history, this play is a typical example of the class of drama known as the "chronicle history," which flourished in the last two decades of the sixteenth century, and culminated in Shakespeare's "Henry IV" and "Henry V." While the order of events in history determines for the most part the succession of scenes, the author condenses, omits, elaborates, and re-arranges in order to gain dramatic effectiveness, and to bring out the character of Edward and the results of his weakness. Thus the action covers a historical period of some twenty-two years, though no such stretch of time is suggested by the play; the military operations in Ireland and Scotland, and especially the battle of Bannockburn, are antedated in order to connect them with Gaveston, who was, in fact, dead before any of them occurred; and the adherence of Spencer to the king is made to follow immediately, instead of several years, after the death of the earlier favorite.

Yet, with all this freedom in the handling of details, Marlowe succeeds in giving a substantially true, as well as a powerfully affecting, picture of the character and fate of Edward II. The play is the ripest and most masterly of Marlowe's productions, showing in the delineation of character, the construction of the plot and the freedom and variety of the verse, a striking advance over his earlier work. Nowhere else does he rival so closely his great successor, Shakespeare.

"The reluctant pangs of abdicating Royalty in Edward furnished hints which Shakespeare scarcely improved in his 'Richard the Second'; and the death-scene of Marlowe's King moves pity and terror beyond any scene, ancient or modern, with which I am acquainted."

CHARLES LAMB.

EDWARD THE SECOND

[DRAMATIS PERSONÆ

KING EDWARD THE SECOND.
PRINCE EDWARD, his Son, afterwards King Edward the Third.
EARL OF KENT, Brother to King Edward the Second.
GAVESTON.
ARCHBISHOP OF CANTERBURY.
BISHOP OF COVENTRY.
BISHOP OF WINCHESTER.
WARWICK.
LANCASTER.
PEMBROKE.
ARUNDEL.
LEICESTER.
BERKELEY.
MORTIMER, the elder.
MORTIMER, the younger, his Nephew.
SPENSER, the elder.
SPENSER, the younger, his Son.
BALDOCK.
BEAUMONT.
TRUSSEL.
GURNEY.
MATREVIS.
LIGHTBORN.
SIR JOHN OF HAINAULT.
LEVUNE.
RICE AP HOWEL.
Abbot, Monks, Herald, Lords, Poor Men, James, Mower, Champion, Messengers, Soldiers, and Attendants.

QUEEN ISABELLA, Wife to King Edward the Second.
Niece to King Edward the Second, daughter to the Duke of Gloucester.
Ladies.]

[ACT THE FIRST]

[SCENE I]

Enter GAVESTON, *reading on a letter that was brought him from the* KING

Gaveston.

"MY FATHER is deceas'd! Come, Gaveston,
And share the kingdom with thy dearest friend,"
Ah! words that make me surfeit with delight!
What greater bliss can hap to Gaveston
Than live and be the favourite of a king!
Sweet prince, I come; these, these thy amorous lines
Might have enforc'd me to have swum from France,
And, like Leander, gasp'd upon the sand,
So thou would'st smile, and take me in thine arms.
The sight of London to my exil'd eyes

Is as Elysium to a new-come soul;
Not that I love the city, or the men,
But that it harbours him I hold so dear—
The king, upon whose bosom let me die,[1]
And with the world be still at enmity.
What need the arctic people love starlight,
To whom the sun shines both by day and night?
Farewell base stooping to the lordly peers!
My knee shall bow to none but to the king.
As for the multitude, that are but sparks,
Rak'd up in embers of their poverty;—
Tanti;[2] I'll fawn first on the wind
That glanceth at my lips, and flieth away.

Enter three Poor Men

But how now, what are these?
Poor Men. Such as desire your worship's service.
Gav. What canst thou do?
1st P. Man. I can ride.
Gav. But I have no horses.—What art thou?
2nd P. Man. A traveller.
Gav. Let me see: thou would'st do well
To wait at my trencher and tell me lies at dinner time;
And as I like your discoursing, I'll have you.—
And what art thou?
3rd P. Man. A soldier, that hath serv'd against the Scot.
Gav. Why, there are hospitals for such as you.
I have no war, and therefore, sir, begone.
3rd P. Man. Farewell, and perish by a soldier's hand,
That would'st reward them with an hospital.
Gav. Ay, ay, these words of his move me as much
As if a goose should play the porcupine,
And dart her plumes, thinking to pierce my breast.
But yet it is no pain to speak men fair;
I'll flatter these, and make them live in hope.— [*Aside.*]
You know that I came lately out of France,

[1] Dyce emends to *lie*. *Die* may be used in the sense of "swoon." [2] So much for them.

And yet I have not view'd my lord the king;
If I speed well, I'll entertain you all.
All. We thank your worship.
Gav. I have some business: leave me to myself.
All. We will wait here about the court. *Exeunt.*
Gav. Do. These are not men for me:
I must have wanton poets, pleasant wits,
Musicians, that with touching of a string
May draw the pliant king which way I please.
Music and poetry is his delight;
Therefore I'll have Italian masks by night,
Sweet speeches, comedies, and pleasing shows;
And in the day, when he shall walk abroad,
Like sylvan nymphs my pages shall be clad;
My men, like satyrs grazing on the lawns,
Shall with their goat-feet dance an antic hay.[3]
Sometime a lovely boy in Dian's shape,
With hair that gilds the water as it glides,
Crownets of pearl about his naked arms,
And in his sportful hands an olive tree,
To hide those parts which men delight to see,
Shall bathe him in a spring; and there hard by,
One like Actæon peeping through the grove
Shall by the angry goddess be transform'd,
And running in the likeness of an hart
By yelping hounds pull'd down, and seem to die;—
Such things as these best please his majesty,
My lord.—Here comes the king, and the nobles
From the parliament. I'll stand aside. [*Retires.*]

Enter KING EDWARD, LANCASTER, *the* Elder MORTIMER, Young MORTIMER; EDMUND, EARL *of* KENT; GUY, EARL *of* WARWICK, *and* [Attendants]

K. Edw. Lancaster!
Lan. My lord.
Gav. That Earl of Lancaster do I abhor. [*Aside.*]

[3] A rural dance.

K. Edw. Will you not grant me this?—In spite of them
I'll have my will; and these two Mortimers,
That cross me thus, shall know I am displeas'd. [*Aside.*]
E. Mor. If you love us, my lord, hate Gaveston.
Gav. That villain Mortimer! I'll be his death. [*Aside.*]
Y. Mor. Mine uncle here, this earl, and I myself
Were sworn to your father at his death,
That he should ne'er return into the realm;
And know, my lord, ere I will break my oath,
This sword of mine, that should offend your foes,
Shall sleep within the scabbard at thy need,
And underneath thy banners march who will,
For Mortimer will hang his armour up.
Gav. Mort Dieu! [*Aside.*]
K. Edw. Well, Mortimer, I'll make thee rue these words.
Beseems it thee to contradict thy king?
Frown'st thou thereat, aspiring Lancaster?
The sword shall plane the furrows of thy brows,
And hew these knees that now are grown so stiff.
I will have Gaveston; and you shall know
What danger 'tis to stand against your king.
Gav. Well done, Ned! [*Aside.*]
Lan. My lord, why do you thus incense your peers,
That naturally would love and honour you
But for that base and obscure Gaveston?
Four earldoms have I, besides Lancaster—
Derby, Salisbury, Lincoln, Leicester,—
These will I sell, to give my soldiers pay,
Ere Gaveston shall stay within the realm;
Therefore, if he be come, expel him straight.
Kent. Barons and earls, your pride hath made me mute;
But now I'll speak, and to the proof, I hope.
I do remember, in my father's days,
Lord Percy of the north, being highly mov'd,
Braved Moubery[4] in presence of the king;
For which, had not his highness lov'd him well,

[4] Mowbray, but the Qto. spelling indicates the pronunciation.

He should have lost his head; but with his look
The undaunted spirit of Percy was appeas'd,
And Moubery and he were reconcil'd:
Yet dare you brave the king unto his face?—
Brother, revenge it, and let these their heads
Preach upon poles, for trespass of their tongues.
War. O, our heads!
K. Edw. Ay, yours; and therefore I would wish you grant—
War. Bridle thy anger, gentle Mortimer.
Y. Mor. I cannot, nor I will not; I must speak.—
Cousin, our hands I hope shall fence our heads,
And strike off his that makes you threaten us.
Come, uncle, let us leave the brain-sick king,
And henceforth parley with our naked swords.
E. Mor. Wiltshire hath men enough to save our heads.
War. All Warwickshire will love him for my sake.[5]
Lan. And northward Gaveston hath many friends.—
Adieu, my lord; and either change your mind,
Or look to see the throne, where you should sit,
To float in blood; and at thy wanton head,
The glozing[6] head of thy base minion thrown.
Exeunt [*all except* KING EDWARD, KENT, GAVESTON *and* Attendants]
K. Edw. I cannot brook these haughty menaces.
Am I a king, and must be overrul'd?—
Brother, display my ensigns in the field;
I'll bandy[7] with the barons and the earls,
And either die or live with Gaveston.
Gav. I can no longer keep me from my lord. [*Comes forward.*]
K. Edw. What, Gaveston! welcome!—Kiss not my hand—
Embrace me, Gaveston, as I do thee.
Why should'st thou kneel? Know'st thou not who I am?
Thy friend, thyself, another Gaveston!
Not Hylas was more mourn'd of Hercules,
Than thou hast been of me since thy exile.
Gav. And since I went from hence, no soul in hell

[5] This line and the next are ironical. [6] Flattering. [7] Contend.

Hath felt more torment than poor Gaveston.
K. Edw. I know it.—Brother, welcome home my friend.
Now let the treacherous Mortimers conspire,
And that high-minded Earl of Lancaster:
I have my wish, in that I joy thy sight;
And sooner shall the sea o'erwhelm my land,
Than bear the ship that shall transport thee hence.
I here create thee Lord High Chamberlain,
Chief Secretary to the state and me,
Earl of Cornwall, King and Lord of Man.
Gav. My lord, these titles far exceed my worth.
Kent. Brother, the least of these may well suffice
For one of greater birth than Gaveston.
K. Edw. Cease, brother, for I cannot brook these words.
Thy worth, sweet friend, is far above my gifts,
Therefore, to equal it, receive my heart.
If for these dignities thou be envied,
I'll give thee more; for, but to honour thee,
Is Edward pleas'd with kingly regiment.[8]
Fear'st[9] thou thy person? Thou shalt have a guard.
Wantest thou gold? Go to my treasury.
Wouldst thou be lov'd and fear'd? Receive my seal;
Save or condemn, and in our name command
Whatso thy mind affects, or fancy likes.
Gav. It shall suffice me to enjoy your love,
Which whiles I have, I think myself as great
As Cæsar riding in the Roman street,
With captive kings at his triumphant car.

Enter the Bishop *of* Coventry

K. Edw. Whither goes my lord of Coventry so fast?
B. of Cov. To celebrate your father's exequies.
But is that wicked Gaveston return'd?
K. Edw. Ay, priest, and lives to be reveng'd on thee,
That wert the only cause of his exile.
Gav. 'Tis true; and but for reverence of these robes,

[8] Rule. [9] Fear'st for.

Thou should'st not plod one foot beyond this place.
B. of Cov. I did no more than I was bound to do;
And, Gaveston, unless thou be reclaim'd,
As then I did incense the parliament,
So will I now, and thou shalt back to France.
Gav. Saving your reverence, you must pardon me.
K. Edw. Throw off his golden mitre, rend his stole,
And in the channel[10] christen him anew.
Kent. Ah, brother, lay not violent hands on him!
For he'll complain unto the see of Rome.
Gav. Let him complain unto the see of hell;
I'll be reveng'd on him for my exile.
K. Edw. No, spare his life, but seize upon his goods.
Be thou lord bishop and receive his rents,
And make him serve thee as thy chaplain.
I give him thee—here, use him as thou wilt.
Gav. He shall to prison, and there die in bolts.
K. Edw. Ay, to the Tower, the Fleet, or where thou wilt.
B. of Cov. For this offence, be thou accurst of God!
K. Edw. Who's there? Convey this priest to the Tower.
B. of Cov. True, true.[11]
K. Edw. But in the meantime, Gaveston, away,
And take possession of his house and goods.
Come, follow me, and thou shalt have my guard
To see it done, and bring thee safe again.
Gav. What should a priest do with so fair a house?
A prison may best beseem his holiness. [*Exeunt.*]

[SCENE II. *The scene is at Westminster*]

Enter [*on one side*] *both the* MORTIMERS; [*on the other,*] WARWICK *and* LANCASTER

War. 'Tis true, the bishop is in the Tower,
And goods and body given to Gaveston.
Lan. What! will they tyrannise upon the church?
Ah, wicked king! accursed Gaveston!

10 Gutter. 11 *I. e.,* You have used the true word 'Convey' (=steal).

This ground, which is corrupted with their steps,
Shall be their timeless[1] sepulchre or mine.

Y. Mor. Well, let that peevish Frenchman guard him sure;
Unless his breast be sword-proof he shall die.

E. Mor. How now! why droops the Earl of Lancaster?

Y. Mor. Wherefore is Guy of Warwick discontent?

Lan. That villain Gaveston is made an earl.

E. Mor. An earl!

War. Ay, and besides Lord Chamberlain of the realm,
And Secretary too, and Lord of Man.

E. Mor. We may not, nor we will not suffer this.

Y. Mor. Why post we not from hence to levy men?

Lan. "My Lord of Cornwall" now at every word!
And happy is the man whom he vouchsafes,
For vailing of his bonnet,[2] one good look.
Thus, arm in arm, the king and he doth march:
Nay more, the guard upon his lordship waits;
And all the court begins to flatter him.

War. Thus leaning on the shoulder of the king,
He nods and scorns and smiles at those that pass.

E. Mor. Doth no man take exceptions at the slave?

Lan. All stomach[3] him, but none dare speak a word.

Y. Mor. Ah, that bewrays their baseness, Lancaster!
Were all the earls and barons of my mind,
We'll hale him from the bosom of the king,
And at the court-gate hang the peasant up,
Who, swoln with venom of ambitious pride,
Will be the ruin of the realm and us.

Enter the [ARCH]BISHOP *of* CANTERBURY [*and an* Attendant]

War. Here comes my lord of Canterbury's grace.

Lan. His countenance bewrays[4] he is displeas'd.

A. of Cant. First were his sacred garments rent and torn,
Then laid they violent hands upon him; next
Himself imprisoned, and his goods asseiz'd:
This certify the Pope;—away, take horse. [*Exit* Attendant]

[1] Untimely. [2] Removing it as a mark of respect. [3] Feel resentment at. [4] Shows.

Lan. My lord, will you take arms against the king?
A. of Cant. What need I? God himself is up in arms,
When violence is offered to the church.
Y. Mor. Then will you join with us, that be his peers,
To banish or behead that Gaveston?
A. of Cant. What else, my lords? for it concerns me near;
The bishopric of Coventry is his.

Enter QUEEN [ISABELLA]

Y. Mor. Madam, whither walks your majesty so fast?
Q. Isab. Unto the forest, gentle Mortimer,
To live in grief and baleful discontent;
For now, my lord, the king regards me not,
But doats upon the love of Gaveston.
He claps his cheeks, and hangs about his neck,
Smiles in his face, and whispers in his ears;
And when I come he frowns, as who should say,
"Go whither thou wilt, seeing I have Gaveston."
E. Mor. Is it not strange that he is thus bewitch'd?
Y. Mor. Madam, return unto the court again.
That sly inveigling Frenchman we'll exile,
Or lose our lives; and yet, ere that day come,
The king shall lose his crown; for we have power,
And courage too, to be reveng'd at full.
Q. Isab. But yet lift not your swords against the king.
Lan. No; but we will lift Gaveston from hence.
War. And war must be the means, or he'll stay still.
Q. Isab. Then let him stay; for rather than my lord
Shall be oppress'd with civil mutinies,
I will endure a melancholy life,
And let him frolic with his minion.
A. of Cant. My lords, to ease all this, but hear me speak:—
We and the rest, that are his counsellors,
Will meet, and with a general consent
Confirm his banishment with our hands and seals.
Lan. What we confirm the king will frustrate.
Y. Mor. Then may we lawfully revolt from him.

War. But say, my lord, where shall this meeting be?
A. of Cant. At the New Temple.
Y. Mor. Content.
A. of Cant. And, in the meantime, I'll entreat you all
To cross to Lambeth, and there stay with me.
Lan. Come then, let's away.
Y. Mor. Madam, farewell!
Q. Isab. Farewell, sweet Mortimer; and, for my sake,
Forbear to levy arms against the king.
Y. Mor. Ay, if words will serve; if not, I must. [*Exeunt.*]

[SCENE III]

Enter GAVESTON *and* KENT

Gav. Edmund, the mighty Prince of Lancaster,
That hath more earldoms than an ass can bear,
And both the Mortimers, two goodly men,
With Guy of Warwick, that redoubted knight,
Are gone toward Lambeth—there let them remain! *Exeunt.*

[SCENE IV]

Enter [LANCASTER, WARWICK, PEMBROKE, *the* Elder MORTIMER, Young MORTIMER, *the* ARCHBISHOP *of* CANTERBURY *and* Attendants]

Lan. Here is the form of Gaveston's exile:
May it please your lordship to subscribe your name.
A. of Cant. Give me the paper.
[*He subscribes, as do the others after him.*]
Lan. Quick, quick, my lord; I long to write my name.
War. But I long more to see him banish'd hence.
Y. Mor. The name of Mortimer shall fright the king,
Unless he be declin'd from that base peasant.

Enter KING EDWARD, GAVESTON, [*and* KENT]

K. Edw. What, are you mov'd that Gaveston sits here?
It is our pleasure; we will have it so.

Lan. Your grace doth well to place him by your side,
For nowhere else the new earl is so safe.
E. Mor. What man of noble birth can brook this sight?
Quam male conveniunt![1]
See what a scornful look the peasant casts!
Pem. Can kingly lions fawn on creeping ants?
War. Ignoble vassal, that like Phaeton
Aspir'st unto the guidance of the sun!
Y. Mor. Their downfall is at hand, their forces down;
We will not thus be fac'd and over-peer'd.
K. Edw. Lay hands on that traitor Mortimer!
E. Mor. Lay hands on that traitor Gaveston!
Kent. Is this the duty that you owe your king?
War. We know our duties—let him know his peers.
K. Edw. Whither will you bear him? Stay, or ye shall die.
E. Mor. We are no traitors; therefore threaten not.
Gav. No, threaten not, my lord, but pay them home!
Were I a king——
Y. Mor. Thou villain, wherefore talk'st thou of a king,
That hardly art a gentleman by birth?
K. Edw. Were he a peasant, being my minion,
I'll make the proudest of you stoop to him.
Lan. My lord, you may not thus disparage us.—
Away, I say, with hateful Gaveston!
E. Mor. And with the Earl of Kent that favours him.
[Attendants *remove* Kent *and* Gaveston.]
K. Edw. Nay, then, lay violent hands upon your king.
Here, Mortimer, sit thou in Edward's throne;
Warwick and Lancaster, wear you my crown.
Was ever king thus over-rul'd as I?
Lan. Learn then to rule us better, and the realm.
Y. Mor. What we have done, our heart-blood shall maintain.
War. Think you that we can brook this upstart pride?
K. Edw. Anger and wrathful fury stops my speech.
A. of Cant. Why are you mov'd? Be patient, my lord,
And see what we your counsellors have done.

[1] How ill they agree!

Y. Mor. My lords, now let us all be resolute,
And either have our wills, or lose our lives.
K. Edw. Meet you for this, proud overbearing peers?
Ere my sweet Gaveston shall part from me,
This isle shall fleet[2] upon the ocean,
And wander to the unfrequented Inde.
A. of Cant. You know that I am legate to the Pope.
On your allegiance to the see of Rome,
Subscribe, as we have done, to his exile.
Y. Mor. Curse him, if he refuse; and then may we
Depose him and elect another king.
K. Edw. Ay, there it goes! but yet I will not yield.
Curse me, depose me, do the worst you can.
Lan. Then linger not, my lord, but do it straight.
A. of Cant. Remember how the bishop was abus'd!
Either banish him that was the cause thereof,
Or I will presently discharge these lords
Of duty and allegiance due to thee.
K. Edw. [*Aside.*] It boots me not to threat; I must speak fair.—
The legate of the Pope will be obey'd.
My lord, you shall be Chancellor of the realm;
Thou, Lancaster, High Admiral of our fleet;
Young Mortimer and his uncle shall be earls;
And you, Lord Warwick, President of the North;
And thou, of Wales. If this content you not,
Make several kingdoms of this monarchy,
And share it equally amongst you all,
So I may have some nook or corner left,
To frolic with my dearest Gaveston.
A. of Cant. Nothing shall alter us, we are resolv'd.
Lan. Come, come, subscribe.
Y. Mor. Why should you love him whom the world hates so?
K. Edw. Because he loves me more than all the world.
Ah, none but rude and savage-minded men
Would seek the ruin of my Gaveston;
You that be noble-born should pity him.

[2] Float.

War. You that are princely-born should shake him off.
For shame subscribe, and let the lown[3] depart.
E. Mor. Urge him, my lord.
A. of Cant. Are you content to banish him the realm?
K. Edw. I see I must, and therefore am content.
Instead of ink, I'll write it with my tears. [*Subscribes.*]
Y. Mor. The king is love-sick for his minion.
K. Edw. 'Tis done; and now, accursed hand, fall off!
Lan. Give it me; I'll have it publish'd in the streets.
Y. Mor. I'll see him presently despatch'd away.
A. of Cant. Now is my heart at ease.
War. And so is mine.
Pem. This will be good news to the common sort.
E. Mor. Be it or no, he shall not linger here.
Exeunt all except KING EDWARD.
K. Edw. How fast they run to banish him I love!
They would not stir, were it to do me good.
Why should a king be subject to a priest?
Proud Rome! that hatchest such imperial grooms,
For these thy superstitious taper-lights,
Wherewith thy antichristian churches blaze,
I'll fire thy crazed buildings, and enforce
The papal towers to kiss the lowly ground!
With slaughtered priests make Tiber's channel swell,
And banks rais'd higher with their sepulchres!
As for the peers, that back the clergy thus,
If I be king, not one of them shall live.

Re-enter GAVESTON

Gav. My lord, I hear it whispered everywhere,
That I am banish'd, and must fly the land.
K. Edw. 'Tis true, sweet Gaveston—O! were it false!
The legate of the Pope will have it so,
And thou must hence, or I shall be depos'd.
But I will reign to be reveng'd of them;
And therefore, sweet friend, take it patiently.

[3] Fellow.

Live where thou wilt, I'll send thee gold enough;
And long thou shalt not stay, or if thou dost,
I'll come to thee; my love shall ne'er decline.

Gav. Is all my hope turn'd to this hell of grief?

K. Edw. Rend not my heart with thy too-piercing words:
Thou from this land, I from myself am banish'd.

Gav. To go from hence grieves not poor Gaveston;
But to forsake you, in whose gracious looks
The blessedness of Gaveston remains,
For nowhere else seeks he felicity.

K. Edw. And only this torments my wretched soul
That, whether I will or no, thou must depart.
Be governor of Ireland in my stead,
And there abide till fortune call thee home.
Here take my picture, and let me wear thine;
[*They exchange pictures.*]
O, might I keep thee here as I do this,
Happy were I! but now most miserable!

Gav. 'Tis something to be pitied of a king.

K. Edw. Thou shalt not hence—I'll hide thee, Gaveston.

Gav. I shall be found, and then 'twill grieve me more.

K. Edw. Kind words and mutual talk makes our grief greater;
Therefore, with dumb embracement, let us part.—
Stay, Gaveston, I cannot leave thee thus.

Gav. For every look, my lord[4] drops down a tear.
Seeing I must go, do not renew my sorrow.

K. Edw. The time is little that thou hast to stay,
And, therefore, give me leave to look my fill.
But come, sweet friend, I'll bear thee on thy way.

Gav. The peers will frown.

K. Edw. I pass[5] not for their anger—Come, let's go;
O that we might as well return as go.

Enter EDMUND *and* QUEEN ISABELLA

Q. Isab. Whither goes my lord?

K. Edw. Fawn not on me, French strumpet! Get thee gone!

[4] Altered to "love" in Dodsley, &c. [5] Care.

Q. Isab. On whom but on my husband should I fawn?
Gav. On Mortimer! with whom, ungentle queen—
I say no more. Judge you the rest, my lord.
Q. Isab. In saying this, thou wrong'st me, Gaveston.
Is't not enough that thou corrupt'st my lord,
And art a bawd to his affections,
But thou must call mine honour thus in question?
Gav. I mean not so; your grace must pardon me.
K. Edw. Thou art too familiar with that Mortimer,
And by thy means is Gaveston exil'd;
But I would wish thee reconcile the lords,
Or thou shalt ne'er be reconcil'd to me.
Q. Isab. Your highness knows it lies not in my power.
K. Edw. Away then! touch me not.—Come, Gaveston.
Q. Isab. Villain! 'tis thou that robb'st me of my lord.
Gav. Madam, 'tis you that rob me of my lord.
K. Edw. Speak not unto her; let her droop and pine.
Q. Isab. Wherein, my lord, have I deserv'd these words?
Witness the tears that Isabella sheds,
Witness this heart, that, sighing for thee, breaks,
How dear my lord is to poor Isabel.
K. Edw. And witness Heaven how dear thou art to me!
There weep; for till my Gaveston be repeal'd,
Assure thyself thou com'st not in my sight.
Exeunt EDWARD *and* GAVESTON.
Q. Isab. O miserable and distressed queen!
Would, when I left sweet France and was embark'd,
That charming Circe, walking on the waves,
Had chang'd my shape, or at the marriage-day
The cup of Hymen had been full of poison,
Or with those arms that twin'd about my neck
I had been stifled, and not liv'd to see
The king my lord thus to abandon me!
Like frantic Juno will I fill the earth
With ghastly murmur of my sighs and cries;
For never doated Jove on Ganymede
So much as he on cursed Gaveston.

But that will more exasperate his wrath;
I must entreat him, I must speak him fair,
And be a means to call home Gaveston.
And yet he'll ever doat on Gaveston;
And so am I for ever miserable.

Re-enter LANCASTER, WARWICK, PEMBROKE, *the* Elder MORTIMER, *and* Young MORTIMER

Lan. Look where the sister of the King of France
Sits wringing of her hands, and beats her breast!
War. The king, I fear, hath ill-entreated her.
Pem. Hard is the heart that injures such a saint.
Y. *Mor.* I know 'tis 'long of Gaveston she weeps.
E. *Mor.* Why? He is gone.
Y. *Mor.* Madam, how fares your grace?
Q. Isab. Ah, Mortimer! now breaks the king's hate forth,
And he confesseth that he loves me not.
Y. *Mor.* Cry quittance, madam, then; and love not him.
Q. Isab. No, rather will I die a thousand deaths!
And yet I love in vain;—he'll ne'er love me.
Lan. Fear ye not, madam; now his minion's gone,
His wanton humour will be quickly left.
Q. Isab. O never, Lancaster! I am enjoin'd
To sue upon you all for his repeal;
This wills my lord, and this must I perform,
Or else be banish'd from his highness' presence.
Lan. For his repeal? Madam, he comes not back,
Unless the sea cast up his shipwreck'd body.
War. And to behold so sweet a sight as that,
There's none here but would run his horse to death.
Y. *Mor.* But, madam, would you have us call him home?
Q. Isab. Ay, Mortimer, for till he be restor'd,
The angry king hath banish'd me the court;
And, therefore, as thou lov'st and tend'rest me,
Be thou my advocate unto these peers.
Y. *Mor.* What! would you have me plead for Gaveston?
E. *Mor.* Plead for him he that will, I am resolv'd.

Lan. And so am I, my lord. Dissuade the queen.
Q. Isab. O Lancaster! let him dissuade the king,
For 'tis against my will he should return.
War. Then speak not for him, let the peasant go.
Q. Isab. 'Tis for myself I speak, and not for him.
Pem. No speaking will prevail, and therefore cease.
Y. *Mor.* Fair queen, forbear to angle for the fish
Which, being caught, strikes him that takes it dead;
I mean that vile torpedo, Gaveston,
That now, I hope, floats on the Irish seas.
Q. Isab. Sweet Mortimer, sit down by me awhile,
And I will tell thee reasons of such weight
As thou wilt soon subscribe to his repeal.
Y. *Mor.* It is impossible; but speak your mind.
Q. Isab. Then thus, but none shall hear it but ourselves.
[*Talks to* Young MORTIMER *apart.*]
Lan. My lords, albeit the queen win Mortimer,
Will you be resolute, and hold with me?
E. Mor. Not I, against my nephew.
Pem. Fear not, the queen's words cannot alter him.
War. No? Do but mark how earnestly she pleads!
Lan. And see how coldly his looks make denial!
War. She smiles; now for my life his mind is chang'd!
Lan. I'll rather lose his friendship, I, than grant.
Y. *Mor.* Well, of necessity it must be so.
My lords, that I abhor base Gaveston,
I hope your honours make no question,
And therefore, though I plead for his repeal,
'Tis not for his sake, but for our avail;
Nay for the realm's behoof, and for the king's.
Lan. Fie, Mortimer, dishonour not thyself!
Can this be true, 'twas good to banish him?
And is this true, to call him home again?
Such reasons make white black, and dark night day.
Y. *Mor.* My lord of Lancaster, mark the respect.[6]
Lan. In no respect can contraries be true.

[6] Consideration.

Q. Isab. Yet, good my lord, hear what he can allege.
War. All that he speaks is nothing; we are resolv'd.
Y. Mor. Do you not wish that Gaveston were dead?
Pem. I would he were!
Y. Mor. Why, then, my lord, give me but leave to speak.
E. Mor. But, nephew, do not play the sophister.
Y. Mor. This which I urge is of a burning zeal
To mend the king, and do our country good.
Know you not Gaveston hath store of gold,
Which may in Ireland purchase him such friends
As he will front the mightest of us all?
And whereas he shall live and be belov'd,
'Tis hard for us to work his overthrow.
War. Mark you but that, my lord of Lancaster.
Y. Mor. But were he here, detested as he is,
How easily might some base slave be suborn'd
To greet his lordship with a poniard,
And none so much as blame the murderer,
But rather praise him for that brave attempt,
And in the chronicle enrol his name
For purging of the realm of such a plague!
Pem. He saith true.
Lan. Ay, but how chance this was not done before?
Y. Mor. Because, my lords, it was not thought upon.
Nay, more, when he shall know it lies in us
To banish him, and then to call him home,
'Twill make him vail[7] the top-flag of his pride,
And fear to offend the meanest nobleman.
E. Mor. But how if he do not, nephew?
Y. Mor. Then may we with some colour rise in arms;
For howsoever we have borne it out,
'Tis treason to be up against the king.
So we shall have the people of our side,
Which for his father's sake lean to the king,
But cannot brook a night-grown mushroom,
Such a one as my lord of Cornwall is,

[7] Lower.

Should bear us down of the nobility.
And when the commons and the nobles join,
'Tis not the king can buckler Gaveston;
We'll pull him from the strongest hold he hath.
My lords, if to perform this I be slack,
Think me as base a groom as Gaveston.
Lan. On that condition, Lancaster will grant.
War. And so will Pembroke and I.
E. Mor. And I.
Y. Mor. In this I count me highly gratified,
And Mortimer will rest at your command.
Q. Isab. And when this favour Isabel forgets,
Then let her live abandon'd and forlorn.—
But see, in happy time, my lord the king,
Having brought the Earl of Cornwall on his way,
Is new return'd. This news will glad him much,
Yet not so much as me. I love him more
Than he can Gaveston; would he lov'd me
But half so much, then were I treble-bless'd

Re-enter King Edward, *mourning*

K. Edw. He's gone, and for his absence thus I mourn.
Did never sorrow go so near my heart
As doth the want of my sweet Gaveston;
And could my crown's revenue bring him back,
I would freely give it to his enemies,
And think I gain'd, having bought so dear a friend.
Q. Isab. Hark! how he harps upon his minion.
K. Edw. My heart is as an anvil unto sorrow,
Which beats upon it like the Cyclops' hammers,
And with the noise turns up my giddy brain,
And makes me frantic for my Gaveston.
Ah! had some bloodless Fury rose from hell,
And with my kingly sceptre struck me dead,
When I was forc'd to leave my Gaveston!
Lan. Diablo! What passions call you these?
Q. Isab. My gracious lord, I come to bring you news.

K. Edw. That you have parley'd with your Mortimer!
Q. Isab. That Gaveston, my lord, shall be repeal'd.
K. Edw. Repeal'd! The news is too sweet to be true?
Q. Isab. But will you love me, if you find it so?
K. Edw. If it be so, what will not Edward do?
Q. Isab. For Gaveston, but not for Isabel.
K. Edw. For thee, fair queen, if thou lov'st Gaveston.
I'll hang a golden tongue about thy neck,
Seeing thou hast pleaded with so good success.
Q. Isab. No other jewels hang about my neck
Than these, my lord; nor let me have more wealth
Than I may fetch from this rich treasury.
O how a kiss revives poor Isabel!
K. Edw. Once more receive my hand; and let this be
A second marriage 'twixt thyself and me.
Q. Isab. And may it prove more happy than the first!
My gentle lord, bespeak these nobles fair,
That wait attendance for a gracious look,
And on their knees salute your majesty.
K. Edw. Courageous Lancaster, embrace thy king!
And, as gross vapours perish by the sun,
Even so let hatred with thy sovereign's smile.
Live thou with me as my companion.
Lan. This salutation overjoys my heart.
K. Edw. Warwick shall be my chiefest counsellor:
These silver hairs will more adorn my court
Than gaudy silks, or rich embroidery.
Chide me, sweet Warwick, if I go astray.
War. Slay me, my lord, when I offend your grace.
K. Edw. In solemn triumphs, and in public shows,
Pembroke shall bear the sword before the king.
Pem. And with this sword Pembroke will fight for you.
K. Edw. But wherefore walks young Mortimer aside?
Be thou commander of our royal fleet;
Or, if that lofty office like thee not,
I make thee here Lord Marshal of the realm.
Y. Mor. My lord, I'll marshal so your enemies,

As England shall be quiet, and you safe.
K. Edw. And as for you, Lord Mortimer of Chirke,
Whose great achievements in our foreign war
Deserves no common place nor mean reward,
Be you the general of the levied troops,
That now are ready to assail the Scots.
E. Mor. In this your grace hath highly honoured me,
For with my nature war doth best agree.
Q. Isab. Now is the King of England rich and strong,
Having the love of his renowned peers.
K. Edw. Ay, Isabel, ne'er was my heart so light.
Clerk of the crown, direct our warrant forth
For Gaveston to Ireland:

[*Enter* BEAUMONT *with warrant.*]

Beaumont, fly
As fast as Iris or Jove's Mercury.
Bea. It shall be done, my gracious lord. [*Exit.*]
K. Edw. Lord Mortimer, we leave you to your charge.
Now let us in, and feast it royally.
Against our friend the Earl of Cornwall comes,
We'll have a general tilt and tournament;
And then his marriage shall be solemnis'd.
For wot you not that I have made him sure[8]
Unto our cousin, the Earl of Gloucester's heir?
Lan. Such news we hear, my lord.
K. Edw. That day, if not for him, yet for my sake,
Who in the triumph will be challenger,
Spare for no cost; we will requit your love.
War. In this, or aught, your highness shall command us.
K. Edw. Thanks, gentle Warwick: come, let's in and revel.
Exeunt all except the MORTIMERS.
E. Mor. Nephew, I must to Scotland; thou stayest here.
Leave now t'oppose thyself against the king.
Thou seest by nature he is mild and calm,
And, seeing his mind so doats on Gaveston,

[8] Affianced him.

Let him without controlment have his will.
The mightiest kings have had their minions:
Great Alexander loved Hephestion;
The conquering Hercules[9] for Hylas wept;
And for Patroclus stern Achilles drooped
And not kings only, but the wisest men:
The Roman Tully lov'd Octavius;
Grave Socrates, wild Alcibiades.
Then let his grace, whose youth is flexible,
And promiseth as much as we can wish,
Freely enjoy that vain, light-headed earl;
For riper years will wean him from such toys.
Y. Mor. Uncle, his wanton humour grieves not me;
But this I scorn, that one so basely born
Should by his sovereign's favour grow so pert,
And riot it with the treasure of the realm.
While soldiers mutiny for want of pay,
He wears a lord's revenue on his back,
And Midas-like, he jets[10] it in the court,
With base outlandish cullions[11] at his heels,
Whose proud fantastic liveries make such show
As if that Proteus, god of shapes, appear'd.
I have not seen a dapper Jack so brisk;
He wears a short Italian hooded cloak
Larded with pearl, and, in his Tuscan cap,
A jewel of more value than the crown.
While others walk below, the king and he
From out a window laugh at such as we,
And flout our train, and jest at our attire.
Uncle, 'tis this that makes me impatient.
E. Mor. But, nephew, now you see the king is chang'd.
Y. Mor. Then so am I, and live to do him service:
But whiles I have a sword, a hand, a heart,
I will not yield to any such upstart.
You know my mind; come, uncle, let's away. *Exeunt.*

[9] Qq. *Hector*. [10] Struts. [11] Scoundrels.

'Tis not a black coat and a little band,
A velvet-cap'd coat, fac'd before with serge,
And smelling to a nosegay all the day,
Or holding of a napkin in your hand,
Or saying a long grace at a table's end,
Or making low legs[1] to a nobleman,
Or looking downward with your eyelids close,
And saying, "Truly, an't[2] may please your honour,"
Can get you any favour with great men;
You must be proud, bold, pleasant, resolute,
And now and then stab, as occasion serves.

Bald. Spencer, thou know'st I hate such formal toys,
And use them but of mere hypocrisy.
Mine old lord whiles he liv'd was so precise,
That he would take exceptions at my buttons,
And being like pin's heads, blame me for the bigness;
Which made me curate-like in mine attire,
Though inwardly licentious enough
And apt for any kind of villainy.
I am none of these common pedants, I,
That cannot speak without *propterea quod.*[3]

Y. Spen. But one of those that saith *quandoquidem,*[4]
And hath a special gift to form a verb.

Bald. Leave off this jesting, here my lady comes.

Enter the Lady [KING EDWARD'S NIECE.]

Niece. The grief for his exile was not so much
As is the joy of his returning home.
This letter came from my sweet Gaveston:—
What need'st thou, love, thus to excuse thyself?
I know thou could'st not come and visit me.
[*Reads.*] "I will not long be from thee, though I die."
This argues the entire love of my lord;
[*Reads.*] "When I forsake thee, death seize on my heart:"
But stay thee here where Gaveston shall sleep.
[*Puts the letter into her bosom.*]

[1] Bows. [2] If it. [3] Lat. *because.* [4] Lat. *since.*

[ACT THE SECOND]

[Scene I. *Gloucester's house*]

Enter Young Spencer *and* Baldock

Bald. Spencer,
Seeing that our lord the Earl of Gloucester's dead,
Which of the nobles dost thou mean to serve?
Y. Spen. Not Mortimer, nor any of his side,
Because the king and he are enemies.
Baldock, learn this of me, a factious lord
Shall hardly do himself good, much less us;
But he that hath the favour of a king,
May with one word advance us while we live.
The liberal Earl of Cornwall is the man
On whose good fortune Spencer's hopes depends.
Bald. What, mean you then to be his follower?
Y. Spen. No, his companion; for he loves me well,
And would have once preferr'd me to the king.
Bald. But he is banish'd; there's small hope of him.
Y. Spen. Ay, for a while; but, Baldock, mark the end.
A friend of mine told me in secrecy
That he's repeal'd, and sent for back again;
And even now a post came from the court
With letters to our lady from the king;
And as she read she smil'd, which makes me think
It is about her lover Gaveston.
Bald. 'Tis like enough; for since he was exil'd
She neither walks abroad, nor comes in sight.
But I had thought the match had been broke off,
And that his banishment had chang'd her mind.
Y. Spen. Our lady's first love is not wavering;
My life for thine, she will have Gaveston.
Bald. Then hope I by her means to be preferr'd,
Having read unto her since she was a child.
Y. Spen. Then, Baldock, you must cast the scholar off,
And learn to court it like a gentleman.

Now to the letter of my lord the king.—
He wills me to repair unto the court,
And meet my Gaveston? Why do I stay,
Seeing that he talks thus of my marriage-day?
Who's there? Baldock!
See that my coach be ready, I must hence.
Bald. It shall be done, madam.
Niece. And meet me at the park-pale presently. *Exit* BALDOCK.
Spencer, stay you and bear me company,
For I have joyful news to tell thee of.
My lord of Cornwall is a-coming over,
And will be at the court as soon as we.
Y. Spen. I knew the king would have him home again.
Niece. If all things sort[5] out as I hope they will,
Thy service, Spencer, shall be thought upon.
Y. Spen. I humbly thank your ladyship.
Niece. Come, lead the way; I long till I am there. [*Exeunt.*]

[SCENE II]

Enter KING EDWARD, QUEEN ISABELLA, KENT, LANCASTER, Young MORTIMER, WARWICK, PEMBROKE, *and* Attendants

K. Edw. The wind is good, I wonder why he stays;
I fear me he is wrack'd upon the sea.
Q. Isab. Look, Lancaster, how passionate[1] he is,
And still his mind runs on his minion!
Lan. My lord,—
K. Edw. How now! what news? Is Gaveston arriv'd?
Y. Mor. Nothing but Gaveston!—What means your grace?
You have matters of more weight to think upon;
The King of France sets foot in Normandy.
K. Edw. A trifle! we'll expel him when we please.
But tell me, Mortimer, what's thy device
Against the stately triumph we decreed?
Y. Mor. A homely one, my lord, not worth the telling.
K. Edw. Pray thee let me know it.

[5] Turn. [1] Sorrowful.

Y. Mor. But, seeing you are so desirous, thus it is:
A lofty cedar-tree, fair flourishing,
On whose top-branches kingly eagles perch,
And by the bark a canker[2] creeps me up,
And gets into the highest bough of all:
The motto, *Æque tandem.*[3]
K. Edw. And what is yours, my lord of Lancaster?
Lan. My lord, mine's more obscure than Mortimer's.
Pliny reports there is a flying fish
Which all the other fishes deadly hate,
And therefore, being pursued, it takes the air:
No sooner is it up, but there's a fowl
That seizeth it; this fish, my lord, I bear:
The motto this: *Undique mors est.*[4]
K. Edw. Proud Mortimer! ungentle Lancaster!
Is this the love you bear your sovereign?
Is this the fruit your reconcilement bears?
Can you in words make show of amity,
And in your shields display your rancorous minds!
What call you this but private libelling
Against the Earl of Cornwall and my brother?
Q. Isab. Sweet husband, be content, they all love you.
K. Edw. They love me not that hate my Gaveston.
I am that cedar, shake me not too much;
And you the eagles; soar ye ne'er so high,
I have the jesses[5] that will pull you down;
And *Æque tandem* shall that canker cry
Unto the proudest peer of Britainy.
Though thou compar'st him to a flying fish,
And threatenest death whether he rise or fall,
'Tis not the hugest monster of the sea,
Nor foulest harpy that shall swallow him.
Y. Mor. If in his absence thus he favours him,
What will he do whenas he shall be present?
Lan. That shall we see; look where his lordship comes.

[2] Canker-worn. [3] Lat. *Justly at length.* [4] Lat. *On all sides is death.*
[5] The straps round a hawk's legs, to which the falconer's leash was fastened.

Enter GAVESTON

K. Edw. My Gaveston!
Welcome to Tynemouth! Welcome to thy friend!
Thy absence made me droop and pine away;
For, as the lovers of fair Danae,
When she was lock'd up in a brazen tower,
Desired her more, and wax'd outrageous,
So did it fare[6] with me; and now thy sight
Is sweeter far than was thy parting hence
Bitter and irksome to my sobbing heart.
Gav. Sweet lord and king, your speech preventeth[7] mine,
Yet have I words left to express my joy:
The shepherd nipt with biting winter's rage
Frolics not more to see the painted spring,
Than I do to behold your majesty.
K. Edw. Will none of you salute my Gaveston?
Lan. Salute him? yes. Welcome, Lord Chamberlain!
Y. Mor. Welcome is the good Earl of Cornwall!
War. Welcome, Lord Governor of the Isle of Man!
Pem. Welcome, Master Secretary!
Kent. Brother, do you hear them?
K. Edw. Still will these earls and barons use me thus.
Gav. My lord, I cannot brook these injuries.
Q. Isab. Aye me, poor soul, when these begin to jar. [*Aside.*]
K. Edw. Return it to their throats, I'll be thy warrant.
Gav. Base, leaden earls, that glory in your birth,
Go sit at home and eat your tenants' beef;
And come not here to scoff at Gaveston,
Whose mounting thoughts did never creep so low
As to bestow a look on such as you.
Lan. Yet I disdain not to do this for you.
[*Draws his sword and offers to stab* GAVESTON.]
K. Edw. Treason! treason! where's the traitor?
Pem. Here! here!
K. Edw. Convey hence Gaveston; they'll murder him.

[6] Qq. 1594–1612, *sure*. [7] Anticipateth.

Gav. The life of thee shall salve this foul disgrace.
Y. Mor. Villain! thy life, unless I miss mine aim.
[*Wounds* GAVESTON.]
Q. Isab. Ah! furious Mortimer, what hast thou done?
Y. Mor. No more than I would answer, were he slain.
[*Exit* GAVESTON *with* Attendants.]
K. Edw. Yes, more than thou canst answer, though he live.
Dear shall you both abye[8] this riotous deed.
Out of my presence! Come not near the court.
Y. Mor. I'll not be barr'd the court for Gaveston.
Lan. We'll hale him by the ears unto the block.
K. Edw. Look to your own heads; his is sure enough.
War. Look to your own crown, if you back him thus.
Kent. Warwick, these words do ill beseem thy years.
K. Edw. Nay, all of them conspire to cross me thus;
But if I live, I'll tread upon their heads
That think with high looks thus to tread me down.
Come, Edmund, let's away and levy men,
'Tis war that must abate these barons' pride.
Exeunt KING EDWARD, [QUEEN ISABELLA *and* KENT.]
War. Let's to our castles, for the king is mov'd.
Y. Mor. Mov'd may he be, and perish in his wrath!
Lan. Cousin, it is no dealing with him now,
He means to make us stoop by force of arms;
And therefore let us jointly here protest,
To persecute that Gaveston to the death.
Y. Mor. By heaven, the abject villain shall not live!
War. I'll have his blood, or die in seeking it.
Pem. The like oath Pembroke takes.
Lan. And so doth Lancaster.
Now send our heralds to defy the king;
And make the people swear to put him down.

[*Enter a* Messenger]

Y. Mor. Letters! From whence?
Mess. From Scotland, my lord. [*Giving letters to* MORTIMER.]

[8] Pay for.

Lan. Why, how now, cousin, how fares all our friends?
Y. Mor. My uncle's taken prisoner by the Scots.
Lan. We'll have him ransom'd, man; be of good cheer.
Y. Mor. They rate his ransom at five thousand pound.
Who should defray the money but the king,
Seeing he is taken prisoner in his wars?
I'll to the king.
Lan. Do, cousin, and I'll bear thee company.
War. Meantime, my lord of Pembroke and myself
Will to Newcastle here, and gather head.[9]
Y. Mor. About it then, and we will follow you.
Lan. Be resolute and full of secrecy.
War. I warrant you. [*Exit with* PEMBROKE.]
Y. Mor. Cousin, and if he will not ransom him,
I'll thunder such a peal into his ears,
As never subject did unto his king.
Lan. Content, I'll bear my part—Holla! who's there?

[*Enter* Guard]

Y. Mor. Ay, marry, such a guard as this doth well.
Lan. Lead on the way.
Guard. Whither will your lordships?
Y. Mor. Whither else but to the king.
Guard. His highness is dispos'd to be alone.
Lan. Why, so he may, but we will speak to him.
Guard. You may not in, my lord.
Y. Mor. May we not?

[*Enter* KING EDWARD *and* KENT]

K. Edw. How now!
What noise is this? Who have we there? Is't you? [*Going.*]
Y. Mor. Nay, stay, my lord, I come to bring you news;
Mine uncle's taken prisoner by the Scots.
K. Edw. Then ransom him.
Lan. 'Twas in your wars; you should ransom him.
Y. Mor. And you shall ransom him, or else——

[9] An army.

Kent. What! Mortimer, you will not threaten him?
K. Edw. Quiet yourself, you shall have the broad seal,
To gather for him throughout the realm.
Lan. Your minion Gaveston hath taught you this.
Y. Mor. My lord, the family of the Mortimers
Are not so poor, but, would they sell their land,
'Twould levy men enough to anger you.
We never beg, but use such prayers as these.
K. Edw. Shall I still be haunted thus?
Y. Mor. Nay, now you're here alone, I'll speak my mind.
Lan. And so will I, and then, my lord, farewell.
Y. Mor. The idle triumphs, masks, lascivious shows,
And prodigal gifts bestow'd on Gaveston,
Have drawn thy treasury dry, and made thee weak;
The murmuring commons, overstretched, break.
Lan. Look for rebellion, look to be depos'd.
Thy garrisons are beaten out of France,
And, lame and poor, lie groaning at the gates.
The wild O'Neill, with swarms of Irish kerns,[10]
Lives uncontroll'd within the English pale.
Unto the walls of York the Scots made road,[11]
And unresisted drave away rich spoils.
Y. Mor. The haughty Dane commands the narrow seas,
While in the harbour ride thy ships unrigg'd.
Lan. What foreign prince sends thee ambassadors?
Y. Mor. Who loves thee, but a sort[12] of flatterers?
Lan. Thy gentle queen, sole sister to Valois,
Complains that thou hast left her all forlorn.
Y. Mor. Thy court is naked, being bereft of those
That make a king seem glorious to the world;
I mean the peers, whom thou should'st dearly love.
Libels are cast again thee in the street;
Ballads and rhymes made of thy overthrow.
Lan. The Northern borderers seeing their houses burnt,
Their wives and children slain, run up and down,
Cursing the name of thee and Gaveston.

[10] Foot soldiers. [11] Inroad. [12] Band.

Y. Mor. When wert thou in the field with banner spread,
But once? and then thy soldiers marched like players,
With garish robes, not armour; and thyself,
Bedaub'd with gold, rode laughing at the rest,
Nodding and shaking of thy spangled crest,
Where women's favours hung like labels down.
Lan. And therefore came it, that the fleering[13] Scots,
To England's high disgrace, have made this jig;
"Maids of England, sore may you mourn,—
For your lemans[14] you have lost at Bannocksbourn,—[15]
With a heave and a ho!
What weeneth the King of England,
So soon to have won Scotland?—
With a rombelow!"
Y. Mor. Wigmore[16] shall fly, to set my uncle free.
Lan. And when 'tis gone, our swords shall purchase more.
If ye be mov'd, revenge it as you can;
Look next to see us with our ensigns spread.
Exit with Young MORTIMER
K. Edw. My swelling heart for very anger breaks!
How oft have I been baited by these peers,
And dare not be reveng'd, for their power is great!
Yet, shall the crowing of these cockerels
Affright a lion? Edward, unfold thy paws,
And let their lives' blood slake thy fury's hunger.
If I be cruel and grow tyrannous,
Now let them thank themselves, and rue too late.
Kent. My lord, I see your love to Gaveston
Will be the ruin of the realm and you,
For now the wrathful nobles threaten wars,
And therefore, brother, banish him for ever.
K. Edw. Art thou an enemy to my Gaveston?
Kent. Ay, and it grieves me that I favoured him.
K. Edw. Traitor, begone! whine thou with Mortimer.
Kent. So will I, rather than with Gaveston.

[13] Jeering. [14] Lovers.
[15] Bannockburn was not yet fought. The rhyme is taken from the Chronicles.
[16] Young Mortimer's estate.

K. Edw. Out of my sight, and trouble me no more!
Kent. No marvel though thou scorn thy noble peers,
When I thy brother am rejected thus.
K. Edw. Away! *Exit* KENT.
Poor Gaveston, that has no friend but me,
Do what they can, we'll live in Tynemouth here,
And, so I walk with him about the walls,
What care I though the earls begirt us round?—
Here comes she that is cause of all these jars.

Enter QUEEN ISABELLA *with* [KING EDWARD'S Niece, *two*] Ladies, [GAVESTON,] BALDOCK *and* Young SPENCER

Q. Isab. My lord, 'tis thought the earls are up in arms.
K. Edw. Ay, and 'tis likewise thought you favour 'em.
Q. Isab. Thus do you still suspect me without cause?
Niece. Sweet uncle! speak more kindly to the queen.
Gav. My lord, dissemble with her, speak her fair.
K. Edw. Pardon me, sweet, I forgot myself.
Q. Isab. Your pardon is quickly got of Isabel.
K. Edw. The younger Mortimer is grown so brave,
That to my face he threatens civil wars.
Gav. Why do you not commit him to the Tower?
K. Edw. I dare not, for the people love him well.
Gav. Why, then we'll have him privily made away.
K. Edw. Would Lancaster and he had both carous'd
A bowl of poison to each other's health!
But let them go, and tell me what are these?
Niece. Two of my father's servants whilst he liv'd,—
May'st please your grace to entertain them now.
K. Edw. Tell me, where wast thou born? What is thine arms?
Bald. My name is Baldock, and my gentry
I fetch from Oxford, not from heraldry.
K. Edw. The fitter art thou, Baldock, for my turn.
Wait on me, and I'll see thou shalt not want.
Bald. I humbly thank your majesty.
K. Edw. Knowest thou him, Gaveston?

Gav. Ay, my lord;
His name is Spencer, he is well allied;
For my sake, let him wait upon your grace;
Scarce shall you find a man of more desert.
K. Edw. Then, Spencer, wait upon me; for his sake
I'll grace thee with a higher style ere long.
Y. Spen. No greater titles happen unto me,
Than to be favoured of your majesty!
K. Edw. Cousin, this day shall be your marriage-feast.
And, Gaveston, think that I love thee well,
To wed thee to our niece, the only heir
Unto the Earl of Gloucester late deceas'd.
Gav. I know, my lord, many will stomach[17] me,
But I respect neither their love nor hate.
K. Edw. The headstrong barons shall not limit me;
He that I list to favour shall be great.
Come, let's away; and when the marriage ends,
Have at the rebels, and their 'complices! *Exeunt.*

[SCENE III. *Near Tynemouth Castle*]

Enter KENT, LANCASTER, Young MORTIMER, WARWICK, PEMBROKE, *and others*

Kent. My lords, of love to this our native land
I come to join with you and leave the king;
And in your quarrel and the realm's behoof
Will be the first that shall adventure life.
Lan. I fear me, you are sent of policy,
To undermine us with a show of love.
War. He is your brother, therefore have we cause
To cast[1] the worst, and doubt of your revolt.
Kent. Mine honour shall be hostage of my truth;
If that will not suffice, farewell, my lords.
Y. Mor. Stay, Edmund; never was Plantagenet
False to his word, and therefore trust we thee.
Pem. But what's the reason you should leave him now?

[17] Feel resentment at. [1] Suspect.

Kent. I have inform'd the Earl of Lancaster.
Lan. And it sufficeth. Now, my lords, know this,
That Gaveston is secretly arriv'd,
And here in Tynemouth frolics with the king.
Let us with these our followers scale the walls,
And suddenly surprise them unawares.
Y. Mor. I'll give the onset.
War. And I'll follow thee.
Y. Mor. This tottered[2] ensign of my ancestors
Which swept the desert shore of that dead sea
Whereof we got the name of Mortimer,
Will I advance upon these castle-walls.
Drums, strike alarum, raise them from their sport,
And ring aloud the knell of Gaveston!
Lan. None be so hardy as to touch the king;
But neither spare you Gaveston nor his friends. *Exeunt.*

[SCENE IV. *Near Tynemouth Castle*]

Enter KING EDWARD *and* Young SPENCER

K. Edw. O tell me, Spencer, where is Gaveston?
Spen. I fear he is slain, my gracious lord.
K. Edw. No, here he comes; now let them spoil and kill.

[*Enter* QUEEN ISABELLA, KING EDWARD'S Niece, GAVESTON, *and* Nobles]

Fly, fly, my lords, the earls have got the hold;
Take shipping and away to Scarborough;
Spencer and I will post away by land.
Gav. O stay, my lord, they will not injure you.
K. Edw. I will not trust them; Gaveston, away!
Gav. Farewell, my lord.
K. Edw. Lady, farewell.
Niece. Farewell, sweet uncle, till we meet again.
K. Edw. Farewell, sweet Gaveston; and farewell, niece.
Q. Isab. No farewell to poor Isabel thy queen?

[2] Tattered.

K. Edw. Yes, yes, for Mortimer, your lover's sake.

Exeunt all but QUEEN ISABELLA.

Q. Isab. Heavens can witness I love none but you:
From my embracements thus he breaks away.
O that mine arms could close this isle about,
That I might pull him to me where I would!
Or that these tears that drizzle from mine eyes
Had power to mollify his stony heart,
That when I had him we might never part.

Enter LANCASTER, WARWICK, Young MORTIMER, *and others. Alarums*

Lan. I wonder how he scap'd!
Y. Mor. Who's this? The queen!
Q. Isab. Ay, Mortimer, the miserable queen,
Whose pining heart her inward sighs have blasted,
And body with continual mourning wasted:
These hands are tir'd with haling of my lord
From Gaveston, from wicked Gaveston,
And all in vain; for, when I speak him fair,
He turns away, and smiles upon his minion.
Y. Mor. Cease to lament, and tell us where's the king?
Q. Isab. What would you with the king? Is't him you seek?
Lan. No, madam, but that cursed Gaveston.
Far be it from the thought of Lancaster
To offer violence to his sovereign.
We would but rid the realm of Gaveston:
Tell us where he remains, and he shall die.
Q. Isab. He's gone by water unto Scarborough;
Pursue him quickly, and he cannot 'scape;
The king hath left him, and his train is small.
War. Foreslow[1] no time, sweet Lancaster; let's march.
Y. Mor. How comes it that the king and he is parted?
Q. Isab. That thus your army, going several ways,
Might be of lesser force; and with the power
That he intendeth presently[2] to raise,
Be easily suppress'd; therefore be gone.

[1] Delay. [2] Immediately.

Y. Mor. Here in the river rides a Flemish hoy;
Let's all aboard, and follow him amain.
Lan. The wind that bears him hence will fill our sails:
Come, come aboard, 'tis but an hour's sailing.
Y. Mor. Madam, stay you within this castle here.
Q. Isab. No, Mortimer, I'll to my lord the king.
Y. Mor. Nay, rather sail with us to Scarborough.
Q. Isab. You know the king is so suspicious,
As if he hear I have but talk'd with you,
Mine honour will be call'd in question;
And therefore, gentle Mortimer, be gone.
Y. Mor. Madam, I cannot stay to answer you,
But think of Mortimer as he deserves.
[*Exeunt all except* QUEEN ISABELLA.]
Q. Isab. So well hast thou deserv'd sweet Mortimer,
As Isabel could live with thee for ever!
In vain I look for love at Edward's hand,
Whose eyes are fix'd on none but Gaveston;
Yet once more I'll importune him with prayers.
If he be strange and not regard my words,
My son and I will over into France,
And to the king my brother there complain,
How Gaveston hath robb'd me of his love:
But yet I hope my sorrows will have end,
And Gaveston this blessed day be slain. *Exit.*

[SCENE V]

Enter GAVESTON, *pursued*

Gav. Yet, lusty lords, I have escap'd your hands,
Your threats, your 'larums, and your hot pursuits;
And though divorced from King Edward's eyes,
Yet liveth Pierce of Gaveston unsurpris'd,[1]
Breathing, in hope (*malgrado*[2] all your beards,
That muster rebels thus against your king),
To see his royal sovereign once again.

[1] Uncaptured. [2] Ital. *in spite of.*

Enter [WARWICK, LANCASTER, PEMBROKE, Young MORTIMER, Soldiers, JAMES, *and other* Attendants of PEMBROKE]

War. Upon him, soldiers, take away his weapons.
Y. Mor. Thou proud disturber of thy country's peace,
Corrupter of thy king, cause of these broils,
Base flatterer, yield! and were it not for shame,
Shame and dishonour to a soldier's name,
Upon my weapon's point here should'st thou fall,
And welter in thy gore.
Lan. Monster of men!
That, like the Greekish strumpet,[3] train'd[4] to arms
And bloody wars so many valiant knights;
Look for no other fortune, wretch, than death!
King Edward is not here to buckler thee.
War. Lancaster, why talk'st thou to the slave?
Go, soldiers, take him hence, for, by my sword,
His head shall off. Gaveston, short warning
Shall serve thy turn; it is our country's cause
That here severely we will execute
Upon thy person. Hang him at a bough.
Gav. My lord!—
War. Soldiers, have him away;—
But for thou wert the favourite of a king,
Thou shalt have so much honour at our hands—
Gav. I thank you all, my lords: then I perceive,
That heading is one, and hanging is the other,
And death is all.

Enter EARL OF ARUNDEL

Lan. How now, my lord of Arundel?
Arun. My lords, King Edward greets you all by me.
War. Arundel, say your message.
Arun. His majesty,
Hearing that you had taken Gaveston,
Entreateth you by me, yet but he may
See him before he dies; for why, he says,

[3] Helen of Troy. [4] Drew.

And sends you word, he knows that die he shall;
And if you gratify his grace so far,
He will be mindful of the courtesy.
War. How now?
Gav. Renownèd Edward, how thy name
Revives poor Gaveston!
War. No, it needeth not;
Arundel, we will gratify the king
In other matters; he must pardon us in this.
Soldiers, away with him!
Gav. Why, my lord of Warwick,
Will not these delays beget my hopes?
I know it, lords, it is this life you aim at,
Yet grant King Edward this.
Y. Mor. Shalt thou appoint
What we shall grant? Soldiers, away with him!
Thus we'll gratify the king:
We'll send his head by thee; let him bestow
His tears on that, for that is all he gets
Of Gaveston, or else his senseless trunk.
Lan. Not so, my lords, lest he bestow more cost
In burying him than he hath ever earn'd.
Arun. My lords, it is his majesty's request,
And in the honour of a king he swears,
He will but talk with him, and send him back.
War. When? can you tell? Arundel, no; we wot
He that the care of his realm remits,
And drives his nobles to these exigents[5]
For Gaveston, will, if he sees[6] him once,
Violate any promises to possess him.
Arun. Then if you will not trust his grace in keep,
My lords, I will be pledge for his return.
Y. Mor. 'Tis honourable in thee to offer this;
But for we know thou art a noble gentleman,
We will not wrong thee so, to make away
A true man for a thief.

[5] Extremities. [6] Cunningham's emendation for *Q. zease.*

Gav. How mean'st thou, Mortimer? That is over-base.
Y. Mor. Away, base groom, robber of king's renown!
Question with thy companions and thy mates.
Pem. My Lord Mortimer, and you, my lords, each one,
To gratify the king's request therein,
Touching the sending of this Gaveston,
Because his majesty so earnestly
Desires to see the man before his death,
I will upon mine honour undertake
To carry him, and bring him back again;
Provided this, that you my lord of Arundel
Will join with me.
War. Pembroke, what wilt thou do?
Cause yet more bloodshed? Is it not enough
That we have taken him, but must we now
Leave him on "had I wist,"[7] and let him go?
Pem. My lords, I will not over-woo your honours,
But if you dare trust Pembroke with the prisoner,
Upon mine oath, I will return him back.
Arun. My lord of Lancaster, what say you in this?
Lan. Why, I say, let him go on Pembroke's word.
Pem. And you, Lord Mortimer?
Y. Mor. How say you, my lord of Warwick?
War. Nay, do your pleasures, I know how 'twill prove.
Pem. Then give him me.
Gav. Sweet sovereign, yet I come
To see thee ere I die.
War. Yet not perhaps,
If Warwick's wit and policy prevail. [*Aside.*]
Y. Mor. My lord of Pembroke, we deliver him you;
Return him on your honour. Sound, away!
Exeunt all except PEMBROKE, ARUNDEL, GAVESTON, [JAMES,] *and other* Attendants *of* PEMBROKE.
Pem. [My lord of Arundel,] you shall go with me.
My house is not far hence; out of the way

[7] "Had I known—the exclamation of those who repent of what they have rashly done." Dyce.

A little, but our men shall go along.
We that have pretty wenches to our wives,
Sir, must not come so near and baulk their lips.
Arun. 'Tis very kindly spoke, my lord of Pembroke;
Your honour hath an adamant of power
To draw a prince.
Pem. So, my lord. Come hither, James:
I do commit this Gaveston to thee,
Be thou this night his keeper; in the morning
We will discharge thee of thy charge. Be gone.
Gav. Unhappy Gaveston, whither goest thou now?
Exit with James *and the other* Attendants.
Horse-boy. My lord, we'll quickly be at Cobham. *Exeunt.*

[ACT THE THIRD]

[Scene I]

Enter Gaveston *mourning,* James, *and other* Attendants *of* Pembroke

Gav. O treacherous Warwick! thus to wrong thy friend.
James. I see it is your life these arms pursue.
Gav. Weaponless must I fall, and die in bands?
O! must this day be period of my life?
Centre of all my bliss! An ye be men,
Speed to the king.
War. My lord of Pembroke's men,
Strive you no longer—I will have that Gaveston.
James. Your lordship does dishonour to yourself,
And wrong our lord, your honourable friend.
War. No, James, it is my country's cause I follow.
Go, take the villain; soldiers, come away.
We'll make quick work. Commend me to your master,
My friend, and tell him that I watch'd it well.
Come, let thy shadow[1] parley with King Edward.

[1] Ghost.

Gav. Treacherous earl, shall I not see the king?
War. The king of Heaven, perhaps; no other king.
Away! *Exeunt* WARWICK *and* Soldiers *with* GAVESTON.
James. Come, fellows, it booted not for us to strive,
We will in haste go certify our lord. *Exeunt.*

[SCENE II]

Enter KING EDWARD *and* [Young] SPENCER, [BALDOCK, *and* Nobles *of the* KING'S *side, and* Soldiers] *with drums and fifes*

K. Edw. I long to hear an answer from the barons
Touching my friend, my dearest Gaveston.
Ah! Spencer, not the riches of my realm
Can ransom him! Ah, he is mark'd to die!
I know the malice of the younger Mortimer,
Warwick I know is rough, and Lancaster
Inexorable, and I shall never see
My lovely Pierce, my Gaveston again!
The barons overbear me with their pride.
Y. Spen. Were I King Edward, England's sovereign,
Son to the lovely Eleanor of Spain,
Great Edward Longshanks' issue, would I bear
These braves, this rage, and suffer uncontroll'd
These barons thus to beard me in my land,
In mine own realm? My lord, pardon my speech:
Did you retain your father's magnanimity,
Did you regard the honour of your name,
You would not suffer thus your majesty
Be counterbuff'd of[1] your nobility.
Strike off their heads, and let them preach on poles!
No doubt, such lessons they will teach the rest,
As by their preachments they will profit much,
And learn obedience to their lawful king.
K. Edw. Yea, gentle Spencer, we have been too mild,
Too kind to them; but now have drawn our sword,
And if they send me not my Gaveston,

[1] Checked by.

We'll steel it on their crest, and poll their tops.
Bald. This haught[2] resolve becomes your majesty,
Not to be tied to their affection,
As though your highness were a schoolboy still,
And must be aw'd and govern'd like a child.

Enter the Elder SPENCER, *with his truncheon and* Soldiers

E. Spen. Long live my sovereign, the noble Edward,
In peace triumphant, fortunate in wars!
K. Edw. Welcome, old man, com'st thou in Edward's aid?
Then tell thy prince of whence, and what thou art.
E. Spen. Lo, with a band of bowmen and of pikes,
Brown bills and targeteers, four hundred strong,
Sworn to defend King Edward's royal right,
I come in person to your majesty,
Spencer, the father of Hugh Spencer there,
Bound to your highness everlastingly,
For favour done, in him, unto us all.
K. Edw. Thy father, Spencer?
Y. Spen. True, an it like your grace,
That pours, in lieu of all your goodness shown,
His life, my lord, before your princely feet.
K. Edw. Welcome ten thousand times, old man, again.
Spencer, this love, this kindness to thy king,
Argues thy noble mind and disposition.
Spencer, I here create thee Earl of Wiltshire,
And daily will enrich thee with our favour,
That, as the sunshine, shall reflect o'er thee.
Beside, the more to manifest our love,
Because we hear Lord Bruce doth sell his land,
And that the Mortimers are in hand withal,
Thou shalt have crowns of us t' outbid the barons:
And, Spencer, spare them not, but lay it on.
Soldiers, a largess, and thrice welcome all!
Y. Spen. My lord, here comes the queen.

[2] High-spirited.

Enter QUEEN ISABELLA, *and her son* [PRINCE EDWARD,] *and* LEVUNE, a Frenchman

K. Edw. Madam, what news?
Q. Isab. News of dishonour, lord, and discontent.
Our friend Levune, faithful and full of trust,
Informeth us, by letters and by words,
That Lord Valois our brother, King of France,
Because your highness hath been slack in homage,
Hath seized Normandy into his hands.
These be the letters, this the messenger.
K. Edw. Welcome, Levune. Tush, Sib, if this be all
Valois and I will soon be friends again.—
But to my Gaveston; shall I never see,
Never behold thee now?—Madam, in this matter,
We will employ you and your little son;
You shall go parley with the King of France.—
Boy, see you bear you bravely to the king,
And do your message with a majesty.
P. Edw. Commit not to my youth things of more weight
Than fits a prince so young as I to bear,
And fear not, lord and father, Heaven's great beams
On Atlas' shoulder shall not lie more safe,
Than shall your charge committed to my trust.
Q. Isab. Ah, boy! this towardness makes thy mother fear
Thou art not mark'd to many days on earth.
K. Edw. Madam, we will that you with speed be shipp'd,
And this our son; Levune shall follow you
With all the haste we can despatch him hence.
Choose of our lords to bear you company,
And go in peace; leave us in wars at home.
Q. Isab. Unnatural wars, where subjects brave their king;
God end them once! My lords, I take my leave,
To make my preparation for France.
[*Exit with* PRINCE EDWARD.]

[Enter ARUNDEL.][3]

K. Edw. What, Lord Arundel, dost thou come alone?
Arun. Yea, my good lord, for Gaveston is dead.
K. Edw. Ah, traitors! have they put my friend to death?
Tell me, Arundel, died he ere thou cam'st,
Or didst thou see my friend to take his death?
Arun. Neither, my lord; for as he was surpris'd,
Begirt with weapons and with enemies round,
I did your highness' message to them all;
Demanding him of them, entreating rather,
And said, upon the honour of my name,
That I would undertake to carry him
Unto your highness, and to bring him back.
K. Edw. And tell me, would the rebels deny me that?
Y. Spen. Proud recreants!
K. Edw. Yea, Spencer, traitors all.
Arun. I found them at the first inexorable;
The Earl of Warwick would not bide the hearing,
Mortimer hardly; Pembroke and Lancaster
Spake least: and when they flatly had denied,
Refusing to receive me pledge for him,
The Earl of Pembroke mildly thus bespake;
"My lords, because our sovereign sends for him,
And promiseth he shall be safe return'd,
I will this undertake, to have him hence,
And see him re-delivered to your hands."
K. Edw. Well, and how fortunes [it] that he came not?
Y. Spen. Some treason, or some villainy, was the cause.
Arun. The Earl of Warwick seiz'd him on his way;
For being delivered unto Pembroke's men,
Their lord rode home thinking his prisoner safe;
But ere he came, Warwick in ambush lay,
And bare him to his death; and in a trench
Strake off his head, and march'd unto the camp.
Y. Spen. A bloody part, flatly 'gainst law of arms!

[3] Qq. Lord Matre[vis]) throughout the scene. Corrected by Dyce.

K. Edw. O shall I speak, or shall I sigh and die!
Y. Spen. My lord, refer your vengeance to the sword
Upon these barons; hearten up your men;
Let them not unreveng'd murder your friends!
Advance your standard, Edward, in the field,
And march to fire them from their starting holes.
K. Edw. (*kneeling.*) By earth, the common mother of us all,
By Heaven, and all the moving orbs thereof,
By this right hand, and by my father's sword,
And all the honours 'longing to my crown,
I will have heads, and lives for him, as many
As I have manors, castles, towns, and towers!— [*Rises.*]
Treacherous Warwick! traitorous Mortimer!
If it be England's king, in lakes of gore
Your headless trunks, your bodies will I trail,
That you may drink your fill, and quaff in blood,
And stain my royal standard with the same,
That so my bloody colours may suggest
Remembrance of revenge immortally
On your accursed traitorous progeny,
You villains, that have slain my Gaveston!
And in this place of honour and of trust,
Spencer, sweet Spencer, I adopt thee here:
And merely of our love we do create thee
Earl of Gloucester, and Lord Chamberlain,
Despite of times, despite of enemies.
Y. Spen. My lord, here's a messenger from the barons.
Desires access unto your majesty.
K. Edw. Admit him near.

Enter the Herald, *with his coat of arms*

Her. Long live King Edward, England's lawful lord!
K. Edw. So wish not they, I wis, that sent thee hither.
Thou com'st from Mortimer and his 'complices,
A ranker rout of rebels never was.
Well, say thy message.
Her. The barons up in arms, by me salute

Your highness with long life and happiness;
And bid me say, as plainer to your grace,
That if without effusion of blood
You will this grief have ease and remedy,
That from your princely person you remove
This Spencer, as a putrifying branch,
That deads the royal vine, whose golden leaves
Empale your princely head, your diadem,
Whose brightness such pernicious upstarts dim,
Say they; and lovingly advise your grace,
To cherish virtue and nobility,
And have old servitors in high esteem,
And shake off smooth dissembling flatterers.
This granted, they, their honours, and their lives,
Are to your highness vow'd and consecrate.

Y. Spen. Ah, traitors! will they still display their pride?

K. Edw. Away, tarry no answer, but be gone!
Rebels, will they appoint their sovereign
His sports, his pleasures, and his company?
Yet, ere thou go, see how I do divorce *Embraces* SPENCER.
Spencer from me.—Now get thee to thy lords,
And tell them I will come to chastise them
For murdering Gaveston; hie thee, get thee gone!
Edward with fire and sword follows at thy heels. [*Exit* Herald.]
My lords, perceive you how these rebels swell?
Soldiers, good hearts, defend your sovereign's right,
For now, even now, we march to make them stoop.
Away! *Exeunt. Alarums, excursions, a great fight, and a retreat* [*sounded, within*].

[SCENE III. *Battlefield at Boroughbridge in Yorkshire*]

Re-enter KING EDWARD, *the* Elder SPENCER, Young SPENCER, *and* Noblemen *of the* KING'S *side*

K. Edw. Why do we sound retreat? Upon them, lords!
This day I shall pour vengeance with my sword
On those proud rebels that are up in arms
And do confront and countermand their king.

Y. Spen. I doubt it not, my lord, right will prevail.
E. Spen. 'Tis not amiss, my liege, for either part
To breathe awhile; our men, with sweat and dust
All choked well near, begin to faint for heat;
And this retire refresheth horse and man.
Y. Spen. Here come the rebels.

Enter Young MORTIMER, LANCASTER, WARWICK, PEMBROKE, *and others.*

Y. Mor. Look, Lancaster, yonder is Edward
Among his flatterers.
Lan. And there let him be
Till he pay dearly for their company.
War. And shall, or Warwick's sword shall smite in vain.
K. Edw. What, rebels, do you shrink and sound retreat?
Y. Mor. No, Edward, no; thy flatterers faint and fly.
Lan. They'd best betimes forsake thee, and their trains,[1]
For they'll betray thee, traitors as they are.
Y. Spen. Traitor on thy face, rebellious Lancaster!
Pem. Away, base upstart, bravest thou nobles thus?
E. Spen. A noble attempt and honourable deed,
Is it not, trow ye, to assemble aid,
And levy arms against your lawful king!
K. Edw. For which ere long their heads shall satisfy,
To appease the wrath of their offended king.
Y. Mor. Then, Edward, thou wilt fight it to the last,
And rather bathe thy sword in subjects' blood,
Than banish that pernicious company?
K. Edw. Ay, traitors all, rather than thus be brav'd,
Make England's civil towns huge heaps of stones,
And ploughs to go about our palace-gates.
War. A desperate and unnatural resolution!
Alarum! To the fight!
St. George for England, and the barons' right!
K. Edw. Saint George for England, and King Edward's right!
[*Alarums. Exeunt the two parties severally.*]

[1] Plots.

[SCENE IV]

Re-enter KING EDWARD [*and his followers,*] *with the* Barons [*and* KENT], *captives*

K. Edw. Now, lusty lords, now, not by chance of war,
But justice of the quarrel and the cause,
Vail'd[2] is your pride; methinks you hang the heads,
But we'll advance them, traitors. Now 'tis time
To be avenged on you for all your braves,
And for the murder of my dearest friend,
To whom right well you knew our soul was knit,
Good Pierce of Gaveston, my sweet favourite.
Ah, rebels! recreants! you made him away.
Kent. Brother, in regard of thee, and of thy land,
Did they remove that flatterer from thy throne.
K. Edw. So, sir, you have spoke; away, avoid our presence.
[*Exit* KENT.]
Accursed wretches, was't in regard of us,
When we had sent our messenger to request
He might be spar'd to come to speak with us,
And Pembroke undertook for his return,
That thou, proud Warwick, watch'd the prisoner,
Poor Pierce, and headed him 'gainst law of arms?
For which thy head shall overlook the rest,
As much as thou in rage outwent'st the rest.
War. Tyrant, I scorn thy threats and menaces;
It is but temporal that thou canst inflict.
Lan. The worst is death, and better die to live
Than live in infamy under such a king.
K. Edw. Away with them, my lord of Winchester!
These lusty leaders, Warwick and Lancaster,
I charge you roundly—off with both their heads!
Away!
War. Farewell, vain world!
Lan. Sweet Mortimer, farewell.

[2] Lowered.

Y. Mor. England, unkind to thy nobility,
Groan for this grief, behold how thou art maim'd!

K. Edw. Go take that haughty Mortimer to the Tower,
There see him safe bestow'd; and for the rest,
Do speedy execution on them all.
Begone!

Y. Mor. What, Mortimer! can ragged stony walls
Immure thy virtue that aspires to Heaven?
No, Edward, England's scourge, it may not be;
Mortimer's hope surmounts his fortune far.

[*The captive* Barons *are led off.*]

K. Edw. Sound drums and trumpets! March with me, my friends,
Edward this day hath crown'd him king anew.

Exeunt all except Young SPENCER, LEVUNE, *and* BALDOCK.

Y. Spen. Levune, the trust that we repose in thee,
Begets the quiet of King Edward's land.
Therefore begone in haste, and with advice
Bestow that treasure on the lords of France,
That, therewith all enchanted, like the guard
That suffered Jove to pass in showers of gold
To Danae, all aid may be denied
To Isabel, the queen, that now in France
Makes friends, to cross the seas with her young son,
And step into his father's regiment.[3]

Levune. That's it these barons and the subtle queen
Long levell'd at.

Bal. Yea, but, Levune, thou seest
These barons lay their heads on blocks together;
What they intend, the hangman frustrates clean.

Levune. Have you no doubt, my lords, I'll clap so close
Among the lords of France with England's gold,
That Isabel shall make her plaints in vain,
And France shall be obdurate with her tears.

Y. Spen. Then make for France, amain—Levune, away!
Proclaim King Edward's wars and victories. *Exeunt.*

[3] Rule.

[ACT THE FOURTH]

[Scene I. *Near the Tower of London*]

Enter Kent

Kent. Fair blows the wind for France; blow gentle gale,
Till Edmund be arriv'd for England's good!
Nature, yield to my country's cause in this.
A brother? No, a butcher of thy friends!
Proud Edward, dost thou banish me thy presence?
But I'll to France, and cheer the wronged queen,
And certify what Edward's looseness is.
Unnatural king! to slaughter noblemen
And cherish flatterers! Mortimer, I stay
Thy sweet escape: stand gracious, gloomy night,
To his device.

Enter Young Mortimer, *disguised*

Y. Mor. Holla! who walketh there?
Is't you, my lord?
Kent. Mortimer, 'tis I;
But hath thy potion wrought so happily?
Y. Mor. It hath, my Lord; the warders all asleep,
I thank them, gave me leave to pass in peace.
But hath your grace got shipping unto France?
Kent. Fear it not. *Exeunt.*

[Scene II. *Paris*]

Enter Queen Isabella *and* Prince Edward

Q. Isab. Ah, boy! our friends do fail us all in France.
The lords are cruel, and the king unkind;
What shall we do?
P. Edw. Madam, return to England,
And please my father well, and then a fig
For all my uncle's friendship here in France.
I warrant you, I'll win his highness quickly;
'A loves me better than a thousand Spencers.

Q. Isab. Ah, boy, thou art deceiv'd, at least in this,
To think that we can yet be tun'd together;
No, no, we jar too far. Unkind Valois!
Unhappy Isabel! when France rejects,
Whither, oh! whither dost thou bend thy steps?

Enter Sir John of Hainault

Sir J. Madam, what cheer?
Q. Isab. Ah! good Sir John of Hainault,
Never so cheerless, nor so far distrest.
Sir J. I hear, sweet lady, of the king's unkindness;
But droop not, madam; noble minds contemn
Despair. Will your grace with me to Hainault,
And there stay time's advantage with your son?
How say you, my lord, will you go with your friends,
And shake off all our fortunes equally?
P. Edw. So pleaseth the queen, my mother, me it likes.
The King of England, nor the court of France,
Shall have me from my gracious mother's side,
Till I be strong enough to break a staff;
And then have at the proudest Spencer's head.
Sir J. Well said, my lord.
Q. Isab. O, my sweet heart, how do I moan thy wrongs,
Yet triumph in the hope of thee, my joy!
Ah, sweet Sir John! even to the utmost verge
Of Europe, or the shore of Tanais,
Will we with thee to Hainault—so we will:—
The marquis is a noble gentleman;
His grace, I dare presume, will welcome me.
But who are these?

Enter Kent *and* Young Mortimer

Kent. Madam, long may you live,
Much happier than your friends in England do!
Q. Isab. Lord Edmund and Lord Mortimer alive!
Welcome to France! The news was here, my lord,
That you were dead, or very near your death.

Y. Mor. Lady, the last was truest of the twain;
But Mortimer, reserv'd for better hap,
Hath shaken off the thraldom of the Tower,
And lives t' advance your standard, good my lord.
P. Edw. How mean you? An[1] the king, my father, lives?
No, my Lord Mortimer, not I, I trow.
Q. Isab. Not, son! why not? I would it were no worse.
But, gentle lords, friendless we are in France.
Y. Mor. Monsieur le Grand, a noble friend of yours,
Told us, at our arrival, all the news:
How hard the nobles, how unkind the king
Hath show'd himself; but, madam, right makes room
Where weapons want; and, though a many friends
Are made away, as Warwick, Lancaster,
And others of our party and faction;
Yet have we friends, assure your grace, in England
Would cast up caps, and clap their hands for joy,
To see us there, appointed[2] for our foes.
Kent. Would all were well, and Edward well reclaim'd,
For England's honour, peace, and quietness.
Y. Mor. But by the sword, my lord, 't must be deserv'd;[3]
The king will ne'er forsake his flatterers.
Sir. J. My lord of England, sith th' ungentle king
Of France refuseth to give aid of arms
To this distressed queen his sister here,
Go you with her to Hainault. Doubt ye not,
We will find comfort, money, men, and friends
Ere long, to bid the English king a base.[4]
How say, young prince? What think you of the match?
P. Edw. I think King Edward will outrun us all.
Q. Isab. Nay, son, not so; and you must not discourage
Your friends, that are so forward in your aid.
Kent. Sir John of Hainault, pardon us, I pray;
These comforts that you give our woful queen
Bind us in kindness all at your command.

[1] If. [2] Equipped. [3] Earned. [4] Challenge. A reference to the game of prisoner's base.

Q. Isab. Yea, gentle brother; and the God of heaven
Prosper your happy motion, good Sir John.
Y. Mor. This noble gentleman, forward in arms,
Was born, I see, to be our anchor-hold.
Sir John of Hainault, be it thy renown,
That England's queen and nobles in distress,
Have been by thee restor'd and comforted.
Sir J. Madam, along, and you my lords, with me,
That England's peers may Hainault's welcome see. [*Exeunt.*]

[Scene III]

Enter King Edward, Arundel, *the* Elder *and* Younger Spencer, *and others*

K. Edw. Thus after many threats of wrathful war,
Triumpheth England's Edward with his friends;
And triumph, Edward, with his friends uncontroll'd!
My lord of Gloucester, do you hear the news?
Y. Spen. What news, my lord?
K. Edw. Why, man, they say there is great execution
Done through the realm; my lord of Arundel,
You have the note, have you not?
Arun. From the Lieutenant of the Tower, my lord.
K. Edw. I pray let us see it. [*Takes the note.*] What have we there?
Read it, Spencer. [*Hands the note to*] Young Spencer, [*who*] *reads the names.*
Why, so; they bark'd apace a month ago:
Now, on my life, they'll neither bark nor bite.
Now, sirs, the news from France? Gloucester, I trow
The lords of France love England's gold so well
As Isabella gets no aid from thence.
What now remains? Have you proclaim'd, my lord,
Reward for them can bring in Mortimer?
Y. Spen. My lord, we have; and if he be in England,
'A will be had ere long, I doubt it not.

K. Edw. If, dost thou say? Spencer, as true as death,
He is in England's ground; our portmasters
Are not so careless of their king's command.

Enter a Messenger

How now, what news with thee? From whence come these?
Mess. Letters, my lord, and tidings forth of France;—
To you, my lord of Gloucester, from Levune.
[*Gives letters to* Young SPENCER.]
K. Edw. Read.
Y. Spen. (reads).

"My duty to your honour premised, &c., I have, according to instructions in that behalf, dealt with the King of France his lords, and effected that the queen, all discontented and discomforted, is gone: whither, if you ask, with Sir John of Hainault, brother to the marquis, into Flanders. With them are gone Lord Edmund, and the Lord Mortimer, having in their company divers of your nation, and others; and, as constant report goeth, they intend to give King Edward battle in England, sooner than he can look for them. This is all the news of import.

Your honour's in all service, LEVUNE."

K. Edw. Ah, villains! hath that Mortimer escap'd?
With him is Edmund gone associate?
And will Sir John of Hainault lead the round?
Welcome, a God's name, madam, and your son;
England shall welcome you and all your rout.
Gallop apace, bright Phœbus, through the sky,
And dusky night, in rusty iron car,
Between you both shorten the time, I pray,
That I may see that most desired day
When we may meet these traitors in the field.
Ah, nothing grieves me, but my little boy
Is thus misled to countenance their ills.
Come, friends, to Bristow,[1] there to make us strong;

[1] Bristol.

And, winds, as equal be to bring them in,
As you injurious were to bear them forth! [*Exeunt.*]

[SCENE IV. *Near Harwich*]

Enter QUEEN ISABELLA, PRINCE EDWARD, KENT, Young MORTIMER, *and* SIR JOHN OF HAINAULT

Q. Isab. Now, lords, our loving friends and countrymen,
Welcome to England all, with prosperous winds!
Our kindest friends in Belgia have we left,
To cope with friends at home; a heavy case
When force to force is knit, and sword and glaive
In civil broils make kin and countrymen
Slaughter themselves in others, and their sides
With their own weapons gore! But what's the help?
Misgoverned kings are cause of all this wrack;
And, Edward, thou art one among them all,
Whose looseness hath betray'd thy land to spoil,
Who made the channels overflow with blood.
Of thine own people patron shouldst thou be,
But thou——

Y. Mor. Nay, madam, if you be a warrior,
You must not grow so passionate in speeches.
Lords,
Sith that we are by sufferance of Heaven
Arriv'd, and armed in this prince's right,
Here for our country's cause swear we to him
All homage, fealty, and forwardness;
And for the open wrongs and injuries
Edward hath done to us; his queen and land,
We come in arms to wreak it with the sword;
That England's queen in peace may repossess
Her dignities and honours; and withal
We may remove these flatterers from the king,
That havoc England's wealth and treasury.

Sir J. Sound trumpets, my lord, and forward let us march.
Edward will think we come to flatter him.
Kent. I would he never had been flattered more! [*Exeunt.*]

[Scene V. *Near Bristol*]

Enter King Edward, Baldock, *and* Young Spencer, *flying about the stage*

Y. Spen. Fly, fly, my lord! the queen is over-strong;
Her friends do multiply, and yours do fail.
Shape we our course to Ireland, there to breathe.
K. Edw. What! was I born to fly and run away,
And leave the Mortimers conquerors behind?
Give me my horse, and let's reinforce our troops:
And in this bed of honour die with fame.
Bald. O no, my lord, this princely resolution
Fits not the time; away! we are pursued. [*Exeunt.*]

Enter Kent, *with sword and target*

Kent. This way he fled, but I am come too late
Edward, alas! my heart relents for thee.
Proud traitor, Mortimer, why dost thou chase
Thy lawful king, thy sovereign, with thy sword?
Vile wretch! and why hast thou, of all unkind,
Borne arms against thy brother and thy king?
Rain showers of vengeance on my cursed head,
Thou God, to whom in justice it belongs
To punish this unnatural revolt!
Edward, this Mortimer aims at thy life!
O fly him, then! But, Edmund, calm this rage,
Dissemble, or thou diest; for Mortimer
And Isabel do kiss, while they conspire;
And yet she bears a face of love forsooth.
Fie on that love that hatcheth death and hate!
Edmund, away! Bristow to Longshanks' blood
Is false. Be not found single for suspect:
Proud Mortimer pries near unto thy walks.

Enter QUEEN ISABELLA, PRINCE EDWARD, Young MORTIMER, *and* SIR JOHN OF HAINAULT

Q. Isab. Successful battle gives the God of kings
To them that fight in right and fear his wrath.
Since then successfully we have prevailed,
Thanked be Heaven's great architect, and you.
Ere farther we proceed, my noble lords,
We here create our well-beloved son,
Of love and care unto his royal person,
Lord Warden of the realm, and sith the fates
Have made his father so infortunate,
Deal you, my lords, in this, my loving lords,
As to your wisdoms fittest seems in all.
Kent. Madam, without offence, if I may ask,
How will you deal with Edward in his fall?
P. Edw. Tell me, good uncle, what Edward do you mean?
Kent. Nephew, your father; I dare not call him king.
Y. Mor. My lord of Kent, what needs these questions?
'Tis not in her controlment, nor in ours,
But as the realm and parliament shall please,
So shall your brother be disposed of.—
I like not this relenting mood in Edmund.
Madam, 'tis good to look to him betimes. [*Aside to the* QUEEN.]
Q. Isab. My lord, the Mayor of Bristow knows our mind.
Y. Mor. Yea, madam, and they scape not easily
That fled the field.
Q. Isab Baldock is with the king.
A goodly chancellor, is he not, my lord?
Sir J. So are the Spencers, the father and the son.
Kent. This Edward is the ruin of the realm.

Enter RICE AP HOWELL *and the* Mayor of Bristow, *with the* Elder SPENCER [*prisoner, and* Attendants]

Rice. God save Queen Isabel, and her princely son!
Madam, the mayor and citizens of Bristow,
In sign of love and duty to this presence,

Present by me this traitor to the state,
Spencer, the father to that wanton Spencer,
That, like the lawless Catiline of Rome,
Revelled in England's wealth and treasury.

Q. Isab. We thank you all.

Y. Mor. Your loving care in this
Deserveth princely favours and rewards.
But where's the king and the other Spencer fled?

Rice. Spencer the son, created Earl of Gloucester,
Is with that smooth-tongu'd scholar Baldock gone
And shipped but late for Ireland with the king.

Y. Mor. Some whirlwind fetch them back or sink them all!—
[*Aside.*]
They shall be started thence, I doubt it not.

P. Edw. Shall I not see the king my father yet?

Kent. Unhappy's Edward, chas'd from England's bounds.
[*Aside.*]

Sir J. Madam, what resteth, why stand you in a muse?

Q. Isab. I rue my lord's ill-fortune; but alas!
Care of my country call'd me to this war.

Y. Mor. Madam, have done with care and sad complaint;
Your king hath wrong'd your country and himself,
And we must seek to right it as we may.
Meanwhile, have hence this rebel to the block.
Your lordship cannot privilege your head.

E. Spen. Rebel is he that fights against his prince;
So fought not they that fought in Edward's right.

Y. Mor. Take him away, he prates;
[*Exeunt* Attendants *with the* Elder SPENCER.)
You, Rice ap Howell,
Shall do good service to her majesty,
Being of countenance in your country here,
To follow these rebellious runagates.
We in meanwhile, madam, must take advice,
How Baldock, Spencer, and their complices,
May in their fall be followed to their end. *Exeunt.*

[SCENE VI. *The scene is in the abbey of Neath*]

Enter the Abbot, Monks, KING EDWARD, Young SPENCER, *and* BALDOCK (*the three latter disguised*)

Abbot. Have you no doubt, my lord; have you no fear;
As silent and as careful we will be,
To keep your royal person safe with us,
Free from suspect and fell invasion
Of such as have your majesty in chase,
Yourself, and those your chosen company,
As danger of this stormy time requires.
K. Edw. Father, thy face should harbour no deceit.
O! hadst thou ever been a king, thy heart,
Pierced deeply with sense of my distress,
Could not but take compassion of my state.
Stately and proud, in riches and in train,
Whilom I was, powerful, and full of pomp:
But what is he whom rule and empery
Have not in life or death made miserable?
Come, Spencer; come, Baldock, come, sit down by me;
Make trial now of that philosophy,
That in our famous nurseries of arts
Thou suck'dst from Plato and from Aristotle.
Father, this life contemplative is Heaven.
O that I might this life in quiet lead!
But we, alas! are chas'd; and you, my friends,
Your lives and my dishonour they pursue.
Yet, gentle monks, for treasure, gold, nor fee,
Do you betray us and our company.
Monk. Your grace may sit secure, if none but we
Do wot of your abode.
Y. Spen. Not one alive; but shrewdly I suspect
A gloomy fellow in a mead below.
'A gave a long look after us, my lord;
And all the land I know is up in arms,
Arms that pursue our lives with deadly hate.

Bald. We were embark'd for Ireland, wretched we!
With awkward winds and [with] sore tempests driven
To fall on shore, and here to pine in fear
Of Mortimer and his confederates.
K. Edw. Mortimer! who talks of Mortimer?
Who wounds me with the name of Mortimer,
That bloody man? Good father, on thy lap
Lay I this head, laden with mickle care.
O might I never open these eyes again!
Never again lift up this drooping head!
O never more lift up this dying heart!
Y. Spen. Look up, my lord.—Baldock, this drowsiness
Betides no good; here even we are betray'd.

Enter, with Welsh hooks, RICE AP HOWELL, *a* Mower, *and* LEICESTER

Mow. Upon my life, these be the men ye seek.
Rice. Fellow, enough.—My lord, I pray be short,
A fair commission warrants what we do.
Leices. The queen's commission, urged by Mortimer;
What cannot gallant Mortimer with the queen?
Alas! see where he sits, and hopes unseen
To escape their hands that seek to reave his life.
Too true it is, *Quem dies vidit veniens superbum,*
Hunc dies vidit fugiens jacentem.[1]
But, Leicester, leave to grow so passionate.
Spencer and Baldock, by no other names,
I do arrest you of high treason here.
Stand not on titles, but obey the arrest;
'Tis in the name of Isabel the queen.
My lord, why droop you thus?
K. Edw. O day, the last of all my bliss on earth!
Centre of all misfortune! O my stars,
Why do you lour unkindly on a king?
Comes Leicester, then, in Isabella's name
To take my life, my company from me?

[1] Whom the dawn sees proud, evening sees prostrate. Seneca, *Thyestes,* 613.

Here, man, rip up this panting breast of mine,
And take my heart in rescue of my friends!
Rice. Away with them!
Y. Spen. It may become thee yet
To let us take our farewell of his grace.
Abbot. My heart with pity earns[2] to see this sight,—
A king to bear these words and proud commands. [*Aside.*]
K. Edw. Spencer, ah, sweet Spencer, thus then must we part?
Y. Spen. We must, my lord, so will the angry Heavens.
K. Edw. Nay, so will hell and cruel Mortimer;
The gentle Heavens have not to do in this.
Bald. My lord, it is in vain to grieve or storm.
Here humbly of your grace we take our leaves;
Our lots are cast; I fear me, so is thine.
K. Edw. In Heaven we may, in earth ne'er shall we meet:
And, Leicester, say, what shall become of us?
Leices. Your majesty must go to Killingworth.[3]
K. Edw. Must! it is somewhat hard, when kings *must* go.
Leices. Here is a litter ready for your grace,
That waits your pleasure, and the day grows old.
Rice. As good be gone, as stay and be benighted.
K. Edw. A litter hast thou? Lay me in a hearse,
And to the gates of hell convey me hence;
Let Pluto's bells ring out my fatal knell,
And hags howl for my death at Charon's shore,
For friends hath Edward none but these,
And these must die under a tyrant's sword.
Rice. My lord, be going; care not for these,
For we shall see them shorter by the heads.
K. Edw. Well, that shall be, shall be: part we must!
Sweet Spencer, gentle Baldock, part we must!
Hence feigned weeds! unfeigned are my woes;
[*Throws off his disguise.*]
Father, farewell! Leicester, thou stay'st for me,
And go I must. Life, farewell, with my friends.
[*Exeunt* KING EDWARD *and* LEICESTER.]

[2] Yearns. [3] Kenilworth.

Y. Spen. O! is he gone? Is noble Edward gone?
Parted from hence, never to see us more?
Rend, sphere of Heaven! and, fire, forsake thy orb!
Earth, melt to air! gone is my sovereign,
Gone, gone, alas! never to make return.

Bald. Spencer, I see our souls are fleeted hence;
We are depriv'd the sunshine of our life:
Make for a new life, man; throw up thy eyes,
And heart, and hands to Heaven's immortal throne;
Pay nature's debt with cheerful countenance;
Reduce we all our lessons unto this:
To die, sweet Spencer, therefore live we all;
Spencer, all live to die, and rise to fall.

Rice. Come, come, keep these preachments till you come to the place appointed. You, and such as you are, have made wise work in England. Will your lordships away?

Mow. Your lordship, I trust, will remember me?

Rice. Remember thee, fellow! what else? Follow me to the town.
[*Exeunt.*]

[ACT THE FIFTH]

[SCENE I. *A room in Kenilworth Castle*]

Enter KING EDWARD, LEICESTER, *the* BISHOP OF WINCHESTER, [*and* TRUSSEL.]

Leices. Be patient, good my lord, cease to lament.
Imagine Killingworth Castle were your court,
And that you lay for pleasure here a space,
Not of compulsion or necessity.

K. Edw. Leicester, if gentle words might comfort me,
Thy speeches long ago had eas'd my sorrows;
For kind and loving hast thou always been.
The griefs of private men are soon allay'd,
But not of kings. The forest deer, being struck,
Runs to an herb that closeth up the wounds;
But, when the imperial lion's flesh is gored,

He rends and tears it with his wrathful paw,
And highly scorning that the lowly earth
Should drink his blood, mounts up into the air.
And so it fares with me, whose dauntless mind
The ambitious Mortimer would seek to curb,
And that unnatural queen, false Isabel,
That thus hath pent and mew'd me in a prison;
For such outrageous passions cloy my soul,
As with the wings of rancour and disdain,
Full often am I soaring up to Heaven,
To plain me to the gods against them both.
But when I call to mind I am a king,
Methinks I should revenge me of my wrongs,
That Mortimer and Isabel have done.
But what are kings, when regiment[1] is gone,
But perfect shadows in a sunshine day?
My nobles rule, I bear the name of king;
I wear the crown, but am controll'd by them,
By Mortimer, and my unconstant queen,
Who spots my nuptial bed with infamy;
Whilst I am lodg'd within this cave of care,
Where sorrow at my elbow still attends,
To company my heart with sad laments,
That bleeds within me for this strange exchange.
But tell me, must I now resign my crown,
To make usurping Mortimer a king?

B. of Win. Your grace mistakes; it is for England's good,
And princely Edward's right we crave the crown.

K. Edw. No, 'tis for Mortimer, not Edward's head;
For he's a lamb, encompassed by wolves,
Which in a moment will abridge his life.
But if proud Mortimer do wear this crown,
Heavens turn it to a blaze of quenchless fire!
Or like the snaky wreath of Tisiphon,
Engirt the temples of his hateful head;
So shall not England's vine be perished,

[1] Rule.

But Edward's name survives, though Edward dies.
Leices. My lord, why waste you thus the time away?
They stay your answer; will you yield your crown?
K. Edw. Ah, Leicester, weigh how hardly I can brook
To lose my crown and kingdom without cause;
To give ambitious Mortimer my right,
That like a mountain overwhelms my bliss,
In which extreme my mind here murdered is.
But what the heavens appoint, I must obey!
Here, take my crown; the life of Edward too;
[*Taking off the crown.*]
Two kings in England cannot reign at once.
But stay awhile, let me be king till night,
That I may gaze upon this glittering crown;
So shall my eyes receive their last content,
My head, the latest honour due to it,
And jointly both yield up their wished right.
Continue ever thou celestial sun;
Let never silent night possess this clime:
Stand still you watches of the element;
All times and seasons, rest you at a stay,
That Edward may be still fair England's king!
But day's bright beam doth vanish fast away,
And needs I must resign my wished crown.
Inhuman creatures! nurs'd with tiger's milk!
Why gape you for your sovereign's overthrow!
My diadem I mean, and guiltless life.
See, monsters, see, I'll wear my crown again!
[*He puts on the crown.*]
What, fear you not the fury of your king?
But, hapless Edward, thou art fondly[2] led;
They pass[3] not for thy frowns as late they did,
But seek to make a new-elected king;
Which fills my mind with strange despairing thoughts,
Which thoughts are martyred with endless torments,
And in this torment comfort find I none,

[2] Foolishly. [3] Care.

But that I feel the crown upon my head;
And therefore let me wear it yet awhile.

Trus. My lord, the parliament must have present news,
And therefore say, will you resign or no? *The* KING *rageth.*

K. Edw. I'll not resign, but whilst I live be king.
Traitors, be gone and join with Mortimer!
Elect, conspire, install, do what you will:—
Their blood and yours shall seal these treacheries!

B. of Win. This answer we'll return, and so farewell.
[*Going with* TRUSSEL.]

Leices. Call them again, my lord, and speak them fair;
For if they go, the prince shall lose his right.

K. Edw. Call thou them back, I have no power to speak.

Leices. My lord, the king is willing to resign.

B. of Win. If he be not, let him choose.

K. Edw. O would I might, but heavens and earth conspire
To make me miserable! Here receive my crown;
Receive it? No, these innocent hands of mine
Shall not be guilty of so foul a crime.
He of you all that most desires my blood,
And will be called the murderer of a king,
Take it. What, are you moved? Pity you me?
Then send for unrelenting Mortimer,
And Isabel, whose eyes, being turned to steel,
Will sooner sparkle fire than shed a tear.
Yet stay, for rather than I'll look on them,
Here, here! [*Gives the crown.*]
Now, sweet God of Heaven,
Make me despise this transitory pomp,
And sit for aye enthronized in Heaven!
Come, death, and with thy fingers close my eyes,
Or if I live, let me forget myself.

B. of Win. My lord—

K. Edw. Call me not lord; away—out of my sight!
Ah, pardon me: grief makes me lunatic!
Let not that Mortimer protect my son;
More safety is there in a tiger's jaws,

Than his embracements. Bear this to the queen,
Wet with my tears, and dried again with sighs;
[*Gives a handkerchief.*]
If with the sight thereof she be not mov'd,
Return it back and dip it in my blood.
Commend me to my son, and bid him rule
Better than I. Yet how have I transgress'd,
Unless it be with too much clemency?
Trus. And thus most humbly do we take our leave.
K. Edw. Farewell;
[*Exeunt the* BISHOP OF WINCHESTER *and* TRUSSEL.]
I know the next news that they bring
Will be my death; and welcome shall it be;
To wretched men, death is felicity.

Enter BERKELEY, [*who gives a paper to* LEICESTER]

Leices. Another post! what news brings he?
K. Edw. Such news as I expect—come, Berkeley, come,
And tell thy message to my naked breast.
Berk. My lord, think not a thought so villainous
Can harbour in a man of noble birth.
To do your highness service and devoir,
And save you from your foes, Berkeley would die.
Leices. My lord, the council of the queen commands
That I resign my charge.
K. Edw. And who must keep me now? Must you, my lord?
Berk. Ay, my most gracious lord; so 'tis decreed.
K. Edw. [*taking the paper.*] By Mortimer, whose name is written here!
Well may I rend his name that rends my heart! [*Tears it.*]
This poor revenge has something eas'd my mind.
So may his limbs be torn, as is this paper!
Hear me, immortal Jove, and grant it too!
Berk. Your grace must hence with me to Berkeley straight.
K. Edw. Whither you will; all places are alike,
And every earth is fit for burial.

Leices. Favour him, my lord, as much as lieth in you.
Berk. Even so betide my soul as I use him.
K. Edw. Mine enemy hath pitied my estate,
And that's the cause that I am now remov'd.
Berk. And thinks your grace that Berkeley will be cruel?
K. Edw. I know not; but of this am I assured,
That death ends all, and I can die but once.
Leicester, farewell!
Leices. Not yet, my lord; I'll bear you on your way. *Exeunt.*

[Scene II. *The royal palace*]

Enter Queen Isabella *and* Young Mortimer

Y. Mor. Fair Isabel, now have we our desire;
The proud corrupters of the light-brain'd king
Have done their homage to the lofty gallows,
And he himself lies in captivity.
Be rul'd by me, and we will rule the realm.
In any case take heed of childish fear,
For now we hold an old wolf by the ears,
That, if he slip, will seize upon us both,
And gripe the sorer, being grip'd himself.
Think therefore, madam, that imports us much
To erect your son with all the speed we may,
And that I be protector over him;
For our behoof will bear the greater sway
Whenas a king's name shall be under writ.
Q. Isab. Sweet Mortimer, the life of Isabel,
Be thou persuaded that I love thee well,
And therefore, so the prince my son be safe,
Whom I esteem as dear as these mine eyes,
Conclude against his father what thou wilt,
And I myself will willingly subscribe.
Y. Mor. First would I hear news that he were depos'd,
And then let me alone to handle him.

Enter MESSENGER

Letters! from whence?
Mess. From Killingworth, my lord.
Q. Isab. How fares my lord the king?
Mess. In health, madam, but full of pensiveness.
Q. Isab. Alas, poor soul, would I could ease his grief!
[*Enter the* BISHOP OF WINCHESTER *with the crown.*]
Thanks, gentle Winchester. [*To the* Messenger.] Sirrah, be gone.
[*Exit* Messenger.]
B. of Win. The king hath willingly resign'd his crown.
Q. Isab. O happy news! send for the prince, my son.
B. of Win. Further, or this letter was seal'd, Lord Berkeley came,
So that he now is gone from Killingworth;
And we have heard that Edmund laid a plot
To set his brother free; no more but so.
The lord of Berkeley is as pitiful
As Leicester that had charge of him before.
Q. Isab. Then let some other be his guardian.
Y. Mor. Let me alone, here is the privy seal.
[*Exit the* BISHOP OF WINCHESTER.]
Who's there?—Call hither Gurney and Matrevis.
[*To* Attendants *within.*]
To dash the heavy-headed Edmund's drift,
Berkeley shall be discharg'd, the king remov'd,
And none but we shall know where he lieth.
Q. Isab. But, Mortimer, as long as he survives,
What safety rests for us, or for my son?
Y. Mor. Speak, shall he presently be despatch'd and die?
Q. Isab. I would he were, so 'twere not by my means.

Enter MATREVIS *and* GURNEY

Y. Mor. Enough.—
Matrevis, write a letter presently
Unto the lord of Berkeley from ourself
That he resign the king to thee and Gurney;
And when 'tis done, we will subscribe our name.

Mat. It shall be done, my lord. [*Writes.*]
Y. Mor. Gurney.
Gur. My lord.
Y. Mor. As thou intend'st to rise by Mortimer,
Who now makes Fortune's wheel turn as he please,
Seek all the means thou canst to make him droop,
And neither give him kind word nor good look.
Gur. I warrant you, my lord.
Y. Mor. And this above the rest: because we hear
That Edmund casts[1] to work his liberty,
Remove him still from place to place by night,
Till at the last he come to Killingworth,
And then from thence to Berkeley back again;
And by the way, to make him fret the more,
Speak curstly to him, and in any case
Let no man comfort him; if he chance to weep,
But amplify his grief with bitter words.
Mat. Fear not, my lord, we'll do as you command.
Y. Mor. So now away; post thitherwards amain.
Q. Isab. Whither goes this letter? To my lord the king?
Commend me humbly to his majesty,
And tell him that I labour all in vain
To ease his grief, and work his liberty;
And bear him this as witness of my love. [*Gives a ring.*]
Mat. I will, madam. *Exit with* GURNEY.

Enter PRINCE EDWARD, *and* KENT *talking with him*

Y. Mor. Finely dissembled. Do so still, sweet queen.
Here comes the young prince with the Earl of Kent.
Q. Isab. Something he whispers in his childish ears.
Y. Mor. If he have such access unto the prince,
Our plots and stratagems will soon be dash'd.
Q. Isab. Use Edmund friendly, as if all were well.
Y. Mor. How fares my honourable lord of Kent?
Kent. In health, sweet Mortimer. How fares your grace?
Q. Isab. Well, if my lord your brother were enlarg'd.

[1] Plots.

Kent. I hear of late he hath depos'd himself.

Q. Isab. The more my grief.

Y. Mor. And mine.

Kent. Ah, they do dissemble! [*Aside.*]

Q. Isab. Sweet son, come hither, I must talk with thee.

Y. Mor. You being his uncle, and the next of blood,
Do look to be protector o'er the prince.

Kent. Not I, my lord; who should protect the son,
But she that gave him life? I mean the queen.

P. Edw. Mother, persuade me not to wear the crown:
Let him be king—I am too young to reign.

Q. Isab. But be content, seeing 'tis his highness' pleasure.

P. Edw. Let me but see him first, and then I will.

Kent. Ay, do, sweet nephew.

Q. Isab. Brother, you know it is impossible.

P. Edw. Why, is he dead?

Q. Isab. No, God forbid!

Kent. I would those words proceeded from your heart.

Y. Mor. Inconstant Edmund, dost thou favour him,
That wast the cause of his imprisonment?

Kent. The more cause have I now to make amends.

Y. Mor. [*Aside to* Q. Isab.] I tell thee, 'tis not meet that one so false
Should come about the person of a prince.—
My lord, he hath betray'd the king his brother,
And therefore trust him not.

P. Edw. But he repents, and sorrows for it now.

Q. Isab. Come, son, and go with this gentle lord and me.

P. Edw. With you I will, but not with Mortimer.

Y. Mor. Why, youngling, 'sdain'st thou so of Mortimer?
Then I will carry thee by force away.

P. Edw. Help, uncle Kent! Mortimer will wrong me.

Q. Isab. Brother Edmund, strive not; we are his friends;
Isabel is nearer than the Earl of Kent.

Kent. Sister, Edward is my charge, redeem him.

Q. Isab. Edward is my son, and I will keep him.

Kent. Mortimer shall know that he hath wrong'd me!—
Hence will I haste to Killingworth Castle,

And rescue aged Edward from his foes,
To be reveng'd on Mortimer and thee.

[*Aside.*] *Exeunt* [*on one side* QUEEN ISABELLA, PRINCE EDWARD, *and* Young MORTIMER; *on the other* KENT.]

[SCENE III. *Kenilworth Castle*]

Enter MATREVIS *and* GURNEY [*and* Soldiers,] *with* KING EDWARD

Mat. My lord, be not pensive, we are your friends;
Men are ordain'd to live in misery,
Therefore come,—dalliance dangereth our lives.

K. Edw. Friends, whither must unhappy Edward go?
Will hateful Mortimer appoint no rest?
Must I be vexed like the nightly bird,
Whose sight is loathsome to all winged fowls?
When will the fury of his mind assuage?
When will his heart be satisfied with blood?
If mine will serve, unbowel straight this breast,
And give my heart to Isabel and him;
It is the chiefest mark they level at.

Gur. Not so my liege, the queen hath given this charge
To keep your grace in safety;
Your passions make your dolours to increase.

K. Edw. This usage makes my misery to increase.
But can my air of life continue long
When all my senses are annoy'd with stench?
Within a dungeon England's king is kept,
Where I am starv'd for want of sustenance.
My daily diet is heart-breaking sobs,
That almost rents the closet of my heart.
Thus lives old Edward not reliev'd by any,
And so must die, though pitied by many.
O, water, gentle friends, to cool my thirst,
And clear my body from foul excrements!

Mat. Here's channel[1] water, as our charge is given.
Sit down, for we'll be barbers to your grace.

[1] Gutter.

K. Edw. Traitors, away! What, will you murder me,
Or choke your sovereign with puddle water?
Gur. No; but wash your face, and shave away your beard,
Lest you be known and so be rescued.
Mat. Why strive you thus? Your labour is in vain!
K. Edw. The wren may strive against the lion's strength,
But all in vain: so vainly do I strive
To seek for mercy at a tyrant's hand.

They wash him with puddle water, and shave his beard away.

Immortal powers! that knows the painful cares
That wait upon my poor distressed soul,
O level all your looks upon these daring men,
That wrongs their liege and sovereign, England's king!
O Gaveston, 'tis for thee that I am wrong'd,
For me, both thou and both the Spencers died!
And for your sakes a thousand wrongs I'll take.
The Spencers' ghosts, wherever they remain,
Wish well to mine; then tush, for them I'll die.
Mat. 'Twixt theirs and yours shall be no enmity.
Come, come away; now put the torches out,
We'll enter in by darkness to Killingworth.

Enter KENT

Gur. How now, who comes there?
Mat. Guard the king sure: it is the Earl of Kent.
K. Edw. O gentle brother, help to rescue me!
Mat. Keep them asunder; thrust in the king.
Kent. Soldiers, let me but talk to him one word.
Gur. Lay hands upon the earl for his assault.
Kent. Lay down your weapons, traitors! Yield the king!
Mat. Edmund, yield thou thyself, or thou shalt die.
Kent. Base villains, wherefore do you gripe me thus?
Gur. Bind him and so convey him to the court.
Kent. Where is the court but here? Here is the king;
And I will visit him; why stay you me?

Mat. The court is where Lord Mortimer remains;
Thither shall your honour go; and so farewell.

Exeunt MATREVIS *and* GURNEY, *with* KING EDWARD.

Kent. O miserable is that commonweal,
Where lords keep courts, and kings are locked in prison!

Sol. Wherefore stay we? On, sirs, to the court!

Kent. Ay, lead me whither you will, even to my death,
Seeing that my brother cannot be releas'd. *Exeunt.*

[SCENE IV. *The royal palace*]

Enter Young MORTIMER

Y. Mor. The king must die, or Mortimer goes down;
The commons now begin to pity him.
Yet he that is the cause of Edward's death,
Is sure to pay for it when his son's of age;
And therefore will I do it cunningly.
This letter, written by a friend of ours,
Contains his death, yet bids them save his life. [*Reads.*]
"Edwardum occidere nolite timere, bonum est
Fear not to kill the king, 'tis good he die."
But read it thus, and that's another sense:
"Edwardum occidere nolite, timere bonum est
Kill not the king, 'tis good to fear the worst."
Unpointed as it is, thus shall it go,
That, being dead, if it chance to be found,
Matrevis and the rest may bear the blame,
And we be quit that caus'd it to be done.
Within this room is lock'd the messenger
That shall convey it, and perform the rest;
And by a secret token that he bears,
Shall he be murdered when the deed is done.—
Lightborn, come forth!

Enter LIGHTBORN

Art thou as resolute as thou wast?

Light. What else, my lord? And far more resolute.

Y. Mor. And hast thou cast[1] how to accomplish it?
Light. Ay, ay, and none shall know which way he died.
Y. Mor. But at his looks, Lightborn, thou wilt relent.
Light. Relent! ha, ha! I use much to relent.
Y. Mor. Well, do it bravely, and be secret.
Light. You shall not need to give instructions;
'Tis not the first time I have kill'd a man.
I learn'd in Naples how to poison flowers;
To strangle with a lawn thrust through the throat;
To pierce the windpipe with a needle's point;
Or whilst one is asleep, to take a quill
And blow a little powder in his ears;
Or open his mouth and pour quicksilver down.
And yet I have a braver way than these.
Y. Mor. What's that?
Light. Nay, you shall pardon me; none shall know my tricks.
Y. Mor. I care not how it is, so it be not spied.
Deliver this to Gurney and Matrevis. [*Gives letter.*]
At every ten mile end thou hast a horse.
Take this; [*Gives money*] away! and never see me more.
Light. No!
Y. Mor. No;
Unless thou bring me news of Edward's death.
Light. That will I quickly do. Farewell, my lord. [*Exit.*]
Y. Mor. The prince I rule, the queen do I command,
And with a lowly congé to the ground,
The proudest lords salute me as I pass;
I seal, I cancel, I do what I will.
Fear'd am I more than lov'd;—let me be fear'd,
And when I frown, make all the court look pale.
I view the prince with Aristarchus' eyes,
Whose looks were as a breeching to a boy.
They thrust upon me the protectorship,
And sue to me for that that I desire.
While at the council-table, grave enough,
And not unlike a bashful puritan,

[1] Planned.

First I complain of imbecility,
Saying it is *onus quam gravissimum*;[2]
Till being interrupted by my friends,
Suscepi that *provinciam*[3] as they term it;
And to conclude, I am Protector now.
Now is all sure: the queen and Mortimer
Shall rule the realm, the king; and none rule us.
Mine enemies will I plague, my friends advance;
And what I list command who dare control?
Major sum quam cui possit fortuna nocere.[4]
And that this be the coronation-day,
It pleaseth me, and Isabel the queen. [*Trumpets within.*]
The trumpets sound, I must go take my place.

Enter the Young KING, QUEEN ISABELLA, *the* ARCHBISHOP OF CANTERBURY, Champion *and* Nobles

A. of Cant. Long live King Edward, by the grace of God
King of England and Lord of Ireland!
Cham. If any Christian, Heathen, Turk, or Jew,
Dares but affirm that Edward's not true king,
And will avouch his saying with the sword,
I am the champion that will combat him.
Y. Mor. None comes, sound trumpets. [*Trumpets sound.*]
K. Edw. Third. Champion, here's to thee.
[*Gives a purse.*]
Q. Isab. Lord Mortimer, now take him to your charge.

Enter Soldiers, *with* KENT *prisoner*

Y. Mor. What traitor have we there with blades and bills?
Sol. Edmund, the Earl of Kent.
K. Edw. Third. What hath he done?
Sol. 'A would have taken the king away perforce,
As we were bringing him to Killingworth.
Y. Mor. Did you attempt this rescue, Edmund? Speak.

[2] *A very heavy burden.* [3] *I have undertaken that office.* [4] *I am too great for fortune to injure.* Ovid, *Metam.* VI. 195.

Kent. Mortimer, I did; he is our king,
And thou compell'st this prince to wear the crown.
Y. Mor. Strike off his head! he shall have martial law.
Kent. Strike off my head! Base traitor, I defy thee!
K. Edw. Third. My lord, he is my uncle, and shall live.
Y. Mor. My lord, he is your enemy, and shall die.
Kent. Stay, villains!
K. Edw. Third. Sweet mother, if I cannot pardon him,
Entreat my Lord Protector for his life.
Q. Isab. Son, be content; I dare not speak a word.
K. Edw. Third. Nor I, and yet methinks I should command;
But, seeing I cannot, I'll entreat for him—
My lord, if you will let my uncle live,
I will requite it when I come to age.
Y. Mor. 'Tis for your highness' good, and for the realm's.—
How often shall I bid you bear him hence?
Kent. Art thou king? Must I die at thy command?
Y. Mor. At our command—Once more away with him.
Kent. Let me but stay and speak; I will not go.
Either my brother or his son is king,
And none of both them thirst for Edmund's blood:
And therefore, soldiers, whither will you hale me?
Soldiers *hale* KENT *away, to be beheaded.*
K. Edw. Third. What safety may I look for at his hands,
If that my uncle shall be murdered thus?
Q. Isab. Fear not, sweet boy, I'll guard thee from thy foes;
Had Edmund lived, he would have sought thy death.
Come, son, we'll ride a-hunting in the park.
K. Edw. Third. And shall my uncle Edmund ride with us?
Q. Isab. He is a traitor; think not on him; come. *Exeunt.*

[SCENE V. *Berkeley Castle*]

Enter MATREVIS *and* GURNEY

Mat. Gurney, I wonder the king dies not,
Being in a vault up to the knees in water,
To which the channels of the castle run,

From whence a damp continually ariseth,
That were enough to poison any man,
Much more a king brought up so tenderly.
Gur. And so do I, Matrevis: yesternight
I opened but the door to throw him meat,
And I was almost stifled with the savour.
Mat. He hath a body able to endure
More than we can inflict: and therefore now
Let us assail his mind another while.
Gur. Send for him out thence, and I will anger him.
Mat. But stay, who's this?

Enter LIGHTBORN

Light. My Lord Protector greets you. [*Gives letter.*]
Gur. What's here? I know not how to construe it.
Mat. Gurney, it was left unpointed for the nonce;
"Edwardum occidere nolite timere,"
That's his meaning.
Light. Know ye this token? I must have the king.
[*Gives token.*]
Mat. Ay, stay awhile, thou shalt have answer straight.
This villain's sent to make away the king. [*Aside.*]
Gur. I thought as much. [*Aside.*]
Mat. And when the murder's done,
See how he must be handled for his labour.
Pereat iste![1] Let him have the king. [*Aside.*]
What else? Here is the key, this is the lake,[2]
Do as you are commanded by my lord.
Light. I know what I must do. Get you away.
Yet be not far off, I shall need your help;
See that in the next room I have a fire,
And get me a spit, and let it be red-hot.
Mat. Very well.
Gur. Need you anything besides?
Light. What else? A table and a feather-bed.
Gur. That's all?

[1] *Let this man die.* [2] Perhaps for "lock."

Light. Ay, ay; so, when I call you, bring it in.
Mat. Fear not thou that.
Gur. Here's a light, to go into the dungeon.
[*Gives a light, and then exit with* MATREVIS.]
Light. So now
Must I about this gear;[3] ne'er was there any
So finely handled as this king shall be.
For, here's a place indeed, with all my heart!
K. Edw. Who's there? What light is that? wherefore com'st thou?
Light. To comfort you, and bring you joyful news.
K. Edw. Small comfort finds poor Edward in thy looks.
Villain, I know thou com'st to murder me.
Light. To murder you, my most gracious lord!
Far is it from my heart to do you harm.
The queen sent me to see how you were used,
For she relents at this your misery:
And what eyes can refrain from shedding tears,
To see a king in this most piteous state?
K. Edw. Weep'st thou already? List awhile to me
And then thy heart, were it as Gurney's is,
Or as Matrevis', hewn from the Caucasus,
Yet will it melt, ere I have done my tale.
This dungeon where they keep me is the sink
Wherein the filth of all the castle falls.
Light. O villains!
K. Edw. And there in mire and puddle have I stood
This ten days' space; and, lest that I should sleep,
One plays continually upon a drum.
They give me bread and water, being a king;
So that, for want of sleep and sustenance,
My mind's distempered, and my body's numb'd,
And whether I have limbs or no I know not.
O, would my blood dropp'd out from every vein,
As doth this water from my tattered robes.
Tell Isabel, the queen, I look'd not thus,

[3] Business.

When for her sake I ran at tilt in France,
And there unhors'd the Duke of Cleremont.
Light. O speak no more, my lord! this breaks my heart.
Lie on this bed, and rest yourself awhile.
K. Edw. These looks of thine can harbour nought but death:
I see my tragedy written in thy brows.
Yet stay a while; forbear thy bloody hand,
And let me see the stroke before it comes,
That even then when I shall lose my life,
My mind may be more steadfast on my God.
Light. What means your highness to mistrust me thus?
K. Edw. What mean'st thou to dissemble with me thus?
Light. These hands were never stain'd with innocent blood,
Nor shall they now be tainted with a king's.
K. Edw. Forgive my thought for having such a thought.
One jewel have I left; receive thou this. [*Giving jewel.*]
Still fear I, and I know not what's the cause,
But every joint shakes as I give it thee.
O, if thou harbour'st murder in thy heart,
Let this gift change thy mind, and save thy soul!
Know that I am a king: O, at that name
I feel a hell of grief! Where is my crown?
Gone, gone! and do I still remain alive?
Light. You're overwatch'd, my lord; lie down and rest.
K. Edw. But that grief keeps me waking, I should sleep;
For not these ten days have these eye-lids clos'd.
Now as I speak they fall, and yet with fear
Open again. O wherefore sitt'st thou here?
Light. If you mistrust me, I'll begone, my lord.
K. Edw. No, no, for if thou mean'st to murder me,
Thou wilt return again, and therefore stay. [*Sleeps.*]
Light. He sleeps.
K. Edw. [*waking*]. O let me not die yet! O stay a while!
Light. How now, my lord?
K. Edw. Something still buzzeth in mine ears,
And tells me if I sleep I never wake;
This fear is that which makes me tremble thus.

And therefore tell me, wherefore art thou come?
Light. To rid thee of thy life.—Matrevis, come!

Enter MATREVIS *and* GURNEY

K. Edw. I am too weak and feeble to resist:—
Assist me, sweet God, and receive my soul!
Light. Run for the table.
K. Edw. O spare me, or despatch me in a trice.
[MATREVIS *brings in a table.*]
Light. So, lay the table down, and stamp on it,
But not too hard, lest that you bruise his body.
[KING EDWARD *is murdered.*]
Mat. I fear me that this cry will raise the town,
And therefore, let us take horse and away.
Light. Tell me, sirs, was it not bravely done?
Gur. Excellent well: take this for thy reward.
GURNEY *stabs* LIGHTBORN [*who dies.*]
Come, let us cast the body in the moat,
And bear the king's to Mortimer our lord:
Away! *Exeunt* [*with the bodies.*]

[SCENE VI. *The royal palace, London*]

Enter Young MORTIMER *and* MATREVIS

Y. Mor. Is't done, Matrevis, and the murderer dead?
Mat. Ay, my good lord; I would it were undone!
Y. Mor. Matrevis, if thou now growest penitent
I'll be thy ghostly father; therefore choose,
Whether thou wilt be secret in this,
Or else die by the hand of Mortimer.
Mat. Gurney, my lord, is fled, and will, I fear
Betray us both, therefore let me fly.
Y. Mor. Fly to the savages!
Mat. I humbly thank your honour. [*Exit.*]
Y. Mor. As for myself, I stand as Jove's huge tree,
And others are but shrubs compar'd to me.
All tremble at my name, and I fear none;
Let's see who dare impeach me for his death!

Enter QUEEN ISABELLA

Q. Isab. Ah, Mortimer, the king my son hath news
His father's dead, and we have murdered him!
Y. Mor. What if he have? The king is yet a child.
Q. Isab. Ay, but he tears his hair, and wrings his hands,
And vows to be reveng'd upon us both.
Into the council-chamber he is gone,
To crave the aid and succour of his peers.
Ay me! see here he comes, and they with him.
Now, Mortimer, begins our tragedy.

Enter KING EDWARD THE THIRD, LORDS, *and* Attendants.

1st Lord. Fear not, my lord, know that you are a king.
K. Edw. Third. Villain!—
Y. Mor. How now, my lord!
K. Edw. Third. Think not that I am frighted with thy words!
My father's murdered through thy treachery;
And thou shalt die, and on his mournful hearse
Thy hateful and accursed head shall lie,
To witness to the world, that by thy means
His kingly body was too soon interr'd.
Q. Isab. Weep not, sweet son!
K. Edw. Third. Forbid me not to weep; he was my father;
And, had you lov'd him half so well as I,
You could not bear his death thus patiently.
But you, I fear, conspir'd with Mortimer.
1st Lord. Why speak you not unto my lord the king?
Y. Mor. Because I think scorn to be accus'd.
Who is the man dares say I murdered him?
K. Edw. Third. Traitor! in me my loving father speaks,
And plainly saith, 'twas thou that murd'redst him.
Y. Mor. But has your grace no other proof than this?
K. Edw. Third. Yes, if this be the hand of Mortimer.
[*Shewing letter.*]
Y. Mor. False Gurney hath betray'd me and himself. [*Aside.*]
Q. Isab. I fear'd as much; murder cannot be hid. [*Aside.*]

Y. Mor. It is my hand; what gather you by this?
K. Edw. Third. That thither thou didst send a murderer.
Y. Mor. What murderer? Bring forth the man I sent.
K. Edw. Third. Ah, Mortimer, thou knowest that he is slain;
And so shalt thou be too.—Why stays he here
Bring him unto a hurdle, drag him forth;
Hang him, I say, and set his quarters up;
But bring his head back presently to me.
Q. Isab. For my sake, sweet son, pity Mortimer!
Y. Mor. Madam, entreat not, I will rather die,
Than sue for life unto a paltry boy.
K. Edw. Third. Hence with the traitor! with the murderer!
Y. Mor. Base Fortune, now I see, that in thy wheel
There is a point, to which when men aspire,
They tumble headlong down: that point I touch'd,
And, seeing there was no place to mount up higher,
Why should I grieve at my declining fall?—
Farewell, fair queen; weep not for Mortimer,
That scorns the world, and, as a traveller,
Goes to discover countries yet unknown.
K. Edw. Third. What! suffer you the traitor to delay?
[Young MORTIMER *is taken away by* First Lord *and* Attendants.]
Q. Isab. As thou receivedest thy life from me,
Spill not the blood of gentle Mortimer!
K. Edw. Third. This argues that you spilt my father's blood,
Else would you not entreat for Mortimer.
Q. Isab. I spill his blood? No.
K. Edw. Third. Ay, madam, you; for so the rumour runs.
Q. Isab. That rumour is untrue; for loving thee,
Is this report rais'd on poor Isabel.
K. Edw. Third. I do not think her so unnatural.
2nd Lord. My lord, I fear me it will prove too true.
K. Edw. Third. Mother, you are suspected for his death
And therefore we commit you to the Tower
Till farther trial may be made thereof;
If you be guilty, though I be your son,

Think not to find me slack or pitiful.
Q. Isab. Nay, to my death, for too long have I liv'd
Whenas my son thinks to abridge my days.
K. Edw. Third. Away with her, her words enforce these tears,
And I shall pity her if she speak again.
Q. Isab. Shall I not mourn for my beloved lord,
And with the rest accompany him to his grave?
2nd Lord. Thus, madam, 'tis the king's will you shall hence.
Q. Isab. He hath forgotten me; stay, I am his mother.
2nd Lord. That boots not; therefore, gentle madam, go.
Q. Isab. Then come, sweet death, and rid me of this grief.
[*Exit.*]

[*Re-enter* 1st Lord, *with the head of* Young MORTIMER]

1st Lord. My lord, here is the head of Mortimer.
K. Edw. Third. Go fetch my father's hearse, where it shall lie;
And bring my funeral robes. [*Exeunt* Attendants.]
Accursed head,
Could I have rul'd thee then, as I do now,
Thou had'st not hatch'd this monstrous treachery!—
Here comes the hearse; help me to mourn, my lords.

[*Re-enter* Attendants *with the hearse and funeral robes*]

Sweet father, here unto thy murdered ghost
I offer up this wicked traitor's head;
And let these tears, distilling from mine eyes,
Be witness of my grief and innocency. [*Exeunt.*]

THE TRAGEDY OF HAMLET PRINCE OF DENMARK

BY

WILLIAM SHAKESPEARE

INTRODUCTORY NOTE

The tragedy of "Hamlet," the most renowned of English dramas, is based on a legend found in the "History of the Danes," written by Saxo Grammaticus about 1200. It came to England through the French, and was already on the stage in a version now lost, before Shakespeare took it up. The earliest edition of our play was printed in a corrupt form in 1603, and was written at least as early as 1602. A more correct edition appeared in 1604, and further alterations appeared in the version printed in the first collected edition of Shakespeare's plays in 1623. The author seems to have worked over and revised this tragedy more than any other of his dramas.

The main situation of the tragedy goes back to the prose tale. There we have a king murdered by his brother, who had previously seduced and has now married the queen; and the son of the king, aiming at revenge, finally achieving it, and using the device of pretended madness to protect himself in the meantime. The prototype of Polonius is killed while eavesdropping, but his character bears little resemblance to Shakespeare's Lord Chamberlain; Ophelia and Horatio are merely hinted at; while Laertes, Fortinbras, and several of the minor characters, such as the grave-diggers and Osric, are altogether absent. The original Hamlet goes to England without interruption from pirates, witnesses the death of his two companions, returns and kills not only the king, but all his courtiers, goes to England again and marries two wives, one of whom betrays him to his death.

Other elements of the tragedy that are probably not due to Shakespeare's invention have been gathered from a study of contemporary "tragedies of revenge." How many of such additions were made by Shakespeare, how many by the author of the lost play, cannot be decided. But for those things which have raised "Hamlet" to its preeminent position in the history of literature,—the magnificence of the poetry, the amazing truth and subtlety of the psychology, and the intensity of the tragic emotion, it is not hard to assign the credit.

THE TRAGEDY OF HAMLET PRINCE OF DENMARK

DRAMATIS PERSONÆ

CLAUDIUS, King of Denmark.
HAMLET, son to the late, and nephew to the present King.
POLONIUS, Lord Chamberlain.
HORATIO, friend to Hamlet.
LAERTES, son to Polonius.
VOLTIMAND, CORNELIUS, ROSENCRANTZ, GUILDENSTERN, OSRIC, A Gentleman, } courtiers.
MARCELLUS, BERNARDO, } officers.
FRANCISCO, a soldier.
REYNALDO, servant to Polonius.
A Priest.
Players.
Two Clowns, grave-diggers.
FORTINBRAS, Prince of Norway.
A Captain.
English Ambassadors.

GERTRUDE, Queen of Denmark, and mother to Hamlet.
OPHELIA, daughter to Polonius.

Ghost of Hamlet's Father.

Lords, Ladies, Officers, Soldiers, Sailors, Messengers, and other Attendants

[SCENE: ELSINORE, DENMARK]

ACT I

SCENE I. [*Elsinore. A platform before the castle*]

FRANCISCO [*at his post. Enter to him*] BERNARDO

Bernardo

WHO's there?
Fran. Nay, answer me. Stand, and unfold yourself.
Ber. Long live the king!
Fran. Bernardo?
Ber. He.
Fran. You come most carefully upon your hour.
Ber. 'Tis now struck twelve. Get thee to bed, Francisco.
Fran. For this relief much thanks. 'Tis bitter cold,
And I am sick at heart.

Ber. Have you had quiet guard?
Fran. Not a mouse stirring.
Ber. Well, good-night.
If you do meet Horatio and Marcellus,
The rivals[1] of my watch, bid them make haste.

Enter HORATIO *and* MARCELLUS

Fran. I think I hear them. Stand, ho! Who's there?
Hor. Friends to this ground.
Mar. And liegemen to the Dane.
Fran. Give you good-night.
Mar. O, farewell, honest soldier.
Who hath reliev'd you?
Fran. Bernardo has my place.
Give you good-night. *Exit.*
Mar. Holla! Bernardo!
Ber. Say,
What, is Horatio there?
Hor. A piece of him.
Ber. Welcome, Horatio; welcome, good Marcellus.
Hor. What, has this thing appear'd again to-night?
Ber. I have seen nothing.
Mar. Horatio says 'tis but our fantasy,
And will not let belief take hold of him
Touching this dreaded sight, twice seen of us;
Therefore I have entreated him along
With us to watch the minutes of this night,
That if again this apparition come,
He may approve our eyes and speak to it.
Hor. Tush, tush, 'twill not appear.
Ber. Sit down a while,
And let us once again assail your ears,
That are so fortified against our story,
What we two nights have seen.
Hor. Well, sit we down,
And let us hear Bernardo speak of this.

[1] Partners.

Ber. Last night of all,
When yond same star that's westward from the pole
Had made his course to illume that part of heaven
Where now it burns, Marcellus and myself,
The bell then beating one,—

Enter Ghost

Mar. Peace, break thee off! Look, where it comes again!
Ber. In the same figure, like the king that's dead.
Mar. Thou art a scholar; speak to it, Horatio.
Ber. Looks it not like the King? Mark it, Horatio.
Hor. Most like; it harrows me with fear and wonder.
Ber. It would be spoke to.
Mar. Question it, Horatio.
Hor. What art thou that usurp'st this time of night,
Together with that fair and warlike form
In which the majesty of buried Denmark
Did sometimes march? By heaven I charge thee, speak!
Mar. It is offended.
Ber. See, it stalks away!
Hor. Stay! speak, speak! I charge thee, speak! *Exit* Ghost.
Mar. 'Tis gone, and will not answer.
Ber. How now, Horatio! you tremble and look pale.
Is not this something more than fantasy?
What think you on 't?
Hor. Before my God, I might not this believe
Without the sensible[2] and true avouch[3]
Of mine own eyes.
Mar. Is it not like the King?
Hor. As thou art to thyself.
Such was the very armour he had on
When he the ambitious Norway combated.
So frown'd he once, when, in an angry parle,
He smote the sledded Polacks on the ice.
'Tis strange.

[2] Appealing to the senses.
[3] Evidence.

Mar. Thus twice before, and jump[4] at this dead hour,
With martial stalk hath he gone by our watch.
Hor. In what particular thought to work I know not;
But, in the gross and scope[5] of my opinion,
This bodes some strange eruption to our state.
Mar. Good now, sit down, and tell me, he that knows,
Why this same strict and most observant watch
So nightly toils the subject of the land,
And why such daily cast of brazen cannon,
And foreign mart for implements of war;
Why such impress of shipwrights, whose sore task
Does not divide the Sunday from the week.
What might be toward, that this sweaty haste
Doth make the night joint-labourer with the day,
Who is't that can inform me?
Hor. That can I;
At least, the whisper goes so. Our last king,
Whose image even but now appear'd to us,
Was, as you know, by Fortinbras of Norway,
Thereto prick'd on by a most emulate pride,
Dar'd to the combat; in which our valiant Hamlet—
For so this side of our known world esteem'd him—
Did slay this Fortinbras; who, by a seal'd compact,
Well ratified by law and heraldry,
Did forfeit, with his life, all those his lands
Which he stood seiz'd of,[6] to the conqueror;
Against the which, a moiety competent
Was gaged[7] by our king; which had return'd
To the inheritance of Fortinbras,
Had he been vanquisher; as, by the same covenant,
And carriage of the article design'd,[8]
His fell to Hamlet. Now, sir, young Fortinbras,
Of unimproved mettle hot and full,
Hath in the skirts of Norway here and there
Shark'd up[9] a list of landless resolutes,

[4] Precisely. [5] General view.
[6] Possessed of. [7] Pledged. [8] Tenor of the agreement. [9] Gathered in.

For food and diet, to some enterprise
That hath a stomach[10] in 't; which is no other—
As it doth well appear unto our state—
But to recover of us, by strong hand
And terms compulsative,[11] those foresaid lands
So by his father lost; and this, I take it,
Is the main motive of our preparations,
The source of this our watch, and the chief head
Of this post-haste and romage[12] in the land.
[*Ber.* I think it be no other but e'en so.
Well may it sort[13] that this portentous figure
Comes armed through our watch, so like the King
That was and is the question of these wars.
Hor. A mote it is to trouble the mind's eye.
In the most high and palmy state of Rome,
A little ere the mightiest Julius fell,
The graves stood tenantless and the sheeted dead
Did squeak and gibber in the Roman streets.

. . . .

As stars with trains of fire and dews of blood,
Disasters in the sun; and the moist star
Upon whose influence Neptune's empire stands
Was sick almost to doomsday with eclipse.
And even the like precurse of fierce events,
As harbingers[14] preceding still the fates
And prologue to the omen coming on,
Have heaven and earth together demonstrated
Unto our climatures[15] and countrymen.]

Re-enter Ghost

But soft, behold! Lo, where it comes again!
I'll cross it, though it blast me. Stay, illusion!
If thou hast any sound, or use of voice,
Speak to me;
If there be any good thing to be done
That may to thee do ease and grace to me,

10 Relish. 11 Compulsory. 12 Turmoil. 13 Agree. 14 Fore-runners. 15 Regions.

Speak to me;
If thou art privy to thy country's fate,
Which, happily, foreknowing may avoid,
O speak!
Or if thou hast uphoarded in thy life
Extorted treasure in the womb of earth,
For which, they say, you spirits oft walk in death,
Speak of it; stay, and speak! (*Cock crows.*)
Stop it, Marcellus.
Mar. Shall I strike at it with my partisan?[16]
Hor. Do, if it will not stand.
Ber. 'Tis here!
Hor. 'Tis here!
Mar. 'Tis gone! *Exit* Ghost.
We do it wrong, being so majestical,
To offer it the show of violence;
For it is, as the air, invulnerable,
And our vain blows malicious mockery.
Ber. It was about to speak, when the cock crew.
Hor. And then it started like a guilty thing
Upon a fearful summons. I have heard,
The cock, that is the trumpet to the morn,
Doth with his lofty and shrill-sounding throat
Awake the god of day; and, at his warning,
Whether in sea or fire, in earth or air,
The extravagant[17] and erring[17] spirit hies
To his confine; and of the truth herein
This present object made probation.
Mar. It faded on the crowing of the cock.
Some say that ever 'gainst that season comes
Wherein our Saviour's birth is celebrated,
The bird of dawning singeth all night long;
And then, they say, no spirit can walk abroad;
The nights are wholesome; then no planets strike,[18]
No fairy takes,[19] nor witch hath power to charm,
So hallow'd and so gracious is the time.

[16] Halberd. [17] Wandering beyond bounds. [18] Exert evil influence. [19] Charms.

Hor. So have I heard and do in part believe it.
But, look, the morn, in russet mantle clad,
Walks o'er the dew of yon high eastern hill.
Break we our watch up; and, by my advice,
Let us impart what we have seen to-night
Unto young Hamlet; for, upon my life,
This spirit, dumb to us, will speak to him.
Do you consent we shall acquaint him with it,
As needful in our loves, fitting our duty?
Mar. Let's do 't, I pray; and I this morning know
Where we shall find him most conveniently. *Exeunt.*

[SCENE II. *A room of state in the castle*]

Flourish. Enter the KING, QUEEN, HAMLET, POLONIUS, LAERTES, OPHELIA, Lords, *and* Attendants

King. Though yet of Hamlet our dear brother's death
The memory be green, and that it us befitted
To bear our hearts in grief, and our whole kingdom
To be contracted in one brow of woe,
Yet so far hath discretion fought with nature
That we with wisest sorrow think on him
Together with remembrance of ourselves.
Therefore our sometime sister, now our queen,
The imperial jointress of this warlike state,
Have we, as 'twere with a defeated[1] joy,—
With one auspicious and one dropping eye,
With mirth in funeral and with dirge in marriage,
In equal scale weighing delight and dole,—
Taken to wife; nor have we herein barr'd
Your better wisdoms, which have freely gone
With this affair along. For all, our thanks.
Now follows that you know: young Fortinbras,
Holding a weak supposal of our worth,
Or thinking by our late dear brother's death
Our state to be disjoint and out of frame,

[1] Disfigured.

Colleagued with the dream of his advantage,
He hath not fail'd to pester us with message
Importing the surrender of those lands
Lost by his father, with all bonds of law,
To our most valiant brother. So much for him.

Enter VOLTIMAND *and* CORNELIUS

Now for ourself and for this time of meeting,
Thus much the business is: we have here writ
To Norway, uncle of young Fortinbras,—
Who, impotent and bed-rid, scarcely hears
Of this his nephew's purpose,—to suppress
His further gait[2] herein, in that the levies,
The lists and full proportions, are all made
Out of his subject;[3] and we here dispatch
You, good Cornelius, and you, Voltimand,
For bearers of this greeting to old Norway;
Giving to you no further personal power
To business with the king, more than the scope
Of these delated[4] articles allow. [*Giving a paper.*
Farewell, and let your haste commend your duty.

[*Cor.*] } *Vol.* } In that and all things will we show our duty.

King. We doubt it nothing; heartily farewell.

Exeunt VOLTIMAND *and* CORNELIUS.

And now, Laertes, what's the news with you?
You told us of some suit; what is 't, Laertes?
You cannot speak of reason to the Dane,
And lose your voice. What wouldst thou beg, Laertes,
That shall not be my offer, not thy asking?
The head is not more native to the heart,
The hand more instrumental to the mouth,
Than is the throne of Denmark to thy father.
What wouldst thou have, Laertes?

Laer. Dread my lord,
Your leave and favour to return to France;

[2] Progress. [3] People. [4] Offered.

From whence though willingly I came to Denmark
To show my duty in your coronation,
Yet now, I must confess, that duty done,
My thoughts and wishes bend again towards France
And bow them to your gracious leave and pardon.

King. Have you your father's leave? What says Polonius?

Pol. He hath, my lord, [wrung from me my slow leave
By laboursome petition, and at last
Upon his will I seal'd my hard consent.]
I do beseech you, give him leave to go.

King. Take thy fair hour, Laertes. Time be thine,
And thy best graces spend it at thy will!
But now, my cousin Hamlet, and my son,—

Ham. [*Aside.*] A little more than kin, and less than kind.

King. How is it that the clouds still hang on you?

Ham. Not so, my lord; I am too much i' the sun.

Queen. Good Hamlet, cast thy nighted colour off,
And let thine eye look like a friend on Denmark.
Do not for ever with thy vailed[5] lids
Seek for thy noble father in the dust.
Thou know'st 'tis common; all that lives must die,
Passing through nature to eternity.

Ham. Ay, madam, it is common.

Queen. If it be,
Why seems it so particular with thee?

Ham. Seems, madam! Nay, it is; I know not "seems."
'Tis not alone my inky cloak, good mother,
Nor customary suits of solemn black,
Nor windy suspiration of forc'd breath,
No, nor the fruitful river in the eye,
Nor the dejected haviour[6] of the visage,
Together with all forms, moods, shows of grief,
That can denote me truly. These indeed seem,
For they are actions that a man might play;
But I have that within which passeth show,
These but the trappings and the suits of woe.

[5] Lowered. [6] Behavior.

King. 'Tis sweet and commendable in your nature, Hamlet,
To give these mourning duties to your father.
But, you must know, your father lost a father;
That father lost, lost his; and the survivor bound
In filial obligation for some term
To do obsequious sorrow. But to persever
In obstinate condolement is a course
Of impious stubbornness; 'tis unmanly grief;
It shows a will most incorrect to heaven,
A heart unfortified, a mind impatient,
An understanding simple and unschool'd;
For what we know must be, and is as common
As any the most vulgar thing to sense,
Why should we in our peevish opposition
Take it to heart? Fie! 'tis a fault to heaven,
A fault against the dead, a fault to nature,
To reason most absurd, whose common theme
Is death of fathers, and who still hath cried,
From the first corse till he that died to-day,
"This must be so." We pray you, throw to earth
This unprevailing woe, and think of us
As of a father; for, let the world take note,
You are the most immediate to our throne,
And with no less nobility of love
Than that which dearest father bears his son,
Do I impart towards you. For your intent
In going back to school in Wittenberg,
It is most retrograde[7] to our desire;
And we beseech you, bend you to remain
Here in the cheer and comfort of our eye,
Our chiefest courtier, cousin, and our son.
Queen. Let not thy mother lose her prayers, Hamlet,
I prithee, stay with us; go not to Wittenberg.
Ham. I shall in all my best obey you, madam.
King. Why, 'tis a loving and a fair reply.
Be as ourself in Denmark. Madam, come;

[7] Opposed.

This gentle and unforc'd accord of Hamlet
Sits smiling to my heart; in grace whereof,
No jocund health that Denmark drinks to-day,
But the great cannon to the clouds shall tell,
And the King's rouse[8] the heavens shall bruit[9] again,
Re-speaking earthly thunder. Come away.

Flourish. Exeunt all but HAMLET.

Ham. O, that this too too solid flesh would melt,
Thaw, and resolve itself into a dew!
Or that the Everlasting had not fix'd
His canon 'gainst self-slaughter! O God! God!
How weary, stale, flat, and unprofitable,
Seems to me all the uses of this world!
Fie on't! oh fie, fie! 'Tis an unweeded garden,
That grows to seed; things rank and gross in nature
Possess it merely.[10] That it should come to this!
But two months dead! Nay, not so much, not two.
So excellent a king; that was, to this,
Hyperion to a satyr; so loving to my mother
That he might not beteem[11] the winds of heaven
Visit her face too roughly. Heaven and earth!
Must I remember? Why, she would hang on him,
As if increase of appetite had grown
By what it fed on; and yet, within a month,—
Let me not think on 't!—Frailty, thy name is woman!—
A little month, or e'er those shoes were old
With which she followed my poor father's body,
Like Niobe, all tears,—why she, even she—
O God! a beast, that wants discourse of reason,[12]
Would have mourn'd longer—married with mine uncle,
My father's brother, but no more like my father
Than I to Hercules; within a month,
Ere yet the salt of most unrighteous tears
Had left the flushing[13] of her galled eyes,
She married. O, most wicked speed, to post

[8] Carouse. [9] Report noisily. [10] Entirely. [11] Allow.
[12] Reasoning power. [13] Redness, or filling full.

With such dexterity to incestuous sheets!
It is not, nor it cannot come to good.—
But break, my heart, for I must hold my tongue.

Enter HORATIO, MARCELLUS, *and* BERNARDO

Hor. Hail to your lordship!
Ham. I am glad to see you well,
Horatio!—or I do forget myself.
Hor. The same, my lord, and your poor servant ever.
Ham. Sir, my good friend; I'll change that name with you.
And what make you from Wittenberg, Horatio?
Marcellus?
Mar. My good lord!
Ham. I am very glad to see you. [*To* BER.] Good even, sir.—
But what, in faith, make you from Wittenberg?
Hor. A truant disposition, good my lord.
Ham. I would not hear your enemy say so,
Nor shall you do mine ear that violence,
To make it truster of your own report
Against yourself. I know you are no truant.
But what is your affair in Elsinore?
We'll teach you to drink deep ere you depart.
Hor. My lord, I came to see your father's funeral.
Ham. I pray thee, do not mock me, fellow-student.
I think it was to see my mother's wedding.
Hor. Indeed, my lord, it followed hard upon.
Ham. Thrift, thrift, Horatio! The funeral bak'd-meats
Did coldly furnish forth the marriage tables.
Would I had met my dearest foe in heaven
Ere I had ever seen that day, Horatio!
My father!—methinks I see my father.
Hor. Oh, where, my lord?
Ham. In my mind's eye, Horatio,
Hor. I saw him once; he was a goodly king.
Ham. He was a man, take him for all in all,
I shall not look upon his like again.

Hor. My lord, I think I saw him yesternight.
Ham. Saw? Who?
Hor. My lord, the King your father.
Ham. The King my father!
Hor. Season your admiration[14] for a while
With an attent ear, till I may deliver,
Upon the witness of these gentlemen,
This marvel to you.
Ham. For God's love, let me hear.
Hor. Two nights together had these gentlemen,
Marcellus and Bernardo, on their watch,
In the dead waste and middle of the night,
Been thus encount'red. A figure like your father,
Arm'd at all points exactly, cap-a-pie,
Appears before them, and with solemn march
Goes slow and stately by them. Thrice he walk'd
By their oppress'd and fear-surprised eyes,
Within his truncheon's length; whilst they, distill'd[15]
Almost to jelly with the act of fear,
Stand dumb and speak not to him. This to me
In dreadful secrecy impart they did,
And I with them the third night kept the watch;
Where, as they had deliver'd, both in time,
Form of the thing, each word made true and good,
The apparition comes. I knew your father;
These hands are not more like.
Ham. But where was this!
Mar. My lord, upon the platform where we watch'd.
Ham. Did you not speak to it?
Hor. My lord, I did;
But answer made it none. Yet once methought
It lifted up it[16] head and did address
Itself to motion, like as it would speak;
But even then the morning cock crew loud,
And at the sound it shrunk in haste away,
And vanish'd from our sight.

[14] Wonder. [15] Melted. [16] Its.

Ham. 'Tis very strange.
Hor. As I do live, my honour'd lord, 'tis true,
And we did think it writ down in our duty
To let you know of it.
Ham. Indeed, indeed, sirs. But this troubles me.
Hold you the watch to-night?
Mar., *Ber.* We do, my lord.
Ham. Arm'd, say you?
Mar., *Ber.* Arm'd, my lord.
Ham. From top to toe?
Mar., *Ber.* My lord, from head to foot.
Ham. Then saw you not his face?
Hor. O, yes, my lord; he wore his beaver up.
Ham. What, look'd he frowningly?
Hor. A countenance more
In sorrow than in anger.
Ham. Pale, or red?
Hor. Nay, very pale.
Ham. And fix'd his eyes upon you?
Hor. Most constantly.
Ham. I would I had been there.
Hor. It would have much amaz'd you.
Ham. Very like, very like. Stay'd it long?
Hor. While one with moderate haste might tell a hundred
Mar., *Ber.* Longer, longer.
Hor. Not when I saw 't.
Ham. His beard was grizzly? No?
Hor. It was, as I have seen it in his life,
A sable silver'd.
Ham. I will watch to-night;
Perchance 'twill walk again.
Hor. I warrant you it will.

Ham. If it assume my noble father's person,
I'll speak to it, though hell itself should gape
And bid me hold my peace. I pray you all,
If you have hitherto conceal'd this sight,
Let it be tenable[17] in your silence still;
And whatsoever else shall hap to-night,
Give it an understanding, but no tongue.
I will requite your loves. So, fare ye well.
Upon the platform 'twixt eleven and twelve,
I'll visit you.
All. Our duty to your honour.
Ham. Your love, as mine to you; farewell.
Exeunt [*all but* HAMLET].
My father's spirit in arms! All is not well;
I doubt some foul play. Would the night were come!
Till then sit still, my soul. Foul deeds will rise,
Though all the earth o'erwhelm them, to men's eyes. *Exit.*

SCENE III. [*A room in Polonius's house*]

Enter LAERTES *and* OPHELIA

Laer. My necessaries are embark'd, farewell;
And, sister, as the winds give benefit
And convoy is assistant, do not sleep,
But let me hear from you.
Oph. Do you doubt that?
Laer. For Hamlet and the trifling of his favours,
Hold it a fashion and a toy in blood,
A violet in the youth of primy[1] nature,
Forward, not permanent, sweet, not lasting,
The [perfume and] suppliance[2] of a minute;
No more.
Oph. No more but so?
Laer. Think it no more:
For nature crescent does not grow alone

[17] Held. [1] In the spring, lusty. [2] What fills in.

In thews[3] and bulk, but, as this temple waxes,
The inward service of the mind and soul
Grows wide withal. Perhaps he loves you now,
And now no soil nor cautel[4] doth besmirch
The virtue of his will; but you must fear,
His greatness weigh'd, his will is not his own;
For he himself is subject to his birth.
He may not, as unvalued persons do,
Carve for himself, for on his choice depends
The sanity and health of the whole state;
And therefore must his choice be circumscrib'd
Unto the voice and yielding[5] of that body
Whereof he is the head. Then, if he says he loves you,
It fits your wisdom so far to believe it
As he in his particular act and place
May give his saying deed; which is no further
Than the main voice of Denmark goes withal.
Then weigh what loss your honour may sustain
If with too credent[6] ear you list his songs,
Or lose your heart, or your chaste treasure open
To his unmast'red importunity.
Fear it, Ophelia, fear it, my dear sister,
And keep you in the rear of your affection,
Out of the shot and danger of desire.
The chariest maid is prodigal enough,
If she unmask her beauty to the moon.
Virtue itself scapes not calumnious strokes.
The canker[7] galls the infants of the spring
Too oft before the buttons[8] be disclos'd,
And in the morn and liquid dew of youth
Contagious blastments are most imminent.
Be wary then, best safety lies in fear;
Youth to itself rebels, though none else near.

Oph. I shall the effect of this good lesson keep,
As watchman to my heart. But, good my brother,
Do not, as some ungracious pastors do,

[3] Muscles. [4] Deceit. [5] Consent. [6] Credulous. [7] Canker-worm. [8] Buds.

Show me the steep and thorny way to heaven,
Whilst, like a puff'd and reckless libertine,
Himself the primrose path of dalliance treads,
And recks not his own rede.[9]

Laer. O, fear me not.

Enter POLONIUS

I stay too long: but here my father comes.
A double blessing is a double grace;
Occasion smiles upon a second leave.

Pol. Yet here, Laertes? Aboard, aboard, for shame!
The wind sits in the shoulder of your sail,
And you are stay'd for. There; my blessing with you!
And these few precepts in thy memory
See thou character. Give thy thoughts no tongue,
Nor any unproportion'd thought his act.
Be thou familiar, but by no means vulgar.
The friends thou hast, and their adoption tried,
Grapple them to thy soul with hoops of steel;
But do not dull thy palm with entertainment
Of each new-hatch'd, unfledg'd comrade. Beware
Of entrance to a quarrel; but being in,
Bear 't that the opposed may beware of thee.
Give every man thine ear, but few thy voice;
Take each man's censure,[10] but reserve thy judgement.
Costly thy habit as thy purse can buy,
But not express'd in fancy; rich, not gaudy;
For the apparel oft proclaims the man,
And they in France of the best rank and station
Are most select and generous in that.
Neither a borrower nor a lender be;
For loan oft loses both itself and friend,
And borrowing dulls the edge of husbandry.[11]
This above all: to thine own self be true,
And it must follow, as the night the day,
Thou canst not then be false to any man.

[9] Advice. [10] Opinion. [11] Thrift.

Farewell; my blessing season this in thee!
Laer. Most humbly do I take my leave, my lord.
Pol. The time invites you; go, your servants tend.
Laer. Farewell, Ophelia, and remember well
What I have said to you.
Oph. 'Tis in my memory lock'd,
And you yourself shall keep the key of it.
Laer. Farewell. *Exit.*
Pol. What is 't, Ophelia, he hath said to you?
Oph. So please you, something touching the Lord Hamlet.
Pol. Marry, well bethought.
'Tis told me, he hath very oft of late
Given private time to you, and you yourself
Have of your audience been most free and bounteous.
If it be so—as so 'tis put on me,
And that in way of caution—I must tell you,
You do not understand yourself so clearly
As it behoves my daughter and your honour.
What is between you? Give me up the truth.
Oph. He hath, my lord, of late made many tenders[12]
Of his affection to me.
Pol. Affection! pooh! You speak like a green girl,
Unsifted in such perilous circumstance.
Do you believe his tenders, as you call them?
Oph. I do not know, my lord, what I should think.
Pol. Marry, I'll teach you: think yourself a baby
That you have ta'en his tenders for true pay,
Which are not sterling. Tender yourself more dearly,
Or—not to crack the wind of the poor phrase,
Running it thus—you'll tender me a fool.
Oph. My lord, he hath importun'd me with love
In honourable fashion.
Pol. Ay, fashion you may call it. Go to, go to.
Oph. And hath given countenance to his speech, my lord,
With almost all the holy vows of heaven.
Pol. Ay, springes[13] to catch woodcocks. I do know,

[12] Offers. [13] Snares.

When the blood burns, how prodigal the soul
Lends the tongue vows. These blazes, daughter,
Giving more light than heat, extinct in both
Even in their promise, as it is a-making,
You must not take for fire. From this time, daughter,
Be somewhat scanter of your maiden presence.
Set your entreatments[14] at a higher rate
Than a command to parley. For Lord Hamlet,
Believe so much in him, that he is young,
And with a larger tether may he walk
Than may be given you. In few, Ophelia,
Do not believe his vows; for they are brokers,
Not of that dye which their investments[15] show,
But mere implorators[16] of unholy suits,
Breathing like sanctified and pious bawds,
The better to beguile. This is for all:
I would not, in plain terms, from this time forth,
Have you so slander any moment leisure
As to give words or talk with the Lord Hamlet.
Look to 't, I charge you. Come your ways.
Oph. I shall obey, my lord. *Exeunt.*

[Scene IV. *The platform*]

Enter Hamlet, Horatio, *and* Marcellus

Ham. The air bites shrewdly; it is very cold.
Hor. It is a nipping and an eager air.
Ham. What hour now?
Hor. I think it lacks of twelve.
Mar. No, it is struck.
Hor. Indeed? I heard it not. Then it draws near the season
Wherein the spirit held his wont to walk.
A flourish of trumpets, and two pieces go off [*within*].
What does this mean, my lord?
Ham. The King doth wake to-night and takes his rouse,
Keeps wassail, and the swaggering up-spring[1] reels;

[14] Invitations. [15] Garments. [16] Pleaders. [1] A wild dance.

And, as he drains his draughts of Rhenish down,
The kettle-drum and trumpet thus bray out
The triumph of his pledge.
Hor. Is it a custom?
Ham. Ay, marry, is 't,
But to my mind, though I am native here
And to the manner born, it is a custom
More honour'd in the breach than the observance.
[This heavy-headed revel east and west
Makes us traduc'd and tax'd[2] of other nations.
They clepe[3] us drunkards, and with swinish phrase
Soil our addition;[4] and indeed it takes
From our achievements, though perform'd at height,
The pith and marrow of our attribute.
So, oft it chances in particular men,
That for some vicious mole[5] of nature in them,
As, in their birth—wherein they are not guilty,
Since nature cannot choose his origin—
By their o'ergrowth of some complexion[6]
Oft breaking down the pales and forts of reason,
Or by some habit that too much o'er-leavens
The form of plausive[7] manners, that these men,
Carrying, I say, the stamp of one defect,
Being nature's livery, or fortune's star,[8]—
His virtues else—be they as pure as grace,
As infinite as man may undergo—
Shall in the general censure[9] take corruption
From that particular fault. The dram of eale[10]
Doth all the noble substance often dout[11]
To his own scandal.]

Enter Ghost

Hor. Look, my lord, it comes!
Ham. Angels and ministers of grace defend us!
Be thou a spirit of health or goblin damn'd,

[2] Accused. [3] Call. [4] Title. [5] Flaw. [6] Disposition. [7] Pleasing. [8] Whether due to nature or fortune. [9] Opinion. [10] Small quantity of evil (?). [11] Drive out, efface (?). The passage is probably corrupt.

Bring with thee airs from heaven or blasts from hell,
Be thy intents wicked or charitable,
Thou com'st in such a questionable[12] shape
That I will speak to thee. I'll call thee Hamlet,
King, father; royal Dane, O, answer me!
Let me not burst in ignorance, but tell
Why thy canoniz'd bones, hearsed in death,
Have burst their cerements;[13] why the sepulchre,
Wherein we saw thee quietly inurn'd,
Hath op'd his ponderous and marble jaws,
To cast thee up again. What may this mean,
That thou, dead corse, again in complete steel
Revisits thus the glimpses of the moon,
Making night hideous, and we fools of nature
So horridly to shake our disposition
With thoughts beyond the reaches of our souls?
Say, why is this? Wherefore? What should we do?

Ghost *beckons* HAMLET.

Hor. It beckons you to go away with it,
As if it some impartment did desire
To you alone.

Mar. Look, with what courteous action
It wafts you to a more removed ground.
But do not go with it.

Hor. No, by no means.

Ham. It will not speak; then will I follow it.

Hor. Do not, my lord.

Ham. Why, what should be the fear?
I do not set my life at a pin's fee,
And for my soul, what can it do to that,
Being a thing immortal as itself?
It waves me forth again. I'll follow it.

Hor. What if it tempt you toward the flood, my lord,
Or to the dreadful summit of the cliff
That beetles o'er his base into the sea,
And there assume some other horrible form,

[12] Inviting discussion. [13] Waxed shroud.

Which might deprive your sovereignty of reason
And draw you into madness? Think of it.
[The very place puts toys of desperation,
Without more motive, into every brain
That looks so many fathoms to the sea
And hears it roar beneath.]

Ham. It wafts me still.
Go on, I'll follow thee.

Mar. You shall not go, my lord.

Ham. Hold off your hand.

Hor. Be rul'd; you shall not go.

Ham. My fate cries out,
And makes each petty artery in this body
As hardy as the Nemean lion's nerve.
Still am I call'd. Unhand me, gentlemen.
By heaven, I'll make a ghost of him that lets[14] me!
I say, away!—Go on, I'll follow thee. *Exeunt* Ghost *and* HAMLET.

Hor. He waxes desperate with imagination.

Mar. Let's follow. 'Tis not fit thus to obey him.

Hor. Have after. To what issue will this come?

Mar. Something is rotten in the state of Denmark.

Hor. Heaven will direct it.

Mar. Nay, let's follow him. *Exeunt.*

[SCENE V. *Another part of the platform*]

Enter Ghost *and* HAMLET

Ham. Where wilt thou lead me? Speak, I'll go no further.

Ghost. Mark me.

Ham. I will.

Ghost. My hour is almost come,
When I to sulphurous and tormenting flames
Must render up myself.

Ham. Alas, poor ghost!

Ghost. Pity me not, but lend thy serious hearing

[14] Hinders.

To what I shall unfold.
Ham. Speak; I am bound to hear.
Ghost. So art thou to revenge, when thou shalt hear.
Ham. What?
Ghost. I am thy father's spirit,
Doom'd for a certain term to walk the night,
And for the day confin'd to fast in fires,
Till the foul crimes done in my days of nature
Are burnt and purg'd away. But that I am forbid
To tell the secrets of my prison-house,
I could a tale unfold whose lightest word
Would harrow up thy soul, freeze thy young blood,
Make thy two eyes, like stars, start from their spheres,
Thy knotty and combined locks to part
And each particular hair to stand on end,
Like quills upon the fretful porpentine.[1]
But this eternal blazon[2] must not be
To ears of flesh and blood. List, Hamlet, O, list!
If thou didst ever thy dear father love—
Ham. O God!
Ghost. Revenge his foul and most unnatural murder.
Ham. Murder!
Ghost. Murder most foul, as in the best it is,
But this most foul, strange, and unnatural.
Ham. Haste me to know 't, that I, with wings as swift
As meditation or the thoughts of love,
May sweep to my revenge.
Ghost. I find thee apt;
And duller shouldst thou be than the fat weed
That roots itself in ease on Lethe wharf,[3]
Wouldst thou not stir in this. Now, Hamlet, hear.
It's given out that, sleeping in mine orchard,
A serpent stung me; so the whole ear of Denmark
Is by a forged process[4] of my death
Rankly abus'd;[5] but know, thou noble youth,

[1] Porcupine. [2] Declaration about the eternal world. [3] Bank. [4] Account. [5] Deceived.

The serpent that did sting thy father's life
Now wears his crown.
Ham. O my prophetic soul!
Mine uncle!
Ghost. Ay, that incestuous, that adulterate beast,
With witchcraft of his wit, with traitorous gifts,—
O wicked wit and gifts, that have the power
So to seduce!—won to his shameful lust
The will of my most seeming-virtuous queen.
O Hamlet, what a falling-off was there!
From me, whose love was of that dignity
That it went hand in hand even with the vow
I made to her in marriage, and to decline
Upon a wretch whose natural gifts were poor
To those of mine!
But virtue, as it never will be moved,
Though lewdness court it in a shape of heaven,
So lust, though to a radiant angel link'd,
Will sate itself in a celestial bed
And prey on garbage.
But, soft! methinks I scent the morning's air.
Brief let me be. Sleeping within mine orchard,
My custom always in the afternoon,
Upon my secure hour thy uncle stole,
With juice of cursed hebenon[6] in a vial,
And in the porches of mine ears did pour
The leperous distilment; whose effect
Holds such an enmity with blood of man
That swift as quicksilver it courses through
The natural gates and alleys of the body,
And with a sudden vigour it doth posset[7]
And curd, like eager[8] droppings into milk,
The thin and wholesome blood. So did it mine,
And a most instant tetter[9] bark'd about,
Most lazar-like, with vile and loathsome crust,
All my smooth body.

[6] An unknown poison. [7] Thicken. [8] Sour. [9] Scurf.

Thus was I, sleeping, by a brother's hand
Of life, of crown, and queen, at once dispatch'd;
Cut off even in the blossoms of my sin,
Unhousel'd,[10] disappointed,[11] unanel'd,[12]
No reckoning made, but sent to my account
With all my imperfections on my head.
O, horrible! O, horrible! most horrible!
If thou hast nature in thee, bear it not;
Let not the royal bed of Denmark be
A couch for luxury and damned incest.
But, howsoever thou pursuest this act,
Taint not thy mind, nor let thy soul contrive
Against thy mother aught. Leave her to heaven
And to those thorns that in her bosom lodge,
To prick and sting her. Fare thee well at once!
The glow-worm shows the matin to be near,
And 'gins to pale his uneffectual fire.
Adieu, adieu! Hamlet, remember me. *Exit.*
Ham. O all you host of heaven! O earth! What else?
And shall I couple hell? O, fie! Hold, my heart,
And you, my sinews, grow not instant old,
But bear me stiffly up. Remember thee!
Ay, thou poor ghost, while memory holds a seat
In this distracted globe. Remember thee!
Yea, from the table of my memory
I'll wipe away all trivial fond[13] records,
All saws[14] of books, all forms, all pressures past,
That youth and observation copied there,
And thy commandment all alone shall live
Within the book and volume of my brain,
Unmix'd with baser matter. Yes, yes, by heaven!
O most pernicious woman!
O villain, villain, smiling, damned villain!
My tables, my tables,—meet it is I set it down!
That one may smile, and smile, and be a villain!

[10] Without the sacrament. [11] Unprepared. [12] Without extreme unction.
[13] Foolish. [14] Sayings.

At least I 'm sure it may be so in Denmark.
So, uncle, there you are. Now to my word;
It is "Adieu, adieu! remember me."
I have sworn 't.

Mar. } *Hor.* } (*Within.*) My lord, my lord!

Mar. [*Within.*] Lord Hamlet!

Hor. [*Within.*] Heaven secure him!

Ham. So be it!

Mar. [*Within.*] Illo, ho, ho, my lord!

Ham. Hillo, ho, ho, boy! Come, bird, come.

Enter Horatio *and* Marcellus

Mar. How is 't, my noble lord?

Hor. What news, my lord?

Ham. O, wonderful!

Hor. Good my lord, tell it.

Ham. No, you'll reveal it.

Hor. Not I, my lord, by heaven.

Mar. Nor I, my lord.

Ham. How say you, then, would heart of man once think it?—
But you'll be secret?

Hor. } *Mar.* } Ay, by heaven, my lord.

Ham. There's ne'er a villain dwelling in all Denmark—
But he's an arrant knave.

Hor. There needs no ghost, my lord, come from the grave
To tell us this.

Ham. Why, right, you are i' the right.
And so, without more circumstance at all,
I hold it fit that we shake hands and part;
You, as your business and desires shall point you,
For every man has business and desire,
Such as it is; and for mine own poor part,
Look you, I'll go pray.

Hor. These are but wild and whirling words, my lord.

Ham. I'm sorry they offend you, heartily;

Yes, faith, heartily.

Hor. There's no offence, my lord.

Ham. Yes, by Saint Patrick, but there is, Horatio,
And much offence too. Touching this vision here,
It is an honest ghost, that let me tell you.
For your desire to know what is between us,
O'ermaster 't as you may. And now, good friends,
As you are friends, scholars, and soldiers,
Give me one poor request.

Hor. What is 't, my lord? We will.

Ham. Never make known what you have seen to-night.

Hor. } *Mar.* } My lord, we will not.

Ham. Nay, but swear 't.

Hor. In faith,
My lord, not I.

Mar. Nor I, my lord, in faith.

Ham. Upon my sword.

Mar. We have sworn, my lord, already.

Ham. Indeed, upon my sword, indeed.

Ghost. Swear! Ghost *cries under the stage.*

Ham. Ah, ha, boy! say'st thou so? Art thou there, truepenny?
Come on; you hear this fellow in the cellarage.
Consent to swear.

Hor. Propose the oath, my lord.

Ham. Never to speak of this that you have seen.
Swear by my sword.

Ghost. [*Beneath.*] Swear.

Ham. *Hic et ubique?*[15] Then we'll shift our ground.
Come thither, gentlemen,
And lay your hands again upon my sword.
Never to speak of this that you have heard,
Swear by my sword.

Ghost. [*Beneath.*] Swear.

Ham. Well said, old mole! Canst work i' the earth so fast?
A worthy pioner![16] Once more remove, good friends.

[15] Lat. *Here and everywhere.* [16] Pioneer.

Hor. O day and night, but this is wondrous strange!
Ham. And therefore as a stranger give it welcome.
There are more things in heaven and earth, Horatio,
Than are dreamt of in your philosophy.
But come;
Here, as before, never, so help you mercy,
How strange or odd soe'er I bear myself,—
As I perchance hereafter shall think meet
To put an antic disposition on—
That you, at such time seeing me, never shall,
With arms encumb'red thus, or this headshake,
Or by pronouncing of some doubtful phrase,
As "Well, we know," or "We could, an if we would,"
Or "If we list to speak," or "There be, an if they might,"
Or such ambiguous giving out, to note
That you know aught of me,—this not to do,
So grace and mercy at your most need help you,
Swear.
Ghost. [*Beneath.*] Swear.
Ham. Rest, rest, perturbed spirit! [*They swear.*] So, gentlemen,
With all my love I do commend me to you.
And what so poor a man as Hamlet is
May do, to express his love and friending to you,
God willing, shall not lack. Let us go in together;
And still your fingers on your lips, I pray.
The time is out of joint;—O cursed spite,
That ever I was born to set it right!
Nay, come, let's go together. *Exeunt.*

ACT II

[Scene I. *A room in Polonius's house*]

Enter Polonius *and* Reynaldo

Pol. Give him this money and these notes, Reynaldo.
Rey. I will, my lord.
Pol. You shall do marvellous wisely, good Reynaldo,

Before you visit him, to make inquiry
Of his behaviour.
Rey. My lord, I did intend it.
Pol. Marry, well said, very well said. Look you, sir,
Inquire me first what Danskers[1] are in Paris,
And how, and who, what means, and where they keep,
What company, at what expense; and finding
By this encompassment and drift[2] of question
That they do know my son, come you more nearer
Than your particular demands will touch it.
Take you, as 'twere, some distant knowledge of him,
As thus, "I know his father and his friends,
And in part him." Do you mark this, Reynaldo?
Rey. Ay, very well, my lord.
Pol. "And in part him; but," you may say, "not well.
But, if 't be he I mean, he's very wild,
Addicted so and so;" and there put on him
What forgeries[3] you please; marry, none so rank
As may dishonour him,—take heed of that;
But, sir, such wanton, wild, and usual slips
As are companions noted and most known
To youth and liberty.
Rey. As gaming, my lord?
Pol. Ay, or drinking, fencing, swearing, quarrelling,
Drabbing; you may go so far.
Rey. My lord, that would dishonour him.
Pol. Faith, no, as you may season[4] it in the charge.
You must not put another scandal on him,
That he is open to incontinency.
That's not my meaning. But breathe his faults so quaintly[5]
That they may seem the taints of liberty,
The flash and outbreak of a fiery mind,
A savageness in unreclaimed blood,
Of general assault.[6]

[1] Danes. [2] Roundabout method. [3] False accusations. [4] Modify.
[5] Carefully, delicately. [6] To which any man is subject.

Rey. But, my good lord,—
Pol. Wherefore should you do this?
Rey. Ay, my lord,
I would know that.
Pol. Marry, sir, here's my drift,
And, I believe, it is a fetch of warrant:[7]
You laying these slight sullies on my son,
As 'twere a thing a little soil'd i' the working,
Mark you,
Your party in converse, him you would sound,
Having ever seen in the prenominate[8] crimes
The youth you breathe of guilty, be assur'd
He closes with you in this consequence;[9]
"Good sir," or so, or "friend," or "gentleman,"
According to the phrase and the addition[10]
Of man and country.
Rey. Very good, my lord.
Pol. And then, sir, does he this—he does—
What was I about to say? [By the mass,] I was about to say something. Where did I leave?
Rey. At "closes in the consequence," at "friend or so," and "gentleman."
Pol. At "closes in the consequence," ay, marry.
He closes with you thus: "I know the gentleman.
I saw him yesterday, or t' other day,
Or then, or then, with such and such; and, as you say,
There was he gaming; there o'ertook in 's rouse;[11]
There falling out at tennis;" or, perchance,
"I saw him enter such a house of sale,"
Videlicet, a brothel, or so forth.
See you now;
Your bait of falsehood takes this carp of truth;
And thus do we of wisdom and of reach,
With windlasses and with assays of bias,[12]
By indirections find directions out.

[7] Warranted device. [8] Before-mentioned. [9] Conclusion. [10] Title.
[11] Overcome in drinking. [12] Circuitous methods.

So by my former lecture and advice,
Shall you my son. You have me, have you not?
Rey. My lord, I have.
Pol. God buy you; fare you well.
Rey. Good my lord.
Pol. Observe his inclination in yourself.
Rey. I shall, my lord.
Pol. And let him ply his music.
Rey. Well, my lord.
Pol. Farewell! *Exit* REYNALDO.

Enter OPHELIA

How now, Ophelia! what's the matter?
Oph. Alas, my lord, I have been so affrighted!
Pol. With what, in the name of God?
Oph. My lord, as I was sewing in my chamber,
Lord Hamlet, with his doublet all unbrac'd,[13]
No hat upon his head, his stockings foul'd,
Ungart'red, and down-gyved[14] to his ankle,
Pale as his shirt, his knees knocking each other,
And with a look so piteous in purport
As if he had been loosed out of hell
To speak of horrors,—he comes before me.
Pol. Mad for thy love?
Oph. My lord, I do not know,
But truly, I do fear it.
Pol. What said he?
Oph. He took me by the wrist and held me hard;
Then goes he to the length of all his arm,
And, with his other hand thus o'er his brow,
He falls to such perusal of my face
As he would draw it. Long stay'd he so.
At last, a little shaking of mine arm,
And thrice his head thus waving up and down
He rais'd a sigh so piteous and profound
That it did seem to shatter all his bulk

[13] Ungirt. [14] Hanging in rings like fetters.

And end his being. That done, he lets me go;
And, with his head over his shoulder turn'd,
He seem'd to find his way without his eyes,
For out o' doors he went without their help,
And, to the last, bended their light on me.

Pol. [Come,] go with me, I will go seek the King.
This is the very ecstasy of love,
Whose violent property fordoes itself
And leads the will to desperate undertakings
As oft as any passion under heaven
That does afflict our natures. I am sorry,—
What, have you given him any hard words of late?

Oph. No, my good lord, but, as you did command,
I did repel his letters and deni'd
His access to me.

Pol. That hath made him mad.
I am sorry that with better heed and judgement
I had not quoted[15] him. I fear'd he did but trifle
And meant to wreck thee; but beshrew my jealousy!
By heaven, it is as proper to our age
To cast beyond ourselves in our opinions
As it is common for the younger sort
To lack discretion. Come, go we to the King.
This must be known, which, being kept close, might move
More grief to hide than hate to utter love.
[Come.] *Exeunt.*

SCENE II. [*A room in the castle*]

Flourish. Enter KING, QUEEN, ROSENCRANTZ, GUILDENSTERN, *with others*

King. Welcome, dear Rosencrantz and Guildenstern!
Moreover that we much did long to see you,
The need we have to use you did provoke
Our hasty sending. Something have you heard

[15] Observed.

Of Hamlet's transformation; so I call it,
Since not the exterior nor the inward man
Resembles that it was. What it should be,
More than his father's death, that thus hath put him
So much from the understanding of himself,
I cannot dream of. I entreat you both,
That, being of so young days brought up with him
And since so neighbour'd to his youth and humour,
That you vouchsafe your rest here in our court
Some little time; so by your companies
To draw him on to pleasures, and to gather
So much as from occasions you may glean,
[Whether aught, to us unknown, afflicts him thus,]
That, open'd, lies within our remedy.

Queen. Good gentlemen, he hath much talk'd of you;
And sure I am two men there are not living
To whom he more adheres. If it will please you
To show us so much gentry[1] and good will
As to expend your time with us a while
For the supply and profit of our hope,
Your visitation shall receive such thanks
As fits a king's remembrance.

Ros. Both your Majesties
Might, by the sovereign power you have of us,
Put your dread pleasures more into command
Than to entreaty.

Guil. We both obey,
And here give up ourselves, in the full bent
To lay our services freely at your feet,
To be commanded.

King. Thanks, Rosencrantz and gentle Guildenstern.

Queen. Thanks, Guildenstern and gentle Rosencrantz,
And I beseech you instantly to visit
My too much changed son. Go, some of ye,
And bring the gentlemen where Hamlet is.

[1] Courtesy.

Guil. Heavens make our presence and our practices
Pleasant and helpful to him!
Queen. Amen!
Exeunt [ROSENCRANTZ, GUILDENSTERN, *and some* Attendants].

Enter POLONIUS

Pol. The ambassadors from Norway, my good lord,
Are joyfully return'd.
King. Thou still hast been the father of good news.
Pol. Have I, my lord? Assure you, my good liege,
I hold my duty as I hold my soul,
Both to my God and to my gracious king.
And I do think, or else this brain of mine
Hunts not the trail of policy so sure
As it hath us'd to do, that I have found
The very cause of Hamlet's lunacy.
King. O, speak of that; that I do long to hear.
Pol. Give first admittance to the ambassadors.
My news shall be the fruit to that great feast.
King. Thyself do grace to them, and bring them in.
[*Exit* POLONIUS.]
He tells me, my sweet queen, that he hath found
The head and source of all your son's distemper.
Queen. I doubt it is no other but the main,
His father's death and our o'erhasty marriage.

Re-enter POLONIUS, *with* VOLTIMAND *and* CORNELIUS

King. Well, we shall sift him.—Welcome, my good friends!
Say, Voltimand, what from our brother Norway?
Volt. Most fair return of greetings and desires.
Upon our first,[2] he sent out to suppress
His nephew's levies, which to him appear'd
To be a preparation 'gainst the Polack,
But, better look'd into, he truly found
It was against your Highness. Whereat grieved.

[2] First request.

That so his sickness, age, and impotence
Was falsely borne in hand,[3] sends out arrests
On Fortinbras; which he, in brief, obeys,
Receives rebuke from Norway, and in fine
Makes vow before his uncle never more
To give the assay of arms against your Majesty.
Whereon old Norway, overcome with joy,
Gives him three thousand crowns in annual fee,
And his commission to employ those soldiers,
So levied as before, against the Polack;
With an entreaty, herein further shown, [*Giving a paper.*]
That it might please you to give quiet pass
Through your dominions for his enterprise,
On such regards of safety and allowance
As therein are set down.
King. It likes us well;
And at our more consider'd time[4] we'll read,
Answer, and think upon this business.
Meantime we thank you for your well-took labour.
Go to your rest; at night we'll feast together.
Most welcome home! *Exeunt* VOLTIMAND *and* CORNELIUS.
Pol. This business is well ended.
My liege, and madam, to expostulate
What majesty should be, what duty is,
Why day is day, night night, and time is time,
Were nothing but to waste night, day, and time;
Therefore, since brevity is the soul of wit
And tediousness the limbs and outward flourishes,
I will be brief. Your noble son is mad.
Mad call I it; for, to define true madness,
What is 't but to be nothing else but mad?
But let that go.
Queen. More matter, with less art.
Pol. Madam, I swear I use no art at all.
That he is mad, 'tis true; 'tis true 'tis pity,
And pity 'tis 'tis true. A foolish figure!

[3] Deceived. [4] Time for deliberation.

But farewell it, for I will use no art.
Mad let us grant him then; and now remains
That we find out the cause of this effect,
Or rather say, the cause of this defect,
For this effect defective comes by cause.
Thus it remains, and the remainder thus.
Perpend.[5]
I have a daughter—have whilst she is mine—
Who, in her duty and obedience, mark,
Hath given me this. Now gather, and surmise. [*Reads*] *the letter.*
"To the celestial and my soul's idol, the most beautified Ophelia,"—
That's an ill phrase, a vile phrase; "beautified" is a vile phrase. But you shall hear. Thus:
"In her excellent white bosom, these."

Queen. Came this from Hamlet to her?

Pol. Good madam, stay a while. I will be faithful. [*Reads.*]

"Doubt thou the stars are fire,
Doubt that the sun doth move,
Doubt truth to be a liar,
But never doubt I love.

"O dear Ophelia, I am ill at these numbers. I have not art to reckon my groans; but that I love thee best, O most best, believe it. Adieu.

Thine evermore, most dear lady,
Whilst this machine is to him,
HAMLET."

This in obedience hath my daughter show'd me,
And more above, hath his solicitings,
As they fell out by time, by means, and place,
All given to mine ear.

King. But how hath she
Receiv'd his love?

Pol. What do you think of me?

King. As of a man faithful and honourable.

Pol. I would fain prove so. But what might you think,

[5] Consider.

When I had seen this hot love on the wing,—
As I perceiv'd it, I must tell you that,
Before my daughter told me,—what might you,
Or my dear Majesty your queen here, think,
If I had play'd the desk or table-book,
Or given my heart a winking, mute and dumb,
Or look'd upon this love with idle sight,
What might you think? No, I went round to work,
And my young mistress thus I did bespeak:
"Lord Hamlet is a prince, out of thy star.[6]
This must not be;" and then I precepts gave her,
That she should lock herself from his resort,
Admit no messengers, receive no tokens.
Which done, she took the fruits of my advice;
And he, repulsed—a short tale to make—
Fell into a sadness, then into a fast,
Thence to a watch, thence into a weakness,
Thence to a lightness, and, by this declension,
Into the madness wherein now he raves,
And all we wail for.

King. Do you think 'tis this?

Queen. It may be, very likely.

Pol. Hath there been such a time—I'd fain know that—
That I have positively said, " 'Tis so,"
When it prov'd otherwise?

King. Not that I know.

Pol. Take this from this, if this be otherwise.
If circumstances lead me, I will find
Where truth is hid, though it were hid indeed
Within the centre.

King. How may we try it further?

Pol. You know, sometimes he walks four hours together
Here in the lobby.

Queen. So he has, indeed.

Pol. At such a time I'll loose my daughter to him.
Be you and I behind an arras[7] then;

[6] Range of fortune. [7] Tapestry.

Mark the encounter. If he love her not
And be not from his reason fallen thereon,
Let me be no assistant for a state,
But keep a farm and carters.

King. We will try it.

Enter HAMLET, *reading on a book*

Queen. But look where sadly the poor wretch comes reading.

Pol. Away, I do beseech you, both away.
I'll board[8] him presently.

Exeunt KING, QUEEN [*and* Attendants].

O, give me leave,
How does my good Lord Hamlet?

Ham. Well, God-a-mercy.

Pol. Do you know me, my lord?

Ham. Excellent well; you are a fishmonger.

Pol. Not I, my lord.

Ham. Then I would you were so honest a man.

Pol. Honest, my lord!

Ham. Ay, sir. To be honest, as this world goes, is to be one man pick'd out of ten thousand.

Pol. That's very true, my lord.

Ham. For if the sun breed maggots in a dead dog, being a good kissing carrion,—Have you a daughter?

Pol. I have, my lord.

Ham. Let her not walk i' the sun. Conception is a blessing, but not as your daughter may conceive. Friend, look to 't.

Pol. [*Aside.*] How say you by that? Still harping on my daughter. Yet he knew me not at first; he said I was a fishmonger. He is far gone, far gone. And truly in my youth I suff'red much extremity for love; very near this. I'll speak to him again.—What do you read, my lord?

Ham. Words, words, words.

Pol. What is the matter, my lord?

Ham. Between who?

[8] Accost.

Pol. I mean, the matter you read, my lord.

Ham. Slanders, sir; for the satirical slave says here that old men have grey beards, that their faces are wrinkled, their eyes purging thick amber or plum-tree gum, and that they have a plentiful lack of wit, together with weak hams; all which, sir, though I most powerfully and potently believe, yet I hold it not honesty to have it thus set down; for you yourself, sir, should be old as I am, if like a crab you could go backward.

Pol. [*Aside.*] Though this be madness, yet there is method in 't—Will you walk out of the air, my lord?

Ham. Into my grave?

Pol. Indeed, that is out o' the air. [*Aside.*] How pregnant sometimes his replies are! a happiness that often madness hits on, which reason and sanity could not so prosperously be deliver'd of. I will leave him, and suddenly contrive the means of meeting between him and my daughter.—My honourable lord, I will most humbly take my leave of you.

Ham. You cannot, sir, take from me anything that I will more willingly part withal,—[*Aside*] except my life, my life.

Pol. Fare you well, my lord.

Ham. These tedious old fools!

Enter ROSENCRANTZ *and* GUILDENSTERN

Pol. You go to seek my Lord Hamlet? There he is.

Ros. [*To* POLONIUS.] God save you, sir! [*Exit* POLONIUS.]

Guil. Mine honour'd lord!

Ros. My most dear lord!

Ham. My excellent good friends! How dost thou, Guildenstern? Oh, Rosencrantz! Good lads, how do ye both?

Ros. As the indifferent children of the earth.

Guil. Happy, in that we are not over-happy.
On Fortune's cap we are not the very button.

Ham. Nor the soles of her shoe?

Ros. Neither, my lord.

Ham. Then you live about her waist, or in the middle of her favour?

Guil. Faith, her privates we.

Ham. In the secret parts of Fortune? Oh, most true; she is a strumpet. What's the news?

Ros. None, my lord, but that the world's grown honest.

Ham. Then is doomsday near. But your news is not true. Let me question more in particular. What have you, my good friends, deserved at the hands of Fortune, that she sends you to prison hither?

Guil. Prison, my lord?

Ham. Denmark's a prison.

Ros. Then is the world one.

Ham. A goodly one, in which there are many confines, wards, and dungeons, Denmark being one o' the worst.

Ros. We think not so, my lord.

Ham. Why, then 'tis none to you; for there is nothing either good or bad, but thinking makes it so. To me it is a prison.

Ros. Why, then your ambition makes it one. 'Tis too narrow for your mind.

Ham. O God, I could be bounded in a nutshell and count myself a king of infinite space, were it not that I have bad dreams.

Guil. Which dreams indeed are ambition, for the very substance of the ambitious is merely the shadow of a dream.

Ham. A dream itself is but a shadow.

Ros. Truly, and I hold ambition of so airy and light a quality that it is but a shadow's shadow.

Ham. Then are our beggars bodies, and our monarchs and outstretch'd heroes the beggars' shadows. Shall we to the court? for, by my fay, I cannot reason.

Ros.
Guil. } We'll wait upon you.

Ham. No such matter. I will not sort you with the rest of my servants, for, to speak to you like an honest man, I am most dreadfully attended. But in the beaten way of friendship, what make you at Elsinore?

Ros. To visit you, my lord; no other occasion.

Ham. Beggar that I am, I am even poor in thanks, but I thank you; and sure, dear friends, my thanks are too dear a halfpenny.

Were you not sent for? Is it your own inclining? Is it a free visitation? Come, deal justly with me. Come, come. Nay, speak.

Guil. What should we say, my lord?

Ham. Why, anything, but to the purpose. You were sent for; and there is a kind of confession in your looks which your modesties have not craft enough to colour. I know the good king and queen have sent for you.

Ros. To what end, my lord?

Ham. That you must teach me. But let me conjure you, by the rights of our fellowship, by the consonancy of our youth, by the obligation of our ever-preserved love, and by what more dear a better proposer could charge you withal, be even and direct with me, whether you were sent for or no!

Ros. [*Aside to* GUIL.] What say you?

Ham. [*Aside.*] Nay, then, I have an eye of you.—If you love me, hold not off.

Guil. My lord, we were sent for.

Ham. I will tell you why; so shall my anticipation prevent[9] your discovery,[10] and your secrecy to the King and Queen moult no feather. I have of late—but wherefore I know not—lost all my mirth, foregone all custom of exercise; and indeed it goes so heavily with my disposition that this goodly frame, the earth, seems to me a sterile promontory, this most excellent canopy, the air, look you, this brave o'erhanging firmament, this majestical roof fretted[11] with golden fire, why, it appears no other thing to me than a foul and pestilent congregation of vapours. What a piece of work is a man! How noble in reason! How infinite in faculty! In form and moving how express[12] and admirable! In action how like an angel! In apprehension how like a god! The beauty of the world! The paragon of animals! And yet, to me, what is this quintessence of dust? Man delights not me,—no, nor woman neither, though by your smiling you seem to say so.

Ros. My lord, there was no such stuff in my thoughts.

Ham. Why did you laugh then, when I said, "Man delights not me"?

[9] Anticipate. [10] Revelation. [11] Adorned. [12] Exact.

Ros. To think, my lord, if you delight not in man, what lenten entertainment the players shall receive from you. We coted[13] them on the way, and hither are they coming to offer you service.

Ham. He that plays the king shall be welcome; his majesty[14] shall have tribute of me; the adventurous knight[14] shall use his foil and target; the lover[14] shall not sigh gratis; the humorous man[15] shall end his part in peace; the clown shall make those laugh whose lungs are tickle o' the sere[16], and the lady shall say her mind freely, or the blank verse shall halt for 't. What players are they?

Ros. Even those you were wont to take delight in, the tragedians of the city.

Ham. How chances it they travel? Their residence, both in reputation and profit, was better both ways.

Ros. I think their inhibition[17] comes by the means of the late innovation.[18]

Ham. Do they hold the same estimation they did when I was in the city? Are they so follow'd?

Ros. No, indeed, they are not.

Ham. How comes it? Do they grow rusty?

Ros. Nay, their endeavour keeps in the wonted pace; but there is, sir, an aery of children, little eyases,[19] that cry out on the top of question, and are most tyrannically clapp'd for 't. These are now the fashion, and so berattle the common stages[20]—so they call them—that many wearing rapiers are afraid of goose-quills[21] and dare scarce come thither.

Ham. What, are they children? Who maintains 'em? How are they escoted?[22] Will they pursue the quality[23] no longer than they can sing? Will they not say afterwards, if they should grow themselves to common players,—as it is most like, if their means are no better—their writers do them wrong, to make them exclaim against their own succession?[24]

Ros. Faith, there has been much to do on both sides, and the nation holds it no sin to tarre[25] them to controversy. There was for a

[13] Overtook and passed.
[14] Stock characters in the drama. [15] The actor who plays whimsical parts.
[16] Easily moved to laughter. "Sere" is the balance-lever of a gun-lock.
[17] Stopping of their playing in the city. [18] The vogue of the children's companies.
[19] Unfledged hawks. [20] Public theatres. [21] A reference to personal satire on the stage.
[22] Paid. [23] Profession of acting. [24] Against themselves when they grow up.
[25] Urge on.

while no money bid for argument unless the poet and the player went to cuffs in the question.

Ham. Is 't possible?

Guil. O, there has been much throwing about of brains.

Ham. Do the boys carry it away?[26]

Ros. Ay, that they do, my lord; Hercules and his load too.[27]

Ham. It is not strange; for mine uncle is King of Denmark, and those that would make mows at him while my father lived, give twenty, forty, [fifty,] an hundred ducats apiece for his picture in little. ['Sblood,] there is something in this more than natural, if philosophy could find it out. *Flourish for the* Players.

Guil. There are the players.

Ham. Gentlemen, you are welcome to Elsinore. Your hands, come. The appurtenance of welcome is fashion and ceremony. Let me comply with you in the garb,[28] lest my extent[29] to the players, which, I tell you, must show fairly outward, should more appear like entertainment than yours. You are welcome; but my uncle-father and aunt-mother are deceiv'd.

Guil. In what, my dear lord?

Ham. I am but mad north-north-west.[30] When the wind is southerly I know a hawk from a handsaw.[31]

Enter Polonius

Pol. Well be with you, gentlemen!

Ham. [*Aside to them.*] Hark you, Guildenstern, and you too, at each ear a hearer: that great baby you see there is not yet out of his swathing-clouts.

Ros. Happily he is the second time come to them, for they say an old man is twice a child.

Ham. I will prophesy he comes to tell me of the players; mark it. [*Aloud.*] You say right, sir; for o' Monday morning 'twas so indeed.

Pol. My lord, I have news to tell you.

Ham. My lord, I have news to tell you. When Roscius was an actor in Rome,—

[26] Win. [27] The sign of the Globe Theatre.
[28] Observe the fashionable ceremonies. [29] Behavior. [30] Only in one direction.
[31] The meaning is disputed. Perhaps, "In other matters I can tell chalk from cheese."

Pol. The actors are come hither, my lord.

Ham. Buzz, buzz!

Pol. Upon mine honour,—

Ham. "Then came each actor on his ass,"—

Pol. The best actors in the world, either for tragedy, comedy, history, pastoral, pastoral-comical, historical-pastoral, tragical-historical, tragical-comical-historical-pastoral, scene individable, or poem unlimited; Seneca cannot be too heavy, nor Plautus too light. For the law of writ and the liberty,[32] these are the only men.

Ham. O Jephthah, judge of Israel, what a treasure hadst thou!

Pol. What a treasure had he, my lord?

Ham. Why,

"One fair daughter, and no more,
The which he loved passing well."

Pol. [*Aside.*] Still on my daughter.

Ham. Am I not i' the right, old Jephthah?

Pol. If you call me Jephthah, my lord, I have a daughter that I love passing well.

Ham. Nay, that follows not.

Pol. What follows, then, my lord?

Ham. Why,

"As by lot, God wot,"

and then, you know,

"It came to pass, as most like it was,"—

The first row of the pious chanson[33] will show you more, for look where my abridgements[34] come.

Enter four or five Players

You're welcome, masters, welcome all. I am glad to see thee well. Welcome, good friends. O, my old friend! Thy face is valanc'd[35] since I saw thee last; com'st thou to beard me in Denmark? What, my young lady and mistress! By 'r lady, your ladyship is nearer heaven than when I saw you last, by the altitude of a chopine.[36] Pray God, your voice, like a piece of uncurrent gold, be not crack'd

[32] Sticking to the text, or improvising.
[33] Song. [34] Pastime. [35] Fringed.
[36] A high-soled shoe. The "lady" is, of course, a boy who played women's parts.

within the ring.[37] Masters, you are all welcome. We'll e'en to 't like French falconers—fly at any thing we see; we'll have a speech straight. Come, give us a taste of your quality; come, a passionate speech.

1. Play. What speech, my lord?

Ham. I heard thee speak me a speech once, but it was never acted; or, if it was, not above once. For the play, I remember, pleas'd not the million; 'twas caviare to the general;[38] but it was—as I receiv'd it, and others, whose judgement in such matters cried in the top of mine[39]—an excellent play, well digested in the scenes, set down with as much modesty as cunning. I remember, one said there were no sallets[40] in the lines to make the matter savoury, nor no matter in the phrase that might indict the author of affectation; but call'd it an honest method, [as wholesome as sweet, and by very much more handsome than fine.] One speech in it I chiefly lov'd; 'twas Æneas' tale to Dido, and thereabout of it especially where he speaks of Priam's slaughter. If it live in your memory, begin at this line: let me see, let me see—

"The rugged Pyrrhus, like the Hyrcanian beast,"

—It is not so. It begins with Pyrrhus:—

"The rugged Pyrrhus, he whose sable arms,
Black as his purpose, did the night resemble
When he lay couched in the ominous horse,
Hath now this dread and black complexion smear'd
With heraldry more dismal. Head to foot
Now is he total gules,[41] horribly trick'd[42]
With blood of fathers, mothers, daughters, sons,
Bak'd and impasted with the parching streets
That lend a tyrannous and damned light
To their vile murders. Roasted in wrath and fire,
And thus o'er-sized with coagulate gore.
With eyes like carbuncles, the hellish Pyrrhus
Old grandsire Priam seeks."

[So, proceed you.]

[37] The circle round the sovereign's head on a coin. [38] Multitude.
[39] With higher authority. [40] Spicy herbs—improprieties.
[41] Red. Heraldic term. [42] Drawn. Heraldic term.

Pol. 'Fore God, my lord, well spoken, with good accent and good discretion.

1. Play. "Anon he finds him
Striking too short at Greeks. His antique sword,
Rebellious to his arm, lies where it falls,
Repugnant to command. Unequal match,
Pyrrhus at Priam drives, in rage strikes wide.
But with the whiff and wind of his fell sword
The unnerved father falls. Then senseless Ilium,
Seeming to feel this blow, with flaming top
Stoops to his base, and with a hideous crash
Takes prisoner Pyrrhus' ear; for, lo! his sword,
Which was declining on the milky head
Of reverend Priam, seem'd i' the air to stick.
So, as a painted tyrant, Pyrrhus stood
And like a neutral to his will and matter,
Did nothing.
But, as we often see, against some storm,
A silence in the heavens, the rack[43] stand still,
The bold winds speechless and the orb below
As hush as death, anon the dreadful thunder
Doth rend the region;[44] so, after Pyrrhus' pause,
Aroused vengeance sets him new a-work;
And never did the Cyclops' hammers fall
On Mars his armour forg'd for proof eterne
With less remorse than Pyrrhus' bleeding sword
Now falls on Priam.
Out, out, thou strumpet Fortune! All you gods,
In general synod take away her power!
Break all the spokes and fellies from her wheel,
And bowl the round nave down the hill of heaven
As low as to the fiends!"

Pol. This is too long.

Ham. It shall to the barber's, with your beard. Prithee, say on; he's for a jig[45] or a tale of bawdry, or he sleeps. Say on; come to Hecuba.

[43] Vapory clouds. [44] Sky, air. [45] Merry ballad.

1. Play. "But who, O, who had seen the mobled queen"—

Ham. "The mobled[46] queen?"

Pol. That's good; "mobled queen" is good.

1. Play. "Run barefoot up and down, threat'ning the flame
With bisson[47] rheum, a clout about that head
Where late the diadem stood, and for a robe,
About her lank and all o'er-teemed[48] loins,
A blanket, in the alarm of fear caught up;—
Who this had seen, with tongue in venom steep'd,
'Gainst Fortune's state would treason have pronounc'd.
But if the gods themselves did see her then,
When she saw Pyrrhus make malicious sport
In mincing with his sword her husband's limbs,
The instant burst of clamour that she made,
Unless things mortal move them not at all,
Would have made milch[49] the burning eyes of heaven,
And passion in the gods."

Pol. Look, whe'er he has not turn'd his colour and has tears in 's eyes. Pray you, no more.

Ham. 'Tis well; I 'll have thee speak out the rest soon. Good my lord, will you see the players well bestow'd?[50] Do ye hear? Let them be well us'd, for they are the abstracts and brief chronicles of the time; after your death you were better have a bad epitaph than their ill report while you live.

Pol. My lord, I will use them according to their desert.

Ham. God's bodykins, man, better. Use every man after his desert, and who should scape whipping? Use them after your own honour and dignity. The less they deserve, the more merit is in your bounty. Take them in.

Pol. Come, sirs. [*Exit.*

Ham. Follow him, friends; we'll hear a play to-morrow. [*Exeunt all the* Players *but the* First.] Dost thou hear me, old friend? Can you play "The Murder of Gonzago"?

1. Play. Ay, my lord.

Ham. We'll ha 't to-morrow night. You could, for a need, study

[46] Muffled. [47] Blinding.
[48] Exhausted by child-bearing. [49] Moist. [50] Lodged.

a speech of some dozen or sixteen lines, which I would set down and insert in 't, could ye not?

1. Play. Ay, my lord.

Ham. Very well. Follow that lord,—and look you mock him not. [*Exit* First Player.] My good friends, I'll leave you till night. You are welcome to Elsinore.

Ros. Good my lord! *Exeunt* [ROSENCRANTZ *and* GUILDENSTERN.]

Ham. Ay, so, God buy ye.—Now I am alone.
O, what a rogue and peasant slave am I!
Is it not monstrous that this player here,
But in a fiction, in a dream of passion,
Could force his soul so to his own conceit
That from her working all his visage wann'd,
Tears in his eyes, distraction in 's aspect,
A broken voice, and his whole function suiting
With forms to his conceit? And all for nothing!
For Hecuba!
What's Hecuba to him, or he to Hecuba,
That he should weep for her? What would he do,
Had he the motive and the cue for passion
That I have? He would drown the stage with tears
And cleave the general ear with horrid speech,
Make mad the guilty and appall the free,[51]
Confound the ignorant, and amaze indeed
The very faculties of eyes and ears.
Yet I,
A dull and muddy-mettled rascal, peak
Like John-a-dreams, unpregnant of[52] my cause,
And can say nothing; no, not for a king,
Upon whose property and most dear life
A damn'd defeat[53] was made. Am I a coward?
Who calls me villain, breaks my pate across,
Plucks off my beard and blows it in my face,
Tweaks me by the nose, gives me the lie i' the throat
As deep as to the lungs, who does me this?
Ha!

[51] Innocent. [52] Unquickened by. [53] Destruction.

['Swounds,] I should take it; for it cannot be
But I am pigeon-liver'd and lack gall
To make oppression bitter, or ere this
I should have fatted all the region[54] kites
With this slave's offal. Bloody, bawdy villain!
Remorseless, treacherous, lecherous, kindless[55] villain!
O, vengeance!
Why, what an ass am I! Sure, this is most brave,
That I, the son of a dear father murdered,
Prompted to my revenge by heaven and hell,
Must, like a whore, unpack my heart with words,
And fall a-cursing, like a very drab,
A scullion!
Fie upon 't! Foh! About, my brain! I have heard
That guilty creatures sitting at a play
Have by the very cunning of the scene
Been struck so to the soul that presently[56]
They have proclaim'd their malefactions;
For murder, though it have no tongue, will speak
With most miraculous organ. I'll have these players
Play something like the murder of my father
Before mine uncle. I'll observe his looks;
I'll tent[57] him to the quick. If he but blench,
I know my course. The spirit that I have seen
May be the devil; and the devil hath power
To assume a pleasing shape; yea, and perhaps
Out of my weakness and my melancholy,
As he is very potent with such spirits,
Abuses me to damn me. I'll have grounds
More relative[58] than this. The play's the thing
Wherein I'll catch the conscience of the King. *Exit.*

[54] Of the air. [55] Unnatural. [56] At once. [57] Probe. [58] Conclusive.

[ACT III]

[SCENE I. *A room in the castle*]

Enter KING, QUEEN, POLONIUS, OPHELIA, ROSENCRANTZ, *and* GUILDENSTERN

King. And can you, by no drift of circumstance,[1]
Get from him why he puts on this confusion,
Grating so harshly all his days of quiet
With turbulent and dangerous lunacy?
Ros. He does confess he feels himself distracted;
But from what cause he will by no means speak.
Guil. Nor do we find him forward to be sounded,
But, with a crafty madness, keeps aloof
When we would bring him on to some confession
Of his true state.
Queen. Did he receive you well?
Ros. Most like a gentleman.
Guil. But with much forcing of his disposition.
Ros. Niggard of question; but, of our demands,
Most free in his reply.
Queen. Did you assay him
To any pastime?
Ros. Madam, it so fell out, that certain players
We o'er-raught[2] on the way; of these we told him,
And there did seem in him a kind of joy
To hear of it. They are about the court,
And, as I think, they have already order
This night to play before him.
Pol. 'Tis most true.
And he beseech'd me to entreat your Majesties
To hear and see the matter.
King. With all my heart; and it doth much content me
To hear him so inclin'd.
Good gentlemen, give him a further edge,
And drive his purpose on to these delights.

[1] Indirect method. [2] Overtook.

Ros. We shall, my lord.

Exeunt [ROSENCRANTZ *and* GUILDENSTERN.]

King. Sweet Gertrude, leave us too,
For we have closely sent for Hamlet hither,
That he, as 'twere by accident, may here
Affront[3] Ophelia.
Her father and myself, lawful espials,[4]
Will so bestow[5] ourselves that, seeing unseen,
We may of their encounter frankly judge,
And gather by him, as he is behaved,
If 't be the affliction of his love or no
That thus he suffers for.

Queen. I shall obey you.
And for your part, Ophelia, I do wish
That your good beauties be the happy cause
Of Hamlet's wildness. So shall I hope your virtues
Will bring him to his wonted way again,
To both your honours.

Oph. Madam, I wish it may. [*Exit* QUEEN.]

Pol. Ophelia, walk you here. Gracious, so please ye,
We will bestow ourselves. [*To* OPHELIA.] Read on this book,
That show of such an exercise may colour
Your loneliness. We are oft to blame in this,—
'Tis too much prov'd—that with devotion's visage
And pious action we do sugar o'er
The devil himself.

King. O, 'tis true!
[*Aside.*] How smart a lash that speech doth give my conscience!
The harlot's cheek, beautied with plast'ring art,
Is not more ugly to[6] the thing that helps it
Than is my deed to my most painted word.
O heavy burden!

Pol. I hear him coming. Let's withdraw, my lord.

Exeunt [KING *and* POLONIUS.]

[3] Encounter. [4] Spies. [5] Place. [6] Compared to.

Enter HAMLET

Ham. To be, or not to be: that is the question.
Whether 'tis nobler in the mind to suffer
The slings and arrows of outrageous fortune,
Or to take arms against a sea of troubles,
And by opposing end them. To die; to sleep;
No more; and by a sleep to say we end
The heart-ache and the thousand natural shocks
That flesh is heir to. 'Tis a consummation
Devoutly to be wish'd. To die; to sleep;—
To sleep? Perchance to dream! Ay, there 's the rub;[7]
For in that sleep of death what dreams may come,
When we have shuffl'd off this mortal coil,[8]
Must give us pause. There's the respect
That makes calamity of so long life.
For who would bear the whips and scorns of time,
The oppressor's wrong, the proud man's contumely,
The pangs of dispriz'd[9] love, the law's delay,
The insolence of office, and the spurns
That patient merit of the unworthy takes,
When he himself might his quietus[10] make
With a bare bodkin?[11] Who would fardels[12] bear,
To grunt and sweat under a weary life,
But that the dread of something after death,
The undiscovered country from whose bourn[13]
No traveller returns, puzzles the will
And makes us rather bear those ills we have
Than fly to others that we know not of?
Thus conscience does make cowards of us all;
And thus the native hue of resolution
Is sicklied o'er with the pale cast of thought,[14]
And enterprises of great pith and moment
With this regard their currents turn awry,
And lose the name of action.—Soft you now!

[7] Impediment. [8] Turmoil of life. [9] Undervalued. [10] Acquittance. [11] Dagger. [12] Burdens. [13] Boundary. [14] Brooding, anxiety.

The fair Ophelia! Nymph, in thy orisons
Be all my sins rememb'red.

Oph. Good my Lord,
How does your honour for this many a day?

Ham. I humbly thank you, well, well, well.

Oph. My lord, I have remembrances of yours
That I have longed long to re-deliver.
I pray you, now receive them.

Ham. No, no;
I never gave you aught.

Oph. My honour'd lord, I know right well you did,
And, with them, words of so sweet breath compos'd
As made the things more rich. Their perfume lost,
Take these again; for to the noble mind
Rich gifts wax poor when givers prove unkind.
There, my lord.

Ham. Ha ha! are you honest?[15]

Oph. My lord!

Ham. Are you fair?

Oph. What means your lordship?

Ham. That if you be honest and fair, your honesty should admit no discourse to your beauty.

Oph. Could beauty, my lord, have better commerce[16] than with honesty?

Ham. Ay, truly; for the power of beauty will sooner transform honesty from what it is to a bawd than the force of honesty can translate beauty into his likeness. This was sometime a paradox, but now the time gives it proof. I did love you once.

Oph. Indeed, my lord you made me believe so.

Ham. You should not have believ'd me, for virtue cannot so inoculate[17] our old stock but we shall relish of it. I loved you not.

Oph. I was the more deceived.

Ham. Get thee to a nunnery; why wouldst thou be a breeder of sinners? I am myself indifferent honest, but yet I could accuse me of such things that it were better my mother had not borne me. I

[15] Chaste. [16] Intercourse. [17] Graft.

am very proud, revengeful, ambitious, with more offences at my beck than I have thoughts to put them in, imagination to give them shape, or time to act them in. What should such fellows as I do crawling between heaven and earth? We are arrant knaves all; believe none of us. Go thy ways to a nunnery. Where's your father?

Oph. At home, my lord.

Ham. Let the doors be shut upon him, that he may play the fool nowhere but in 's own house. Farewell!

Oph. O, help him, you sweet heavens!

Ham. If thou dost marry, I'll give thee this plague for thy dowry: be thou as chaste as ice, as pure as snow, thou shalt not escape calumny. Get thee to a nunnery, go. Farewell! Or, if thou wilt needs marry, marry a fool; for wise men know well enough what monsters you make of them. To a nunnery, go, and quickly too. Farewell!

Oph. O heavenly powers, restore him!

Ham. I have heard of your paintings too, well enough. God has given you one face and you make yourselves another. You jig, you amble, and you lisp and nick-name God's creatures and make your wantonness your ignorance. Go to, I'll no more on 't; it hath made me mad. I say, we will have no more marriages. Those that are married already, all but one, shall live; the rest shall keep as they are. To a nunnery, go. *Exit.*

Oph. O, what a noble mind is here o'erthrown!
The courtier's, soldier's, scholar's, eye, tongue, sword;
The expectancy and rose of the fair state,
The glass of fashion and the mould of form,
The observ'd of all observers, quite, quite down!
And I, of ladies most deject and wretched,
That suck'd the honey of his music vows,
Now see that noble and most sovereign reason,
Like sweet bells jangled out of tune and harsh;
That unmatch'd form and feature of blown[18] youth
Blasted with ecstasy.[19] O, woe is me,
To have seen what I have seen, see what I see!

[18] Full-blown. [19] Madness.

Re-enter KING *and* POLONIUS

King. Love! his affections do not that way tend;
Nor what he spake, though it lack'd form a little,
Was not like madness. There's something in his soul
O'er which his melancholy sits on brood,
And I do doubt the hatch and the disclose[20]
Will be some danger; which for to prevent,
I have in quick determination
Thus set it down: he shall with speed to England
For the demand of our neglected tribute.
Haply the seas and countries different
With variable objects shall expel
This something-settled matter in his heart,
Whereon his brains still beating puts him thus
From fashion of himself. What think you on't?
Pol. It shall do well; but yet do I believe
The origin and commencement of this grief
Sprung from neglected love. How now, Ophelia!
You need not tell us what Lord Hamlet said;
We heard it all. My lord, do as you please,
But, if you hold it fit, after the play
Let his queen mother all alone entreat him
To show his griefs. Let her be round[21] with him,
And I'll be plac'd, so please you, in the ear
Of all their conference. If she find him not,
To England send him, or confine him where
Your wisdom best shall think.
King. It shall be so.
Madness in great ones must not unwatch'd go. *Exeunt.*

[SCENE II. *A hall in the castle*]

Enter HAMLET *and* Players

Ham. Speak the speech, I pray you, as I pronounc'd it to you, trippingly on the tongue; but if you mouth it, as many of your

[20] Breaking of the shell; outcome. [21] Direct.

players do, I had as lief the town-crier spoke my lines. Nor do not saw the air too much with your hand, thus, but use all gently; for in the very torrent, tempest, and, as I may say, the whirlwind of passion, you must acquire and beget a temperance that may give it smoothness. O, it offends me to the soul to see a robustious[1] periwig-pated fellow tear a passion to tatters, to very rags, to split the ears of the groundlings[2] who for the most part are capable of nothing but inexplicable dumb-shows and noise. I could have such a fellow whipp'd for o'erdoing Termagant.[3] It out-herods Herod.[4] Pray you, avoid it.

1. Play. I warrant your honour.

Ham. Be not too tame neither, but let your own discretion be your tutor. Suit the action to the word, the word to the action; with this special observance, that you o'erstep not the modesty[5] of nature. For anything so overdone is from the purpose of playing, whose end, both at the first and now, was and is, to hold, as 'twere, the mirror up to nature; to show virtue her own feature, scorn her own image, and the very age[6] and body of the time his form and pressure.[7] Now this overdone, or come tardy off,[8] though it make the unskilful laugh, cannot but make the judicious grieve; the censure[9] of the which one must, in your allowance, o'erweigh a whole theatre of others. O, there be players that I have seen play, and heard others praise, and that highly, not to speak it profanely, that, neither having the accent of Christians nor the gait of Christian, pagan, nor man, have so strutted and bellowed that I have thought some of Nature's journeymen had made men and not made them well, they imitated humanity so abominably.

1. Play. I hope we have reform'd that indifferently with us, sir.

Ham. O, reform it altogether. And let those that play your clowns speak no more than is set down for them; for there be of them that will themselves laugh to set on some quantity of barren spectators to laugh too, though in the mean time some necessary question of the play be then to be considered. That's villanous, and shows a most pitiful ambition in the Fool that uses it. Go, make you ready.

Exeunt Players.

[1] Sturdy. [2] Spectators standing in the pit, then the cheapest part of the theatre.
[3] Believed to be the god of the Saracens. A figure in the old plays and romances.
[4] The raging Herod of the miracle-plays. [5] Moderation. [6] Generation.
[7] Impress. [8] Hanging fire. [9] Opinion.

Enter POLONIUS, ROSENCRANTZ, *and* GUILDENSTERN

How now, my lord! Will the King hear this piece of work?
Pol. And the Queen too, and that presently.
Ham. Bid the players make haste. *Exit* POLONIUS.
Will you two help to hasten them?
Ros. / *Guil.* We will, my lord.

Exeunt ROSENCRANTZ *and* GUILDENSTERN.

Ham. What ho! Horatio.

Enter HORATIO

Hor. Here, sweet lord, at your service.
Ham. Horatio, thou art e'en as just a man
As e'er my conversation cop'd[10] withal.
Hor. O, my dear lord,—
Ham. Nay, do not think I flatter,
For what advancement may I hope from thee
That no revenue hast but thy good spirits
To feed and clothe thee? Why should the poor be flatter'd?
No, let the candied tongue lick absurd pomp,
And crook the pregnant[11] hinges of the knee
Where thrift[12] may follow fawning. Dost thou hear?
Since my dear soul was mistress of my choice
And could of men distinguish, her election
Hath seal'd thee for herself; for thou hast been
As one, in suffering all, that suffers nothing,
A man that Fortune's buffets and rewards
Hath ta'en with equal thanks; and blest are those
Whose blood and judgement are so well commingled,
That they are not a pipe for Fortune's finger
To sound what stop she please. Give me that man
That is not passion's slave, and I will wear him
In my heart's core, ay, in my heart of heart,
As I do thee.—Something too much of this.—
There is a play to-night before the King.

[10] As I ever encountered in my intercourse with men. [11] Ready (to bend). [12] Profit.

One scene of it comes near the circumstance
Which I have told thee of my father's death.
I prithee, when thou seest that act a-foot,
Even with the very comment of thy soul
Observe mine uncle. If his occulted guilt
Do not itself unkennel in one speech,
It is a damned ghost that we have seen,
And my imaginations are as foul
As Vulcan's stithy.[13] Give him heedful note;
For I mine eyes will rivet to his face,
And after we will both our judgements join
To censure[14] of his seeming.

Hor. Well, my lord.
If he steal aught the whilst this play is playing,
And scape detecting, I will pay the theft.

Danish march. A flourish. Enter KING, QUEEN, POLONIUS, OPHELIA, ROSENCRANTZ, GUILDENSTERN, *and other* Lords *attendant, with the* guard *carrying torches*

Ham. They are coming to the play; I must be idle. Get you a place.

King. How fares our cousin Hamlet?

Ham. Excellent, i' faith,—of the chameleon's dish. I eat the air, promise-cramm'd. You cannot feed capons so.

King. I have nothing with this answer, Hamlet; these words are not mine.

Ham. No, nor mine now. [*To* POLONIUS.] My lord, you play'd once i' the university, you say?

Pol. That I did, my lord, and was accounted a good actor.

Ham. And what did you enact?

Pol. I did enact Julius Cæsar. I was kill'd i' the Capitol; Brutus kill'd me.

Ham. It was a brute part of him to kill so capital a calf there.—Be the players ready?

Ros. Ay, my lord, they stay upon your patience.

Queen. Come hither, my good Hamlet, sit by me.

[13] Forge, anvil. [14] Judge.

Ham. No, good mother, here's metal more attractive.

[*Lying down at* OPHELIA'S *feet.*]

Pol. [*To the King.*] O, ho! do you mark that?

Ham. Lady, shall I lie in your lap?

Oph. No, my lord.

Ham. I mean, my head upon your lap?

Oph. Ay, my lord.

Ham. Do you think I meant country matters?

Oph. I think nothing, my lord.

Ham. That's a fair thought to lie between maid's legs.

Oph. What is, my lord?

Ham. Nothing.

Oph. You are merry, my lord.

Ham. Who, I?

Oph. Ay, my lord.

Ham. O God, your only jig-maker. What should a man do but be merry? For, look you, how cheerfully my mother looks, and my father died within 's two hours.

Oph. Nay, 'tis twice two months, my lord.

Ham. So long? Nay then, let the devil wear black, for I'll have a suit of sables.[15] O heavens! die two months ago, and not forgotten yet? Then there's hope a great man's memory may outlive his life half a year; but, by 'r lady, he must build churches then, or else shall he suffer not thinking on, with the hobby-horse, whose epitaph is, "For, O, for, O, the hobby-horse is forgot."

Hautboys play. The dumb-show enters.

Enter a King *and* Queen *very lovingly, the* Queen *embracing him. She kneels and makes show of protestation unto him. He takes her up and declines his head upon her neck; lays him down upon a bank of flowers. She, seeing him asleep, leaves him. Anon comes in a fellow, takes off his crown, kisses it, and pours poison in the* King's *ears, and exit. The* Queen *returns, finds the* King *dead, and makes passionate action. The* poisoner, *with some two or three* Mutes, *comes in again, seeming to lament with her. The dead body is carried away. The* poisoner *woos the* Queen *with*

[15] Furs, or black garments. Probably intentionally ambiguous.

gifts; she seems loath and unwilling a while, but in the end accepts his love. *Exeunt.*

Oph. What means this, my lord?

Ham. Marry, this is miching mallecho;[16] that means mischief.

Oph. Belike this show imports the argument of the play?

Enter PROLOGUE

Ham. We shall know by this fellow. The players cannot keep counsel, they'll tell all.

Oph. Will they tell us what this show meant?

Ham. Ay, or any show that you'll show him. Be not you asham'd to show, he'll not shame to tell you what it means.

Oph. You are naught,[17] you are naught. I'll mark the play.

Pro. For us, and for our tragedy,
Here stooping to your clemency,
We beg your hearing patiently. [*Exit.*]

Ham. Is this a prologue, or the posy of a ring?

Oph. 'Tis brief, my lord.

Ham. As woman's love.

Enter [*two* Players,] *a* King *and his* Queen

P. King. Full thirty times hath Phœbus' cart[18] gone round
Neptune's salt wash and Tellus' orbed ground,
And thirty dozen moons with borrowed sheen
About the world have times twelve thirties been,
Since love our hearts and Hymen did our hands
Unite commutual in most sacred bands.

P. Queen. So many journeys may the sun and moon
Make us again count o'er ere love be done!
But, woe is me, you are so sick of late,
So far from cheer and from your former state,
That I distrust you. Yet, though I distrust,
Discomfort you, my lord, it nothing must;
For women's fear and love holds quantity,[19]
In neither aught, or in extremity.
Now, what my love is, proof hath made you know;

[16] Skulking mischief. [17] Improper. [18] Chariot. [19] Keep proportion.

And as my love is siz'd, my fear is so.
[Where love is great, the littlest doubts are fear;
Where little fears grow great, great love grows there.]
P. King. Faith, I must leave thee, love, and shortly too.
My operant powers their functions leave to do;
And thou shalt live in this fair world behind,
Honour'd, belov'd; and haply one as kind.
For husband shalt thou—
P. Queen. O, confound the rest!
Such love must needs be treason in my breast!
In second husband let me be accurst!
None wed the second but who kill'd the first.
Ham. [*Aside.*] Wormwood, wormwood!
P. Queen. The instances that second marriage move
Are base respects of thrift, but none of love.
A second time I kill my husband dead,
When second husband kisses me in bed.
P. King. I do believe you think what now you speak,
But what we do determine oft we break.
Purpose is but the slave to memory,
Of violent birth, but poor validity;
Which now, like fruit unripe, sticks on the tree,
But fall unshaken when they mellow be.
Most necessary 'tis that we forget
To pay ourselves what to ourselves is debt.
What to ourselves in passion we propose,
The passion ending, doth the purpose lose.
The violence of either grief or joy
Their own enactures[20] with themselves destroy.
Where joy most revels, grief doth most lament;
Grief joys, joy grieves, on slender accident.
This world is not for aye, nor 'tis not strange
That even our loves should with our fortunes change,
For 'tis a question left us yet to prove,
Whether love lead fortune, or else fortune love.
The great man down, you mark his favourite flies;

[20] Acts.

The poor advanc'd makes friends of enemies.
And hitherto doth love on fortune tend,
For who not needs shall never lack a friend;
And who in want a hollow friend doth try,
Directly seasons him his enemy.
But, orderly to end where I begun,
Our wills and fates do so contrary run
That our devices still are overthrown;
Our thoughts are ours, their ends none of our own.
So think thou wilt no second husband wed;
But die thy thoughts when thy first lord is dead.

P. Queen. Nor earth to me give food, nor heaven light!
Sport and repose lock from me day and night!
[To desperation turn my trust and hope!
An anchor's cheer[21] in prison be my scope!]
Each opposite[22] that blanks[23] the face of joy
Meet what I would have well and it destroy!
Both here and hence pursue me lasting strife,
If, once a widow, ever I be wife!

Ham. If she should break it now!

P. King. 'Tis deeply sworn. Sweet, leave me here a while.
My spirits grow dull, and fain I would beguile
The tedious day with sleep. *Sleeps.*

P. Queen. Sleep rock thy brain,
And never come mischance between us twain! *Exit.*

Ham. Madam, how like you this play?

Queen. The lady protests too much, methinks.

Ham. O, but she'll keep her word.

King. Have you heard the argument? Is there no offence in 't?

Ham. No, no, they do but jest, poison in jest.
No offence i' the world.

King. What do you call the play?

Ham. The Mouse-trap. Marry, how? Tropically.[24] This play is the image of a murder done in Vienna. Gonzago is the duke's name; his wife, Baptista. You shall see anon. 'Tis a knavish piece of work, but what o' that? Your Majesty and we that have free souls, it

[21] Hermit's fare. [22] Contrary thing. [23] Makes pale. [24] Figuratively.

touches us not. Let the gall'd jade wince, our withers are unwrung.

Enter LUCIANUS

This is one Lucianus, nephew to the king.

Oph. You are a good chorus, my lord.

Ham. I could interpret between you and your love,[25] if I could see the puppets dallying.[26]

Oph. You are keen, my lord, you are keen.

Ham. It would cost you a groaning to take off my edge.

Oph. Still better, and worse.

Ham. So you mistake[27] your husbands. Begin, murderer; pox, leave thy damnable faces and begin. Come, "the croaking raven doth bellow for revenge."

Luc. Thoughts black, hands apt, drugs fit, and time agreeing;
Confederate season, else no creature seeing.
Thou mixture rank, of midnight weeds collected,
With Hecate's ban thrice blasted, thrice infected,
Thy natural magic and dire property
On wholesome life usurp immediately.

Pours the poison in [to the sleeper's] ears.

Ham. He poisons him i' the garden for 's estate. His name's Gonzago; the story is extant, and writ in choice Italian. You shall see anon how the murderer gets the love of Gonzago's wife.

Oph. The King rises.

Ham. What, frighted with false fire?[28]

Queen. How fares my lord?

Pol. Give o'er the play.

King. Give me some light. Away!

All. Lights, lights, lights!

Exeunt all but HAMLET *and* HORATIO.

Ham. Why, let the strucken deer go weep,
The hart ungalled play;
For some must watch, while some must sleep,—
So runs the world away.

[25] Lover. [26] Referring to the interpreter who explains the action in a puppet show.
[27] Implying that wives, having promised to take their husbands for better, for worse, break their word. [28] Fire-works.

Would not this, sir, and a forest of feathers[29]—if the rest of my fortunes turn Turk with me—with two Provincial roses[30] on my raz'd[31] shoes, get me a fellowship in a cry of players, sir?

Hor. Half a share.

Ham. A whole one, I.

For thou dost know, O Damon dear,
This realm dismantled was
Of Jove himself; and now reigns here
A very, very—pajock.

Hor. You might have rhym'd.

Ham. O good Horatio, I'll take the ghost's word for a thousand pound. Didst perceive?

Hor. Very well, my lord.

Ham. Upon the talk of the poisoning?

Hor. I did very well note him.

Re-enter ROSENCRANTZ *and* GUILDENSTERN

Ham. Ah, ha! Come, some music! Come, the recorders!
For if the king like not the comedy,
Why, then, belike, he likes it not, perdy.
Come, some music!

Guil. Good my lord, vouchsafe me a word with you.

Ham. Sir, a whole history.

Guil. The King, sir,—

Ham. Ay, sir, what of him?

Guil. Is in his retirement marvellous distemper'd.[32]

Ham. With drink, sir?

Guil. No, my lord, rather with choler.[33]

Ham. Your wisdom should show itself more richer to signify this to his doctor; for, for me to put him to his purgation would perhaps plunge him into far more choler.

Guil. Good my lord, put your discourse into some frame, and start not so wildly from my affair.

Ham. I am tame, sir; pronounce.

[29] Feather head-dresses were much worn by actors. [30] Rosettes of ribbon.
[31] Slashed. [32] Perturbed. [33] Anger.

Guil. The Queen, your mother, in most great affliction of spirit, hath sent me to you.

Ham. You are welcome.

Guil. Nay, good my lord, this courtesy is not of the right breed. If it shall please you to make me a wholesome answer I will do your mother's commandment; if not, your pardon and my return shall be the end of my business.

Ham. Sir, I cannot.

Guil. What, my lord?

Ham. Make you a wholesome answer. My wit 's diseas'd. But, sir, such answers as I can make, you shall command, or, rather, as you say, my mother. Therefore no more, but to the matter. My mother, you say,—

Ros. Then thus she says: your behaviour hath struck her into amazement and admiration.[34]

Ham. O wonderful son, that can so astonish a mother! But is there no sequel at the heels of this mother's admiration? [Impart.]

Ros. She desires to speak with you in her closet ere you go to bed.

Ham. We shall obey, were she ten times our mother. Have you any further trade with us?

Ros. My lord, you once did love me.

Ham. So I do still, by these pickers and stealers.[35]

Ros. Good my lord, what is your cause of distemper?
You do surely bar the door upon your own liberty if you deny your griefs to your friend.

Ham. Sir, I lack advancement.

Ros. How can that be, when you have the voice of the King himself for your succession in Denmark?

Ham. Ay, but "While the grass grows,"—[36] the proverb is something musty.

Re-enter one with a recorder

O, the recorder! Let me see.—To withdraw[37] with you:—why do you go about to recover the wind of me, as if you would drive me into a toil?

[34] Wonder. [35] Hands. [36] "—the steed starves." [37] Talk apart.

Guil. O, my lord, if my duty be too bold, my love is too unmannerly.

Ham. I do not well understand that. Will you play upon this pipe?

Guil. My lord, I cannot.

Ham. I pray you.

Guil. Believe me, I cannot.

Ham. I do beseech you.

Guil. I know no touch of it, my lord.

Ham. 'Tis as easy as lying. Govern these ventages[38] with your finger and thumb, give it breath with your mouth, and it will discourse most excellent music. Look you, these are the stops.

Guil. But these cannot I command to any utterance of harmony. I have not the skill.

Ham. Why, look you now, how unworthy a thing you make of me! You would play upon me, you would seem to know my stops, you would pluck out the heart of my mystery, you would sound me from my lowest note to the top of my compass; and there is much music, excellent voice, in this little organ, yet cannot you make it [speak. 'Sblood,] do you think that I am easier to be play'd on than a pipe? Call me what instrument you will, though you can fret[39] me, you cannot play upon me.

Enter POLONIUS

God bless you, sir.

Pol. My lord, the Queen would speak with you, and presently.

Ham. Do you see that cloud that's almost in shape like a camel?

Pol. By the mass, and it's like a camel, indeed.

Ham. Methinks it is like a weasel.

Pol. It is back'd like a weasel.

Ham. Or like a whale?

Pol. Very like a whale.

Ham. Then will I come to my mother by and by. [*Aside.*] They fool me to the top of my bent.—I will come by and by.

Pol. I will say so. *Exit.*

38 Wind-holes.

39 A pun on fret, to irritate and fret, a bar on a stringed instrument to guide the fingers.

Ham. "By and by" is easily said. Leave me, friends.
[*Exeunt all but* HAMLET.]
'Tis now the very witching time of night
When churchyards yawn and hell itself breathes out
Contagion to this world. Now could I drink hot blood,
And do such bitter business as the day
Would quake to look on. Soft! now to my mother,
O heart, lose not thy nature! Let not ever
The soul of Nero enter this firm bosom;
Let me be cruel, not unnatural.
I will speak daggers to her, but use none.
My tongue and soul in this be hypocrites;
How in my words soever she be shent[40]
To give them seals never, my soul, consent! *Exit.*

[SCENE III. *A room in the castle*]

Enter KING, ROSENCRANTZ, *and* GUILDENSTERN

King. I like him not, nor stands it safe with us
To let his madness range. Therefore prepare you.
I your commission will forthwith dispatch,
And he to England shall along with you.
The terms of our estate may not endure
Hazard so dangerous as doth hourly grow
Out of his lunacies.
Guil. We will ourselves provide.
Most holy and religious fear it is
To keep those many many bodies safe
That live and feed upon your Majesty.
Ros. The single and peculiar life is bound
With all the strength and armour of the mind
To keep itself from noyance,[1] but much more
That spirit upon whose weal depends and rests
The lives of many. The cease of majesty
Dies not alone, but, like a gulf,[2] doth draw
What's near it with it. It is a massy wheel,

[40] Rebuked. [1] Harm. [2] Whirlpool.

Fixed on the summit of the highest mount,
To whose huge spokes ten thousand lesser things
Are mortis'd and adjoin'd; which, when it falls
Each small annexment, petty consequence,
Attends the boisterous ruin. Never alone
Did the King sigh, but with a general groan.

King. Arm you, I pray you, to this speedy voyage,
For we will fetters put upon this fear,
Which now goes too free-footed.

Ros. }
Guil. } We will haste us.

Exeunt ROSENCRANTZ *and* GUILDENSTERN.

Enter POLONIUS

Pol. My lord, he's going to his mother's closet.
Behind the arras I'll convey myself,
To hear the process. I'll warrant she'll tax him home;
And, as you said, and wisely was it said,
'Tis meet that some more audience than a mother,
Since nature makes them partial, should o'erhear
The speech, of vantage.[3] Fare you well, my liege.
I'll call upon you ere you go to bed,
And tell you what I know.

King. Thanks, dear my lord.

[*Exit* POLONIUS.]

O, my offence is rank, it smells to heaven;
It hath the primal eldest curse upon 't,
A brother's murder. Pray can I not,
Though inclination be as sharp as will.
My stronger guilt defeats my strong intent,
And, like a man to double business bound,
I stand in pause where I shall first begin,
And both neglect. What if this cursed hand
Were thicker than itself with brother's blood,
Is there not rain enough in the sweet heavens
To wash it white as snow? Whereto serves mercy

[3] From an advantageous position.

But to confront the visage of offence?
And what's in prayer but this twofold force,
To be forestalled ere we come to fall,
Or pardon'd being down? Then I'll look up;
My fault is past. But, O, what form of prayer
Can serve my turn? "Forgive me my foul murder"?
That cannot be; since I am still possess'd
Of those effects for which I did the murder,
My crown, mine own ambition, and my queen.
May one be pardon'd and retain the offence?[4]
In the corrupted currents of this world
Offence's gilded hand may shove by justice,
And oft 'tis seen the wicked prize itself
Buys out the law. But 'tis not so above.
There is no shuffling, there the action lies
In his true nature; and we ourselves compell'd,
Even to the teeth and forehead of our faults,
To give in evidence. What then? What rests?
Try what repentance can. What can it not?
Yet what can it when one cannot repent?
O wretched state! O bosom black as death!
O limed soul, that, struggling to be free,
Art more engag'd! Help, angels! Make assay!
Bow, stubborn knees, and, heart with strings of steel,
Be soft as sinews of the new-born babe!
All may be well. *[Retires and] kneels.*

Enter HAMLET

Ham. Now might I do it pat, now he is praying.
And now I'll do 't.—And so he goes to heaven;
And so am I reveng'd. That would be scann'd.
A villain kills my father, and for that,
I, his sole son, do this same villain send
To heaven.
Oh, this is hire and salary, not revenge.
He took my father grossly, full of bread,

[4] The profit of the crime.

With all his crimes broad blown, as flush as May;
And how his audit stands who knows save Heaven?
But in our circumstance and course of thought
'Tis heavy with him. And am I then reveng'd,
To take him in the purging of his soul,
When he is fit and season'd for his passage?
No!
Up, sword, and know thou a more horrid hent.[5]
When he is drunk asleep, or in his rage,
Or in the incestuous pleasure of his bed,
At gaming, swearing, or about some act
That has no relish of salvation in 't,—
Then trip him, that his heels may kick at heaven,
And that his soul may be as damn'd and black
As hell, whereto it goes. My mother stays.
This physic but prolongs thy sickly days. *Exit.*

King. [*Rising.*] My words fly up, my thoughts remain below.
Words without thoughts never to heaven go. *Exit.*

[SCENE IV. *The Queen's closet*]

Enter QUEEN *and* POLONIUS

Pol. He will come straight. Look you lay home to him.
Tell him his pranks have been too broad to bear with,
And that your Grace hath screen'd and stood between
Much heat and him. I'll silence me e'en here.
Pray you, be round with him.

Ham. (*Within.*) Mother, mother, mother!

Queen. I'll warrant you, fear me not. Withdraw, I hear him coming. [POLONIUS *hides behind the arras.*]

Enter HAMLET

Ham. Now, mother, what's the matter?

Queen. Hamlet, thou hast thy father much offended.

Ham. Mother, you have my father much offended.

Queen. Come, come, you answer with an idle tongue.

[5] Grip.

Ham. Go, go, you question with a wicked tongue.
Queen. Why, how now, Hamlet!
Ham. What's the matter now?
Queen. Have you forgot me?
Ham. No, by the rood, not so.
You are the Queen, your husband's brother's wife;
But would you were not so! You are my mother.
Queen. Nay, then, I'll set those to you that can speak.
Ham. Come, come, and sit you down. You shall not budge.
You go not till I set you up a glass
Where you may see the inmost part of you.
Queen. What wilt thou do? Thou wilt not murder me?
Help, help, ho!
Pol. [*Behind.*] What, ho! help, help, help!
Ham. [*Drawing.*] How now! A rat? Dead, for a ducat, dead!
Kills POLONIUS [*through the arras*].
Pol. [*Behind.*] O, I am slain!
Queen. O me, what hast thou done?
Ham. Nay, I know not.
Is it the King?
Queen. O, what a rash and bloody deed is this!
Ham. A bloody deed! Almost as bad, good mother,
As kill a king, and marry with his brother.
Queen. As kill a king!
Ham. Ay, lady, 'twas my word.
[*Lifts up the arras and discovers* POLONIUS.]
Thou wretched, rash, intruding fool, farewell!
I took thee for thy better. Take thy fortune.
Thou find'st to be too busy is some danger.
—Leave wringing of your hands. Peace! Sit you down,
And let me wring your heart; for so I shall,
If it be made of penetrable stuff,
If damned custom have not braz'd it so
That it is proof and bulwark against sense.[1]
Queen. What have I done, that thou dar'st wag thy tongue
In noise so rude against me?

[1] Feeling.

Ham. Such an act
That blurs the grace and blush of modesty,
Calls virtue hypocrite, takes off the rose
From the fair forehead of an innocent love
And sets a blister there, makes marriage-vows
As false as dicers' oaths; O, such a deed
As from the body of contraction[2] plucks
The very soul, and sweet religion makes
A rhapsody of words. Heaven's face doth glow,
Yea, this solidity and compound mass,
With tristful[3] visage, as against the doom,[4]
Is thought-sick at the act.
Queen. Ay me, what act,
That roars so loud and thunders in the index?[5]
Ham. Look here, upon this picture, and on this,
The counterfeit presentment[6] of two brothers.
See, what a grace was seated on this brow:
Hyperion's curls, the front of Jove himself,
An eye like Mars, to threaten or command,
A station like the herald Mercury
New-lighted on a heaven-kissing hill,
A combination and a form indeed,
Where every god did seem to set his seal,
To give the world assurance of a man.
This was your husband. Look you now what follows:
Here is your husband, like a mildew'd ear,
Blasting his wholesome brother. Have you eyes?
Could you on this fair mountain leave to feed,
And batten[7] on this moor? Ha! have you eyes?
You cannot call it love, for at your age
The hey-day in the blood is tame, it's humble,
And waits upon the judgement; and what judgement
Would step from this to this? [Sense sure you have,
Else could you not have motion; but sure, that sense

[2] The marriage contract. [3] Sorrowful. [4] Judgment day.
[5] Prelude. [6] Portrait. [7] Feed.

Is apoplex'd; for madness would not err,
Nor sense to ecstasy was ne'er so thrall'd
But it reserv'd some quantity[8] of choice,
To serve in such a difference.] What devil was 't
That thus hath cozen'd you at hoodman-blind?[9]
[Eyes without feeling, feeling without sight,
Ears without hands or eyes, smelling sans all,
Or but a sickly part of one true sense
Could not so mope.[10]]
O shame! where is thy blush? Rebellious hell,
If thou canst mutine in a matron's bones,
To flaming youth let virtue be as wax,
And melt in her own fire. Proclaim no shame
When the compulsive ardour gives the charge,
Since frost itself as actively doth burn
And reason panders will.

Queen. O Hamlet, speak no more!
Thou turn'st mine eyes into my very soul,
And there I see such black and grained[11] spots
As will not leave their tinct.[12]

Ham. Nay, but to live
In the rank sweat of an enseamed[13] bed,
Stew'd in corruption, honeying and making love
Over the nasty sty,—

Queen. O, speak to me no more!
These words like daggers enter in mine ears.
No more, sweet Hamlet!

Ham. A murderer and a villain!
A slave that is not twentieth part the tithe
Of your precedent lord! A vice[14] of kings!
A cutpurse of the empire and the rule,
That from a shelf the precious diadem stole,
And put it in his pocket!

Queen. No more!

[8] Portion. [9] Blind-man's buff. [10] Be stupid. [11] Ingrained.
[12] Abandon their stain. [13] Filthy, greasy. [14] The roguish buffoon of the old plays.

Enter Ghost

Ham. A king of shreds and patches,—
Save me, and hover o'er me with your wings,
You heavenly guards! What would your gracious figure?
Queen. Alas, he's mad!
Ham. Do you not come your tardy son to chide,
That, laps'd in time and passion,[15] lets go by
The important acting of your dread command?
O, say!
Ghost. Do not forget! This visitation
Is but to whet thy almost blunted purpose.
But, look, amazement on thy mother sits.
O, step between her and her fighting soul.
Conceit[16] in weakest bodies strongest works.
Speak to her, Hamlet.
Ham. How is it with you, lady?
Queen. Alas, how is 't with you,
That you do bend your eye on vacancy
And with the incorporal air do hold discourse?
Forth at your eyes your spirits wildly peep,
And, as the sleeping soldiers in the alarm,
Your bedded hair, like life in excrements,[17]
Start up and stand on end. O gentle son,
Upon the heat and flame of thy distemper
Sprinkle cool patience. Whereon do you look?
Ham. On him, on him! Look you, how pale he glares!
His form and cause conjoin'd, preaching to stones,
Would make them capable.[18] Do not look upon me,
Lest with this piteous action you convert
My stern effects;[19] then what I have to do
Will want true colour, tears perchance for blood.
Queen. To whom do you speak this?
Ham. Do you see nothing there?
Queen. Nothing at all, yet all that is I see.

[15] Having allowed time and passion to go past.
[16] Imagination. [17] Any outgrowth; here, hair. [18] Susceptible. [19] Actions.

Ham. Nor did you nothing hear?
Queen. No, nothing but ourselves.
Ham. Why, look you there! Look, how it steals away!
My father, in his habit as he lived!
Look, where he goes, even now, out at the portal! *Exit* Ghost.
Queen. This is the very coinage of your brain.
This bodiless creation ecstasy[20]
Is very cunning in.
Ham. Ecstasy!
My pulse, as yours, doth temperately keep time,
And makes as healthful music. It is not madness
That I have uttered. Bring me to the test,
And I the matter will re-word, which madness
Would gambol from. Mother, for love of grace,
Lay not that flattering unction to your soul,
That not your trespass, but my madness speaks.
It will but skin and film the ulcerous place,
Whilst rank corruption, mining all within,
Infects unseen. Confess yourself to Heaven;
Repent what's past, avoid what is to come,
And do not spread the compost on the weeds,
To make them rank. Forgive me this my virtue,
For in the fatness of these pursy[21] times
Virtue itself of vice must pardon beg,
Yea, curb and woo for leave to do him good.
Queen. O Hamlet, thou hast cleft my heart in twain.
Ham. O, throw away the worser part of it,
And live the purer with the other half.
Good-night; but go not to mine uncle's bed.
Assume a virtue, if you have it not.
[That monster, custom, who all sense[22] doth eat,
Of habits devil, is angel yet in this,
That to the use of actions fair and good
He likewise gives a frock or livery,
That aptly is put on.] Refrain to-night,

[20] Madness. [21] Overfed.
[22] Sensibility.

And that shall lend a kind of easiness
To the next abstinence; [the next more easy;
For use almost can change the stamp of nature,
And either master the devil or throw him out,
With wondrous potency.] Once more, good-night;
And when you are desirous to be blest,
I'll blessing beg of you. For this same lord, [*Pointing to* Polonius.]
I do repent; but Heaven hath pleas'd it so,
To punish me with this and this with me,
That I must be their scourge and minister.
I will bestow him, and will answer well
The death I gave him. So, again, good-night.
I must be cruel, only to be kind.
Thus bad begins and worse remains behind.
[One word more, good lady.]
Queen. What shall I do?
Ham. Not this, by no means, that I bid you do:
Let the bloat king tempt you again to bed,
Pinch wanton on your cheek, call you his mouse,
And let him, for a pair of reechy[23] kisses,
Or paddling in your neck with his damn'd fingers,
Make you to ravel all this matter out,
That I essentially am not in madness,
But mad in craft. 'Twere good you let him know;
For who, that's but a queen, fair, sober, wise,
Would from a paddock, from a bat, a gib,[24]
Such dear concernings hide? Who would do so?
No, in despite of sense and secrecy,
Unpeg the basket on the house's top,
Let the birds fly, and like the famous ape,
To try conclusions[25] in the basket creep,
And break your own neck down.
Queen. Be thou assur'd, if words be made of breath,
And breath of life, I have no life to breathe
What thou hast said to me.
Ham. I must to England; you know that?

[23] Smoky, stinking. [24] Tom-cat. [25] Experiments.

Queen. Alack,
I had forgot. 'Tis so concluded on.
Ham. [There's letters sealed, and my two school-fellows,
Whom I will trust as I will adders fang'd,
They bear the mandate. They must sweep my way,
And marshal me to knavery. Let it work;
For 'tis the sport to have the enginer
Hoist with his own petar;[26] and 't shall go hard
But I will delve one yard below their mines,
And blow them at the moon. O, 'tis most sweet,
When in one line two crafts directly meet.]
This man shall set me packing.
I'll lug the guts into the neighbour room.
Mother, good-night. Indeed this counsellor
Is now most still, most secret, and most grave,
Who was in life a foolish prating knave.
Come, sir, to draw toward an end with you.
Good-night, mother.
Exeunt [severally,] HAMLET *tugging in* POLONIUS.

[ACT IV]

[SCENE I. *A room in the castle*]

Enter KING [QUEEN, ROSENCRANTZ, *and* GUILDENSTERN]

King. There's matter in these sighs; these profound heaves
You must translate; 'tis fit we understand them.
Where is your son?
Queen. [Bestow this place on us a little while.]
[*Exeunt* ROSENCRANTZ *and* GUILDENSTERN.]
Ah, my good lord, what have I seen to-night!
King. What, Gertrude? How does Hamlet?
Queen. Mad as the seas and wind, when both contend
Which is the mightier. In his lawless fit,
Behind the arras hearing something stir,
He whips his rapier out, and cries, "A rat, a rat!"

[26] Bomb.

And, in his brainish[1] apprehension, kills
The unseen good old man.
King. O heavy deed!
It had been so with us, had we been there.
His liberty is full of threats to all,
To you yourself, to us, to every one.
Alas, how shall this bloody deed be answered?
It will be laid to us, whose providence
Should have kept short, restrain'd, and out of haunt,[2]
This mad young man. But so much was our love,
We would not understand what was most fit,
But, like the owner of a foul disease,
To keep it from divulging, let it feed
Even on the pith of life. Where is he gone?
Queen. To draw apart the body he hath kill'd,
O'er whom his very madness, like some ore
Among the mineral of metals base,
Shows itself pure; he weeps for what is done.
King. O Gertrude, come away!
The sun no sooner shall the mountains touch,
But we will ship him hence, and this vile deed
We must, with all our majesty and skill,
Both countenance and excuse. Ho, Guildenstern!

[*Re-*]*enter* ROSENCRANTZ *and* GUILDENSTERN

Friends both, go join you with some further aid.
Hamlet in madness hath Polonius slain,
And from his mother's closet hath he dragg'd him.
Go seek him out; speak fair, and bring the body
Into the chapel. I pray you, haste in this.
Exeunt ROSENCRANTZ *and* GUILDENSTERN.
Come, Gertrude, we'll call up our wisest friends
To let them know both what we mean to do
And what's untimely done; [so, haply, slander]
[Whose whisper o'er the world's diameter,
As level as the cannon to his blank,[3]

[1] Mad, headstrong. [2] Resort. [3] White spot in the center of a target.

Transports his poisoned shot, may miss our name,
And hit the woundless air.] O, come away!
My soul is full of discord and dismay. *Exeunt.*

[SCENE II. *Another room in the castle*]

Enter HAMLET

Ham. Safely stowed.

Ros.
Guil. } (*Within.*) Hamlet! Lord Hamlet!

Ham. What noise? Who calls on Hamlet?
O, here they come.

Enter ROSENCRANTZ *and* GUILDENSTERN

Ros. What have you done, my lord, with the dead body?

Ham. Compounded it with dust, whereto 'tis kin.

Ros. Tell us where 'tis, that we may take it thence
And bear it to the chapel.

Ham. Do not believe it.

Ros. Believe what?

Ham. That I can keep your counsel and not mine own. Besides, to be demanded of a sponge! What replication[1] should be made by the son of a king?

Ros. Take you me for a sponge, my lord?

Ham. Ay, sir, that soaks up the King's countenance, his rewards, his authorities. But such officers do the King best service in the end. He keeps them, as an ape doth nuts, in the corner of his jaw; first mouth'd, to be last swallowed. When he needs what you have glean'd, it is but squeezing you, and, sponge, you shall be dry again.

Ros. I understand you not, my lord.

Ham. I am glad of it. A knavish speech sleeps in a foolish ear.

Ros. My lord, you must tell us where the body is, and go with us to the King.

Ham. The body is with the King, but the King is not with the body. The King is a thing—

[1] Reply.

Guil. A thing, my lord!

Ham. Of nothing. Bring me to him. Hide fox, and all after.[2]

Exeunt.

[SCENE III. *Another room in the castle*]

Enter KING [*and two or three*]

King. I have sent to seek him, and to find the body.
How dangerous is it that this man goes loose!
Yet must not we put the strong law on him.
He's lov'd of the distracted multitude,
Who like not in their judgement, but their eyes,
And where 'tis so, the offender's scourge is weigh'd,
But never the offence. To bear all smooth and even,
This sudden sending him away must seem
Deliberate pause. Diseases desperate grown
By desperate appliance are relieved,
Or not at all.

Enter ROSENCRANTZ

How now! What hath befallen?

Ros. Where the dead body is bestow'd,[1] my lord,
We cannot get from him.

King. But where is he?

Ros. Without, my lord, guarded, to know your pleasure.

King. Bring him before us.

Ros. Ho, Guildenstern! bring in my lord.

Enter HAMLET *and* GUILDENSTERN

King. Now, Hamlet, where's Polonius?

Ham. At supper.

King. At supper! Where?

Ham. Not where he eats, but where he is eaten. A certain convocation of [politic] worms[2] are e'en at him. Your worm is your only emperor for diet. We fat all creatures else to fat us, and we fat

[2] A reference to a game.

[1] Hidden. [2] Worms that eat the bodies of politicians.

ourselves for maggots. Your fat king and your lean beggar is but variable service, two dishes, but to one table; that's the end.

[*King.* Alas, alas!

Ham. A man may fish with the worm that hath eat of a king, and eat of the fish that hath fed of that worm.]

King. What dost thou mean by this?

Ham. Nothing but to show you how a king may go a progress through the guts of a beggar.

King. Where is Polonius?

Ham. In heaven; send thither to see. If your messenger find him not there, seek him i' the other place yourself. But indeed, if you find him not [within] this month, you shall nose him as you go up the stairs into the lobby.

King. Go seek him there. [*To some* Attendants.]

Ham. He will stay till ye come. [*Exeunt* Attendants.]

King. Hamlet, this deed of thine, for thine especial safety,—
Which we do tender, as we dearly grieve
For that which thou hast done,—must send thee hence
With fiery quickness; therefore prepare thyself.
The bark is ready, and the wind at help,
The associates tend, and everything is bent
For England.

Ham. For England?

King. Ay, Hamlet.

Ham. Good.

King. So is it, if thou knew'st our purposes.

Ham. I see a cherub that sees them. But come, for England! Farewell, dear mother.

King. Thy loving father, Hamlet.

Ham. My mother. Father and mother is man and wife, man and wife is one flesh, and so, my mother. Come, for England! [*Exit.*

King. Follow him at foot, tempt him with speed aboard.
Delay it not; I'll have him hence to-night.
Away! for everything is seal'd and done
That else leans on the affair. Pray you, make haste.
[*Exeunt* Rosencrantz *and* Guildenstern.]
And, England, if my love thou hold'st at aught,—

As my great power thereof may give thee sense,
Since yet thy cicatrice[3] looks raw and red
After the Danish sword, and thy free awe
Pays homage to us—thou mayst not coldly set
Our sovereign process,[4] which imports at full,
By letters conjuring to that effect,
The present death of Hamlet. Do it, England;
For like the hectic[5] in my blood he rages,
And thou must cure me. Till I know 'tis done,
Howe'er my haps, my joys were ne'er begun. *Exit.*

[SCENE IV. *A plain in Denmark*]

Enter FORTINBRAS, [*a* Captain,] *and army,* [*marching*]

For. Go, captain, from me greet the Danish king.
Tell him that, by his license, Fortinbras
Claims the conveyance of a promis'd march
Over his kingdom. You know the rendezvous.
If that his Majesty would aught with us,
We shall express our duty in his eye;[1]
And let him know so.

Cap. I will do 't, my lord.

For. Go softly[2] on. *Exeunt* FORTINBRAS [*and* Soldiers].

[*Enter* HAMLET, ROSENCRANTZ, *and others*

Ham. Good sir, whose powers are these?

Cap. They are of Norway, sir.

Ham. How purpos'd, sir, I pray you?

Cap. Against some part of Poland.

Ham. Who commands them, sir?

Cap. The nephew to old Norway, Fortinbras.

Ham. Goes it against the main of Poland, sir,
Or for some frontier?

Cap. Truly to speak, and with no addition,
We go to gain a little patch of ground
That hath in it no profit but the name.

[3] Scar. [4] Procedure. [5] Fever. [1] Presence. [2] Slowly.

To pay five ducats, five, I would not farm it;
Nor will it yield to Norway or the Pole
A ranker rate, should it be sold in fee.

Ham. Why, then the Polack never will defend it.

Cap. Yes, it is already garrison'd.

Ham. Two thousand souls and twenty thousand ducats
Will not debate the question of this straw.
This is the imposthume[3] of much wealth and peace,
That inward breaks, and shows no cause without
Why the man dies. I humbly thank you, sir.

Cap. God buy you, sir. [*Exit.*]

Ros. Will 't please you go, my lord?

Ham. I'll be with you straight. Go a little before.

[*Exeunt all except* HAMLET.]

How all occasions do inform against me,
And spur my dull revenge? What is a man,
If his chief good and market of his time
Be but to sleep and feed? A beast, no more.
Sure, He that made us with such large discourse,
Looking before and after, gave us not
That capability and god-like reason
To fust[4] in us unus'd. Now, whether it be
Bestial oblivion, or some craven scruple
Of thinking too precisely on the event,—
A thought which, quarter'd, hath but one part wisdom
And ever three parts coward,—I do not know
Why yet I live to say, "This thing's to do,"
Sith I have cause and will and strength and means
To do 't. Examples gross as earth exhort me;
Witness this army of such mass and charge[5]
Led by a delicate and tender prince,
Whose spirit with divine ambition puff'd
Makes mouths at the invisible event,
Exposing what is mortal and unsure
To all that fortune, death, and danger dare,
Even for an egg-shell. Rightly to be great

[3] Boil. [4] Mould. [5] Expense.

Is not to stir without great argument,[6]
But greatly to find quarrel in a straw
When honour's at the stake. How stand I then,
That have a father kill'd, a mother stain'd,
Excitements of my reason and my blood,
And let all sleep, while to my shame I see
The imminent death of twenty thousand men,
That for a fantasy and trick[7] of fame
Go to their graves like beds, fight for a plot
Whereon the numbers cannot try the cause,
Which is not tomb enough and continent[8]
To hide the slain? O, from this time forth,
My thoughts be bloody, or be nothing worth!] *Exit.*

[SCENE V. *Elsinore. A room in the castle*]

Enter QUEEN, HORATIO [*and a* Gentleman]

Queen. I will not speak with her.
[*Gent.*] She is importunate, indeed distract.
Her mood will needs be pitied.
Queen. What would she have?
[*Gent.*] She speaks much of her father; says she hears
There's tricks i' the world, and hems, and beats her heart,
Spurns enviously[1] at straws, speaks things in doubt
That carry but half sense. Her speech is nothing,
Yet the unshaped use of it doth move
The hearers to collection.[2] They aim at it
And botch[3] the words up fit to their own thoughts;
Which, as her winks, and nods, and gestures yield them,
Indeed would make one think there would be thought,
Though nothing sure, yet much unhappily.
[*Hor.*] 'Twere good she were spoken with, for she may strew
Dangerous conjectures in ill-breeding minds.
Let her come in. [*Exit* Gentleman.
Queen. [*Aside.*] To my sick soul, as sin's true nature is,
Each toy[4] seems prologue to some great amiss;[5]

[6] Matter of dispute. [7] Trifle. [8] Receptacle. [1] Kicks ill-naturedly.
[2] Inference. [3] Patch together. [4] Trifle. [5] Misfortune.

So full of artless jealousy[6] is guilt,
It spills itself in fearing to be spilt.

Enter OPHELIA, *distracted*

Oph. Where is the beauteous majesty of Denmark?

Queen. How now, Ophelia!

Oph. [*Sings.*]

"How should I your true love know
From another one?
By his cockle hat[7] and staff,
And his sandal shoon."

Queen. Alas, sweet lady, what imports this song?

Oph. Say you? Nay, pray you, mark.

[*Sings.*] "He is dead and gone, lady,
He is dead and gone;
At his head a grass-green turf
At his heels a stone."

Enter KING

Queen. Nay, but, Ophelia,—

Oph. Pray you, mark.

[*Sings.*] "White his shroud as the mountain snow,"—

Queen. Alas, look here, my lord.

Oph. [*Sings.*]

"Larded[8] with sweet flowers;
Which bewept to the grave did not go
With true-love showers."

King. How do you, pretty lady?

Oph. Well, God 'ild you! They say the owl was a baker's daughter. Lord, we know what we are, but know not what we may be. God be at your table!

King. Conceit[9] upon her father.

Oph. Pray you, let's have no words of this, but when they ask you what it means, say you this:

[6]Suspicion. [7]Hat with a cockle-shell—the sign of a pilgrim to the shrine of St. James of Compostella. [8]Garnished. [9]Thought.

[*Sings.*] "Tomorrow is Saint Valentine's day,
All in the morning betime,
And I a maid at your window,
To be your Valentine.

"Then up he rose and donn'd his clothes,
And dupp'd[10] the chamber door;
Let in the maid, that out a maid
Never departed more."

King. Pretty Ophelia!

Oph. Indeed, la, without an oath I'll make an end on 't.

"By Gis,[11] and by Saint Charity,
Alack! and, fie for shame!
Young men will do 't, if they come to 't;
By Cock,[12] they are to blame.

"Quoth she, 'Before you tumbled me,
You promis'd me to wed.'
'So would I ha' done, by yonder sun,
An thou hadst not come to my bed.' "

King. How long hath she been thus?

Oph. I hope all will be well. We must be patient; but I cannot choose but weep, to think they should lay him i' the cold ground. My brother shall know of it; and so I thank you for your good counsel. Come, my coach! Good-night, ladies; good-night, sweet ladies; good-night, good-night. *Exit.*

King. Follow her close; give her good watch, I pray you.
[*Exeunt some.*]
O, this is the poison of deep grief; it springs
All from her father's death. O Gertrude, Gertrude,
When sorrows come, they come not single spies,
But in battalions. First, her father slain;
Next, your son gone; and he most violent author

[10]Opened. [11]Disguised oath: Jesus. [12]Corruption of "God."

Of his own just remove; the people muddied,
Thick and unwholesome in their thoughts and whispers,
For good Polonius' death; and we have done but greenly
In hugger-mugger[13] to inter him; poor Ophelia
Divided from herself and her fair judgement,
Without the which we are pictures, or mere beasts;
Last, and as much containing as all these,
Her brother is in secret come from France,
Feeds on his wonder, keeps himself in clouds,
And wants not buzzers to infect his ear
With pestilent speeches of his father's death.
Wherein necessity, of matter beggar'd,
Will nothing stick our persons to arraign
In ear and ear. O my dear Gertrude, this,
Like to a murdering-piece,[14] in many places
Gives me superfluous death. *A noise within.*

Enter a Messenger

Queen. Alack, what noise is this?

King. Where are my Switzers?[15] Let them guard the door. What is the matter?

Mess. Save yourself, my lord!
The ocean, overpeering of his list,[16]
Eats not the flats with more impetuous haste
Than young Laertes, in a riotous head,[17]
O'erbears your officers. The rabble call him lord;
And, as the world were now but to begin,
Antiquity forgot, custom not known,
(The ratifiers and props of every word,)
They cry, "Choose we! Laertes shall be king!"
Caps, hands, and tongues applaud it to the clouds,
"Laertes shall be king, Laertes king!"

Queen. How cheerfully on the false trail they cry!
O, this is counter,[18] you false Danish dogs!

[13] Secretly. [14] Cannon loaded with grape-shot. [15] Swiss mercenaries, used as a bodyguard. [16] Boundary. [17] Armed force. [18] Hunting in the wrong direction.

Enter LAERTES [*armed;* Danes *following*]

King. The doors are broke. *Noise within.*
Laer. Where is this king? Sirs, stand you all without.
Danes. No, let's come in.
Laer. I pray you, give me leave.
Danes. We will, we will. [*They retire without the door.*]
Laer. I thank you; keep the door. O thou vile king,
Give me my father!
Queen. Calmly, good Laertes.
Laer. That drop of blood that's calm proclaims me bastard,
Cries cuckold to my father, brands the harlot
Even here, between the chaste unsmirched brows
Of my true mother.
King. What is the cause, Laertes,
That thy rebellion looks so giant-like?
Let him go, Gertrude; do not fear our person.
There's such divinity doth hedge a king,
That treason can but peep to what it would,
Acts little of his will. Tell me, Laertes,
Why thou art thus incens'd. Let him go, Gertrude.
Speak, man.
Laer. Where's my father?
King. Dead.
Queen. But not by him.
King. Let him demand his fill.
Laer. How came he dead? I'll not be juggl'd with.
To hell, allegiance! Vows, to the blackest devil!
Conscience and grace, to the profoundest pit!
I dare damnation. To this point I stand,
That both the worlds I give to negligence,
Let come what comes; only I'll be reveng'd
Most throughly for my father.
King. Who shall stay you?
Laer. My will, not all the world.
And for my means, I'll husband them so well,
They shall go far with little.

King. Good Laertes,
If you desire to know the certainty
Of your dear father's death, is 't writ in your revenge
That, swoopstake,[19] you will draw both friend and foe,
Winner and loser?
Laer. None but his enemies.
King. Will you know them then?
Laer. To his good friends thus wide I'll ope my arms,
And like the kind life-rend'ring pelican,
Repast them with my blood.
King. Why, now you speak
Like a good child and a true gentleman.
That I am guiltless of your father's death,
And am most sensibly in grief for it,
It shall as level to your judgement pierce
As day does to your eye.
A noise within: "Let her come in!"

Re-enter OPHELIA

Laer. How now! what noise is that?
O heat, dry up my brains! Tears seven times salt
Burn out the sense and virtue of mine eye!
By heaven, thy madness shall be paid by weight
Till our scale turns the beam. O rose of May!
Dear maid, kind sister, sweet Ophelia!
O heavens! is 't possible, a young maid's wits
Should be as mortal as an old man's life?
Nature is fine[20] in love, and where 'tis fine,
It sends some precious instance[21] of itself
After the thing it loves.
Oph. [*Sings.*]

"They bore him barefac'd on the bier;
Hey non nonny, nonny, hey nonny;
And on his grave rains many a tear,"—

[19] Taking everything in.
[20] Delicate. [21] Token, sample.

Fare you well, my dove!

Laer. Hadst thou thy wits and didst persuade revenge,
It could not move thus.

Oph. You must sing, "Down a-down, and you call him a-down-a." O, how the wheel becomes it![22] It is the false steward, that stole his master's daughter.

Laer. This nothing's more than matter.

Oph. There's rosemary, that's for remembrance; pray, love, remember; and there is pansies, that's for thoughts.

Laer. A document in madness, thoughts and remembrance fitted.

Oph. There's fennel for you, and columbines; there's rue for you, and here's some for me; we may call it herb of grace o' Sundays. O, you must wear your rue with a difference. There's a daisy. I would give you some violets, but they wither'd all when my father died. They say he made a good end,—

[*Sings.*] "For bonny sweet Robin is all my joy."

Laer. Thought[23] and affliction, passion, hell itself,
She turns to favour and to prettiness.

Oph. [*Sings.*]

"And will he not come again?
And will he not come again?
No, no, he is dead;
Go to thy death-bed;
He never will come again.

"His beard as white as snow,
All flaxen was his poll.
He is gone, he is gone,
And we cast away moan.
God ha' mercy on his soul!"

And of all Christian souls, I pray God. God buy ye. *Exit.*

Laer. Do you see this, you gods?

King. Laertes, I must commune with your grief,
Or you deny me right. Go but apart,
Make choice of whom your wisest friends you will,

[22] How well the song goes to the spinning-wheel. [23] Brooding, melancholy thought.

And they shall hear and judge 'twixt you and me.
If by direct or by collateral hand
They find us touch'd,[24] we will our kingdom give,
Our crown, our life, and all that we call ours,
To you in satisfaction; but if not,
Be you content to lend your patience to us,
And we shall jointly labour with your soul
To give it due content.

Laer. Let this be so.
His means of death, his obscure burial—
No trophy, sword, nor hatchment[25] o'er his bones,
No noble rite nor formal ostentation—
Cry to be heard, as 't were from heaven to earth,
That I must call 't in question.

King. So you shall;
And where the offence is let the great axe fall.
I pray you, go with me. *Exeunt.*

[SCENE VI. *Another room in the castle*]

Enter HORATIO *with an* Attendant

Hor. What are they that would speak with me?

Att. Sailors, sir. They say they have letters for you.

Hor. Let them come in. [*Exit* Attendant.]
I do not know from what part of the world
I should be greeted, if not from Lord Hamlet.

Enter Sailor

Sail. God bless you, sir.

Hor. Let Him bless thee too.

Sail. He shall, sir, an 't please Him. There's a letter for you, sir—it comes from the ambassador that was bound for England—if your name be Horatio, as I am let to know it is.

[*Hor.*] (*Reads.*) "Horatio, when thou shalt have overlook'd this, give these fellows some means to the King; they have letters for

[24] Implicated. [25] Escutcheon.

him. Ere we were two days old at sea, a pirate of very warlike appointment gave us chase. Finding ourselves too slow of sail, we put on a compelled valour. In the grapple I boarded them. On the instant they got clear of our ship, so I alone became their prisoner. They have dealt with me like thieves of mercy,[1] but they knew what they did: I am to do a good turn for them. Let the King have the letters I have sent, and repair thou to me with as much haste as thou wouldest fly death. I have words to speak in your ear will make thee dumb, yet are they much too light for the bore[2] of the matter. These good fellows will bring thee where I am. Rosencrantz and Guildenstern hold their course for England; of them I have much to tell thee. Farewell.

"He that thou knowest thine,
HAMLET."

Come, I will give you way for these your letters;
And do 't the speedier, that you may direct me
To him from whom you brought them. *Exeunt.*

[SCENE VII. *Another room in the castle*]

Enter KING *and* LAERTES

King. Now must your conscience my acquittance seal;
And you must put me in your heart for friend,
Sith you have heard, and with a knowing ear,
That he which hath your noble father slain
Pursued my life.
Laer. It well appears. But tell me
Why you proceeded not against these feats,
So crimeful and so capital in nature,
As by your safety, wisdom, all things else,
You mainly were stirr'd up.
King. O, for two special reasons,
Which may to you, perhaps, seem much unsinew'd,
And yet to me they are strong. The Queen his mother
Lives almost by his looks; and for myself—

[1] Merciful thieves. [2] Calibre, greatness.

My virtue or my plague, be it either which—
She's so conjunctive[1] to my life and soul,
That, as the star moves not but in his sphere,
I could not but by her. The other motive
Why to a public count I might not go,
Is the great love the general gender[2] bear him;
Who, dipping all his faults in their affection,
Would, like the spring that turneth wood to stone,
Convert his gyves[3] to graces; so that my arrows,
Too slightly timb'red for so loud a wind,
Would have reverted to my bow again,
And not where I had aim'd them.

Laer. And so have I a noble father lost,
A sister driven into desperate terms,
Whose worth, if praises may go back again,
Stood challenger on mount of all the age
For her perfections. But my revenge will come.

King. Break not your sleeps for that. You must not think
That we are made of stuff so flat and dull
That we can let our beard be shook with danger
And think it pastime. You shortly shall hear more.
I lov'd your father, and we love ourself,
And that, I hope, will teach you to imagine—

Enter a Messenger *with letters*

How now! What news?

Mess. Letters, my lord, from Hamlet.
This to your Majesty; this to the Queen.

King. From Hamlet! Who brought them?

Mess. Sailors, my lord, they say; I saw them not.
They were given me by Claudio. He receiv'd them
[Of him that brought them].

King. Laertes, you shall hear them.
Leave us. *Exit* Messenger.

[*Reads.*] "High and mighty, You shall know I am set naked on your kingdom. To-morrow shall I beg leave to see your kingly eyes,

[1] Closely joined. [2] Multitude. [3] Fetters.

when I shall, first asking your pardon thereunto, recount the occasions of my sudden and more strange return.

HAMLET."

What should this mean? Are all the rest come back?
Or is it some abuse, or no such thing?
Laer. Know you the hand?
King. 'Tis Hamlet's character. "Naked!"
And in a postscript here, he says, "alone."
Can you advise me?
Laer. I'm lost in it, my lord. But let him come.
It warms the very sickness in my heart
That I shall live and tell him to his teeth,
"Thus didest thou."
King. If it be so, Laertes,—
As how should it be so? How otherwise?—
Will you be rul'd by me?
Laer. [Ay, my lord,]
If so you'll not o'errule me to a peace.
King. To thine own peace. If he be now return'd,
As checking[4] at his voyage, and that he means
No more to undertake it, I will work him
To an exploit, now ripe in my device,
Under the which he shall not choose but fall;
And for his death no wind of blame shall breathe,
But even his mother shall uncharge the practice[5]
And call it accident.
[*Laer.* My lord, I will be rul'd;
The rather, if you could devise it so
That I might be the organ.[6]
King. It falls right.
You have been talk'd of since your travel much,
And that in Hamlet's hearing, for a quality
Wherein, they say, you shine. Your sum of parts
Did not together pluck such envy from him
As did that one, and that, in my regard,
Of the unworthiest siege.[7]

[4] Refusing to proceed. [5] Free the plot from blame. [6] Instrument, means. [7] Rank.

Laer. What part is that, my lord?
King. A very riband in the cap of youth,
Yet needful too; for youth no less becomes
The light and careless livery that it wears
Than settled age his sables and his weeds,
Importing health and graveness.] Two months since,
Here was a gentleman of Normandy;—
I've seen myself, and serv'd against, the French,
And they can well on horseback; but this gallant
Had witchcraft in 't. He grew unto his seat,
And to such wondrous doing brought his horse,
As had he been incorps'd[8] and demi-natur'd
With the brave beast. So far he pass'd my thought,
That I, in forgery[9] of shapes and tricks,
Come short of what he did.
Laer. A Norman, was 't?
King. A Norman.
Laer. Upon my life, Lamound.
King. The very same.
Laer. I know him well. He is the brooch[10] indeed
And gem of all the nation.
King. He made confession of you,
And gave you such a masterly report
For art and exercise in your defence,
And for your rapier most especially,
That he cried out, 'twould be a sight indeed
If one could match you. [The scrimers[11] of their nation,
He swore, had neither motion, guard, nor eye,
If you oppos'd them.] Sir, this report of his
Did Hamlet so envenom with his envy
That he could nothing do but wish and beg
Your sudden coming o'er to play with him.
Now, out of this—
Laer. What out of this, my lord?
King. Laertes, was your father dear to you?
Or are you like the painting of a sorrow,

[8] Incorporated. [9] Imagination. [10] Ornament. [11] Fencers.

A face without a heart?
Laer. Why ask you this?
King. Not that I think you did not love your father,
But that I know love is begun by time,
And that I see, in passages of proof,[12]
Time qualifies the spark and fire of it.
[There lives within the very flame of love
A kind of wick or snuff that will abate it,
And nothing is at a like goodness still;
For goodness, growing to a plurisy,[13]
Dies in his own too much. That we would do,
We should do when we would; for this "would" changes,
And hath abatements and delays as many
As there are tongues, are hands, are accidents;
And then this "should" is like a spendthrift sigh,[14]
That hurts by easing. But, to the quick o' the ulcer:—]
Hamlet comes back. What would you undertake,
To show yourself your father's son in deed
More than in words?
Laer. To cut his throat i' the church.
King. No place, indeed, should murder sanctuarize;[15]
Revenge should have no bounds. But, good Laertes,
Will you do this, keep close within your chamber?
Hamlet return'd shall know you are come home.
We'll put on those shall praise your excellence
And set a double varnish on the fame
The Frenchman gave you, bring you, in fine, together
And wager on your heads. He, being remiss,
Most generous and free from all contriving,
Will not peruse the foils, so that, with ease,
Or with a little shuffling, you may choose
A sword unbated,[16] and in a pass of practice[17]
Requite him for your father.
Laer. I will do 't;
And, for that purpose, I'll anoint my sword.

[12] Proved instances. [13] Excess. [14] Sighing was supposed to draw blood from the heart, and so shorten life. [15] Protect, as in a sanctuary.
[16] Unblunted. [17] Treacherous thrust.

I bought an unction of a mountebank,[18]
So mortal that, but dip a knife in it,
Where it draws blood no cataplasm[19] so rare,
Collected from all simples[20] that have virtue
Under the moon, can save the thing from death
That is but scratch'd withal. I'll touch my point
With this contagion, that, if I gall him slightly,
It may be death.

King. Let's further think of this,
Weigh what convenience both of time and means
May fit us to our shape. If this should fail,
And that our drift look through our bad performance,
'Twere better not assay'd; therefore this project
Should have a back or second, that might hold
If this should blast in proof.[21] Soft! let me see.
We'll make a solemn wager on your cunnings,—
I ha 't!
When in your motion you are hot and dry—
As make your bouts more violent to that end—
And that he calls for drink, I'll have prepar'd him
A chalice for the nonce,[22] whereon but sipping,
If he by chance escape your venom'd stuck,[23]
Our purpose may hold there. But stay, what noise?

Enter QUEEN

How, sweet queen!

Queen. One woe doth tread upon another's heel,
So fast they follow. Your sister's drown'd, Laertes.

Laer. Drown'd! O, where?

Queen. There is a willow grows aslant a brook,
That shows his hoar leaves in the glassy stream.
There with fantastic garlands did she come
Of crow-flowers, nettles, daisies, and long purples[24]
That liberal[25] shepherds give a grosser name,
But our cold maids do dead men's fingers call them;

[18] Quack doctor. [19] Poultice. [20] Herbs. [21] Be blighted in trial. [22] Occasion. [23] Thrust. [24] Orchis. [25] Free-spoken.

There, on the pendent boughs her coronet weeds
Clamb'ring to hang, an envious silver broke,
When down her weedy trophies and herself
Fell in the weeping brook. Her clothes spread wide,
And, mermaid-like, awhile they bore her up;
Which time she chanted snatches of old tunes,
As one incapable of[26] her own distress,
Or like a creature native and indued[27]
Unto that element. But long it could not be
Till that her garments, heavy with their drink,
Pull'd the poor wretch from her melodious lay
To muddy death.

Laer. Alas, then, is she drown'd?

Queen. Drown'd, drown'd.

Laer. Too much of water hast thou, poor Ophelia,
And therefore I forbid my tears. But yet
It is our trick. Nature her custom holds,
Let shame say what it will; when these are gone,
The woman will be out. Adieu, my lord;
I have a speech of fire that fain would blaze,
But that this folly douts[28] it. *Exit.*

King. Let's follow, Gertrude.
How much I had to do to calm his rage!
Now fear I this will give it start again,
Therefore let's follow. *Exeunt.*

[ACT V]

[SCENE I. *A churchyard*]

Enter two Clowns [*with spades and pickaxes*]

1\. *Clo.* Is she to be buried in Christian burial that wilfully seeks her own salvation?

2\. *Clo.* I tell thee she is, and therefore make her grave straight. The crowner[1] hath sat on her, and finds it Christian burial.

1\. *Clo.* How can that be, unless she drown'd herself in her own defence?

[26] Insensible of. [27] Fitted to. [28] Extinguishes. [1] Coroner.

2. *Clo.* Why, 'tis found so.

1. *Clo.* It must be *"se offendendo,"*[2] it cannot be else. For here lies the point: if I drown myself wittingly, it argues an act, and an act hath three branches; it is, to act, to do, and to perform; argal,[3] she drown'd herself wittingly.

2. *Clo.* Nay, but hear you, goodman delver,—

1. *Clo.* Give me leave. Here lies the water; good. Here stands the man; good. If the man go to this water and drown himself, it is, will he, nill he, he goes,—mark you that? But if the water come to him and drown him, he drowns not himself; argal, he that is not guilty of his own death shortens not his own life.

2. *Clo.* But is this law?

1. *Clo.* Ay, marry, is 't; crowner's quest law.

2. *Clo.* Will you ha' the truth on 't? If this had not been a gentlewoman, she should have been buried out o' Christian burial.

1. *Clo.* Why, there thou say'st; and the more pity that great folk should have countenance in this world to drown or hang themselves, more than their even Christian.[4] Come, my spade. There is no ancient gentlemen but gardeners, ditchers, and grave-makers; they hold up Adam's profession.

2. *Clo.* Was he a gentleman?

1. *Clo.* He was the first that ever bore arms.

2. *Clo.* Why, he had none.

1. *Clo.* What, art a heathen? How dost thou understand the Scripture? The Scripture says Adam digg'd; could he dig without arms? I'll put another question to thee. If thou answerest me not to the purpose, confess thyself—

2. *Clo.* Go to.

1. *Clo.* What is he that builds stronger than either the mason, the shipwright, or the carpenter?

2. *Clo.* The gallows-maker; for that frame outlives a thousand tenants.

1. *Clo.* I like thy wit well, in good faith. The gallows does well; but how does it well? It does well to those that do ill. Now, thou dost ill to say the gallows is built stronger than the church, argal, the gallows may do well to thee. To 't again, come.

[2] The clown's mistake for "se defendendo." [3] *Ergo,* therefore. [4] Fellow-Christian.

2. *Clo.* "Who builds stronger than a mason, a shipwright, or a carpenter?"

1. *Clo.* Ay, tell me that, and unyoke.

2. *Clo.* Marry, now I can tell.

1. *Clo.* To 't.

2. *Clo.* Mass, I cannot tell.

Enter HAMLET *and* HORATIO, *afar off*

1. *Clo.* Cudgel thy brains no more about it, for your dull ass will not mend his pace with beating; and, when you are ask'd this question next, say "a grave-maker"; the houses that he makes lasts till doomsday. Go, get thee to Yaughan; fetch me a stoup of liquor.

[*Exit* Second Clown.]

[*He digs, and*] *sings.*

"In youth, when I did love, did love,
  Methought it was very sweet,
To contract, O, the time for-a my behove,
  O, methought, there-a was nothing-a meet."

Ham. Has this fellow no feeling of his business, that he sings at grave-making?

Hor. Custom hath made it in him a property of easiness.[5]

Ham. 'Tis e'en so. The hand of little employment hath the daintier sense.

1. *Clo.* (*Sings.*)

"But age, with his stealing steps,
  Hath claw'd me in his clutch,
And hath shipped me intil the land,
  As if I had never been such."

[*Throws up a skull.*]

Ham. That skull had a tongue in it, and could sing once. How the knave jowls[6] it to the ground, as if it were Cain's jaw-bone,[7] that did the first murder! It might be the pate of a politician, which this ass now o'erreaches; one that would circumvent God, might it not?

Hor. It might, my lord.

[5] A function he performs easily. [6] Knocks.

[7] The ass's jawbone with which, according to legend, Cain slew Abel.

Ham. Or of a courtier, which could say, "Good morrow, sweet lord! How dost thou, good lord?" This might be my lord such-a-one, that prais'd my lord such-a-one's horse, when he meant to beg it; might it not?

Hor. Ay, my lord.

Ham. Why, e'en so; and now my Lady Worm's; chapless, and knock'd about the mazzard[8] with a sexton's spade. Here's fine revolution, if we had the trick to see 't. Did these bones cost no more the breeding, but to play at loggats[9] with 'em? Mine ache to think on 't.

1. *Clo.* (*Sings.*)

"A pick-axe, and a spade, a spade,
For and a shrouding sheet;
O, a pit of clay for to be made
For such a guest is meet."

[*Throws up another skull.*]

Ham. There's another. Why might not that be the skull of a lawyer? Where be his quiddits[10] now, his quillets,[10] his cases, his tenures, and his tricks? Why does he suffer this rude knave now to knock him about the sconce[11] with a dirty shovel, and will not tell him of his action of battery? Hum! This fellow might be in 's time a great buyer of land, with his statutes, his recognizances, his fines, his double vouchers, his recoveries.[12] Is this the fine of his fines, and the recovery of his recoveries, to have his fine pate full of fine dirt? Will his vouchers vouch him no more of his purchases, and double ones too, than the length and breadth of a pair of indentures? The very conveyances of his lands will hardly lie in this box, and must the inheritor himself have no more, ha?

Hor. Not a jot more, my lord.

Ham. Is not parchment made of sheep-skins?

Hor. Ay, my lord, and of calf-skins too.

Ham. They are sheep and calves that seek out assurance in that. I will speak to this fellow. Whose grave 's this, sir?

1. *Clo.* Mine, sir.

[*Sings.*] "O, a pit of clay for to be made
For such a guest is meet."

[8] Head. [9] A game played with little logs of wood.
[10] Subtleties and fine distinctions. [11] Head. [12] Technical legal terms.

Ham. I think it be thine indeed, for thou liest in 't.

1. *Clo.* You lie out on 't, sir, and therefore it is not yours. For my part, I do not lie in 't, and yet it is mine.

Ham. Thou dost lie in 't, to be in 't and say 'tis thine. 'Tis for the dead, not for the quick, therefore thou liest.

1. *Clo.* 'Tis a quick[13] lie, sir; 'twill away again, from me to you.

Ham. What man dost thou dig it for?

1. *Clo.* For no man, sir.

Ham. What woman, then?

1. *Clo.* For none, neither.

Ham. Who is to be buried in 't?

1. *Clo.* One that was a woman, sir; but, rest her soul, she's dead.

Ham. How absolute the knave is! We must speak by the card, or equivocation will undo us. By the Lord, Horatio, these three years I have taken note of it; the age is grown so picked[14] that the toe of the peasant comes so near the heels of our courtier, he galls his kibe.[15] How long hast thou been a grave-maker?

1. *Clo.* Of all the days i' the year, I came to 't that day that our last king Hamlet o'ercame Fortinbras.

Ham. How long is that since?

1. *Clo.* Cannot you tell that? Every fool can tell that. It was the very day that young Hamlet was born; he that was mad, and sent into England.

Ham. Ay, marry, why was he sent into England?

1. *Clo.* Why, because 'a was mad. He shall recover his wits there; or, if he do not, it's no great matter there.

Ham. Why?

1. *Clo.* 'Twill not be seen in him there; there the men are as mad as he.

Ham. How came he mad?

1. *Clo.* Very strangely, they say.

Ham. How "strangely"?

1. *Clo.* Faith, e'en with losing his wits.

Ham. Upon what ground?

1. *Clo.* Why, here in Denmark. I have been sexton here, man and boy, thirty years.

Ham. How long will a man lie i' the earth ere he rot?

[13] Living. [14] Smart. [15] Chilblain.

1. *Clo.* I' faith, if he be not rotten before he die—as we have many pocky corses now-a-days, that will scarce hold the laying in—he will last you some eight year or nine year. A tanner will last you nine year.

Ham. Why he more than another?

1. *Clo.* Why, sir, his hide is so tann'd with his trade that he will keep out water a great while, and your water is a sore decayer of your whoreson dead body. Here's a skull now; this skull has lain in the earth three and twenty years.

Ham. Whose was it?

1. *Clo.* A whoreson mad fellow's it was. Whose do you think it was?

Ham. Nay, I know not.

1. *Clo.* A pestilence on him for a mad rogue! 'A pour'd a flagon of Rhenish on my head once. This same skull, sir, was Yorick's skull, the King's jester.

Ham. This?

1. *Clo.* E'en that.

Ham. Let me see. [*Takes the skull.*] Alas, poor Yorick! I knew him, Horatio; a fellow of infinite jest, of most excellent fancy. He hath borne me on his back a thousand times. And now how abhorred in my imagination it is! My gorge rises at it. Here hung those lips that I have kiss'd I know not how oft. Where be your gibes now, your gambols, your songs, your flashes of merriment, that were wont to set the table on a roar? Not one now, to mock your own grinning? Quite chopfallen? Now get you to my lady's chamber, and tell her, let her paint an inch thick, to this favour she must come. Make her laugh at that. Prithee, Horatio, tell me one thing.

Hor. What 's that, my lord?

Ham. Dost thou think Alexander look'd o' this fashion i' the earth?

Hor. E'en so.

Ham. And smelt so? Pah! [*Puts down the skull.*]

Hor. E'en so, my lord.

Ham. To what base uses we may return, Horatio! Why may not imagination trace the noble dust of Alexander, till he find it stopping a bung-hole?

Hor. 'Twere to consider too curiously, to consider so.

Ham. No, faith, not a jot; but to follow him thither with modesty[16] enough and likelihood to lead it; as thus: Alexander died, Alexander was buried, Alexander returneth into dust, the dust is earth, of earth we make loam, and why of that loam whereto he was converted might they not stop a beer-barrel?

Imperial Cæsar, dead and turn'd to clay,
Might stop a hole to keep the wind away.
O, that that earth, which kept the world in awe,
Should patch a wall to expel the winter's flaw![17]

But soft! but soft! Aside! Here comes the King,

Enter [Priests, *etc., in procession;*] KING, QUEEN, LAERTES, *and a Coffin, with* Lords *attendant*

The Queen, the courtiers. Who is that they follow?
And with such maimed rites? This doth betoken
The corse they follow did with desperate hand
Fordo[18] it[19] own life. 'Twas of some estate.
Couch we a while, and mark. [*Retiring with* HORATIO.]

Laer. What ceremony else?

Ham. That is Laertes, a very noble youth. Mark.

Laer. What ceremony else?

Priest. Her obsequies have been as far enlarg'd
As we have warrantise. Her death was doubtful;
And, but that great command o'ersways the order,
She should in ground unsanctified have lodg'd
Till the last trumpet; for charitable prayer,
Shards,[20] flints, and pebbles should be thrown on her.
Yet here she is allowed her virgin rites,
Her maiden strewments,[21] and the bringing home
Of bell and burial.

Laer. Must there no more be done?

Priest. No more be done.
We should profane the service of the dead
To sing such requiem and such rest to her
As to peace-parted souls.

Laer. Lay her i' the earth,

[16] Moderation. [17] Gust. [18] Destroy. [19] Its. [20] Potsherds. [21] Strewing with flowers.

And from her fair and unpolluted flesh
May violets spring! I tell thee, churlish priest
A minist'ring angel shall my sister be,
When thou liest howling.

Ham. What, the fair Ophelia!

Queen. Sweets to the sweet; farewell! [*Scattering flowers.*]
I hop'd thou shouldst have been my Hamlet's wife.
I thought thy bride-bed to have deck'd, sweet maid,
And not to have strew'd thy grave.

Laer. O, treble woe
Fall ten times treble on that cursed head
Whose wicked deed thy most ingenious sense
Depriv'd thee of! Hold off the earth a while,
Till I have caught her once more in mine arms.
Leaps in the grave.
Now pile your dust upon the quick and dead,
Till of this flat a mountain you have made
To o'ertop old Pelion, or the skyish head
Of blue Olympus.

Ham. [*Advancing.*] What is he whose grief
Bears such an emphasis, whose phrase of sorrow
Conjures the wand'ring stars and makes them stand
Like wonder-wounded hearers? This is I,
Hamlet, the Dane! [*Leaps into the grave.*]

Laer. The devil take thy soul! [*Grappling with him.*]

Ham. Thou pray'st not well.
I prithee, take thy fingers from my throat,
For, though I am not splenitive[22] and rash,
Yet have I something in me dangerous,
Which let thy wiseness fear. Away thy hand!

King. Pluck them asunder.

Queen. Hamlet, Hamlet!

[*All.* Gentlemen,—

Hor.] Good my lord, be quiet.

[*The* Attendants *part them, and they come out of the grave.*]

22 Easily angry.

Ham. Why, I will fight with him upon this theme
Until my eyelids will no longer wag.
Queen. O my son, what theme?
Ham. I lov'd Ophelia. Forty thousand brothers
Could not, with all their quantity of love,
Make up my sum. What wilt thou do for her?
King. O, he is mad, Laertes.
Queen. For love of God, forbear him.
Ham. ['Swounds,] show me what thou 'lt do.
Woo 't[23] weep? Woo 't fight? [Woo 't fast?] Woo 't tear thyself?
Woo 't drink up eisel?[24] Eat a crocodile?
I'll do 't. Dost thou come here to whine?
To outface me with leaping in her grave?
Be buried quick with her, and so will I;
And, if thou prate of mountains, let them throw
Millions of acres on us, till our ground,
Singeing his pate against the burning zone,
Make Ossa like a wart! Nay, an thou 'lt mouth,
I'll rant as well as thou.
[*Queen.*] This is mere madness,
And thus a while the fit will work on him.
Anon, as patient as the female dove,
When that her golden couplets[25] are disclos'd,
His silence will sit drooping.
Ham. Hear you, sir,
What is the reason that you use me thus?
I lov'd you ever. But it is no matter.
Let Hercules himself do what he may,
The cat will mew and dog will have his day. *Exit.*
King. I pray you, good Horatio, wait upon him. [*Exit* HORATIO.]
[*To* LAERTES.] Strengthen your patience in our last night's speech;
We'll put the matter to the present push.[26]
Good Gertrude, set some watch over your son.
This grave shall have a living monument.
An hour of quiet shortly shall we see;
Till then, in patience our proceeding be. *Exeunt.*

[23] Wouldst thou. [24] Vinegar. [25] Pair of young doves. [26] Immediate operation.

[SCENE II. *A hall in the castle*]

Enter HAMLET *and* HORATIO

Ham. So much for this, sir; now let me see the other.
You do remember all the circumstance?
Hor. Remember it, my lord!
Ham. Sir, in my heart there was a kind of fighting,
That would not let me sleep. Methought I lay
Worse than the mutines in the bilboes.[1] Rashly,—
And prais'd be rashness for it; let us know
Our indiscretion sometimes serves us well
When our deep plots do pall;[2] and that should teach us
There 's a divinity that shapes our ends,
Rough-hew them how we will,—
Hor. That is most certain.
Ham. Up from my cabin,
My sea-gown scarf'd about me, in the dark
Grop'd I to find out them; had my desire;
Finger'd their packet; and, in fine, withdrew
To mine own room again, making so bold,
My fears forgetting manners, to unseal
Their grand commission; where I found, Horatio,—
O royal knavery!—an exact command,
Larded[3] with many several sorts of reason
Importing Denmark's health and England's too,
With, ho! such bugs[4] and goblins in my life,
That, on the supervise,[5] no leisure bated,
No, not to stay the grinding of the axe,
My head should be struck off.
Hor. Is 't possible?
Ham. Here's the commission; read it at more leisure.
But wilt thou hear me how I did proceed?
Hor. I beseech you.
Ham. Being thus be-netted round with villainies,—
Ere I could make a prologue to my brains,

[1] Mutineers in fetters. [2] Weaken. [3] Garnished. [4] Bugbears. [5] First reading.

They had begun the play,—I sat me down,
Devis'd a new commission, wrote it fair.
I once did hold it, as our statists[6] do,
A baseness to write fair, and labour'd much
How to forget that learning; but, sir, now
It did me yeoman's service. Wilt thou know
The effect[7] of what I wrote?

Hor. Ay, good my lord.

Ham. An earnest conjuration from the King,
As England was his faithful tributary,
As love between them as the palm should flourish,
As Peace should still her wheaten garland wear
And stand a comma[8] 'tween their amities,
And many such-like *as*-es of great charge,
That, on the view and knowing of these contents,
Without debatement further, more or less,
He should the bearers put to sudden death,
Not shriving time allow'd.

Hor. How was this seal'd?

Ham. Why, even in that was Heaven ordinant.[9]
I had my father's signet in my purse,
Which was the model of that Danish seal;
Folded the writ up in form of the other,
Subscrib'd it, gave 't the impression,[10] plac'd it safely,
The changeling never known. Now, the next day
Was our sea-fight; and what to this was sequent
Thou know'st already.

Hor. So Guildenstern and Rosencrantz go to 't.

Ham. Why, man, they did make love to this employment;
They are not near my conscience. Their defeat
Doth by their own insinuation grow.
'Tis dangerous when the baser nature comes
Between the pass[11] and fell incensed points
Of mighty opposites.[12]

Hor. Why, what a king is this!

[6] Statesmen. [7] Substance.
[8] A phrase occurring in the midst of a sentence (?). A link (?). [9] Controlling
[10] I. e. of the seal. [11] Thrust. [12] Opponents.

Ham. Does it not, thinks't thee, stand me now upon—[13]
He that hath kill'd my king and whor'd my mother,
Popp'd in between the election and my hopes,
Thrown out his angle for my proper[14] life,
And with such cozenage[15]—is 't not perfect conscience,
To quit him with this arm? And is 't not to be damn'd,
To let this canker of our nature come
In further evil?

Hor. It must be shortly known to him from England
What is the issue of the business there.

Ham. It will be short; the interim is mine,
And a man's life's no more than to say "One."
But I am very sorry, good Horatio
That to Laertes I forgot myself;
For, by the image of my cause, I see
The portraiture of his. I'll court his favours.
But, sure, the bravery[16] of his grief did put me
Into a tow'ring passion.

Hor. Peace! who comes here?

Enter Young Osric

Osr. Your lordship is right welcome back to Denmark.

Ham. I humbly thank you, sir.—Dost know this waterfly?

Hor. No, my good lord.

Ham. Thy state is the more gracious, for 'tis a vice to know him. He hath much land, and fertile; let a beast be lord of beasts, and his crib shall stand at the King's mess. 'Tis a chough,[17] but, as I say, spacious in the possession of dirt.

Osr. Sweet lord, if your lordship were at leisure, I should impart a thing to you from his Majesty.

Ham. I will receive it with all diligence of spirit. Put your bonnet to his right use; 'tis for the head.

Osr. I thank your lordship, 'tis very hot.

Ham. No, believe me, 'tis very cold; the wind is northerly.

Osr. It is indifferent cold, my lord, indeed.

[13] Is it not my duty? [14] Own. [15] Deceit.
[16] Ostentation. [17] Jackdaw.

Ham. Methinks it is very sultry and hot for my complexion.

Osr. Exceedingly, my lord; it is very sultry,—as 'twere,—I cannot tell how. But, my lord, his Majesty bade me signify to you that he has laid a great wager on your head. Sir, this is the matter,—

Ham. I beseech you, remember—

[HAMLET *moves him to put on his hat.*]

Osr. Nay, in good faith; for mine ease, in good faith. [Sir, here is newly come to court Laertes, believe me, an absolute gentleman, full of most excellent differences,[18] of very soft society and great showing; indeed, to speak feelingly of him, he is the card[19] or calendar[20] of gentry, for you shall find in him the continent[21] of what part a gentleman would see.

Ham. Sir, his definement[22] suffers no perdition[23] in you; though, I know, to divide him inventorially would dizzy the arithmetic of memory, and yet but yaw[24] neither, in respect of his quick sail. But, in the verity of extolment, I take him to be a soul of great article;[25] and his infusion of such dearth and rareness, as, to make true diction of him, his semblable[26] is his mirror; and who else would trace him, his umbrage,[27] nothing more.

Osr. Your lordship speaks most infallibly of him.

Ham. The concernancy,[28] sir? Why do we wrap the gentleman in our more rawer breath?

Osr. Sir?

Hor. Is 't not possible to understand in another tongue? You will do 't, sir, really.

Ham. What imports the nomination of this gentleman?

Osr. Of Laertes?

Hor. His purse is empty already. All 's golden words are spent.

Ham. Of him, sir.

Osr. I know you are not ignorant—

Ham. I would you did, sir; yet, in faith, if you did, it would not much approve me. Well, sir?]

Osr. You are not ignorant of what excellence Laertes is—

[*Ham.* I dare not confess that, lest I should compare with him in excellence; but to know a man well were to know himself.

[18] Distinctions, characteristics. [19] Chart, for guidance. [20] Example.
[21] Abstract, summary. [22] Description. [23] Loss. [24] Move unsteadily.
[25] Importance. [26] Like. [27] Shadow. [28] Import.

Osr. I mean, sir, for his weapon; but in the imputation laid on him by them, in his meed he's unfellowed.]

Ham. What's his weapon?

Osr. Rapier and dagger.

Ham. That's two of his weapons; but well.

Osr. The King, sir, has wag'd with him six Barbary horses, against the which he has impon'd,[29] as I take it, six French rapiers and poniards, with their assigns,[30] as girdle, hanger, or so. Three of the carriages, in faith, are very dear to fancy, very responsive[31] to the hilts, most delicate carriages, and of very liberal conceit.[32]

Ham. What call you the carriages?

[*Hor.* I knew you must be edified by the margent[33] ere you had done.]

Osr. The carriages, sir, are the hangers.

Ham. The phrase would be more germane to the matter, if we could carry cannon by our sides; I would it might be hangers till then. But, on: six Barbary horses against six French swords, their assigns, and three liberal-conceited carriages; that 's the French bet against the Danish. Why is this "impon'd," as you call it?

Osr. The King, sir, hath laid that in a dozen passes between you and him, he shall not exceed you three hits; he hath laid on twelve for nine; and that would come to immediate trial, if your lordship would vouchsafe the answer.

Ham. How if I answer no?

Osr. I mean, my lord, the opposition of your person in trial.

Ham. Sir, I will walk here in the hall; if it please his Majesty, 'tis the breathing[34] time of day with me. Let the foils be brought, the gentleman willing, and the King hold his purpose, I will win for him if I can; if not, I'll gain nothing but my shame and the odd hits.

Osr. Shall I re-deliver you e'en so?

Ham. To this effect, sir; after what flourish your nature will.

Osr. I commend my duty to your lordship.

Ham. Yours, yours. [*Exit* Osric.] He does well to commend it himself; there are no tongues else for 's turn.

[29] Wagered. [30] Appendages. [31] Corresponding. [32] Ornamental design.
[33] Instructed by the marginal comment. [34] For relaxation.

Hor. This lapwing runs away with the shell on his head.

Ham. He did comply[35] with his dug before he suck'd it. Thus has he, and many more of the same bevy that I know the drossy age dotes on, only got the tune of the time and outward habit of encounter; a kind of yesty collection, which carries them through and through the most fond and winnowed[36] opinions; and do but blow them to their trials, the bubbles are out.

[*Enter a* Lord

Lord. My lord, his Majesty commended him to you by young Osric, who brings back to him, that you attend him in the hall. He sends to know if your pleasure hold to play with Laertes, or that you will take longer time.

Ham. I am constant to my purposes; they follow the King's pleasure. If his fitness speaks, mine is ready, now or whensoever, provided I be so able as now.

Lord. The King and Queen and all are coming down.

Ham. In happy time.

Lord. The Queen desires you to use some gentle entertainment to Laertes before you fall to play.

Ham. She well instructs me.] [*Exit* Lord.]

Hor. You will lose this wager, my lord.

Ham. I do not think so; since he went into France, I have been in continual practice. I shall win at the odds. But thou wouldst not think how ill all 's here about my heart. But it is no matter.

Hor. Nay, good my lord,—

Ham. It is but foolery; but it is such a kind of gain-giving,[37] as would perhaps trouble a woman.

Hor. If your mind dislike anything, obey it. I will forestall their repair hither, and say you are not fit.

Ham. Not a whit; we defy augury. There's a special providence in the fall of a sparrow. If it be now, 'tis not to come; if it be not to come, it will be now; if it be not now, yet it will come; the readiness is all. Since no man has aught of what he leaves,[38] what is 't to leave betimes? [Let be.]

[35] Use ceremony. [36] Foolish and over-refined. [37] Misgiving.
[38] Carries anything beyond the grave.

Enter KING, QUEEN, LAERTES, [OSRIC,] Lords, *and other* Attendants *with foils and gauntlets; a table and flagons of wine on it*

King. Come, Hamlet, come, and take this hand from me.
[*The* KING *puts* LAERTES'S *hand into* HAMLET'S.]
Ham. Give me your pardon, sir. I've done you wrong,
But pardon 't, as you are a gentleman.
This presence[39] knows,
And you must needs have heard, how I am punish'd
With sore distraction. What I have done
That might your nature, honour, and exception[40]
Roughly awake, I here proclaim was madness.
Was 't Hamlet wrong'd Laertes? Never Hamlet!
If Hamlet from himself be ta'en away,
And when he's not himself does wrong Laertes,
Then Hamlet does it not, Hamlet denies it.
Who does it, then? His madness. If 't be so,
Hamlet is of the faction that is wrong'd;
His madness is poor Hamlet's enemy.
Sir, in this audience,
Let my disclaiming from a purpos'd evil
Free me so far in your most generous thoughts,
That I have shot mine arrow o'er the house
And hurt my brother.
Laer. I am satisfied in nature,
Whose motive, in this case, should stir me most
To my revenge; but in my terms of honour
I stand aloof, and will no reconcilement,
Till by some elder masters of known honour
I have a voice and precedent of peace,
To keep my name ungor'd.[41] But till that time,
I do receive your offer'd love like love,
And will not wrong it.
Ham. I embrace it freely,
And will this brother's wager frankly play.
Give us the foils. Come on.

[39] The court. [40] Disapproval. [41] Uninjured.

Laer. Come, one for me.

Ham. I'll be your foil, Laertes; in mine ignorance
Your skill shall, like a star i' the darkest night,
Stick fiery off[42] indeed.

Laer. You mock me, sir.

Ham. No, by this hand.

King. Give them the foils, young Osric. Cousin Hamlet,
You know the wager?

Ham. Very well, my lord.
Your Grace hath laid the odds o' the weaker side.

King. I do not fear it, I have seen you both;
But since he is better'd, we have therefore odds.

Laer. This is too heavy, let me see another.

Ham. This likes me well. These foils have all a length?

They prepare to play.

Osr. Ay, my good lord.

King. Set me the stoups of wine upon that table.
If Hamlet give the first or second hit,
Or quit in answer of the third exchange,
Let all the battlements their ordnance fire.
The King shall drink to Hamlet's better breath,
And in the cup an union[43] shall he throw,
Richer than that which four successive kings
In Denmark's crown have worn. Give me the cups,
And let the kettle to the trumpets speak,
The trumpet to the cannoneer without,
The cannons to the heavens, the heaven to earth,
"Now the King drinks to Hamlet." Come, begin;
And you, the judges, bear a wary eye.

Ham. Come on, sir.

Laer. Come, my lord. *They play.*

Ham. One.

Laer. No.

Ham. Judgement.

Osr. A hit, a very palpable hit.

Laer. Well; again.

[42] Stand out in brilliant contrast. [43] Pearl.

King. Stay, give me drink. Hamlet, this pearl is thine;
Here's to thy health! Give him the cup.
[*Trumpets sound, and shot goes off*
[*within.*]
Ham. I'll play this bout first; set it by a while.
Come. [*They play.*] Another hit; what say you?
Laer. A touch, a touch, I do confess.
King. Our son shall win.
Queen. He's fat, and scant of breath.
Here, Hamlet, take my napkin, rub thy brows.
The Queen carouses to thy fortune, Hamlet.
Ham. Good madam!
King. Gertrude, do not drink.
Queen. I will, my lord; I pray you, pardon me.
King. [*Aside.*] It is the poison'd cup; it is too late.
Ham. I dare not drink yet, madam; by and by.
Queen. Come, let me wipe thy face.
Laer. My lord, I'll hit him now.
King. I do not think 't.
Laer. [*Aside.*] And yet 'tis almost 'gainst my conscience.
Ham. Come, for the third, Laertes; you but dally.
I pray you, pass with your best violence.
I am afeard you make a wanton of me.
Laer. Say you so? Come on. *They play.*
Osr. Nothing, neither way.
Laer. Have at you now!
[LAERTES *wounds* HAMLET; *then,*]
in scuffling, they change rapiers.
King. Part them; they are incens'd.
Ham. Nay, come, again.
[HAMLET *wounds* LAERTES. *The* QUEEN *falls.*]
Osr. Look to the Queen there! Ho!
Hor. They bleed on both sides. How is 't, my lord!
Osr. How is 't, Laertes?
Laer. Why, as a woodcock to mine own springe,[44] Osric;
I am justly kill'd with mine own treachery.

[44] Snare.

Ham. How does the Queen?
King. She swounds to see them bleed.
Queen. No, no, the drink, the drink,—O my dear Hamlet,—
The drink, the drink! I am poison'd. [*Dies.*]
Ham. O villainy! Ho! let the door be lock'd:
Treachery! Seek it out.
Laer. It is here, Hamlet. Hamlet, thou art slain.
No medicine in the world can do thee good;
In thee there is not half an hour of life.
The treacherous instrument is in thy hand,
Unbated and envenom'd. The foul practice[45]
Hath turn'd itself on me. Lo, here I lie,
Never to rise again. Thy mother's poison'd.
I can no more:—the King, the King's to blame.
Ham. The point envenom'd too!
Then, venom, to thy work. *Hurts the* KING.
All. Treason! treason!
King. O, yet defend me, friends; I am but hurt.
Ham. Here, thou incestuous, murderous, damned Dane,
Drink off this potion! Is thy union here?
Follow my mother! KING *dies.*
Laer. He is justly serv'd;
It is a poison temp'red[46] by himself.
Exchange forgiveness with me, noble Hamlet.
Mine and my father's death come not upon thee,
Nor thine on me! *Dies.*
Ham. Heaven make thee free of it! I follow thee.
I am dead, Horatio. Wretched queen, adieu!
You that look pale and tremble at this chance,
That are but mutes or audience to this act,
Had I but time—as this fell sergeant, Death,
Is strict in his arrest—O, I could tell you—
But let it be. Horatio, I am dead;
Thou liv'st. Report me and my cause aright
To the unsatisfied.
Hor. Never believe it.

[45] Plot. [46] Mixed.

I am more an antique Roman than a Dane;
Here's yet some liquor left.
Ham. As thou 'rt a man,
Give me the cup. Let go! By heaven, I'll have 't!
O good Horatio, what a wounded name,
Things standing thus unknown, shall live behind me!
If thou didst ever hold me in thy heart,
Absent thee from felicity a while
And in this harsh world draw thy breath in pain
To tell my story. [*March afar off, and shot within.*
What warlike noise is this?
Osr. Young Fortinbras, with conquest come from Poland,
To the ambassadors of England gives
This warlike volley.
Ham. O, I die, Horatio;
The potent poison quite o'er-crows[47] my spirit.
I cannot live to hear the news from England,
But I do prophesy the election lights
On Fortinbras; he has my dying voice.
So tell him, with the occurrents, more and less,
Which have solicited[48]—The rest is silence. *Dies.*
Hor. Now cracks a noble heart. Good-night, sweet prince,
And flights of angels sing thee to thy rest!
Why does the drum come hither? [*March within.*]

Enter Fortinbras *and the* English Ambassador, *with drum, colours. and* Attendants

Fort. Where is this sight?
Hor. What is it ye would see?
If aught of woe or wonder, cease your search.
Fort. This quarry[49] cries on havoc. O proud Death,
What feast is toward in thine eternal cell,
That thou so many princes at a shot
So bloodily hast struck?
Amb. The sight is dismal,
And our affairs from England come too late.

[47] Triumphs over. [48] Prompted. [49] Pile of corpses.

The ears are senseless that should give us hearing,
To tell him his commandment is fulfill'd,
That Rosencrantz and Guildenstern are dead.
Where should we have our thanks?
Hor. Not from his mouth,
Had it the ability of life to thank you.
He never gave commandment for their death.
But since, so jump[50] upon this bloody question,
You from the Polack wars, and you from England,
Are here arrived, give order that these bodies
High on a stage be placed to the view;
And let me speak to the yet unknowing world
How these things came about. So shall you hear
Of carnal, bloody, and unnatural acts,
Of accidental judgements, casual slaughters,
Of deaths put on by cunning and forc'd cause,
And, in this upshot, purposes mistook
Fallen on the inventors' heads: all this can I
Truly deliver.
Fort. Let us haste to hear it,
And call the noblest to the audience.
For me, with sorrow I embrace my fortune.
I have some rights of memory[51] in this kingdom,
Which now to claim, my vantage doth invite me.
Hor. Of that I shall have also cause to speak,
And from his mouth whose voice will draw on more.
But let this same be presently[52] perform'd
Even while men's minds are wild, lest more mischance,
On plots and errors, happen.
Fort. Let four captains
Bear Hamlet, like a soldier, to the stage,
For he was likely, had he been put on,[53]
To have prov'd most royally; and, for his passage,[54]
The soldiers' music and the rites of war
Speak loudly for him.

[50] Precisely. [51] Traditional. [52] Immediately. [53] Tested (as king).
[54] Carrying off the body.

Take up the bodies. Such a sight as this
Becomes the field, but here shows much amiss.
Go, bid the soldiers shoot.

Exeunt marching, [bearing off the dead bodies;] after which a peal of ordnance are shot off.

THE TRAGEDY OF KING LEAR

BY

WILLIAM SHAKESPEARE

INTRODUCTORY NOTE

"KING LEAR" is, in its picture of the tragic effect of human weakness and human cruelty, the most overpowering of the works of Shakespeare. It was written about 1605, in the middle of that period of his activity when he was interested, for whatever reason, in portraying the suffering and disaster that are entailed by defects of character, and the terrible cost at which such defects are purged away; and not even "Hamlet" displays these things so irresistibly.

The germ of the story is found in the folk-lore of many ages and countries. Attached to the name of Lear, the legend assumed pseudo-historical form with Geoffrey of Monmouth in the twelfth century, was handed down through the long line of Latin and English chroniclers, appeared in collections of tales, found a place in Spenser's "Faerie Queene," and was dramatized by an anonymous playwright about ten years before the date of Shakespeare's drama. To Shakespeare himself is due the tragic catastrophe which takes the place of the traditional fortunate ending, according to which the French forces were victorious, and Lear was restored to his kingdom. He first makes Lear go mad; invents the banishment of Kent and his subsequent disguise; creates the Fool; and, finally, connects with Lear the whole story of Gloucester and his sons.

This skilfully interwoven underplot is taken from Sidney's "Arcadia," in which a story is told of a king turned against his legitimate son by the slanders of his bastard. The pretended madness of Edgar, and the love of the wicked daughters for Edmund are inventions of Shakespeare's.

But these details are not the only means by which the improbable legend is converted into the most tremendous of tragedies. This is done chiefly by the intensity with which the characters are conceived: the imperiousness and intellectual grasp of Lear, the force and subtlety of Edmund, the venom of the wicked daughters, the tenderness of Cordelia, the impassioned loyalty of Kent, the unselfishness of Edgar, and the poignant candor of the faithful Fool.

THE TRAGEDY OF KING LEAR

[DRAMATIS PERSONÆ

LEAR, King of Britain.
KING OF FRANCE.
DUKE OF BURGUNDY.
DUKE OF CORNWALL.
DUKE OF ALBANY.
EARL OF KENT.
EARL OF GLOUCESTER.
EDGAR, son to Gloucester.
EDMUND, bastard son to Gloucester.
CURAN, a courtier.
Old Man, tenant to Gloucester.
Doctor.
Fool.
OSWALD, steward to Goneril.
A Captain employed by Edmund.
Gentleman attendant on Cordelia.
A Herald.
Servants to Cornwall.

GONERIL, REGAN, CORDELIA, daughters to Lear.

Knights of Lear's train, Captains, Messengers, Soldiers, and Attendants

SCENE: BRITAIN]

ACT I

SCENE I. [*King Lear's palace*]

Enter KENT, GLOUCESTER, *and* EDMUND

Kent

I THOUGHT the King had more affected[1] the Duke of Albany than Cornwall.

Glou. It did always seem so to us; but now, in the division of the kingdom, it appears not which of the Dukes he values most; for qualities[2] are so weigh'd, that curiosity in neither can make choice of either's moiety.[3]

Kent. Is not this your son, my lord?

Glou. His breeding, sir, hath been at my charge. I have so often blush'd to acknowledge him, that now I am braz'd[4] to 't.

Kent. I cannot conceive you.

Glou. Sir, this young fellow's mother could; whereupon she grew round-womb'd, and had, indeed, sir, a son for her cradle ere she had a husband for her bed. Do you smell a fault?

[1] Liked. [2] The values in each share are so balanced. [3] Portion. [4] Hardened.

Kent. I cannot wish the fault undone, the issue of it being so proper.[5]

Glou. But I have a son, sir, by order of law, some year elder than this, who yet is no dearer in my account.[6] Though this knave came something saucily into the world before he was sent for, yet was his mother fair; there was good sport at his making, and the whoreson must be acknowledged. Do you know this noble gentleman, Edmund?

Edm. No, my lord.

Glou. My Lord of Kent. Remember him hereafter as my honourable friend.

Edm. My services to your lordship.

Kent. I must love you, and sue to know you better.

Edm. Sir, I shall study deserving.

Glou. He hath been out[7] nine years, and away he shall again. The King is coming.

Sennet.[8] *Enter one bearing a coronet, then* KING LEAR, *then the* DUKES OF ALBANY *and* CORNWALL, *next* GONERIL, REGAN, CORDELIA, *with followers*

Lear. Attend the lords of France and Burgundy, Gloucester.

Glou. I shall, my lord. *Exeunt* [GLOUCESTER *and* EDMUND].

Lear. Meantime we shall express our darker purpose.
Give me the map there. Know that we have divided
In three our kingdom; and 'tis our fast intent
To shake all cares and business from our age,
Conferring them on younger strengths, while we
Unburden'd crawl toward death. Our son of Cornwall,
And you, our no less loving son of Albany,
We have this hour a constant will to publish
Our daughters' several dowers, that future strife
May be prevented now. The Princes, France and Burgundy,
Great rivals in our youngest daughter's love,
Long in our court have made their amorous sojourn,
And here are to be answer'd. Tell me, my daughters,—

[5] Handsome. [6] Esteem. [7] Away, making a career.
[8] A set of notes on a trumpet.

Since now we will divest us both of rule,
Interest of territory, cares of state,—
Which of you shall we say doth love us most,
That we our largest bounty may extend
Where nature doth with merit challenge?[9] Goneril,
Our eldest-born, speak first.

Gon. Sir, I love you more than word can wield the matter;
Dearer than eye-sight, space, and liberty;
Beyond what can be valued, rich or rare;
No less than life, with grace, health, beauty, honour;
As much as child e'er lov'd, or father found;
A love that makes breath poor, and speech unable:
Beyond all manner of so much I love you.

Cor. [*Aside.*] What shall Cordelia speak? Love and be silent.

Lear. Of all these bounds, even from this line to this,
With shadowy forests and with champains[10] rich'd,
With plenteous rivers and wide-skirted meads,
We make thee lady. To thine and Albany's issues
Be this perpetual. What says our second daughter,
Our dearest Regan, wife of Cornwall? Speak.

Reg. I am made of that self metal as my sister,
And prize me at her worth. In my true heart
I find she names my very deed of love;
Only she comes too short, that I profess
Myself an enemy to all other joys
Which the most precious square of sense[11] possesses;
And find I am alone felicitate
In your dear Highness' love.

Cor. [*Aside.*] Then poor Cordelia!
And yet not so; since, I am sure, my love 's
More ponderous than my tongue.

Lear. To thee and thine hereditary ever
Remain this ample third of our fair kingdom;
No less in space, validity, and pleasure,
Than that conferr'd on Goneril. Now, our joy,

[9] Where natural affection deservedly claims it. [10] Level country.
[11] Sense in its perfection.

Although our last and least, to whose young love [12]
The vines of France and milk of Burgundy
Strive to be interess'd,[13] what can you say to draw
A third more opulent than your sisters? Speak.
Cor. Nothing, my lord.
Lear. Nothing!
Cor. Nothing.
Lear. Nothing will come of nothing. Speak again.
Cor. Unhappy that I am, I cannot heave
My heart into my mouth. I love your Majesty
According to my bond; no more nor less.
Lear. How, how, Cordelia! Mend your speech a little,
Lest you may mar your fortunes.
Cor. Good my lord,
You have begot me, bred me, lov'd me: I
Return those duties back as are right fit;
Obey you, love you, and most honour you.
Why have my sisters husbands, if they say
They love you all? Haply, when I shall wed,
That lord whose hand must take my plight shall carry
Half my love with him, half my care and duty.
Sure, I shall never marry like my sisters
[To love my father all].
Lear. But goes thy heart with this?
Cor. Ay, my good lord.
Lear. So young, and so untender?
Cor. So young, my lord, and true.
Lear. Let it be so; thy truth, then, be thy dower!
For, by the sacred radiance of the sun,
The mysteries of Hecate, and the night;
By all the operation of the orbs
From whom we do exist, and cease to be;
Here I disclaim all my paternal care,
Propinquity and property[14] of blood,
And as a stranger to my heart and me

[12] The quarto reading is, *Although the last, not least in our dear love.* [13] Attached.
[14] Relationship.

Hold thee, from this, for ever. The barbarous Scythian,
Or he that makes his generation messes[15]
To gorge his appetite, shall to my bosom
Be as well neighbour'd, piti'd, and reliev'd,
As thou my sometime daughter.

Kent. Good my liege,—

Lear. Peace, Kent!
Come not between the dragon and his wrath.
I lov'd her most, and thought to set my rest
On her kind nursery.[16] [*To* Cor.] Hence, and avoid my sight!—
So be my grave my peace, as here I give
Her father's heart from her! Call France.—Who stirs?
Call Burgundy. Cornwall and Albany,
With my two daughters' dowers digest the third;
Let pride, which she calls plainness, marry her.
I do invest you jointly with my power,
Pre-eminence, and all the large effects
That troop with majesty. Ourself, by monthly course,
With reservation of an hundred knights,
By you to be sustain'd, shall our abode
Make with you by due turn. Only we shall retain
The name, and all the addition[17] to a king;
The sway, revenue, execution of the rest,
Beloved sons, be yours; which to confirm,
This coronet part between you.

Kent. Royal Lear,
Whom I have ever honour'd as my king,
Lov'd as my father, as my master follow'd,
As my great patron thought on in my prayers,—

Lear. The bow is bent and drawn; make from the shaft.

Kent. Let it fall rather, though the fork invade
The region of my heart: be Kent unmannerly
When Lear is mad. What wouldst thou do, old man?
Thinkst thou that duty shall have dread to speak,
When power to flattery bows? To plainness honour's bound,
When majesty falls to folly. Reserve thy state;

[15] The Scythians were said to eat their parents. [16] Nursing. [17] Titles.

And, in thy best consideration, check
This hideous rashness. Answer my life my judgement,
Thy youngest daughter does not love thee least;
Nor are those empty-hearted whose low sounds
Reverb[18] no hollowness.

Lear. Kent, on thy life, no more.

Kent. My life I never held but as a pawn
To wage against thy enemies, ne'er fear to lose it.
Thy safety being motive.

Lear. Out of my sight!

Kent. See better, Lear; and let me still remain
The true blank[19] of thine eye.

Lear. Now, by Apollo,—

Kent. Now, by Apollo, king,
Thou swear'st thy gods in vain.

Lear. O, vassal! miscreant!
[*Laying his hand on his sword.*]

Alb. / *Corn.* } Dear sir, forbear.

Kent. Kill thy physician, and thy fee bestow
Upon the foul disease. Revoke thy gift;
Or, whilst I can vent clamour from my throat,
I'll tell thee thou dost evil.

Lear. Hear me, recreant!
On thine allegiance, hear me!
That thou hast sought to make us break our vows,
Which we durst never yet, and with strain'd pride
To come betwixt our sentences and our power,
Which nor our nature nor our place can bear,
Our potency made good, take thy reward.
Five days we do allot thee, for provision
To shield thee from disasters of the world;
And on the sixth to turn thy hated back
Upon our kingdom. If, on the tenth day following,
Thy banish'd trunk be found in our dominions,

18 Reverberate. 19 The white spot in a target.

The moment is thy death. Away! By Jupiter,
This shall not be revok'd.
Kent. Fare thee well, king! Sith thus thou wilt appear,
Freedom lives hence, and banishment is here.
[*To* CORDELIA.] The gods to their dear shelter take thee, maid,
That justly think'st, and hast most rightly said!
[*To* REGAN *and* GONERIL.] And your large speeches may your deeds approve,
That good effects may spring from words of love.
Thus Kent, O princes, bids you all adieu;
He'll shape his old course in a country new. *Exit.*

Flourish. Re-enter GLOUCESTER, *with* FRANCE, BURGUNDY, *and* Attendants

Glou. Here's France and Burgundy, my noble lord.
Lear. My Lord of Burgundy,
We first address toward you, who with this king
Hath rivall'd for our daughter. What, in the least,
Will you require in present dower with her,
Or cease your quest of love?
Bur. Most royal Majesty,
I crave no more than what your Highness offer'd,
Nor will you tender less.
Lear. Right noble Burgundy,
When she was dear to us, we did hold her so;
But now her price is fallen. Sir, there she stands:
If aught within that little-seeming substance,
Or all of it, with our displeasure piec'd,
And nothing more, may fitly like your Grace,
She's there, and she is yours.
Bur. I know no answer.
Lear. Will you, with those infirmities she owes,[20]
Unfriended, new-adopted to our hate,
Dower'd with our curse, and stranger'd with our oath,
Take her, or leave her?

[20] Owns.

Bur. Pardon me, royal sir;
Election makes not up[21] in such conditions.
Lear. Then leave her, sir; for, by the power that made me,
I tell you all her wealth. [*To* FRANCE.] For you, great king,
I would not from your love make such a stray,
To match you where I hate; therefore beseech you
To avert your liking a more worthier way
Than on a wretch whom Nature is asham'd
Almost to acknowledge hers.
France. This is most strange,
That she, whom even but now was your best object,
The argument[22] of your praise, balm of your age,
The best, the dearest, should in this trice of time
Commit a thing so monstrous, to dismantle
So many folds of favour. Sure, her offence
Must be of such unnatural degree,
That monsters[23] it, or your fore-vouch'd affection
Fallen into taint; which to believe of her,
Must be a faith that reason without miracle
Should never plant in me.
Cor. I yet beseech your Majesty,—
If for I want that glib and oily art,
To speak and purpose not; since what I well intend,
I'll do 't before I speak,— that you make known
It is no vicious blot, murder, or foulness,
No unchaste action, or dishonoured step,
That hath depriv'd me of your grace and favour;
But even for want of that for which I am richer,
A still-soliciting eye, and such a tongue
That I am glad I have not, though not to have it
Hath lost me in your liking.
Lear. Better thou
Hadst not been born than not to have pleas'd me better.
France. Is it but this,—a tardiness in nature
Which often leaves the history[24] unspoke
That it intends to do? My Lord of Burgundy,

[21] One does not choose. [22] Subject. [23] Makes a monster of. [24] Statement.

What say you to the lady? Love's not love
When it is mingled with regards[25] that stand
Aloof from the entire point. Will you have her?
She is herself a dowry.
Bur. Royal king,
Give but that portion which yourself propos'd,
And here I take Cordelia by the hand,
Duchess of Burgundy.
Lear. Nothing. I have sworn; I am firm.
Bur. I am sorry, then, you have so lost a father
That you must lose a husband.
Cor. Peace be with Burgundy!
Since that respect and fortunes are his love,
I shall not be his wife.
France. Fairest Cordelia, that art most rich being poor,
Most choice forsaken, and most lov'd despis'd!
Thee and thy virtues here I seize upon,
Be it lawful I take up what's cast away.
Gods, gods! 'tis strange that from their cold'st neglect
My love should kindle to inflam'd respect.
Thy dowerless daughter, king, thrown to my chance,
Is queen of us, of ours, and our fair France.
Not all the dukes of waterish Burgundy
Can buy this unpriz'd precious maid of me.
Bid them farewell, Cordelia, though unkind;
Thou losest here, a better where[26] to find.
Lear. Thou hast her, France. Let her be thine; for we
Have no such daughter, nor shall ever see
That face of hers again.—[*To* COR.] Therefore be gone
Without our grace, our love, our benison.[27]—
Come, noble Burgundy.
Flourish. Exeunt [*all but* FRANCE, GONERIL, REGAN, *and* CORDELIA].
France. Bid farewell to your sisters.
Cor. The jewels of our father, with wash'd eyes
Cordelia leaves you. I know you what you are;

[25] Considerations. [26] Place. [27] Blessing.

And like a sister am most loath to call
Your faults as they are named. Love well our father,
To your professed[28] bosoms I commit him;
But yet, alas, stood I within his grace,
I would prefer[29] him to a better place.
So, farewell to you both.

Reg. Prescribe not us our duty.

Gon. Let your study
Be to content your lord, who hath receiv'd you
At fortune's alms. You have obedience scanted,
And well are worth[30] the want that you have wanted.

Cor. Time shall unfold what plighted[31] cunning hides;
Who covers faults, at last shame them derides.
Well may you prosper!

France. Come, my fair Cordelia.

Exeunt [FRANCE *and* CORDELIA].

Gon. Sister, it is not little I have to say of what most nearly appertains to us both. I think our father will hence to-night.

Reg. That's most certain, and with you; next month with us.

Gon. You see how full of changes his age is; the observation we have made of it hath not been little. He always lov'd our sister most; and with what poor judgement he hath now cast her off appears too grossly.[32]

Reg. 'Tis the infirmity of his age; yet he hath ever but slenderly known himself.

Gon. The best and soundest of his time hath been but rash; then must we look from his age to receive not alone the imperfections of long-engraffed condition,[33] but therewithal the unruly waywardness that infirm and choleric years bring with them.

Reg. Such unconstant starts are we like to have from him as this of Kent's banishment.

Gon. There is further compliment of leave-taking between France and him. Pray you, let us hit together; if our father carry authority with such disposition as he bears, this last surrender of his will but offend us.

[28] Professing. [29] Advance. [30] Deserve. [31] Folded, disguised. [32] Obviously. [33] Long-confirmed disposition.

Reg. We shall further think of it.
Gon. We must do something, and i' the heat. [*Exeunt.*

SCENE II. [*The Earl of Gloucester's castle*]

Enter Bastard [EDMUND *with a letter*]

Edm. Thou, Nature, art my goddess; to thy law
My services are bound. Wherefore should I
Stand in the plague of custom, and permit
The curiosity[1] of nations to deprive me,
For that I am some twelve or fourteen moonshines
Lag of[2] a brother? Why bastard? Wherefore base?
When my dimensions are as well compact,
My mind as generous,[3] and my shape as true,
As honest madam's issue? Why brand they us
With base? with baseness? bastardy? base, base?
Who, in the lusty stealth of nature, take
More composition[4] and fierce quality
Than doth, within a dull, stale, tired bed,
Go to the creating a whole tribe of fops,
Got 'tween asleep and wake? Well, then,
Legitimate Edgar, I must have your land.
Our father's love is to the bastard Edmund
As to the legitimate. Fine word, "legitimate"!
Well, my legitimate, if this letter speed
And my invention thrive, Edmund the base
Shall top the legitimate. I grow; I prosper.
Now, gods, stand up for bastards!

Enter GLOUCESTER

Glou. Kent banish'd thus! and France in choler parted!
And the King gone to-night! subscrib'd[5] his power!
Confin'd to exhibition![6] All this done
Upon the gad![7] Edmund, how now! what news?

[1] Fastidiousness. [2] Younger than. [3] High-spirited. [4] A richer blending.
[5] Having signed away. [6] Allowance. [7] Spur of the moment.

Edm. So please your lordship, none. [*Putting up the letter.*]

Glou. Why so earnestly seek you to put up that letter?

Edm. I know no news, my lord.

Glou. What paper were you reading?

Edm. Nothing, my lord.

Glou. No? What needed, then, that terrible dispatch of it into your pocket? The quality of nothing hath not such need to hide itself. Let's see. Come, if it be nothing, I shall not need spectacles.

Edm. I beseech you, sir, pardon me. It is a letter from my brother, that I have not all o'er-read; and for so much as I have perus'd, I find it not fit for your o'er-looking.

Glou. Give me the letter, sir.

Edm. I shall offend, either to detain or give it. The contents, as in part I understand them, are to blame.

Glou. Let's see, let's see.

Edm. I hope, for my brother's justification, he wrote this but as an essay[8] or taste of my virtue.

Glou. (*Reads.*) "This policy and reverence of age makes the world bitter to the best of our times; keeps our fortunes from us till our oldness cannot relish them. I begin to find an idle and fond bondage in the oppression of aged tyranny; who sways, not as it hath power, but as it is suffer'd. Come to me, that of this I may speak more. If our father would sleep till I wak'd him, you should enjoy half his revenue for ever, and live the beloved of your brother,

EDGAR."

Hum—conspiracy!—"Sleep till I wake him, you should enjoy half his revenue!"—My son Edgar! Had he a hand to write this? a heart and brain to breed it in?—When came this to you? Who brought it?

Edm. It was not brought me, my lord; there's the cunning of it. I found it thrown in at the casement of my closet.

Glou. You know the character to be your brother's?

Edm. If the matter were good, my lord, I durst swear it were his; but, in respect of that, I would fain think it were not.

Glou. It is his.

[8] Trial.

Edm. It is his hand, my lord; but I hope his heart is not in the contents.

Glou. Has he never before sounded you in this business?

Edm. Never, my lord; but I have heard him oft maintain it to be fit that, sons at perfect age, and fathers declin'd, the father should be as ward to the son, and the son manage his revenue.

Glou. O villain, villain! His very opinion in the letter! Abhorred villain! Unnatural, detested, brutish villain! worse than brutish! Go, sirrah, seek him; I'll apprehend him. Abominable villain! Where is he?

Edm. I do not well know, my lord. If it shall please you to suspend your indignation against my brother till you can derive from him better testimony of his intent, you should run a certain course; where, if you violently proceed against him, mistaking his purpose, it would make a great gap in your own honour, and shake in pieces the heart of his obedience. I dare pawn down my life for him, that he hath writ this to feel my affection to your honour, and to no other pretence of danger.

Glou. Think you so?

Edm. If your honour judge it meet, I will place you where you shall hear us confer of this, and by an auricular assurance have your satisfaction; and that without any further delay than this very evening.

Glou. He cannot be such a monster—

[*Edm.* Nor is not, sure.

Glou. To his father, that so tenderly and entirely loves him. Heaven and earth!] Edmund, seek him out; wind me into him, I pray you. Frame the business after your own wisdom. I would unstate[9] myself, to be in a due resolution.[10]

Edm. I will seek him, sir, presently;[11] convey the business as I shall find means, and acquaint you withal.

Glou. These late eclipses in the sun and moon portend no good to us. Though the wisdom of nature can reason it thus and thus, yet nature finds itself scourg'd by the sequent effects. Love cools, friendship falls off, brothers divide: in cities, mutinies; in countries, discord; in palaces, treason; and the bond crack'd 'twixt son and

[9] Give up my rank. [10] Free from doubt. [11] At once.

father. This villain of mine comes under the prediction; there's son against father; the King falls from bias of nature;[12] there's father against child. We have seen the best of our time; machinations, hollowness, treachery, and all ruinous disorders, follow us disquietly to our graves. Find out this villain, Edmund; it shall lose thee nothing; do it carefully. And the noble and true-hearted Kent banish'd! his offence, honesty! 'Tis strange.
Exit.

Edm. This is the excellent foppery of the world, that, when we are sick in fortune,—often the surfeits[13] of our own behaviour,—we make guilty of our disasters the sun, the moon, and the stars; as if we were villains on necessity, fools by heavenly compulsion, knaves, thieves, and treachers by spherical predominance, drunkards, liars, and adulterers by an enforc'd obedience of planetary influence, and all that we are evil in, by a divine thrusting on. An admirable evasion of whoremaster man, to lay his goatish disposition on the charge of a star! My father compounded with my mother under the dragon's tail; and my nativity was under *Ursa Major;* so that it follows, I am rough and lecherous. Fut, I should have been that I am, had the maidenliest star in the firmament twinkled on my bastardizing. Edgar—

Enter EDGAR

and pat he comes like the catastrophe of the old comedy. My cue is villanous melancholy, with a sigh like Tom o' Bedlam[14]—O, these eclipses do portend these divisions! *fa, sol, la, mi.*

Edg. How now, brother Edmund! what serious contemplation are you in?

Edm. I am thinking, brother, of a prediction I read this other day, what should follow these eclipses.

Edg. Do you busy yourself with that?

Edm. I promise you, the effects he writes of succeed unhappily; [as of unnaturalness between the child and the parent; death, dearth, dissolutions of ancient amities; divisions in state, menaces and maledictions against king and nobles; needless diffidences,[15] banishment of friends, dissipation of cohorts, nuptial breaches and I know not what.

[12] Natural inclination. [13] Bad effects. [14] A crazy beggar. [15] Suspicions.

Edg. How long have you been a sectary astronomical?[16]

Edm. Come, come;] when saw you my father last?

Edg. [Why,] the night gone by.

Edm. Spake you with him?

Edg. Ay, two hours together.

Edm. Parted you in good terms? Found you no displeasure in him by word nor countenance?

Edg. None at all.

Edm. Bethink yourself wherein you may have offended him; and at my entreaty forbear his presence until some little time hath qualified the heat of his displeasure, which at this instant so rageth in him, that with the mischief of your person it would scarcely allay.

Edg. Some villain hath done me wrong.

Edm. That's my fear. I pray you, have a continent[17] forbearance till the speed of his rage goes slower; and, as I say, retire with me to my lodging, from whence I will fitly bring you to hear my lord speak. Pray ye, go; there's my key. If you do stir abroad, go arm'd.

Edg. Arm'd, brother!

Edm. Brother, I advise you to the best; go armed; I am no honest man if there be any good meaning toward you. I have told you what I have seen and heard; but faintly, nothing like the image and horror of it. Pray you, away.

Edg. Shall I hear from you anon?

Edm. I do serve you in this business. *Exit* EDGAR.

A credulous father, and a brother noble,
Whose nature is so far from doing harms
That he suspects none; on whose foolish honesty
My practices[18] ride easy. I see the business.
Let me, if not by birth, have lands by wit:
All with me's meet that I can fashion fit. *Exit.*

SCENE III. [*The Duke of Albany's palace*]

Enter GONERIL, *and* [OSWALD, *her*] Steward

Gon. Did my father strike my gentleman for chiding of his Fool?

Osw. Ay, madam.

[16] A believer in astrology. [17] Restrained. [18] Plots.

Gon. By day and night he wrongs me; every hour
He flashes into one gross crime or other
That sets us all at odds. I'll not endure it.
His knights grow riotous, and himself upbraids us
On every trifle. When he returns from hunting,
I will not speak with him; say I am sick.
If you come slack of former services,
You shall do well; the fault of it, I'll answer.

Osw. He's coming, madam; I hear him. [*Horns within.*]

Gon. Put on what weary negligence you please,
You and your fellows; I'd have it come to question.[1]
If he distaste[2] it, let him to my sister,
Whose mind and mine, I know, in that are one,
[Not to be over-rul'd. Idle old man,
That still would manage those authorities
That he hath given away! Now, by my life,
Old fools are babes again, and must be us'd
With checks as flatteries, when they are seen abus'd.]
Remember what I have said.

Osw. Well, madam.

Gon. And let his knights have colder looks among you;
What grows of it, no matter. Advise your fellows so.
[I would breed from hence occasions, and I shall,
That I may speak.] I'll write straight to my sister,
To hold my [very] course. Prepare for dinner. *Exeunt.*

Scene IV. [*A hall in the same*]

Enter Kent [*disguised*]

Kent. If but as well I other accents borrow,
That can my speech defuse,[3] my good intent
May carry through itself to that full issue
For which I raz'd my likeness.[4] Now, banish'd Kent,
If thou canst serve where thou dost stand condemn'd,
So may it come, thy master, whom thou lov'st,
Shall find thee full of labours.

[1] Discussion. [2] Dislike. [3] Confuse, disguise. [4] Changed my appearance.

Horns within. Enter LEAR, [Knights] *and* Attendants

Lear. Let me not stay a jot for dinner; go get it ready. [*Exit an attendant.*] How now! what art thou?

Kent. A man, sir.

Lear. What dost thou profess? What wouldst thou with us?

Kent. I do profess to be no less than I seem; to serve him truly that will put me in trust; to love him that is honest; to converse with him that is wise and says little; to fear judgement; to fight when I cannot choose; and to eat no fish.

Lear. What art thou?

Kent. A very honest-hearted fellow, and as poor as the King.

Lear. If thou be'st as poor for a subject as he's for a king, thou art poor enough. What wouldst thou?

Kent. Service.

Lear. Who wouldst thou serve?

Kent. You.

Lear. Dost thou know me, fellow?

Kent. No, sir; but you have that in your countenance which I would fain call master.

Lear. What's that?

Kent. Authority.

Lear. What services canst thou do?

Kent. I can keep honest counsel, ride, run, mar a curious[5] tale in telling it, and deliver a plain message bluntly. That which ordinary men are fit for, I am qualified in; and the best of me is diligence.

Lear. How old art thou?

Kent. Not so young, sir, to love a woman for singing, nor so old to dote on her for anything. I have years on my back forty-eight.

Lear. Follow me; thou shalt serve me. If I like thee no worse after dinner, I will not part from thee yet. Dinner, ho, dinner! Where's my knave, my Fool? Go you, and call my Fool hither.

Exit an Attendant.

Enter Steward [OSWALD]

You, you, sirrah, where's my daughter?

Osw. So please you,— *Exit.*

[5] Elaborate.

Lear. What says the fellow there? Call the clotpoll[6] back. [*Exit a* knight.] Where's my Fool, ho? I think the world's asleep.

[*Re-enter* Knight]

How now! where's that mongrel?

Knight. He says, my lord, your daughter is not well.

Lear. Why came not the slave back to me when I call'd him?

Knight. Sir, he answered me in the roundest[7] manner, he would not.

Lear. He would not!

Knight. My lord, I know not what the matter is; but, to my judgement, your Highness is not entertain'd with that ceremonious affection as you were wont. There's a great abatement of kindness appears as well in the general dependants as in the Duke himself also and your daughter.

Lear. Ha! say'st thou so?

Knight. I beseech you, pardon me, my lord, if I be mistaken; for my duty cannot be silent when I think your Highness wrong'd.

Lear. Thou but rememb'rest me of mine own conception. I have perceived a most faint neglect of late, which I have rather blamed as mine own jealous curiosity[8] than as a very pretence[9] and purpose of unkindness. I will look further into 't. But where's my Fool? I have not seen him this two days.

Knight. Since my young lady's going into France, sir, the Fool hath much pined away.

Lear. No more of that; I have noted it well. Go you, and tell my daughter I would speak with her. [*Exit an* Attendant.] Go you, call hither my Fool. [*Exit an* Attendant.]

Re-enter Steward [OSWALD]

O, you sir, you, come you hither, sir. Who am I, sir?

Osw. My lady's father.

Lear. "My lady's father"! My lord's knave! You whoreson dog! you slave! you cur!

Osw. I am none of these, my lord; I beseech your pardon.

Lear. Do you bandy looks with me, you rascal? [*Striking him.*]

[6] Blockhead. [7] Bluntest. [8] Punctiliousness. [9] Real plan.

Osw. I'll not be struck, my lord.

Kent. Nor tripp'd neither, you base foot-ball player.

[*Tripping up his heels.*]

Lear. I thank thee, fellow. Thou serv'st me, and I'll love thee.

Kent. Come, sir, arise, away! I'll teach you differences.[10] Away, away! If you will measure your lubber's length again, tarry; but away! go to. Have you wisdom? So. [*Pushes* OSWALD *out.*]

Lear. Now, my friendly knave, I thank thee. There's earnest of thy service. [*Giving* KENT *money.*]

Enter FOOL

Fool. Let me hire him too; here's my coxcomb.

[*Offering* KENT *his cap.*]

Lear. How now, my pretty knave! how dost thou?

Fool. Sirrah, you were best take my coxcomb.

[*Kent.* Why, Fool?]

Fool. Why? For taking one's part that's out of favour. Nay, an thou canst not smile as the wind sits, thou'lt catch cold shortly. There, take my coxcomb. Why, this fellow has banish'd two on 's daughters, and did the third a blessing against his will; if thou follow him, thou must needs wear my coxcomb.—How now, nuncle! Would I had two coxcombs and two daughters!

Lear. Why, my boy?

Fool. If I gave them all my living, I'd keep my coxcombs myself. There's mine; beg another of thy daughters.

Lear. Take heed, sirrah; the whip.

Fool. Truth's a dog must to kennel; he must be whipp'd out, when Lady the brach[11] may stand by the fire and stink.

Lear. A pestilent gall to me!

Fool. Sirrah, I'll teach thee a speech.

Lear. Do.

Fool. Mark it, nuncle:

"Have more than thou showest,
Speak less than thou knowest,
Lend less than thou owest,
Ride more than thou goest,[12]

[10] *I. e.* of rank. [11] Hound. [12] Walkest.

Learn more than thou trowest,
Set less than thou throwest;
Leave thy drink and thy whore,
And keep in-a-door,
And thou shalt have more
Than two tens to a score."

Kent. This is nothing, Fool.

Fool. Then 'tis like the breath of an unfee'd lawyer; you gave me nothing for 't. Can you make no use of nothing, nuncle?

Lear. Why, no, boy; nothing can be made out of nothing.

Fool. [*To* KENT.] Prithee, tell him so much the rent of his land comes to. He will not believe a fool.

Lear. A bitter fool!

Fool. Dost thou know the difference, my boy, between a bitter fool and a sweet one?

Lear. No, lad; teach me.

[*Fool.* "That lord that counsell'd thee
To give away thy land,
Come place him here by me,
Do thou for him stand:
The sweet and bitter fool
Will presently appear;
The one in motley here,
The other found out there."

Lear. Dost thou call me fool, boy?

Fool. All thy other titles thou hast given away; that thou wast born with.

Kent. This is not altogether fool, my lord.

Fool. No, faith, lords and great men will not let me; if I had a monopoly out, they would have part on 't. And ladies, too, they will not let me have all the fool to myself; they'll be snatching.] Nuncle, give me an egg, and I'll give thee two crowns.

Lear. What two crowns shall they be?

Fool. Why, after I have cut the egg i' the middle, and eat up the meat, the two crowns of the egg. When thou clovest thy crown i' the middle, and gav'st away both parts, thou bor'st thine ass on thy back o'er the dirt. Thou hadst little wit in thy bald crown, when thou gav'st thy golden one away. If I speak like myself in this, let him be whipp'd that first finds it so.

"Fools had ne'er less grace in a year;
For wise men are grown foppish,
And know not how their wits to wear,
Their manners are so apish."

Lear. When were you wont to be so full of songs, sirrah?

Fool. I have used it, nuncle, e'er since thou mad'st thy daughters thy mothers; for when thou gav'st them the rod, and puttest down thine own breeches,

"Then they for sudden joy did weep,
And I for sorrow sung,
That such a king should play bo-peep,
And go the fools among."

Prithee, nuncle, keep a schoolmaster that can teach thy Fool to lie. I would fain learn to lie.

Lear. An you lie, sirrah, we'll have you whipp'd.

Fool. I marvel what kin thou and thy daughters are. They'll have me whipp'd for speaking true, thou'lt have me whipp'd for lying; and sometimes I am whipp'd for holding my peace. I had rather be any kind o' thing than a Fool; and yet I would not be thee, nuncle; thou hast pared thy wit o' both sides, and left nothing i' the middle. Here comes one o' the parings.

Enter GONERIL

Lear. How now, daughter! what makes that frontlet[13] on? [Methinks] you are too much of late i' the frown.

Fool. Thou wast a pretty fellow when thou hadst no need to care for her frowning; now thou art an O without a figure. I am better than thou art now; I am a Fool, thou art nothing. [*To* GON.] Yes, forsooth, I will hold my tongue; so your face bids me, though you say nothing. Mum, mum,

"He that keeps nor crust nor crumb,
Weary of all, shall want some."

[*Pointing to* LEAR.] That's a sheal'd[14] peascod.

[13] The scowl on her brow. [14] Empty.

Gon. Not only, sir, this your all-licens'd Fool,
But other of your insolent retinue
Do hourly carp[15] and quarrel, breaking forth
In rank and not-to-be-endured riots. Sir,
I had thought, by making this well known unto you,
To have found a safe redress; but now grow fearful,
By what yourself, too, late have spoke and done,
That you protect this course, and put it on[16]
By your allowance; which if you should, the fault
Would not scape censure, nor the redresses sleep,
Which, in the tender[17] of a wholesome weal,
Might in their working do you that offence,
Which else were shame, that then necessity
Will call discreet proceeding.

Fool. For, you know, nuncle,
"The hedge-sparrow fed the cuckoo so long,
That it had it head bit off by it young."
So, out went the candle, and we were left darkling.[18]

Lear. Are you our daughter?

Gon. [Come, sir,]
I would you would make use of your good wisdom,
Whereof I know you are fraught,[19] and put away
These dispositions, which of late transport you
From what you rightly are.

Fool. May not an ass know when the cart draws the horse? "Whoop, Jug! I love thee."

Lear. Doth any here know me? This is not Lear.
Doth Lear walk thus? speak thus? Where are his eyes?
Either his notion weakens, his discernings
Are lethargied—Ha! waking? 'Tis not so.
Who is it that can tell me who I am?

Fool. Lear's shadow.

[*Lear.* I would learn that; for, by the marks of sovereignty, knowledge, and reason, I should be false persuaded I had daughters.

Fool. Which they will make an obedient father.]

Lear. Your name, fair gentlewoman?

[15] Find fault. [16] Encourage it. [17] Regard, care. [18] In the dark. [19] Endowed.

Gon. This admiration,[20] sir, is much o' the savour
Of other your new pranks. I do beseech you
To understand my purposes aright.
As you are old and reverend, you should be wise.
Here do you keep a hundred knights and squires;
Men so disorder'd, so debosh'd[21] and bold,
That this our court, infected with their manners,
Shows like a riotous inn. Epicurism[22] and lust
Makes it more like a tavern or a brothel
Than a grac'd palace. The shame itself doth speak
For instant remedy. Be then desir'd
By her, that else will take the thing she begs,
A little to disquantity[23] your train;
And the remainders, that shall still depend,
To be such men as may besort[24] your age,
Which know themselves and you.

Lear. Darkness and devils!
Saddle my horses; call my train together!
Degenerate bastard! I'll not trouble thee;
Yet have I left a daughter.

Gon. You strike my people; and your disorder'd rabble
Make servants of their betters.

Enter ALBANY

Lear. Woe, that too late repents!—[O, sir, are you come?]
Is it your will? Speak, sir.—Prepare my horses.—
Ingratitude, thou marble-hearted fiend,
More hideous when thou show'st thee in a child
Than the sea-monster!

Alb. Pray, sir, be patient.

Lear. [*To* GON.] Detested kite! thou liest.
My train are men of choice and rarest parts,
That all particulars of duty know,
And in the most exact regard support
The worships[25] of their name. O most small fault,

[20] Pretended wonder. [21] Debauched. [22] Gluttony. [23] Reduce.
[24] Suit. [25] Honor.

How ugly didst thou in Cordelia show!
Which, like an engine,[26] wrench'd my frame of nature
From the fix'd place; drew from my heart all love,
And added to the gall. O Lear, Lear, Lear!
Beat at this gate, that let thy folly in, [*Striking his head.*]
And thy dear judgement out! Go, go, my people.

Alb. My lord, I am guiltless as I am ignorant
Of what hath moved you.

Lear. It may be so, my lord.
Hear, Nature! hear, dear goddess, hear!
Suspend thy purpose, if thou didst intend
To make this creature fruitful!
Into her womb convey sterility!
Dry up in her the organs of increase,
And from her derogate[27] body never spring
A babe to honour her! If she must teem,[28]
Create her child of spleen, that it may live
And be a thwart[29] disnatur'd torment to her!
Let it stamp wrinkles in her brow of youth,
With cadent[30] tears fret channels in her cheeks,
Turn all her mother's pains and benefits
To laughter and contempt, that she may feel
How sharper than a serpent's tooth it is
To have a thankless child!—Away, away! *Exit.*

Alb. Now, gods that we adore, whereof comes this?

Gon. Never afflict yourself to know more of it;
But let his disposition have that scope
As dotage gives it.

Re-enter LEAR

Lear. What, fifty of my followers at a clap!
Within a fortnight!

Alb. What's the matter, sir?

Lear. I'll tell thee. [*To* GON.] Life and death! I am asham'd
That thou hast power to shake my manhood thus;
That these hot tears, which break from me perforce,

[26] Rack. [27] Degraded. [28] Have children. [29] Twisted in disposition. [30] Falling.

Should make thee worth them. Blasts and fogs upon thee!
The untented[31] woundings of a father's curse
Pierce every sense about thee! Old fond[32] eyes,
Beweep this cause again, I'll pluck ye out,
And cast you, with the waters that you loose,
To temper clay. Ha! [is it come to this?]
Let it be so: I have another daughter,
Who, I am sure, is kind and comfortable.
When she shall hear this of thee, with her nails
She'll flay thy wolvish visage. Thou shalt find
That I'll resume the shape which thou dost think
I have cast off for ever. [Thou shalt, I warrant thee.]

[*Exeunt* LEAR, KENT, *and* Attendants.]

Gon. Do you mark that?

Alb. I cannot be so partial, Goneril,
To the great love I bear you,—

Gon. Pray you, content.—What, Oswald, ho!
[*To the Fool.*] You, sir, more knave than fool, after your master.

Fool. Nuncle Lear, nuncle Lear, tarry! Take the Fool with thee.

A fox, when one has caught her,
And such a daughter,
Should sure to the slaughter,
If my cap would buy a halter.
So the Fool follows after. *Exit.*

Gon. This man hath had good counsel,—a hundred knights!
'Tis politic and safe to let him keep
At point[33] a hundred knights; yes, that, on every dream,
Each buzz,[34] each fancy, each complaint, dislike,
He may enguard his dotage with their powers,
And hold our lives in mercy. Oswald, I say!

Alb. Well, you may fear too far.

Gon. Safer than trust too far.
Let me still take away the harms I fear,
Not fear still to be taken. I know his heart.
What he hath utter'd I have writ my sister.

[31] Too deep to be probed. [32] Foolish. [33] Fully armed. [34] Idle rumor.

If she sustain him and his hundred knights,
When I have show'd the unfitness,—

Re-enter Steward [Oswald]

How now, Oswald!
What, have you writ that letter to my sister?
Osw. Ay, madam.
Gon. Take you some company, and away to horse.
Inform her full of my particular fear;
And thereto add such reasons of your own
As may compact[35] it more. Get you gone;
And hasten your return. [*Exit* Oswald.] No, no, my lord,
This milky gentleness and course of yours
Though I condemn not, yet, under pardon,
You are much more at task[36] for want of wisdom
Than prais'd for harmful mildness.
Alb. How far your eyes may pierce I cannot tell.
Striving to better, oft we mar what's well.
Gon. Nay, then—
Alb. Well, well; the event. *Exeunt.*

Scene V. [*Court before the same*]

Enter Lear, Kent, *and* Fool

Lear. Go you before to Gloucester with these letters. Acquaint my daughter no further with anything you know than comes from her demand out of the letter. If your diligence be not speedy, I shall be there afore you.

Kent. I will not sleep, my lord, till I have delivered your letter. *Exit.*

Fool. If a man's brains were in 's heels, were 't not in danger of kibes?[1]

Lear. Ay, boy.

Fool. Then, I prithee, be merry; thy wit shall not go slip-shod.

Lear. Ha, ha, ha!

[35] Confirm. [36] To be blamed. [1] Chilblains.

Fool. Shalt see thy other daughter will use thee kindly;[2] for though she's as like this as a crab's like an apple, yet I can tell what I can tell.

Lear. What canst tell, boy?

Fool. She will taste as like this as a crab does to a crab. Thou canst tell why one's nose stands i' the middle on 's face?

Lear. No.

Fool. Why, to keep one's eyes of either side 's nose, that what a man cannot smell out, he may spy into.

Lear. I did her wrong—

Fool. Canst tell how an oyster makes his shell?

Lear. No.

Fool. Nor I neither; but I can tell why a snail has a house.

Lear. Why?

Fool. Why, to put 's head in; not to give it away to his daughters, and leave his horns without a case.

Lear. I will forget my nature. So kind a father! Be my horses ready?

Fool. Thy asses are gone about 'em. The reason why the seven stars are no more than seven is a pretty reason.

Lear. Because they are not eight?

Fool. Yes, indeed. Thou wouldst make a good Fool.

Lear. To take 't again perforce![3] Monster ingratitude!

Fool. If thou wert my Fool, nuncle, I'd have thee beaten for being old before thy time.

Lear. How's that?

Fool. Thou shouldst not have been old till thou hadst been wise.

Lear. O, let me not be mad, not mad, sweet heaven!
Keep me in temper; I would not be mad!

[*Enter* Gentleman]

How now! are the horses ready?

Gent. Ready, my lord.

Lear. Come, boy.

Fool. She that's a maid now, and laughs at my departure,
Shall not be a maid long, unless things be cut shorter. *Exeunt.*

[2] A pun: with kindness, and after her kind.
[3] Probably Lear is thinking of regaining his power.

ACT II

SCENE I. [*The Earl of Gloucester's castle*]

Enter Bastard [EDMUND] *and* CURAN, *severally*

Edm. Save thee, Curan.

Cur. And you, sir. I have been with your father, and given him notice that the Duke of Cornwall and Regan his duchess will be here with him this night.

Edm. How comes that?

Cur. Nay, I know not. You have heard of the news abroad; I mean the whisper'd ones, for they are yet but ear-kissing arguments?[1]

Edm. Not I. Pray you, what are they?

Cur. Have you heard of no likely wars toward,[2] 'twixt the Dukes of Cornwall and Albany?

Edm. Not a word.

Cur. You may do, then, in time. Fare you well, sir. *Exit.*

Edm. The Duke be here to-night? The better! best!
This weaves itself perforce into my business.
My father hath set guard to take my brother;
And I have one thing, of a queasy question,[3]
Which I must act. Briefness[4] and fortune, work!

Enter EDGAR

Brother, a word; descend. Brother, I say!
My father watches; O sir, fly this place;
Intelligence is given where you are hid;
You have now the good advantage of the night.
Have you not spoken 'gainst the Duke of Cornwall?
He's coming hither, now, i' the night, i' the haste,
And Regan with him. Have you nothing said
Upon his party 'gainst the Duke of Albany?
Advise yourself.[5]

Edg. I am sure on 't, not a word.

Edm. I hear my father coming. Pardon me,

[1] Subjects of discussion. [2] Coming on.
[3] Requiring delicate handling. [4] Speed. [5] Reflect.

In cunning I must draw my sword upon you.
Draw; seem to defend yourself; now quit you well.
Yield! Come before my father. Light, ho, here!—
Fly, brother.—Torches, torches!—So, farewell. *Exit* EDGAR.
Some blood drawn on me would beget opinion [*Wounds his arm.*]
Of my more fierce endeavour. I have seen drunkards
Do more than this in sport.—Father, father!—
Stop, stop!—No help?

Enter GLOUCESTER, *and* Servants *with torches*

Glou. Now, Edmund, where's the villain?
Edm. Here stood he in the dark, his sharp sword out,
Mumbling of wicked charms, conjuring the moon
To stand auspicious mistress,—
Glou. But where is he?
Edm. Look, sir, I bleed.
Glou. Where is the villain, Edmund?
Edm. Fled this way, sir. When by no means he could—
Glou. Pursue him, ho! Go after. [*Exeunt some* Servants.] By no means what?
Edm. Persuade me to the murder of your lordship;
But that I told him, the revenging gods
'Gainst parricides did all the thunder bend;
Spoke, with how manifold and strong a bond
The child was bound to the father; sir, in fine,
Seeing how loathly opposite I stood
To his unnatural purpose, in fell motion,[6]
With his prepared sword, he charges home
My unprovided body, latch'd[7] mine arm;
And when he saw my best alarum'd spirits,
Bold in the quarrel's right, rous'd to the encounter,
Or whether gasted[8] by the noise I made,
Full suddenly he fled.
Glou. Let him fly far.
Not in this land shall he remain uncaught;
And found,—dispatch. The noble Duke my master,

[6] With a formidable thrust. [7] Caught, hit. [8] Frightened.

My worthy arch[9] and patron, comes to-night.
By his authority I will proclaim it,
That he which finds him shall deserve our thanks,
Bringing the murderous coward to the stake;
He that conceals him, death.

Edm. When I dissuaded him from his intent,
And found him pight[10] to do it, with curst speech
I threaten'd to discover[11] him; he replied,
"Thou unpossessing bastard! dost thou think,
If I would stand against thee, would the reposal
Of any trust, virtue, or worth in thee
Make thy words faith'd?[12] No! what I should deny,—
As this I would; ay, though thou didst produce
My very character,[13]—I'd turn it all
To thy suggestion,[14] plot, and damned practice;
And thou must make a dullard of the world[15]
If they not thought the profits of my death
Were very pregnant and potential spurs[16]
To make thee seek it."

Glou. O strange and fast'ned[17] villain!
Would he deny his letter? [I never got him.] *Tucket within.*
Hark, the Duke's trumpets! I know not why he comes.
All ports I'll bar, the villain shall not scape;
The Duke must grant me that. Besides, his picture
I will send far and near, that all the kingdom
May have due note of him; and of my land,
Loyal and natural boy, I'll work the means
To make thee capable.[18]

Enter CORNWALL, REGAN, *and* Attendants

Corn. How now, my noble friend! since I came hither,
Which I can call but now, I have heard strange news.

Reg. If it be true, all vengeance comes too short
Which can pursue the offender. How dost, my lord?

Glou. O, madam, my old heart is crack'd, it's crack'd!

[9] Chief. [10] Resolved. [11] Reveal. [12] Believed. [13] Handwriting. [14] Tempting.
[15] Suppose the world to be very stupid. [16] Obvious and potent inducements.
[17] Confirmed. [18] Able to inherit.

Reg. What, did my father's godson seek your life?
He whom my father nam'd? your Edgar?
Glou. O, lady, lady, shame would have it hid!
Reg. Was he not companion with the riotous knights
That tended upon my father?
Glou. I know not, madam. 'Tis too bad, too bad.
Edm. Yes, madam, he was of that consort.[19]
Reg. No marvel, then, though he were ill affected:[20]
'Tis they have put him on the old man's death,
To have the expense and waste of his revenues.
I have this present evening from my sister
Been well inform'd of them; and with such cautions,
That if they come to sojourn at my house,
I'll not be there.
Corn. Nor I, assure thee, Regan.
Edmund, I hear that you have shown your father
A child-like office.
Edm. 'Twas my duty, sir.
Glou. He did bewray his practice;[21] and receiv'd
This hurt you see, striving to apprehend him.
Corn. Is he pursued?
Glou. Ay, my good lord.
Corn. If he be taken, he shall never more
Be fear'd of doing harm. Make your own purpose,
How in my strength you please. For you, Edmund,
Whose virtue and obedience doth this instant
So much commend itself, you shall be ours.
Natures of such deep trust we shall much need;
You we first seize on.
Edm. I shall serve you, sir,
Truly, however else.
Glou. For him I thank your Grace.
Corn. You know not why we came to visit you,—
Reg. Thus out of season, threading dark-ey'd night?
Occasions, noble Gloucester, of some poise,[22]
Wherein we must have use of your advice.

[19] Band. [20] Disloyal. [21] Reveal his plot. [22] Weight.

Our father he hath writ, so hath our sister,
Of differences, which I best thought it fit
To answer from[23] our home; the several messengers
From hence attend dispatch.[24] Our good old friend,
Lay comforts to your bosom; and bestow
Your needful counsel to our businesses,
Which craves the instant use.

Glou. I serve you, madam.
Your Graces are right welcome. *Exeunt. Flourish.*

SCENE II. [*Before Gloucester's castle*]

Enter KENT *and* Steward [OSWALD], *severally*

Osw. Good dawning to thee, friend. Art of this house?

Kent. Ay.

Osw. Where may we set our horses?

Kent. I' the mire.

Osw. Prithee, if thou lov'st me, tell me.

Kent. I love thee not.

Osw. Why, then, I care not for thee.

Kent. If I had thee in Lipsbury pinfold, I would make thee care for me.

Osw. Why dost thou use me thus? I know thee not.

Kent. Fellow, I know thee.

Osw. What dost thou know me for?

Kent. A knave; a rascal; an eater of broken meats; a base, proud, shallow, beggarly, three-suited,[1] hundred-pound, filthy, worsted-stocking knave; a lily-livered, action-taking, whoreson, glass-gazing, superserviceable, finical rogue; one-trunk-inheriting[2] slave; one that wouldst be a bawd, in way of good service, and art nothing but the composition of a knave, beggar, coward, pandar, and the son and heir of a mongrel bitch; one whom I will beat into clamorous whining, if thou deni'st the least syllable of thy addition.[3]

Osw. Why, what a monstrous fellow art thou, thus to rail on one that is neither known of thee nor knows thee!

[23] Away from. [24] Wait to be sent off.
[1] Three suits of clothing seem to have been part of a servant's allowance.
[2] All of whose goods go into one trunk. [3] Title.

Kent. What a brazen-fac'd varlet art thou, to deny thou knowest me! Is it two days since I tripp'd up thy heels, and beat thee before the King? Draw, you rogue; for, though it be night, yet the moon shines. I'll make a sop o' the moonshine of you, you whoreson cullionly[4] barber-monger![5] Draw! [*Drawing his sword.*]

Osw. Away! I have nothing to do with thee.

Kent. Draw, you rascal! You come with letters against the King; and take Vanity the puppet's part against the royalty of her father. Draw, you rogue, or I'll so carbonado[6] your shanks,—draw, you rascal! Come your ways.

Osw. Help, ho! murder! help!

Kent. Strike, you slave! Stand, rogue, stand!
You neat slave, strike. [*Beating him.*]

Osw. Help, ho! murder! murder!

Enter Bastard [EDMUND] *with his rapier drawn,* CORNWALL, REGAN, GLOUCESTER, *and* Servants

Edm. How now! What's the matter? Part.

Kent. With you, goodman boy,[7] if you please.
Come, I'll flesh[8] ye; come on, young master.

Glou. Weapons! arms! What's the matter here?

Corn. Keep peace, upon your lives!
He dies that strikes again. What is the matter?

Reg. The messengers from our sister and the King.

Corn. What is your difference? Speak.

Osw. I am scarce in breath, my lord.

Kent. No marvel, you have so bestirr'd your valour. You cowardly rascal, Nature disclaims in[9] thee. A tailor made thee.

Corn. Thou art a strange fellow. A tailor make a man?

Kent. A tailor, sir. A stone-cutter or a painter could not have made him so ill, though they had been but two years o' the trade.

Corn. Speak yet, how grew your quarrel?

Osw. This ancient ruffian, sir, whose life I have spar'd at suit of his grey beard,—

Kent. Thou whoreson zed! thou unnecessary[10] letter! My lord,

[4] Rascally. [5] Haunter of barber-shops.
[6] Slash. [7] Little master. [8] Initiate.
[9] Disavows. [10] Z was often omitted from the old dictionaries.

if you will give me leave, I will tread this unbolted[11] villain into mortar, and daub the wall of a jakes with him. Spare my grey beard, you wagtail?

Corn. Peace, sirrah!
You beastly knave, know you no reverence?

Kent. Yes, sir; but anger hath a privilege.

Corn. Why art thou angry?

Kent. That such a slave as this should wear a sword,
Who wears no honesty. Such smiling rogues as these,
Like rats, oft bite the holy cords a-twain
Which are too intrinse[12] to unloose; smooth every passion
That in the natures of their lords rebel;
Bring oil to fire, snow to their colder moods;
Renege,[13] affirm, and turn their halcyon beaks[14]
With every gale and vary of their masters,
Knowing nought, like dogs, but following.
A plague upon your epileptic visage!
Smile you my speeches, as I were a fool?
Goose, if I had you upon Sarum Plain,
I'd drive ye cackling home to Camelot.

Corn. What, art thou mad, old fellow?

Glou. How fell you out? Say that.

Kent. No contraries hold more antipathy
Than I and such a knave.

Corn. Why dost thou call him knave? What is his fault?

Kent. His countenance likes[15] me not.

Corn. No more, perchance, does mine, nor his, nor hers.

Kent. Sir, 'tis my occupation to be plain;
I have seen better faces in my time
Than stands on any shoulder that I see
Before me at this instant.

Corn. This is some fellow
Who, having been prais'd for bluntness, doth affect
A saucy roughness, and constrains the garb[16]
Quite from his nature. He cannot flatter, he;

[11] Rank. [12] Intricate.
[13] Deny. [14] The halcyon or kingfisher was hung up and used as a weather-cock.
[15] Pleases. [16] Puts on forcibly a manner not natural to him.

An honest mind and plain, he must speak truth!
An[17] they will take it, so; if not, he's plain.
These kind of knaves I know, which in this plainness
Harbour more craft and more corrupter ends
Than twenty silly ducking observants[18]
That stretch their duties nicely.[19]

Kent. Sir, in good sooth, in sincere verity,
Under the allowance of your great aspect,
Whose influence, like the wreath of radiant fire
On flickering Phœbus' front,—

Corn. What mean'st by this?

Kent. To go out of my dialect, which you discommend so much. I know, sir, I am no flatterer. He that beguil'd you in a plain accent was a plain knave; which for my part I will not be, though I should win your displeasure to entreat me to 't.

Corn. What was the offence you gave him?

Osw. I never gave him any.
It pleas'd the King his master very late
To strike at me, upon his misconstruction;
When he, compact,[20] and flattering his displeasure,
Tripp'd me behind; being down, insulted,[21] rail'd,
And put upon him such a deal of man[22]
That 't worthied[23] him, got praises of the King
For him attempting[24] who was self-subdued;
And, in the fleshment[25] of this dread exploit,
Drew on me here again.

Kent. None of these rogues and cowards
But Ajax is their fool.

Corn. Fetch forth the stocks!
You stubborn ancient knave, you reverend braggart,
We'll teach you—

Kent. Sir, I am too old to learn.
Call not your stocks for me; I serve the King,
On whose employment I was sent to you.
You shall do small respects, show too bold malice

[17] If. [18] Obsequious servants. [19] Carry out their duties very punctiliously.
[20] Taking his part. [21] Exulted over me. [22] Made himself such a hero.
[23] Made to seem worthy. [24] For attacking one who. [25] Exhilaration of a first success.

Against the grace and person of my master,
Stocking his messenger.

Corn. Fetch forth the stocks! As I have life and honour,
There shall he sit till noon.

Reg. Till noon! Till night, my lord; and all night too.

Kent. Why, madam, if I were your father's dog,
You should not use me so.

Reg. Sir, being his knave, I will.

Stocks brought out.

Corn. This is a fellow of the self-same colour[26]
Our sister speaks of. Come, bring away the stocks!

Glou. Let me beseech your Grace not to do so.
[His fault is much, and the good King his master
Will check him for 't. Your purpos'd low correction
Is such as basest and contemned'st wretches
For pilferings and most common trespasses
Are punish'd with.] The King must take it ill
That he's so slightly valued in his messenger,
Should have him thus restrained.

Corn. I'll answer that.

Reg. My sister may receive it much more worse
To have her gentleman abus'd, assaulted,
[For following her affairs. Put in his legs.]

[KENT *is put in the stocks.*]

Come, my good lord, away.

Exeunt [*all but* GLOUCESTER *and* KENT].

Glou. I am sorry for thee, friend; 'tis the Duke's pleasure,
Whose disposition, all the world well knows,
Will not be rubb'd[27] nor stopp'd. I'll entreat for thee.

Kent. Pray, do not, sir. I have watch'd and travell'd hard;
Some time I shall sleep out, the rest I'll whistle.
A good man's fortune may grow out at heels.
Give you good morrow!

Glou. The Duke's to blame in this; 'twill be ill taken. *Exit.*

Kent. Good King, that must approve[28] the common saw,
Thou out of heaven's benediction com'st

[26] Kind. [27] Impeded. [28] Confirm.

To the warm sun![29]
Approach, thou beacon to this under globe,
That by thy comfortable beams I may
Peruse this letter! Nothing, almost, sees miracles
But misery. I know 'tis from Cordelia,
Who hath most fortunately been inform'd
Of my obscured[30] course; [*reads*] "—and shall find time
From this enormous[31] state—seeking to give
Losses their remedies."—All weary and o'erwatch'd,
Take vantage, heavy eyes, not to behold
This shameful lodging.
Fortune, good-night! Smile once more; turn thy wheel! [*Sleeps.*]

[Scene III. *The same*]

Enter Edgar

Edg. I heard myself proclaim'd;
And by the happy hollow of a tree
Escap'd the hunt. No port is free; no place
That guard and most unusual vigilance
Does not attend my taking.[1] Whiles I may scape
I will preserve myself, and am bethought
To take the basest and most poorest shape
That ever penury, in contempt of man,
Brought near to beast. My face I'll grime with filth,
Blanket my loins, elf[2] all my hairs in knots,
And with presented nakedness out-face
The winds and persecutions of the sky.
The country gives me proof and precedent
Of Bedlam beggars, who, with roaring voices,
Strike in their numb'd and mortified arms
Pins, wooden pricks, nails, sprigs of rosemary;
And with this horrible object,[3] from low farms,
Poor pelting[4] villages, sheep-cotes, and mills,

[29] From better to worse. [30] Disguised. [31] Monstrous.
[1] Watch to capture me. [2] Tangle in elf-locks.
[3] Appearance. [4] Petty.

Sometimes with lunatic bans,[5] sometimes with prayers,
Enforce their charity. Poor Turlygod! poor Tom!
That's something yet. Edgar I nothing am. *Exit.*

[SCENE IV. *The same*]

Enter LEAR, Fool, *and* Gentleman. [KENT *in the stocks*]

Lear. 'Tis strange that they should so depart from home,
And not send back my messengers.

Gent. As I learn'd,
The night before there was no purpose in them
Of this remove.

Kent. Hail to thee, noble master!

Lear. Ha!
Mak'st thou this shame thy pastime?

Kent. No, my lord.

Fool. Ha, ha! he wears cruel garters. Horses are tied by the heads, dogs and bears by the neck, monkeys by the loins, and men by the legs. When a man's over-lusty at legs, then he wears wooden nether stocks.[1]

Lear. What's he that hath so much thy place mistook
To set thee here?

Kent. It is both he and she;
Your son and daughter.

Lear. No.

Kent. Yes.

Lear. No, I say.

Kent. I say, yea.

[*Lear.* No, no, they would not.

Kent. Yes, they have.]

Lear. By Jupiter, I swear, no.

Kent. By Juno, I swear, ay.

Lear. They durst not do 't;
They could not, would not do 't. 'Tis worse than murder,
To do upon respect[2] such violent outrage.

[5] Curses. [1] Stockings. [2] Deliberately.

Resolve[3] me, with all modest haste, which way
Thou mightst deserve, or they impose, this usage,
Coming from us.
Kent. My lord, when at their home
I did commend[4] your Highness' letters to them,
Ere I was risen from the place that show'd
My duty kneeling, came there a reeking post,
Stew'd in his haste, half breathless, panting forth
From Goneril, his mistress, salutations;
Deliver'd letters, spite of intermission,[5]
Which presently they read. On those contents,
They summon'd up their meiny,[6] straight took horse;
Commanded me to follow, and attend
The leisure of their answer; gave me cold looks:
And meeting here the other messenger,
Whose welcome, I perceiv'd, had poison'd mine,—
Being the very fellow which of late
Display'd[7] so saucily against your Highness,—
Having more man than wit about me, drew.
He rais'd the house with loud and coward cries.
Your son and daughter found this trespass worth
The shame which here it suffers.
Fool. Winter's not gone yet, if the wild geese fly that way.
"Fathers that wear rags
Do make their children blind;
But fathers that bear bags
Shall see their children kind.
Fortune, that arrant whore,
Ne'er turns the key to the poor."
But, for[8] all this, thou shalt have as many dolours[9] for thy daughters as thou canst tell[10] in a year.
Lear. O, how this mother[11] swells up toward my heart!
Hysterica passio, down, thou climbing sorrow,
Thy element's below!—Where is this daughter?
Kent. With the Earl, sir, here within.

[3] Answer. [4] Deliver. [5] Regardless of interrupting me.
[6] Retinue. [7] Behaved. [8] On account of. [9] Pun on "griefs" and "dollars."
[10] Count. [11] Hysteria, suffocation.

Lear. Follow me not;
Stay here. *Exit.*

Gent. Made you no more offence but what you speak of?

Kent. None.
How chance the King comes with so small a number?

Fool. An thou hadst been set i' the stocks for that question, thou'dst well deserv'd it.

Kent. Why, Fool?

Fool. We'll set thee to school to an ant, to teach thee there's no labouring i' the winter. All that follow their noses are led by their eyes but blind men; and there's not a nose among twenty but can smell him that's stinking. Let go thy hold when a great wheel runs down a hill, lest it break thy neck with following; but the great one that goes upward, let him draw thee after. When a wise man gives thee better counsel, give me mine again; I would have none but knaves follow it, since a fool gives it.

"That sir which serves and seeks for gain,
And follows but for form,
Will pack when it begins to rain,
And leave thee in the storm.
But I will tarry; the Fool will stay,
And let the wise man fly.
The knave turns fool that runs away;
The Fool no knave, perdy."

Re-enter Lear *and* Gloucester

Kent. Where learn'd you this, Fool?

Fool. Not i' the stocks, fool.

Lear. Deny to speak with me? They are sick? They are weary?
They have travell'd all the night? Mere fetches;[12]
The images[13] of revolt and flying off.
Fetch me a better answer.

Glou. My dear lord,
You know the fiery quality of the Duke;
How unremovable and fix'd he is
In his own course.

[12] Subterfuges. [13] Signs.

Lear. Vengeance! plague! death! confusion!
"Fiery"? What "quality"? Why, Gloucester, Gloucester,
I'd speak with the Duke of Cornwall and his wife.
Glou. Well, my good lord, I have inform'd them so.
Lear. "Inform'd" them! Dost thou understand me, man?
Glou. Ay, my good lord.
Lear. The King would speak with Cornwall; the dear father
Would with his daughter speak, commands her service.
Are they "inform'd" of this? My breath and blood!
"Fiery"? The fiery duke? Tell the hot duke that—
No, but not yet; may be he is not well.
Infirmity doth still neglect all office
Whereto our health is bound; we are not ourselves
When nature, being oppress'd, commands the mind
To suffer with the body. I'll forbear;
And am fallen out with my more headier[14] will,
To take the indispos'd and sickly fit
For the sound man.—Death on my state! wherefore
[*Looking on* KENT.]
Should he sit here? This act persuades me
That this remotion[15] of the Duke and her
Is practice[16] only. Give me my servant forth.
Go tell the Duke and 's wife I'd speak with them,
Now, presently.[17] Bid them come forth and hear me,
Or at their chamber-door I'll beat the drum
Till it cry sleep to death.
Glou. I would have all well betwixt you. *Exit.*
Lear. O me, my heart, my rising heart! But, down!

Fool. Cry to it, nuncle, as the cockney did to the eels when she put 'em i' the paste alive; she knapp'd 'em o' the coxcombs with a stick, and cried, "Down, wantons, down!" 'Twas her brother that, in pure kindness to his horse, buttered his hay.

Enter CORNWALL, REGAN, GLOUCESTER, *and* Servants

Lear. Good morrow to you both.
Corn. Hail to your Grace!

[14] More impetuous. [15] Seclusion. [16] Craft. [17] At once.

KENT *is set at liberty.*

Reg. I am glad to see your Highness.
Lear. Regan, I think you are; I know what reason
I have to think so. If thou shouldst not be glad,
I would divorce me from thy mother's tomb,
Sepulchring an adulteress. [*To* KENT.] O, are you free?
Some other time for that. Beloved Regan,
Thy sister's naught. O Regan, she hath tied
Sharp-tooth'd unkindness, like a vulture, here.
[*Points to his heart.*]
I can scarce speak to thee; thou'lt not believe
With how deprav'd a quality—O Regan!
Reg. I pray you, sir, take patience. I have hope
You less know how to value her desert
Than she to scant her duty.
Lear. Say, how is that?
Reg. I cannot think my sister in the least
Would fail her obligation. If, sir, perchance
She have restrain'd the riots of your followers,
'Tis on such ground, and to such wholesome end,
As clears her from all blame.
Lear. My curses on her!
Reg. O, sir, you are old;
Nature in you stands on the very verge
Of her confine. You should be rul'd and led
By some discretion that discerns your state
Better than you yourself. Therefore, I pray you,
That to our sister you do make return;
Say you have wrong'd her, sir.
Lear. Ask her forgiveness?
Do you but mark how this becomes the house:[18]
"Dear daughter, I confess that I am old; [*Kneeling.*]
Age is unnecessary. On my knees I beg
That you'll vouchsafe me raiment, bed, and food."
Reg. Good sir, no more; these are unsightly tricks.
Return you to my sister.

[18] Family relation.

Lear. [*Rising.*] Never, Regan:
She hath abated[19] me of half my train;
Look'd black upon me; struck me with her tongue,
Most serpent-like, upon the very heart.
All the stor'd vengeances of heaven fall
On her ingrateful top! Strike her young bones,
You taking[20] airs, with lameness!

Corn. Fie, sir, fie!

Lear. You nimble lightnings, dart your blinding flames
Into her scornful eyes! Infect her beauty,
You fen-suck'd fogs, drawn by the powerful sun,
To fall[21] and blast her pride!

Reg. O the blest gods! so will you wish on me,
When the rash mood is on.

Lear. No, Regan, thou shalt never have my curse.
Thy tender-hefted[22] nature shall not give
Thee o'er to harshness. Her eyes are fierce; but thine
Do comfort and not burn. 'Tis not in thee
To grudge my pleasures, to cut off my train,
To bandy hasty words, to scant my sizes,[23]
And, in conclusion, to oppose the bolt
Against my coming in. Thou better know'
The offices of nature, bond of childhood,
Effects[24] of courtesy, dues of gratitude.
Thy half o' the kingdom hast thou not forgot,
Wherein I thee endow'd.

Reg. Good sir, to the purpose.

Tucket within

Lear. Who put my man i' the stocks?

Enter Steward [OSWALD]

Corn. What trumpet's that?

Reg. I know 't; my sister's. This approves[25] her letter,
That she would soon be here. [*To* OSWALD.] Is your lady come?

[19] Deprived. [20] Infectious. [21] Humble.
[22] Gently disposed. [23] Allowances.
[24] Workings. [25] Confirms.

Lear. This is a slave whose easy-borrowed pride
Dwells in the fickle grace of her he follows.
Out, varlet, from my sight!
Corn. What means your Grace?

Enter GONERIL

Lear. Who stock'd my servant? Regan, I have good hope
Thou didst not know on 't. Who comes here? O heavens,
If you do love old men, if your sweet sway
Allow[26] obedience, if you yourselves are old,
Make it your cause; send down, and take my part!
[*To* GON.] Art not asham'd to look upon this beard?
O Regan, will you take her by the hand?
Gon. Why not by the hand, sir? How have I offended?
All's not offence that indiscretion finds
And dotage terms so.
Lear. O sides, you are too tough;
Will you yet hold? How came my man i' the stocks?
Corn. I set him there, sir; but his own disorders
Deserv'd much less advancement.
Lear. You! did you?
Reg. I pray you, father, being weak, seem so
If, till the expiration of your month,
You will return and sojourn with my sister,
Dismissing half your train, come then to me.
I am now from home, and out of that provision
Which shall be needful for your entertainment.
Lear. Return to her, and fifty men dismiss'd!
No, rather I abjure all roofs, and choose
To wage[27] against the enmity o' the air;
To be a comrade with the wolf and owl,—
Necessity's sharp pinch. Return with her?
Why, the hot-blooded France, that dowerless took
Our youngest born, I could as well be brought
To knee[28] his throne, and, squire-like, pension beg

[26] Approve of. [27] Contend.
[28] Kneel before.

To keep base life afoot. Return with her?
Persuade me rather to be slave and sumpter[29]
To this detested groom. [*Pointing at* OSWALD.]

Gon. At your choice, sir.

Lear. I prithee, daughter, do not make me mad;
I will not trouble thee, my child; farewell!
We'll no more meet, no more see one another.
But yet thou art my flesh, my blood, my daughter;
Or rather a disease that's in my flesh,
Which I must needs call mine; thou art a boil,
A plague-sore, an embossed[30] carbuncle,
In my corrupted blood. But I'll not chide thee;
Let shame come when it will, I do not call it.
I do not bid the thunder-bearer shoot,
Nor tell tales of thee to high-judging Jove.
Mend when thou canst; be better at thy leisure.
I can be patient; I can stay with Regan,
I and my hundred knights.

Reg. Not altogether so;
I look'd not for you yet, nor am provided
For your fit welcome. Give ear, sir, to my sister;
For those that mingle reason with your passion
Must be content to think you old, and so—
But she knows what she does.

Lear. Is this well spoken?

Reg. I dare avouch it, sir. What, fifty followers!
Is it not well? What should you need of more?
Yea, or so many, sith that both charge[31] and danger
Speak 'gainst so great a number? How, in one house,
Should many people, under two commands,
Hold amity? 'Tis hard; almost impossible.

Gon. Why might not you, my lord, receive attendance
From those that she calls servants or from mine?

Reg. Why not, my lord? If then they chanc'd to slack ye,[32]
We could control them. If you will come to me,—

[29] Pack-horse (driver ?). [30] Swollen. [31] Expense.
[32] Be slack in their performance of duties.

For now I spy a danger—I entreat you
To bring but five and twenty; to no more
Will I give place or notice.

Lear. I gave you all.

Reg. And in good time you gave it.

Lear. Made you my guardians, my depositaries;[33]
But kept a reservation to be followed
With such a number. What, must I come to you
With five and twenty, Regan? Said you so?

Reg. And speak 't again, my lord; no more with me.

Lear. Those wicked creatures yet do look well-favour'd
When others are more wicked; not being the worst
Stands in some rank of praise. [*To* GON.] I'll go with thee.
Thy fifty yet doth double five and twenty,
And thou art twice her love.

Gon. Hear me, my lord:
What need you five and twenty, ten, or five,
To follow in a house where twice so many
Have a command to tend you?

Reg. What need one?

Lear. O, reason not the need! Our basest beggars
Are in the poorest thing superfluous.
Allow[34] not nature more than nature needs,
Man's life is cheap as beast's. Thou art a lady;
If only to go warm were gorgeous,
Why, nature needs not what thou gorgeous wear'st,
Which scarcely keeps thee warm. But, for true need,—
You heavens, give me that patience, patience I need!
You see me here, you gods, a poor old man,
As full of grief as age; wretched in both!
If it be you that stirs these daughters' hearts
Against their father, fool me not so much
To bear it tamely; touch me with noble anger,
And let not women's weapons, water-drops,
Stain my man's cheeks! No, you unnatural hags,
I will have such revenges on you both

[33] Stewards and trustees. [34] If you allow not.

That all the world shall—I will do such things,—
What they are, yet I know not; but they shall be
The terrors of the earth. You think I'll weep:
No, I'll not weep.
I have full cause of weeping; but this heart *Storm and tempest.*
Shall break into a hundred thousand flaws,[35]
Or ere I'll weep. O, Fool! I shall go mad!

Exeunt LEAR, GLOUCESTER, KENT, *and* FOOL.

Corn. Let us withdraw; 'twill be a storm.
Reg. This house is little; the old man and 's people
Cannot be well bestow'd.[36]
Gon. 'Tis his own blame; hath put himself from rest,
And must needs taste his folly.
Reg. For his particular,[37] I'll receive him gladly,
But not one follower.
Gon. So am I purpos'd.
Where is my Lord of Gloucester?

Re-enter GLOUCESTER

Corn. Followed the old man forth. He is return'd.
Glou. The King is in high rage.
Corn. Whither is he going?
Glou. He calls to horse; but will I know not whither.
Corn. 'Tis best to give him way; he leads himself.
Gon. My lord, entreat him by no means to stay.
Glou. Alack, the night comes on, and the high winds
Do sorely ruffle;[38] for many miles about
There's scarce a bush.
Reg. O, sir, to wilful men,
The injuries that they themselves procure
Must be their schoolmasters. Shut up your doors.
He is attended with a desperate train;
And what they may incense him to, being apt
To have his ear abus'd,[39] wisdom bids fear.

[35] Fragments. [36] Lodged. [37] Him individually.
[38] Bluster. [39] Deceived.

Corn. Shut up your doors, my lord; 'tis a wild night:
My Regan counsels well. Come out o' the storm. [*Exeunt.*

ACT III

Scene I. [*The open country near Gloucester's castle*]

Storm still. Enter Kent *and a* Gentleman, *severally*

Kent. Who's there, besides foul weather?
Gent. One minded like the weather, most unquietly.
Kent. I know you. Where's the King?
Gent. Contending with the fretful elements;
Bids the wind blow the earth into the sea,
Or swell the curled waters 'bove the main,[1]
That things might change or cease; [tears his white hair,
Which the impetuous blasts, with eyeless rage,
Catch in their fury, and make nothing of;
Strives in his little world of man to out-scorn
The to-and-fro-conflicting wind and rain.
This night, wherein the cub-drawn[2] bear would couch,
The lion and the belly-pinched wolf
Keep their fur dry, unbonneted he runs,
And bids what will take all.]
Kent. But who is with him?
Gent. None but the Fool; who labours to outjest
His heart-struck injuries.
Kent. Sir, I do know you;
And dare, upon the warrant of my note,[3]
Commend a dear[4] thing to you. There is division,
Although as yet the face of it is cover'd
With mutual cunning, 'twixt Albany and Cornwall;
Who have—as who have not, that their great stars[5]
Thron'd and set high?—servants, who seem no less,
Which are to France the spies and speculations[6]
Intelligent of our state; what hath been seen,

[1] Land. [2] Sucked dry, and so fierce. [3] Observation.
[4] Important. [5] Fortunes. [6] Observers.

Either in snuffs[7] and packings[8] of the Dukes,
Or the hard rein which both of them have borne
Against the old kind king, or something deeper,
Whereof perchance these are but furnishings;[9]
[But, true it is, from France there comes a power[10]
Into this scattered[11] kingdom; who already,
Wise in our negligence, have secret feet
In some of our best ports, and are at point[12]
To show their open banner. Now to you:
If on my credit you dare build so far
To make your speed to Dover, you shall find
Some that will thank you, making just report
Of how unnatural and bemadding[13] sorrow
The King hath cause to plain.
I am a gentleman of blood and breeding;
And, from some knowledge and assurance, offer
This office to you.]

Gent. I will talk further with you.

Kent. No, do not.
For confirmation that I am much more
Than my out-wall,[14] open this purse, and take
What it contains. If you shall see Cordelia,—
As fear not but you shall,—show her this ring;
And she will tell you who that fellow is
That yet you do not know. Fie on this storm!
I will go seek the King.

Gent. Give me your hand. Have you no more to say?

Kent. Few words, but, to effect,[15] more than all yet;
That, when we have found the King,—in which your pain[16]
That way, I'll this,—he that first lights on him
Holla the other. *Exeunt* [*severally*].

[7] Offence-takings. [8] Plots. [9] Externals. [10] Army. [11] Divided. [12] Ready.
[13] Maddening. [14] Exterior. [15] Important. [16] Take you pains to search.

SCENE II. [*The same.*] *Storm still*

Enter LEAR *and* Fool

Lear. Blow, winds, and crack your cheeks! Rage! Blow!
You cataracts and hurricanoes, spout
Till you have drench'd our steeples, drown'd the cocks!
You sulphurous and thought-executing[17] fires,
Vaunt-couriers[18] of oak-cleaving thunderbolts,
Singe my white head! And thou, all-shaking thunder,
Strike flat the thick rotundity o' the world!
Crack nature's moulds, all germens[19] spill[20] at once,
That makes ingrateful man!

Fool. O nuncle, court holy-water[21] in a dry house is better than this rain-water out o' door. Good nuncle, in; ask thy daughters' blessing. Here's a night pities neither wise men nor fools.

Lear. Rumble thy bellyful! Spit, fire! Spout, rain!
Nor rain, wind, thunder, fire, are my daughters.
I tax[22] not you, you elements, with unkindness;
I never gave you kingdom, call'd you children;
You owe me no subscription.[23] Then let fall
Your horrible pleasure. Here I stand, your slave,
A poor, infirm, weak, and despis'd old man;
But yet I call you servile ministers,
That will with two pernicious daughters join
Your high engender'd battles[24] 'gainst a head
So old and white as this. Oh! Oh! 'tis foul!

Fool. He that has a house to put 's head in has a good head-piece.

"The cod-piece that will house
Before the head has any,
The head and he shall louse;
So beggars marry many.
The man that makes his toe
What he his heart should make

[17] Quick as thought. [18] Fore-runners. [19] Seeds. [20] Destroy.
[21] Flattery. [22] Blame. [23] Allegiance.
[24] Battalions mustered in the heavens.

Shall of a corn cry woe,
And turn his sleep to wake."[25]
For there was never yet fair woman but she made mouths in a glass.

Enter KENT

Lear. No, I will be the pattern of all patience; I will say nothing.

Kent. Who's there?

Fool. Marry, here's grace and a cod-piece; that's a wise man and a fool.

Kent. Alas, sir, are you here? Things that love night
Love not such nights as these; the wrathful skies
Gallow[26] the very wanderers of the dark,
And make them keep their caves. Since I was man,
Such sheets of fire, such bursts of horrid thunder,
Such groans of roaring wind and rain, I never
Remember to have heard. Man's nature cannot carry
The affliction nor the fear.

Lear. Let the great gods,
That keep this dreadful pudder[27] o'er our heads,
Find out their enemies now. Tremble, thou wretch,
That hast within thee undivulged crimes,
Unwhipp'd of justice! Hide thee, thou bloody hand;
Thou perjur'd, and thou simular[28] of virtue
That art incestuous! Caitiff, to pieces shake,
That under covert and convenient seeming
Has practis'd[29] on man's life! Close pent-up guilts,
Rive your concealing continents,[30] and cry
These dreadful summoners grace.[31] I am a man
More sinn'd against than sinning.

Kent. Alack, bare-headed!
Gracious my lord, hard by here is a hovel;
Some friendship will it lend you 'gainst the tempest.
Repose you there; while I to this hard house—
More harder than the stones whereof 'tis rais'd;

[25] He who cherishes the mean in preference to the worthy, shall suffer from the mean. [26] Frighten. [27] Turmoil.
[28] Simulator. [29] Plotted against. [30] What hides you. [31] For mercy.

Which even but now, demanding after you,
Deni'd[32] me to come in—return, and force
Their scanted courtesy.

Lear. My wits begin to turn.
Come on, my boy. How dost, my boy? Art cold?
I am cold myself. Where is this straw, my fellow?
The art of our necessities is strange,
And can make vile things precious. Come, your hovel.
Poor Fool and knave, I have one part in my heart
That's sorry yet for thee.

Fool. [*Singing.*]

"He that has and a little tiny wit,—
With heigh-ho, the wind and the rain,—
Must make content with his fortunes fit,
For the rain it raineth every day."

Lear. True, boy. Come, bring us to this hovel.

Exeunt [LEAR *and* KENT].

Fool. This is a brave night to cool a courtezan.
I'll speak a prophecy ere I go:

When priests are more in word than matter;
When brewers mar their malt with water;
When nobles are their tailors' tutors;
No heretics burn'd, but wenches' suitors;
When every case in law is right;
No squire in debt, nor no poor knight;
When slanders do not live in tongues;
Nor cutpurses come not to throngs;
When usurers tell their gold i' the field;
And bawds and whores do churches build:
Then shall the realm of Albion
Come to great confusion.
Then comes the time, who lives to see 't,
That going shall be us'd with feet.

This prophecy Merlin shall make; for I live before his time. *Exit.*

[32] Refused to allow.

SCENE III. [*Gloucester's castle*]

Enter GLOUCESTER *and* EDMUND

Glou. Alack, alack, Edmund, I like not this unnatural dealing. When I desired their leave that I might pity him, they took from me the use of mine own house; charg'd me, on pain of perpetual displeasure, neither to speak of him, entreat for him, or any way sustain him.

Edm. Most savage and unnatural!

Glou. Go to; say you nothing. There is division between the Dukes, and a worse matter than that. I have received a letter this night; 'tis dangerous to be spoken; I have lock'd the letter in my closet. These injuries the King now bears will be revenged home;[1] there is part of a power already footed.[2] We must incline to the King. I will look him, and privily relieve him. Go you and maintain talk with the Duke, that my charity be not of him perceived. If he ask for me, I am ill, and gone to bed. If I die for it, as no less is threat'ned me, the King my old master must be relieved. There is strange things toward,[3] Edmund; pray you, be careful. *Exit.*

Edm. This courtesy, forbid thee, shall the Duke
Instantly know; and of that letter too.
This seems a fair deserving,[4] and must draw me
That which my father loses; no less than all.
The younger rises when the old doth fall. *Exit.*

SCENE IV. [*The open country. Before a hovel*]

Enter LEAR, KENT, *and* Fool

Kent. Here is the place, my lord; good my lord, enter.
The tyranny of the open night's too rough
For nature to endure. *Storm still.*

Lear. Let me alone.

Kent. Good my lord, enter here.

Lear. Wilt break my heart?

[1] Fully. [2] Army already on the march. [3] About to happen.
[4] An action deserving reward.

Kent. I had rather break mine own. Good my lord, enter.

Lear. Thou think'st 'tis much that this contentious storm
Invades us to the skin; so 'tis to thee;
But where the greater malady is fix'd,
The lesser is scarce felt. Thou 'dst shun a bear;
But if thy flight lay toward the roaring sea,
Thou 'dst meet the bear i' the mouth. When the mind's free,
The body's delicate;[1] the tempest in my mind
Doth from my senses take all feeling else
Save what beats there. Filial ingratitude!
Is it not as this mouth should tear this hand
For lifting food to 't? But I will punish home.
No, I will weep no more. In such a night
To shut me out! Pour on! I will endure.
In such a night as this! O Regan, Goneril!
Your old kind father, whose frank heart gave all,—
O, that way madness lies; let me shun that;
No more of that.

Kent. Good my lord, enter here.

Lear. Prithee, go in thyself; seek thine own ease.
This tempest will not give me leave to ponder
On things would hurt me more. But I'll go in.
[*To the* Fool.] In, boy; go first. You houseless poverty,—
Nay, get thee in. I'll pray, and then I'll sleep. *Exit* [Fool].
Poor naked wretches, wheresoe'er you are,
That bide the pelting of this pitiless storm,
How shall your houseless heads and unfed sides,
Your loop'd[2] and window'd[2] raggedness, defend you
From seasons such as these? O, I have ta'en
Too little care of this! Take physic, pomp;
Expose thyself to feel what wretches feel,
That thou mayst shake the superflux to them,
And show the heavens more just.

Edg. [*Within.*] Fathom and half, fathom and half! Poor Tom!

[*The* Fool *runs out from the hovel.*]

Fool. Come not in here, nuncle, here's a spirit. Help me, help me!

[1] Sensitive. [2] Full of holes.

Kent. Give me thy hand. Who's there?

Fool. A spirit, a spirit! He says his name 's poor Tom.

Kent. What art thou that dost grumble there i' the straw? Come forth.

[*Enter* EDGAR, *disguised as a madman*]

Edg. Away! the foul fiend follows me!
"Through the sharp hawthorn blow the winds."
Hum! go to thy bed, and warm thee.

Lear. Did'st thou give all to thy daughters, and art thou come to this?

Edg. Who gives anything to poor Tom? whom the foul fiend hath led through fire and through flame, and through ford and whirlpool, o'er bog and quagmire; that hath laid knives under his pillow, and halters in his pew; set ratsbane[3] by his porridge; made him proud of heart, to ride on a bay trotting-horse over four-inch'd bridges, to course his own shadow for a traitor. Bless thy five wits! Tom's a-cold,—O, do de, do de, do de. Bless thee from whirlwinds, starblasting, and taking![4] Do poor Tom some charity, whom the foul fiend vexes. There could I have him now,—and there,—and there again, and there. *Storm still.*

Lear. Has his daughters brought him to this pass?
Couldst thou save nothing? Wouldst thou give 'em all?

Fool. Nay, he reserv'd a blanket, else we had been all sham'd.

Lear. Now, all the plagues that in the pendulous[5] air
Hang fated o'er men's faults light on thy daughters!

Kent. He hath no daughters, sir.

Lear. Death, traitor! nothing could have subdu'd nature
To such a lowness but his unkind daughters.
Is it the fashion, that discarded fathers
Should have thus little mercy on their flesh?
Judicious punishment! 'Twas this flesh begot
Those pelican[6] daughters.

Edg. "Pillicock sat on Pillicock-hill."
Alow, alow, loo, loo!

[3] Poison for rats. [4] Infection. [5] Suspended.
[6] The pelican was believed to feed on its mother's blood.

Fool. This cold night will turn us all to fools and madmen.

Edg. Take heed o' the foul fiend. Obey thy parents; keep thy word justly; swear not; commit[7] not with man's sworn spouse; set not thy sweet heart on proud array. Tom 's a-cold.

Lear. What hast thou been?

Edg. A serving-man, proud in heart and mind; that curl'd my hair; wore gloves in my cap; serv'd the lust of my mistress' heart, and did the act of darkness with her; swore as many oaths as I spake words, and broke them in the sweet face of heaven: one that slept in the contriving of lust, and wak'd to do it. Wine lov'd I dearly, dice dearly; and in woman out-paramour'd the Turk:[8] false of heart, light of ear, bloody of hand; hog in sloth, fox in stealth, wolf in greediness, dog in madness, lion in prey. Let not the creaking of shoes nor the rustling of silks betray thy poor heart to woman. Keep thy foot out of brothels, thy hand out of plackets,[9] thy pen from lenders' books, and defy the foul fiend.

"Still through the hawthorn blows the cold wind."

Says suum, mun, nonny. Dolphin my boy, boy, sessa! let him trot by.

Storm still.

Lear. Thou wert better in a grave than to answer[10] with thy uncover'd body this extremity of the skies. Is man no more than this? Consider him well. Thou ow'st the worm no silk, the beast no hide, the sheep no wool, the cat no perfume. Ha! here's three on 's are sophisticated! Thou art the thing itself; unaccommodated[11] man is no more but such a poor, bare, forked animal as thou art. Off, off, you lendings![12] come, unbutton here. [*Tearing off his clothes.*]

Enter GLOUCESTER, *with a torch*

Fool. Prithee, nuncle, be contented; 'tis a naughty night to swim in. Now a little fire in a wild field were like an old lecher's heart; a small spark, all the rest on 's body cold. Look, here comes a walking fire.

Edg. This is the foul [fiend] Flibbertigibbet; he begins at curfew, and walks till the first cock; he gives the web and the pin,[13] squints

[7] Sin. [8] *I. e.*, the Sultan. [9] Opening in a petticoat.
[10] Encounter. [11] Unfurnished. [12] *I. e.*, clothes. [13] An eye-disease; cataract.

the eye, and makes the hare-lip; mildews the white wheat, and hurts the poor creature of earth.

"St. Withold footed thrice the 'old;[14]
He met the night-mare, and her ninefold;[15]
Bid her alight,
And her troth plight,
And, aroint[16] thee, witch, aroint thee!"

Kent. How fares your Grace?

Lear. What's he?

Kent. Who's there? What is 't you seek?

Glou. What are you there? Your names?

Edg. Poor Tom, that eats the swimming frog, the toad, the tadpole, the wall-newt, and the water; that in the fury of his heart, when the foul fiend rages, eats cow-dung for salads; swallows the old rat and the ditch-dog; drinks the green mantle of the standing pool; who is whipp'd from tithing[17] to tithing, and stock'd punish'd, and imprison'd; who hath three suits to his back, six shirts to his body,

Horse to ride, and weapon to wear;
But mice and rats, and such small deer,
Have been Tom's food for seven long year.

Beware my follower. Peace, Smulkin; peace, thou fiend!

Glou. What, hath your Grace no better company?

Edg. The prince of darkness is a gentleman.
Modo he's call'd, and Mahu.

Glou. Our flesh and blood, my lord, is grown so vile,
That it doth hate what gets it.

Edg. Poor Tom's a-cold.

Glou. Go in with me; my duty cannot suffer
To obey in all your daughters' hard commands.
Though their injunction be to bar my doors
And let this tyrannous night take hold upon you,
Yet have I ventur'd to come seek you out,
And bring you where both fire and food is ready.

Lear. First let me talk with this philosopher.
What is the cause of thunder?

[14] Wold, open country. [15] Nine familiar spirits (?). [16] Avaunt. [17] District.

Kent. Good my lord, take his offer; go into the house.
Lear. I'll talk a word with this same learned Theban.
What is your study?
Edg. How to prevent the fiend, and to kill vermin.
Lear. Let me ask you one word in private.
Kent. Importune him once more to go, my lord;
His wits begin to unsettle.
Glou. Canst thou blame him? *Storm still.*
His daughters seek his death. Ah, that good Kent!
He said it would be thus, poor banish'd man!
Thou say'st the King grows mad; I'll tell thee, friend,
I am almost mad myself. I had a son,
Now outlaw'd from my blood; he sought my life,
But lately, very late. I lov'd him, friend,
No father his son dearer; true to tell thee,
The grief hath craz'd my wits. What a night's this!
I do beseech your Grace,—
Lear. O, cry you mercy,[18] sir.
Noble philosopher, your company.
Edg. Tom's a-cold.
Glou. In, fellow, there, into the hovel; keep thee warm.
Lear. Come, let's in all.
Kent. This way, my lord.
Lear. With him;
I will keep still with my philosopher.
Kent. Good my lord, soothe him; let him take the fellow.
Glou. Take him you on.
Kent. Sirrah, come on; go along with us.
Lear. Come, good Athenian.
Glou. No words, no words: hush.
Edg. "Child Rowland to the dark tower came;
His word was still,—'Fie, foh, and fum,
I smell the blood of a British man.'" [*Exeunt.*

[18] Beg your pardon.

Scene V. [*Gloucester's castle*]

Enter Cornwall *and* Edmund

Corn. I will have my revenge ere I depart his house.

Edm. How, my lord, I may be censured[1] that nature thus gives way to loyalty, something fears me to think of.

Corn. I now perceive, it was not altogether your brother's evil disposition made him seek his death; but a provoking merit, set a-work by a reproveable badness in himself.

Edm. How malicious is my fortune, that I must repent to be just! This is the letter which he spoke of, which approves[2] him an intelligent party to the advantages of France. O heavens! that this treason were not, or not I the detector!

Corn. Go with me to the Duchess.

Edm. If the matter of this paper be certain, you have mighty business in hand.

Corn. True or false, it hath made thee Earl of Gloucester. Seek out where thy father is, that he may be ready for our apprehension.

Edm. [*Aside.*] If I find him comforting the King, it will stuff his suspicion more fully.—I will persevere in my course of loyalty, though the conflict be sore between that and my blood.

Corn. I will lay trust upon thee; and thou shalt find a dearer father in my love. *Exeunt.*

Scene VI. [*A building attached to Gloucester's castle*]

Enter Kent *and* Gloucester

Glou. Here is better than the open air; take it thankfully. I will piece out the comfort with what addition I can. I will not be long from you. *Exit.*

Kent. All the power of his wits have given way to his impatience. The gods reward your kindness!

Enter Lear, Edgar, *and* Fool

Edg. Frateretto calls me; and tells me Nero is an angler in the lake of darkness. Pray, innocent, and beware the foul fiend.

[1] Judged. [2] Proves.

Fool. Prithee, nuncle, tell me whether a madman be a gentleman or a yeoman?

Lear. A king, a king!

Fool. No, he's a yeoman that has a gentleman to his son; for he's a mad yeoman that sees his son a gentleman before him.

Lear. To have a thousand with red burning spits
Come hissing in upon 'em,—

[1][*Edg.* The foul fiend bites my back.

Fool. He's mad that trusts in the tameness of a wolf, a horse's health, a boy's love, or a whore's oath.

Lear. It shall be done; I will arraign them straight.
[*To* EDGAR.] Come, sit thou here, most learned justicer;
[*To the* Fool.] Thou, sapient sir, sit here. Now, you she-foxes!

Edg. Look, where he stands and glares!
Wantest thou eyes at trial, madam?
"Come o'er the bourn,[2] Bessy, to me,"—

Fool. "Her boat hath a leak,
And she must not speak
Why she dares not come over to thee."

Edg. The foul fiend haunts poor Tom in the voice of a nightingale. Hopdance cries in Tom's belly for two white herring. Croak not, black angel; I have no food for thee.

Kent. How do you, sir? Stand you not so amaz'd:
Will you lie down and rest upon the cushions?

Lear. I'll see their trial first. Bring in their evidence.
[*To* EDGAR.] Thou robed man of justice, take thy place;
[*To the* Fool.] And thou, his yoke-fellow of equity,
Bench by his side. [*To* KENT.] You are o' the commission,
Sit you too.

Edg. Let us deal justly.
"Sleepest or wakest thou, jolly shepherd?
Thy sheep be in the corn;
And for one blast of thy minikin[3] mouth,
Thy sheep shall take no harm."
Purr! the cat is grey.

[1] From this speech to "let her scape," forty lines below, the passage is missing from the folio. [2] Stream. [3] Little.

Lear. Arraign her first; 'tis Goneril. I here take my oath before this honourable assembly, she kick'd the poor king her father.

Fool. Come hither, mistress. Is your name Goneril?

Lear. She cannot deny it.

Fool. Cry you mercy, I took you for a joint-stool.

Lear. And here's another, whose warp'd[4] looks proclaim
What store her heart is made on. Stop her there!
Arms, arms, sword, fire! Corruption in the place!
False justicer, why hast thou let her scape?

Edg. Bless thy five wits!

Kent. O pity! Sir, where is the patience now
That you so oft have boasted to retain?

Edg. [*Aside.*] My tears begin to take his part so much,
They mar my counterfeiting.

Lear. The little dogs and all,
Tray, Blanch, and Sweetheart, see, they bark at me.

Edg. Tom will throw his head at them.
Avaunt, you curs!

> Be thy mouth or black or white,
> Tooth that poisons if it bite;
> Mastiff, greyhound, mongrel grim,
> Hound or spaniel, brach[5] or lym,[6]
> Or bobtail tike or trundle-tail,[7]
> Tom will make him weep and wail;
> For, with throwing thus my head,
> Dogs leapt the hatch,[8] and all are fled.

Do de, de, de. Sessa! Come, march to wakes and fairs and market-towns. Poor Tom, thy horn is dry.

Lear. Then let them anatomize[9] Regan; see what breeds about her heart. Is there any cause in nature that make these hard hearts? [*To* Edg.] You, sir, I entertain for one of my hundred; only I do not like the fashion of your garments. You will say they are Persian, but let them be chang'd.

[4] Distorted, unnatural. [5] A small hound. [6] A bloodhound.
[7] A dog with a curling tail. [8] A half-door. [9] Dissect.

Re-enter GLOUCESTER

Kent. Now, good my lord, lie here and rest a while.
Lear. Make no noise, make no noise; draw the curtains; so, so, so. We'll go to supper i' the morning.
Fool. And I'll go to bed at noon.
Glou. Come hither, friend; where is the King my master?
Kent. Here, sir; but trouble him not, his wits are gone.
Glou. Good friend, I prithee, take him in thy arms;
I have o'erheard a plot of death upon him.
There is a litter ready; lay him in 't,
And drive toward Dover, friend, where thou shalt meet
Both welcome and protection. Take up thy master.
If thou shouldst dally half an hour, his life,
With thine, and all that offer to defend him,
Stand in assured loss. Take up, take up;
And follow me, that will to some provision
Give thee quick conduct.
Kent. [Oppressed nature sleeps.
This rest might yet have balm'd thy broken sinews,[10]
Which, if convenience will not allow,
Stand in hard cure.[11] [*To the* Fool.] Come, help to bear thy master;
Thou must not stay behind.]
Glou. Come, come, away.
Exeunt [*all but* EDGAR]

[*Edg.* When we our betters see bearing our woes,
We scarcely think our miseries our foes.
Who alone suffers, suffers most i' the mind,
Leaving free[12] things and happy shows behind;
But then the mind much sufferance doth o'erskip,
When grief hath mates, and bearing fellowship.
How light and portable[13] my pain seems now,
When that which makes me bend makes the King bow,
He childed as I fathered! Tom, away!
Mark the high noises; and thyself bewray,

[10] Nerves. [11] Are in a dangerous condition.
[12] Free from suffering. [13] Tolerable.

When false opinion, whose wrong thoughts defile thee,
In thy just proof repeals and reconciles thee.
What will hap more to-night, safe scape the King!
Lurk, lurk.] [*Exit.*]

Scene VII. [*Gloucester's castle*]

Enter Cornwall, Regan, Goneril, Bastard [Edmund], *and* Servants

Corn. [*To* Gon.] Post speedily to my lord your husband; show him this letter. The army of France is landed.—Seek out the traitor Gloucester. [*Exeunt some of the* Servants.]

Reg. Hang him instantly.

Gon. Pluck out his eyes.

Corn. Leave him to my displeasure.—Edmund, keep you our sister company; the revenges we are bound to take upon your traitorous father are not fit for your beholding. Advise the Duke, where you are going, to a most festinate[1] preparation; we are bound to the like. Our posts shall be swift and intelligent[2] betwixt us. Farewell, dear sister; farewell, my lord of Gloucester.

Enter Steward [Oswald]

How now! where's the King?

Osw. My Lord of Gloucester hath convey'd him hence.
Some five or six and thirty of his knights,
Hot questrists[3] after him, met him at gate,
Who, with some other of the lords dependants,
Are gone with him toward Dover, where they boast
To have well-armed friends.

Corn. Get horses for your mistress.

Gon. Farewell, sweet lord, and sister.

Corn. Edmund, farewell.

Exeunt [Goneril, Edmund, *and* Oswald].

Go seek the traitor Gloucester,
Pinion him like a thief, bring him before us. [*Exeunt other* Servants.]
Though well we may not pass upon his life
Without the form of justice, yet our power

[1] Hasty. [2] Bearing news. [3] Seekers.

Shall do a courtesy to our wrath, which men
May blame, but not control.

Enter GLOUCESTER *and* Servants

Who's there? The traitor?
Reg. Ingrateful fox! 'tis he.
Corn. Bind fast his corky[4] arms.
Glou. What means your Graces? Good my friends, consider
You are my guests. Do me no foul play, friends.
Corn. Bind him, I say. [Servants *bind him.*]
Reg. Hard, hard. O filthy traitor!
Glou. Unmerciful lady as you are, I'm none.
Corn. To this chair bind him. Villain, thou shalt find—
[REGAN *plucks his beard.*]
Glou. By the kind gods, 'tis most ignobly done
To pluck me by the beard.
Reg. So white, and such a traitor!
Glou. Naughty lady,
These hairs, which thou dost ravish from my chin,
Will quicken,[5] and accuse thee. I am your host:
With robber's hands my hospitable favours[6]
You should not ruffle thus. What will you do?
Corn. Come, sir, what letters had you late from France?
Reg. Be simple-answer'd,[7] for we know the truth.
Corn. And what confederacy have you with the traitors
Late footed in the kingdom?
Reg. To whose hands you have sent the lunatic king,
Speak.
Glou. I have a letter guessingly[8] set down,
Which came from one that's of a neutral heart,
And not from one oppos'd.
Corn. Cunning.
Reg. And false.
Corn. Where hast thou sent the King?
Glou. To Dover.

[4] Withered. [5] Become alive. [6] The features of your host.
[7] Direct in your answers. [8] From conjecture.

Reg. Wherefore to Dover? Wast thou not charg'd at peril—
Corn. Wherefore to Dover? Let him answer that.
Glou. I am tied to the stake, and I must stand the course.[9]
Reg. Wherefore to Dover?
Glou. Because I would not see thy cruel nails
Pluck out his poor old eyes; nor thy fierce sister
In his anointed flesh stick boarish fangs.
The sea, with such a storm as his bare head
In hell-black night endur'd, would have buoy'd up
And quench'd the stelled[10] fires;
Yet, poor old heart, he holp the heavens to rain.
If wolves had at thy gate howl'd that stern time,
Thou shouldst have said, "Good porter, turn the key."
All cruels else subscribe;[11] but I shall see
The winged vengeance overtake such children.
Corn. See 't shalt thou never. Fellows, hold the chair.
Upon these eyes of thine I'll set my foot.
Glou. He that will think to live till he be old,
Give me some help!—O cruel! O you gods!
Reg. One side will mock another; the other too.
Corn. If you see vengeance,—
[1.] *Serv.* Hold your hand, my lord!
I have serv'd you ever since I was a child;
But better service have I never done you
Than now to bid you hold.
Reg. How now, you dog!
[1.] *Serv.* If you did wear a beard upon your chin,
I'd shake it on this quarrel. What do you mean?
Corn. My villain! [*They draw and fight.*]
[1.] *Serv.* Nay, then, come on, and take the chance of anger.
Reg. Give me thy sword. A peasant stand up thus?
Takes a sword, and runs at him behind.
[1.] *Serv.* Oh, I am slain! My lord, you have one eye left
To see some mischief on him. Oh! [*Dies.*]
Corn. Lest it see more, prevent it. Out, vile jelly!

[9] The attack of the dogs in bear-baiting.
[10] Fixed (?), starry (?). [11] Perhaps, "all other cruelties yield to this."

Where is thy lustre now?

Glou. All dark and comfortless. Where's my son Edmund?
Edmund, enkindle all the sparks of nature,
To quit this horrid act.

Reg. Out, treacherous villain!
Thou call'st on him that hates thee. It was he
That made the overture[12] of thy treasons to us,
Who is too good to pity thee.

Glou. O my follies! then Edgar was abus'd.[13]
Kind gods, forgive me that, and prosper him!

Reg. Go thrust him out at gates, and let him smell
His way to Dover. *Exit [one] with* GLOUCESTER. How is 't, my lord?
How look you?

Corn. I have received a hurt; follow me, lady.
Turn out that eyeless villain; throw this slave
Upon the dunghill. Regan, I bleed apace;
Untimely comes this hurt. Give me your arm.

[*Exit* CORNWALL, *led by* REGAN.]

[2. *Serv.* I'll never care what wickedness I do,
If this man come to good.

3. *Serv.* If she live long,
And in the end meet the old course of death,
Women will all turn monsters.

2. *Serv.* Let's follow the old earl, and get the Bedlam
To lead him where he would: his roguish madness
Allows itself to anything.[14]

3. *Serv.* Go thou: I'll fetch some flax and whites of eggs
To apply to his bleeding face. Now, Heaven help him!]

Exeunt [severally].

ACT IV

SCENE I. [*The open country near Gloucester's castle*]

Enter EDGAR

Edg. Yet better thus, and known to be contemn'd,
Than, still contemn'd and flatter'd, to be worst,

12 Revealed. 13 Wronged. 14 To be directed to anything.

The lowest and most dejected[1] thing of fortune
Stands still in esperance,[2] lives not in fear.
The lamentable change is from the best;
The worst returns to laughter.[3] Welcome, then,
Thou unsubstantial air that I embrace!
The wretch that thou hast blown unto the worst
Owes nothing to thy blasts.

Enter GLOUCESTER, *led by an* Old Man

But who comes here?
My father, poorly led? World, world, O world!
But that thy strange mutations make us hate thee,
Life would not yield to age.

Old Man. O, my good lord, I have been your tenant, and your father's tenant, these fourscore years.

Glou. Away, get thee away! Good friend, be gone;
Thy comforts can do me no good at all;
Thee they may hurt.

Old Man. [Alack, sir,] you cannot see your way.

Glou. I have no way, and therefore want no eyes;
I stumbled when I saw. Full oft 'tis seen,
Our means secure us,[4] and our mere defects
Prove our commodities.[5] O dear son Edgar,
The food of thy abused[6] father's wrath!
Might I but live to see thee in my touch,
I'd say I had eyes again!

Old Man. How now! Who's there?

Edg. [*Aside.*] O gods! Who is 't can say, "I am at the worst"?
I am worse than e'er I was.

Old Man. 'Tis poor mad Tom.

Edg. [*Aside.*] And worse I may be yet; the worst is not
So long as we can say, "This is the worst."

Old Man. Fellow, where goest?

Glou. Is it a beggar-man?

Old Man. Madman and beggar too.

[1] Abased. [2] Hope. [3] A change from the worst must be towards good.
[4] Render us careless. [5] Advantages. [6] Deceived.

Glou. He has some reason, else he could not beg.
I' the last night's storm I such a fellow saw,
Which made me think a man a worm. My son
Came then into my mind, and yet my mind
Was then scarce friends with him. I have heard more since.
As flies to wanton boys, are we to the gods,
They kill us for their sport.

Edg. [*Aside.*] How should this be?
Bad is the trade that must play fool to sorrow,
Ang'ring itself and others.—Bless thee, master!

Glou. Is that the naked fellow?

Old Man. Ay, my lord.

Glou. [Then, prithee,] get thee away. If, for my sake,
Thou wilt o'ertake us, hence a mile or twain
I' the way toward Dover, do it for ancient love;
And bring some covering for this naked soul,
Which I'll entreat to lead me.

Old Man. Alack, sir, he is mad.

Glou. 'Tis the time's plague, when madmen lead the blind.
Do as I bid thee, or rather do thy pleasure;
Above the rest, be gone

Old Man. I'll bring him the best 'parel that I have,
Come on 't what will. *Exit.*

Glou. Sirrah, naked fellow,—

Edg. Poor Tom's a-cold. [*Aside.*] I cannot daub it[7] further.

Glou. Come hither, fellow.

Edg. [*Aside.*] And yet I must.—Bless thy sweet eyes, they bleed.

Glou. Know'st thou the way to Dover?

Edg. Both stile and gate, horse-way and foot-path. Poor Tom hath been scar'd out of his good wits. Bless thee, good man's son, from the foul fiend! [Five fiends have been in poor Tom at once; of lust, as Obidicut; Hobbididence, prince of dumbness; Mahu, of stealing; Modo, of murder; Flibbertigibbet, of mopping and mowing,[8] who since possesses chambermaids and waiting-women. So, bless thee, master!]

Glou. Here, take this purse, thou whom the heavens' plagues

[7] Keep up the disguise. [8] Making grimaces.

Have humbled to all strokes. That I am wretched
Makes thee the happier; heavens, deal so still!
Let the superfluous and lust-dieted man,
That slaves your ordinance,[9] that will not see
Because he does not feel, feel your power quickly;
So distribution should undo excess,
And each man have enough. Dost thou know Dover?

Edg. Ay, master.

Glou. There is a cliff, whose high and bending head
Looks fearfully in the confined[10] deep.
Bring me but to the very brim of it,
And I'll repair the misery thou dost bear
With something rich about me. From that place
I shall no leading need.

Edg. Give me thy arm;
Poor Tom shall lead thee. *Exeunt.*

SCENE II. [*Before the Duke of Albany's palace*]

Enter GONERIL, Bastard [EDMUND], *and* Steward [OSWALD]

Gon. Welcome, my lord! I marvel our mild husband
Not met us on the way.—Now, where's your master?

Osw. Madam, within; but never man so chang'd.
I told him of the army that was landed;
He smil'd at it. I told him you were coming;
His answer was, "The worse." Of Gloucester's treachery,
And of the loyal service of his son,
When I inform'd him, then he call'd me sot,
And told me I had turn'd the wrong side out.
What most he should dislike seems pleasant to him;
What like, offensive.

Gon. [*To* EDM.] Then shall you go no further.
It is the cowish[1] terror of his spirit,
That dares not undertake; he'll not feel wrongs
Which tie him to an answer.[2] Our wishes on the way

[9] That subordinates instead of obeying your commands (?). The reference is to the command to give to the needy. [10] Restrained by the cliffs.

[1] Cowardly. [2] Retaliation.

May prove effects.[3] Back, Edmund, to my brother;
Hasten his musters and conduct his powers.
I must change names at home, and give the distaff
Into my husband's hands. This trusty servant
Shall pass between us. Ere long you are like to hear,
If you dare venture in your own behalf,
A mistress's command. Wear this; spare speech;
Decline your head. This kiss, if it durst speak,
Would stretch thy spirits up into the air.
Conceive, and fare thee well.

Edm. Yours in the ranks of death. *Exit.*

Gon. My most dear Gloucester!
O, the difference of man and man!
To thee a woman's services are due;
My Fool usurps my body.

Osw. Madam, here comes my lord. *Exit.*

Enter the Duke of Albany

Gon. I have been worth the whistle.[4]

Alb. O Goneril!
You are not worth the dust which the rude wind
Blows in your face. [I fear your disposition.
That nature which contemns its origin
Cannot be bordered certain in itself.[5]
She that herself will sliver[6] and disbranch
From her material[7] sap, perforce must wither
And come to deadly use.[8]

Gon. No more; the text is foolish.

Alb. Wisdom and goodness to the vile seem vile;
Filths savour but themselves. What have you done?
Tigers, not daughters, what have you perform'd?
A father, and a gracious aged man,
Whose reverence even the head-lugg'd[9] bear would lick,
Most barbarous, most degenerate! have you madded.[10]

[3] Come to pass. [4] Worth consideration.
[5] Cannot be counted on to keep within bounds.
[6] Break off. [7] Essential. [8] *I. e.*, to burning.
[9] Pulled by the head. [10] Driven mad.

Could my good brother suffer you to do it?
A man, a prince, by him so benefited!
If that the heavens do not their visible spirits
Send quickly down to tame these vile offences,
It will come,
Humanity must perforce prey on itself,
Like monsters of the deep.]
Gon. Milk-liver'd[11] man!
That bear'st a cheek for blows, a head for wrongs,
Who hast not in thy brows an eye discerning
Thine honour from thy suffering, [that not know'st
Fools do those villains pity who are punish'd
Ere they have done their mischief, where's thy drum?
France spreads his banners in our noiseless[12] land,
With plumed helm thy state begins to threat;
Whiles thou, a moral fool, sits still, and cries,
"Alack, why does he so?"]
Alb. See thyself, devil!
Proper[13] deformity seems not in the fiend
So horrid as in woman.
Gon. O vain fool!
[*Alb.* Thou changed and self-cover'd[14] thing, for shame!
Be-monster not thy feature. Were 't my fitness
To let these hands obey my blood,
They are apt enough to dislocate and tear
Thy flesh and bones. Howe'er thou art a fiend
A woman's shape doth shield thee.
Gon. Marry, your manhood—Mew!

Enter a Messenger

Alb. What news?]
Mess. O, my good lord, the Duke of Cornwall's dead;
Slain by his servant, going to put out
The other eye of Gloucester.
Alb. Gloucester's eyes!

[11] Cowardly. [12] Peaceful. [13] Appropriate to a fiend.
[14] Whose devilish self is covered with a human form (?).

Mess. A servant that he bred, thrill'd with remorse,[15]
Oppos'd against the act, bending[16] his sword
To his great master; who, thereat enrag'd,
Flew on him, and amongst them fell'd him dead;
But not without that harmful stroke, which since
Hath pluck'd him after.

Alb. This shows you are above,
You justicers, that these our nether[17] crimes.
So speedily can venge! But, O poor Gloucester!
Lost he his other eye?

Mess. Both, both, my lord.
This letter, madam, craves a speedy answer.
'Tis from your sister.

Gon. [*Aside.*] One way I like this well;
But being widow, and my Gloucester with her,
May all the building in my fancy pluck
Upon my hateful life.[18] Another way,
The news is not so tart.—I'll read, and answer. *Exit.*

Alb. Where was his son when they did take his eyes?

Mess. Come with my lady hither.

Alb. He is not here.

Mess. No, my good lord; I met him back again.

Alb. Knows he the wickedness?

Mess. Ay, my good lord; 'twas he inform'd against him;
And quit the house on purpose, that their punishment
Might have the freer course.

Alb. Gloucester, I live
To thank thee for the love thou show'dst the King,
And to revenge thine eyes. Come hither, friend;
Tell me what more thou know'st. *Exeunt.*

[SCENE III. *The French camp near Dover*

Enter KENT *and a* Gentleman

Kent. Why the King of France is so suddenly gone back, know you no reason?

[15] Pity. [16] Directing. [17] Committed on earth.
[18] My castles in the air may tumble and make my life hateful to me.

Gent. Something he left imperfect in the state, which since his coming forth is thought of; which imports to the kingdom so much fear and danger that his personal return was most required and necessary.

Kent. Who hath he left behind him General?

Gent. The Marshal of France, Monsieur La Far.

Kent. Did your letters pierce the Queen to any demonstration of grief?

Gent. Ay, sir; she took them, read them in my presence;
And now and then an ample tear trill'd[1] down
Her delicate cheek. It seem'd she was a queen
Over her passion,[2] who, most rebel-like,
Sought to be king o'er her.

Kent. O, then it mov'd her.

Gent. Not to a rage; patience and sorrow strove
Who should express her goodliest. You have seen
Sunshine and rain at once: her smiles and tears
Were like a better way; those happy smilets
That play'd on her ripe lip seem'd not to know
What guests were in her eyes, which, parted thence,
As pearls from diamonds dropp'd. In brief,
Sorrow would be a rarity most beloved,
If all could so become it.

Kent. Made she no verbal question?

Gent. Faith, once or twice she heav'd the name of "father"
Pantingly forth, as if it press'd her heart;
Cried, "Sisters! sisters! Shame of ladies! sisters!
Kent! father! sisters! What, i' the storm? i' the night?
Let pity[3] not be believ'd!" There she shook
The holy water from her heavenly eyes;
And, clamour-moistened, then away she started
To deal with grief alone.

Kent. It is the stars,
The stars above us, govern our conditions;[4]
Else one self mate and make[5] could not beget
Such different issues. You spoke not with her since?

[1] Trickled. [2] Emotion.
[3] The existence of pity. [4] Dispositions. [5] Husband and wife.

Gent. No.

Kent. Was this before the King return'd?

Gent. No, since.

Kent. Well, sir, the poor distressed Lear's i' the town;
Who sometime, in his better tune, remembers
What we are come about, and by no means
Will yield to see his daughter.

Gent. Why, good sir?

Kent. A sovereign shame so elbows[6] him. His own unkindness,
That stripp'd her from his benediction, turn'd her
To foreign casualties, gave her dear rights
To his dog-hearted daughters,—these things sting
His mind so venomously, that burning shame
Detains him from Cordelia.

Gent. Alack, poor gentleman!

Kent. Of Albany's and Cornwall's powers[7] you heard not?

Gent. 'Tis so, they are afoot.

Kent. Well, sir, I'll bring you to our master Lear,
And leave you to attend him. Some dear[8] cause
Will in concealment wrap me up a while;
When I am known aright, you shall not grieve
Lending me this acquaintance. I pray you, go
Along with me.] *Exeunt.*

SCENE [IV. *The same. A tent*]

Enter, with drum and colours, CORDELIA, Doctor, *and* Soldiers

Cor. Alack, 'tis he! Why, he was met even now
As mad as the vex'd sea, singing aloud,
Crown'd with rank fumiter and furrow-weeds,
With hardocks, hemlock, nettles, cuckoo-flowers,
Darnel, and all the idle weeds that grow
In our sustaining corn. A sentry send forth;
Search every acre in the high-grown field,
And bring him to our eye. [*Exit an* Officer.] What can man's wisdom

[6] Shoves him back. [7] Armies. [8] Important and intimate.

In the restoring his bereaved sense?
He that helps him take all my outward worth.
Doct. There is means, madam.
Our foster-nurse of nature is repose,
The which he lacks; that to provoke in him,
Are many simples[1] operative, whose power
Will close the eye of anguish.
Cor. All blest secrets,
All you unpublish'd virtues of the earth,
Spring with my tears! be aidant and remediate[2]
In the good man's distress! Seek, seek for him,
Lest his ungovern'd rage dissolve the life
That wants the means to lead it.

Enter a Messenger

Mess. News, madam!
The British powers are marching hitherward.
Cor. 'Tis known before; our preparation stands
In expectation of them. O dear father,
It is thy business that I go about;
Therefore great France
My mourning and importune[3] tears hath pitied.
No blown[4] ambition doth our arms incite,
But love, dear love, and our ag'd father's right.
Soon may I hear and see him! *Exeunt.*

SCENE [V. *Gloucester's castle*]

Enter REGAN *and* Steward [OSWALD]

Reg. But are my brother's powers set forth?
Osw. Ay, madam.
Reg. Himself in person there?
Osw. Madam, with much ado.[5]
Your sister is the better soldier.
Reg. Lord Edmund spake not with your lord at home?
Osw. No, madam.

[1] Medicinal herbs. [2] Helpful and curative.
[3] Importunate, persistent. [4] Puffed up. [5] Induced with much difficulty.

Reg. What might import my sister's letter to him?
Osw. I know not, lady.
Reg. Faith, he is posted hence on serious matter.
It was great ignorance,[6] Gloucester's eyes being out,
To let him live; where he arrives he moves
All hearts against us. Edmund, I think, is gone,
In pity of his misery, to dispatch
His nighted[7] life; moreover, to descry
The strength o' the enemy.
Osw. I must needs after him, madam, with my letter.
Reg. Our troops set forth to-morrow, stay with us;
The ways are dangerous.
Osw. I may not, madam:
My lady charg'd my duty in this business.
Reg. Why should she write to Edmund? Might not you
Transport her purposes by word? Belike
Some things—I know not what. I'll love thee much,
Let me unseal the letter.
Osw. Madam, I had rather—
Reg. I know your lady does not love her husband;
I am sure of that; and at her late being here
She gave strange œillades[8] and most speaking looks
To noble Edmund. I know you are of her bosom.[9]
Osw. I, madam?
Reg. I speak in understanding; y' are, I know 't.
Therefore I do advise you, take this note:
My lord is dead; Edmund and I have talk'd;
And more convenient is he for my hand
Than for your lady's. You may gather more.
If you do find him, pray you, give him this;
And when your mistress hears thus much from you,
I pray, desire her call her wisdom to her.
So, fare you well.
If you do chance to hear of that blind traitor,
Preferment falls on him that cuts him off.

[6] Folly. [7] Blinded. [8] Amorous glances. [9] In her confidence.

Osw. Would I could meet him, madam! I should show
What party I do follow.
Reg. Fare thee well. [*Exeunt.*

SCENE [VI. *Fields near Dover*]

Enter GLOUCESTER, *and* EDGAR [*dressed like a peasant*]

Glou. When shall I come to the top of that same hill?
Edg. You do climb up it now; look, how we labour.
Glou. Methinks the ground is even.
Edg. Horrible steep.
Hark, do you hear the sea?
Glou. No, truly.
Edg. Why, then, your other senses grow imperfect
By your eyes' anguish.
Glou. So may it be, indeed.
Methinks thy voice is alter'd, and thou speak'st
In better phrase and matter than thou didst.
Edg. You're much deceiv'd. In nothing am I chang'd
But in my garments.
Glou. Methinks you're better spoken.
Edg. Come on, sir, here's the place; stand still. How fearful
And dizzy 'tis, to cast one's eyes so low!
The crows and choughs[1] that wing the midway air
Show scarce so gross[2] as beetles. Half way down
Hangs one that gathers samphire,[3] dreadful trade!
Methinks he seems no bigger than his head.
The fishermen, that walk upon the beach,
Appear like mice; and yond tall anchoring bark,
Diminish'd to her cock;[4] her cock, a buoy
Almost too small for sight. The murmuring surge,
That on the unnumb'red idle pebbles chafes,
Cannot be heard so high. I'll look no more,
Lest my brain turn, and the deficient sight
Topple down headlong.

[1] Jackdaws. [2] Large. [3] A herb used for pickling. [4] Cock-boat.

Glou. Set me where you stand.
Edg. Give me your hand; you are now within a foot
Of the extreme verge. For all beneath the moon
Would I not leap upright.
Glou. Let go my hand.
Here, friend, 's another purse; in it a jewel
Well worth a poor man's taking. Fairies and gods
Prosper it with thee! Go thou further off;
Bid me farewell, and let me hear thee going.
Edg. Now fare ye well, good sir.
Glou. With all my heart.
Edg. Why I do trifle thus with his despair
Is done to cure it.
Glou. [*Kneeling.*] O you mighty gods!
This world I do renounce, and in your sights
Shake patiently my great affliction off.
If I could bear it longer, and not fall
To quarrel with your great opposeless wills,
My snuff[5] and loathed part of nature should
Burn itself out. If Edgar live, O bless him!
Now, fellow, fare thee well.
Edg. Gone, sir; farewell!
—And yet I know not how conceit[6] may rob
The treasury of life, when life itself
Yields[7] to the theft. [Glou. *throws himself forward.*] Had he been where he thought,
By this had thought been past. Alive or dead?—
Ho, you sir! friend! Hear you, sir! speak!—
Thus might he pass[8] indeed; yet he revives.—
What are you, sir?
Glou. Away, and let me die.
Edg. Hadst thou been aught but gossamer, feathers, air,
So many fathom down precipitating,
Thou 'dst shiver'd like an egg: but thou dost breathe;
Hast heavy substance; bleed'st not; speak'st; art sound.
Ten masts at each[9] make not the altitude

[5] Refuse, worthless part. [6] Imagination. [7] Consents to. [8] Die. [9] End to end.

Which thou hast perpendicularly fell.
Thy life's a miracle. Speak yet again.
Glou. But have I fallen, or no?
Edg. From the dread summit of this chalky bourn.[10]
Look up a-height;[11] the shrill-gorg'd[12] lark so far
Cannot be seen or heard. Do but look up.
Glou. Alack, I have no eyes.
Is wretchedness depriv'd that benefit,
To end itself by death? 'Twas yet some comfort,
When misery could beguile the tyrant's rage,
And frustrate his proud will.
Edg. Give me your arm.
Up: so. How is 't? Feel you your legs? You stand.
Glou. Too well, too well.
Edg. This is above all strangeness.
Upon the crown o' the cliff, what thing was that
Which parted from you?
Glou. A poor unfortunate beggar.
Edg. As I stood here below, methought his eyes
Were two full moons; he had a thousand noses,
Horns whelk'd[13] and waved like the enridged sea.
It was some fiend; therefore, thou happy father,
Think that the clearest[14] gods, who make them honours
Of men's impossibilities, have preserv'd thee.
Glou. I do remember now. Henceforth I'll bear
Affliction till it do cry out itself,
"Enough, enough," and die. That thing you speak of,
I took it for a man; often 'twould say,
"The fiend, the fiend!" He led me to that place.
Edg. Bear free and patient thoughts.

Enter LEAR [*fantastically dressed with wild flowers*]

But who comes here?
The safer[15] sense will ne'er accommodate[16]
His master thus.

[10] Boundary. [11] On high. [12] Shrill-throated. [13] Twisted (?).
[14] Most righteous. [15] Saner. [16] Fit out.

Lear. No, they cannot touch me for coining;
I am the King himself.

Edg. O thou side-piercing sight!

Lear. Nature's above art in that respect. There's your press-money. That fellow handles his bow like a crow-keeper; draw me a clothier's yard. Look, look, a mouse! Peace, peace; this piece of toasted cheese will do 't. There's my gauntlet; I'll prove it on a giant. Bring up the brown bills. O, well flown, bird! I' the clout,[17] i' the clout! Hewgh! Give the word.[18]

Edg. Sweet marjoram.

Lear. Pass.

Glou. I know that voice.

Lear. Ha! Goneril, with a white beard! They flatter'd me like a dog, and told me I had the white hairs in my beard ere the black ones were there. To say "ay" and "no" to everything that I said! "Ay" and "no" too was no good divinity. When the rain came to wet me once, and the wind to make me chatter; when the thunder would not peace at my bidding; there I found 'em, there I smelt 'em out. Go to, they are not men o' their words: they told me I was everything; 'tis a lie, I am not ague-proof.

Glou. The trick of that voice I do well remember.
Is 't not the King?

Lear. Ay, every inch a king!
When I do stare, see how the subject quakes.
I pardon that man's life. What was thy cause?[19]
Adultery?
Thou shalt not die. Die for adultery! No:
The wren goes to 't, and the small gilded fly
Does lecher in my sight.
Let copulation thrive; for Gloucester's bastard son
Was kinder to his father than my daughters
Got 'tween the lawful sheets.
To 't, luxury,[20] pell-mell! for I lack soldiers.
Behold yond simp'ring dame,
Whose face between her forks[21] presages snow,
That minces virtue, and does shake the head

[17] Mark. [18] Pass-word. [19] Accusation. [20] Lust. [21] Probably, hair ornaments.

To hear of pleasure's name,—
The fitchew,[22] nor the soiled[23] horse, goes to 't
With a more riotous appetite.
Down from the waist they are Centaurs,
Though women all above;
But to the girdle do the gods inherit,
Beneath is all the fiends';
There's hell, there's darkness, there's the sulphurous pit,
Burning, scalding, stench, consumption; fie, fie, fie! pah, pah!
Give me an ounce of civet; good apothecary, sweeten my imagination.
There's money for thee.

Glou. O, let me kiss that hand!

Lear. Let me wipe it first; it smells of mortality.

Glou. O ruin'd piece of nature! This great world
Shall so wear out to nought. Dost thou know me?

Lear. I remember thine eyes well enough. Dost thou squiny[24] at me? No, do thy worst, blind Cupid; I'll not love. Read thou this challenge; mark but the penning of it.

Glou. Were all thy letters suns, I could not see.

Edg. [*Aside.*] I would not take this from report. It is; and my heart breaks at it.

Lear. Read.

Glou. What, with the case[25] of eyes?

Lear. O, ho, are you there with me? No eyes in your head, nor no money in your purse? Your eyes are in a heavy case, your purse in a light; yet you see how this world goes.

Glou. I see it feelingly.

Lear. What, art mad? A man may see how this world goes with no eyes. Look with thine ears; see how yond justice rails upon yond simple thief. Hark, in thine ear: change places, and, handy-dandy, which is the justice, which is the thief? Thou has seen a farmer's dog bark at a beggar?

Glou. Ay, sir.

Lear. And the creature run from the cur? There thou mightst behold the great image of authority: a dog's obey'd in office.
Thou rascal beadle, hold thy bloody hand!

[22] Pole-cat. [23] Lusty with feeding. [24] Squint. [25] Sockets.

Why dost thou lash that whore? Strip thy own back;
Thou hotly lusts to use her in that kind
For which thou whip'st her. The usurer hangs the cozener.[26]
Through tatter'd clothes great vices do appear;
Robes and furr'd gowns hide all. Plate sins with gold,
And the strong lance of justice hurtless breaks;
Arm it in rags, a pigmy's straw does pierce it.
None does offend, none, I say, none; I'll able[27] 'em.
Take that of me, my friend, who have the power
To seal the accuser's lips. Get thee glass eyes,
And, like a scurvy politician, seem
To see the things thou dost not. Now, now, now, now.
Pull off my boots; harder, harder: so.

Edg. O, matter and impertinency[28] mix'd!
Reason in madness!

Lear. If thou wilt weep my fortunes, take my eyes.
I know thee well enough; thy name is Gloucester.
Thou must be patient; we came crying hither.
Thou know'st, the first time that we smell the air,
We wawl and cry. I will preach to thee; mark.

Glou. Alack, alack the day!

Lear. When we are born, we cry that we are come
To this great stage of fools.—This a good block.[29]
It were a delicate stratagem, to shoe
A troop of horse with felt. I'll put 't in proof;[30]
And when I have stol'n upon these son-in-laws,
Then, kill, kill, kill, kill, kill, kill!

Enter a Gentleman [*with* Attendants]

Gent. O, here he is! Lay hand upon him. Sir,
Your most dear daughter—

Lear. No rescue? What, a prisoner? I am even
The natural fool of fortune. Use me well;
You shall have ransom. Let me have surgeons;
I am cut to the brains.

[26] Swindler. [27] Warrant. [28] Sense and nonsense.
[29] Hat (?). [30] To the test.

Gent. You shall have anything.
Lear. No seconds? All myself?
Why, this would make a man a man of salt,[31]
To use his eyes for garden water-pots,
[Ay, and laying autumn's dust.
Gent. Good sir,—]
Lear. I will die bravely, like a smug[32] bridegroom. What! I will be jovial. Come, come; I am a king,
My masters, know you that?
Gent. You are a royal one, and we obey you.
Lear. Then there's life in 't. Come, an you get it, you shall get it by running. Sa, sa, sa, sa. *Exit* [*running;* Attendants *follow*].
Gent. A sight most pitiful in the meanest wretch,
Past speaking of in a king! Thou hast one daughter
Who redeems Nature from the general curse
Which twain have brought her to.
Edg. Hail, gentle sir.
Gent. Sir, speed you: what's your will?
Edg. Do you hear aught, sir, of a battle toward?
Gent. Most sure and vulgar;[33] every one hears that,
Which can distinguish sound.
Edg. But, by your favour,
How near's the other army?
Gent. Near and on speedy foot; the main descry[34]
Stands on the hourly thought.
Edg. I thank you, sir; that's all.
Gent. Though that the Queen on special cause is here,
Her army is mov'd on. *Exit.*
Edg. I thank you, sir.
Glou. You ever-gentle gods, take my breath from me;
Let not my worser spirit tempt me again
To die before you please!
Edg. Well pray you, father.
Glou. Now, good sir, what are you?
Edg. A most poor man, made tame to fortune's blows;

[31] Tears. [32] Neat, fine. [33] Generally known.
[34] The sight of the main body is hourly expected.

Who, by the art of known and feeling sorrows,
Am pregnant[35] to good pity. Give me your hand,
I'll lead you to some biding.

Glou. Hearty thanks;
The bounty and the benison of Heaven
To boot, and boot!

Enter Steward [OSWALD]

Osw. A proclaim'd prize! Most happy!
That eyeless head of thine was first fram'd flesh
To raise my fortunes. Thou old unhappy traitor,
Briefly thyself remember; the sword is out
That must destroy thee.

Glou. Now let thy friendly hand
Put strength enough to 't. [EDGAR *interposes.*]

Osw. Wherefore, bold peasant,
Dar'st thou support a publish'd[36] traitor? Hence;
Lest that the infection of his fortune take
Like hold on thee. Let go his arm.

Edg. 'Chill[37] not let go, zir, without vurther 'casion.

Osw. Let go, slave, or thou diest!

Edg. Good gentleman, go your gait, and let poor volk pass. An 'chud[38] ha' bin zwagger'd out of my life, 't would not ha' bin zo long as 'tis by a vortnight. Nay, come not near th' old man; keep out, 'che vor ye,[39] or Ise try whether your costard[40] or my ballow[41] be the harder. 'Chill be plain with you.

Osw. Out, dunghill!

Edg. 'Chill pick your teeth, zir. Come, no matter vor your foins.[42]
[*They fight, and* EDGAR *knocks him down.*]

Osw. Slave, thou hast slain me. Villain, take my purse.
If ever thou wilt thrive, bury my body;
And give the letters which thou find'st about me
To Edmund, Earl of Gloucester; seek him out
Upon[43] the English party. O, untimely death!
Death! *Dies.*

[35] Ready. [36] Publicly proclaimed. [37] I will.
[38] If I could. [39] I warn you. [40] Head. [41] Cudgel. [42] Thrusts. [43] Among.

Edg. I know thee well; a serviceable villain,
As duteous to the vices of thy mistress
As badness would desire.

Glou. What, is he dead?

Edg. Sit you down, father; rest you.
Let's see these pockets; the letters that he speaks of
May be my friends. He's dead; I am only sorry
He had no other death's-man. Let us see.
Leave, gentle wax; and, manners, blame us not.
To know our enemies' minds, we rip their hearts;
Their papers, is more lawful.

(*Reads the letter.*) "Let our reciprocal vows be remem'red. You have many opportunities to cut him off; if your will want not, time and place will be fruitfully offer'd. There is nothing done, if he return the conqueror; then am I the prisoner, and his bed my gaol; from the loathed warmth whereof deliver me, and supply the place for your labour.

"Your—wife, so I would say—
"Affectionate servant,
"GONERIL."

O indistinguish'd space[44] of woman's will![45]
A plot upon her virtuous husband's life;
And the exchange my brother! Here, in the sands,
Thee I'll rake up, the post unsanctified
Of murderous lechers; and in the mature time
With this ungracious paper strike the sight
Of the death-practis'd[46] duke. For him 'tis well
That of thy death and business I can tell.

Glou. The King is mad; how stiff is my vile sense
That I stand up and have ingenious[47] feeling
Of my huge sorrows! Better I were distract;
So should my thoughts be sever'd from my griefs,
Drum afar off.
And woes by wrong imaginations lose
The knowledge of themselves.

[44] Unlimited range. [45] Appetites. [46] Whose death was plotted.
[47] Conscious.

Edg. Give me your hand.
Far off, methinks, I hear the beaten drum.
Come, father, I'll bestow[48] you with a friend. *Exeunt.*

SCENE VII. [*A tent in the French camp*]

Enter CORDELIA, KENT, *and* Doctor

Cor. O thou good Kent, how shall I live and work
To match thy goodness? My life will be too short,
And every measure fail me.
Kent. To be acknowledg'd, madam, is o'er-paid.
All my reports go with the modest truth;
Nor more nor clipp'd,[1] but so.
Cor. Be better suited;
These weeds are memories of those worser hours.
I prithee, put them off.
Kent. Pardon, dear madam;
Yet to be known shortens my made intent.[2]
My boon I make it, that you know me not
Till time and I think meet.
Cor. Then be 't so, my good lord. [*To the* Doctor.]
How does the King?
Doct. Madam, sleeps still.
Cor. O you kind gods,
Cure this great breach in his abused nature!
The untun'd and jarring senses, O, wind up
Of this child-changed[3] father!
Doct. So please your Majesty
That we may wake the King? He hath slept long.
Cor. Be govern'd by your knowledge, and proceed
I' the sway of your own will.

Enter LEAR *in a chair carried by* Servants. [Gentleman *in attendance*]

Is he array'd?
Gent. Ay, madam; in the heaviness of sleep
We put fresh garments on him.

[48] Lodge. [1] Shortened. [2] Interferes with the plan I have formed.
[3] Changed by the cruelty of his children.

Doct. Be by, good madam, when we do awake him;
I doubt not of his temperance.[4]
[*Cor.* Very well.
Doct. Please you, draw near.—Louder the music there!]
Cor. O my dear father! Restoration hang
Thy medicine on my lips; and let this kiss
Repair those violent harms that my two sisters
Have in thy reverence made!
Kent. Kind and dear princess!
Cor. Had you not been their father, these white flakes
Did challenge pity of them. Was this a face
To be oppos'd against the warring winds?
[To stand against the deep dread-bolted thunder?
In the most terrible and nimble stroke
Of quick, cross lightning? to watch—poor perdu![5]—
With this thin helm?] Mine enemy's dog,
Though he had bit me, should have stood that night
Against my fire; and wast thou fain, poor father,
To hovel thee with swine and rogues forlorn
In short and musty straw? Alack, alack!
'Tis wonder that thy life and wits at once
Had not concluded all. He wakes; speak to him.
Doct. Madam, do you; 'tis fittest.
Cor. How does my royal lord? How fares your Majesty?
Lear. You do me wrong to take me out o' the grave.
Thou art a soul in bliss; but I am bound
Upon a wheel of fire, that mine own tears
Do scald like molten lead.
Cor. Sir, do you know me?
Lear. You are a spirit, I know; when did you die?
Cor. Still, still, far wide![6]
Doct. He's scarce awake; let him alone a while.
Lear. Where have I been? Where am I? Fair daylight?
I am mightily abus'd. I should even die with pity,
To see another thus. I know not what to say.
I will not swear these are my hands. Let's see;

[4] Sanity. [5] A soldier put on dangerous sentry duty. [6] Delirious.

I feel this pin prick. Would I were assur'd
Of my condition!
Cor. O, look upon me, sir,
And hold your hand in benediction o'er me.
[No, sir,] you must not kneel.
Lear. Pray, do not mock me.
I am a very foolish fond[7] old man,
Fourscore and upward, not an hour more nor less;
And, to deal plainly,
I fear I am not in my perfect mind.
Methinks I should know you, and know this man;
Yet I am doubtful; for I am mainly[8] ignorant
What place this is, and all the skill I have
Remembers not these garments; nor I know not
Where I did lodge last night. Do not laugh at me;
For, as I am a man, I think this lady
To be my child Cordelia.
Cor. And so I am, I am.
Lear. Be your tears wet? Yes, faith. I pray, weep not.
If you have poison for me, I will drink it.
I know you do not love me; for your sisters
Have, as I do remember, done me wrong;
You have some cause, they have not.
Cor. No cause, no cause.
Lear. Am I in France?
Kent. In your own kingdom, sir.
Lear. Do not abuse me.
Doct. Be comforted, good madam; the great rage,[9]
You see, is kill'd in him: [and yet it is danger
To make him even o'er the time he has lost.]
Desire him to go in; trouble him no more
Till further settling.
Cor. Will 't please your Highness walk?
Lear. You must bear with me.
Pray you now, forget and forgive; I am old and foolish.
Exeunt [*all but* KENT *and* Gentleman].

[7] Foolish. [8] Quite. [9] Frenzy.

[*Gent.* Holds it true, sir, that the Duke of Cornwall was so slain?

Kent. Most certain, sir.

Gent. Who is conductor of his people?

Kent. As 'tis said, the bastard son of Gloucester.

Gent. They say Edgar, his banish'd son, is with the Earl of Kent in Germany.

Kent. Report is changeable. 'Tis time to look about; the powers of the kingdom approach apace.

Gent. The arbitrement[10] is like to be bloody.
Fare you well, sir. [*Exit.*]

Kent. My point and period will be throughly wrought,
Or well or ill, as this day's battle's fought.] *Exit.*

ACT V

Scene I. [*The British camp, near Dover*]

Enter, with drum and colours, Edmund, Regan, Gentlemen, and Soldiers

Edm. Know of the Duke if his last purpose hold,
Or whether since he is advis'd[1] by aught
To change the course. He's full of alteration
And self-reproving; bring his constant pleasure.[2]
[*To a* Gentleman, *who goes out.*]

Reg. Our sister's man is certainly miscarried.

Edm. 'Tis to be doubted, madam.

Reg. Now, sweet lord,
You know the goodness I intend upon you.
Tell me—but truly—but then speak the truth,
Do you not love my sister?

Edm. In honour'd love.

Reg. But have you never found my brother's way
To the forfended[3] place?

[*Edm.* That thought abuses you.

Reg. I am doubtful that you have been conjunct
And bosom'd with her,—as far as we call hers.][4]

[10] Decision. [1] Induced. [2] Fixed resolve. [3] Forbidden.
[4] Intimate with her, to the utmost extent.

Edm. No, by mine honour, madam.

Reg. I never shall endure her. Dear my lord,
Be not familiar with her.

Edm. Fear me not.
She and the Duke her husband!

Enter, with drum and colours, ALBANY, GONERIL, *and* Soldiers

[*Gon.* [*Aside.*] I had rather lose the battle than that sister
Should loosen him and me.]

Alb. Our very loving sister, well be-met.
Sir, this I heard: the King is come to his daughter,
With others whom the rigour of our state[5]
Forc'd to cry out. [Where I could not be honest,
I never yet was valiant. For this business,
It toucheth us, as France invades our land,
Not bolds[6] the King, with others, whom, I fear,
Most just and heavy causes make oppose.

Edm. Sir, you speak nobly.]

Reg. Why is this reason'd?[7]

Gon. Combine together 'gainst the enemy;
For these domestic and particular broils
Are not the question here.

Alb. Let's then determine
With the ancient[8] of war on our proceeding.

[*Edm.* I shall attend you presently at your tent.]

Reg. Sister, you'll go with us?

Gon. No.

Reg. 'Tis most convenient; pray you, go with us.

Gon. [*Aside.*] O, ho, I know the riddle.—I will go.

Exeunt both the armies.

[*As they are going out,*] *enter* EDGAR [*disguised.* ALBANY *remains*]

Edg. If e'er your Grace had speech with man so poor,
Hear me one word.

Alb. I'll overtake you.—Speak.

Edg. Before you fight the battle, ope this letter.

[5] Government. [6] Not because it emboldens. [7] Discussed. [8] Veterans.

If you have victory, let the trumpet sound
For him that brought it. Wretched though I seem,
I can produce a champion that will prove
What is avouched[9] there. If you miscarry,
Your business of the world hath so an end,
And machination ceases. Fortune love you!
Alb. Stay till I have read the letter.
Edg. I was forbid it.
When time shall serve, let but the herald cry,
And I'll appear again. *Exit.*
Alb. Why, fare thee well; I will o'erlook[10] thy paper.

Re-enter EDMUND

Edm. The enemy's in view; draw up your powers.
Here is the guess of their true strength and forces
By diligent discovery;[11] but your haste
Is now urg'd on you.
Alb. We will greet the time.[12] *Exit.*
Edm. To both these sisters have I sworn my love;
Each jealous[13] of the other, as the stung
Are of the adder. Which of them shall I take?
Both? one? or neither? Neither can be enjoy'd,
If both remain alive. To take the widow
Exasperates, makes mad her sister Goneril;
And hardly shall I carry out my side,
Her husband being alive. Now then we'll use
His countenance for the battle; which being done,
Let her who would be rid of him devise
His speedy taking off.[14] As for the mercy
Which he intends to Lear and to Cordelia,
The battle done, and they within our power,
Shall never see his pardon; for my state
Stands on me to defend, not to debate.[15] *Exit.*

[9] Asserted. [10] Read. [11] Scouting.
[12] Face the emergency. [13] Suspicious. [14] Murder.
[15] It concerns me to defend my position, not discuss it.

SCENE II. [*A field between the two camps*]

Alarum within. Enter with drum and colours, LEAR, CORDELIA, *and* Soldiers, *over the stage; and exeunt*

Enter EDGAR *and* GLOUCESTER

Edg. Here, father, take the shadow of this tree
For your good host; pray that the right may thrive.
If ever I return to you again,
I'll bring you comfort.
Glou. Grace go with you, sir! *Exit* [EDGAR].

Alarum and retreat within. Re-enter EDGAR

Edg. Away, old man; give me thy hand; away!
King Lear hath lost, he and his daughter ta'en.
Give me thy hand; come on.
Glou. No further, sir; a man may rot even here.
Edg. What, in ill thoughts again? Men must endure
Their going hence, even as their coming hither;
Ripeness is all. Come on.
Glou. And that's true too. *Exeunt.*

SCENE III. [*The British camp near Dover*]

Enter, in conquest, with drum and colours, EDMUND; LEAR *and* CORDELIA *as prisoners:* Captain, Soldiers, *etc.*

Edm. Some officers take them away. Good guard,
Until their greater pleasures first be known
That are to censure[1] them.
Cor. We are not the first
Who, with best meaning, have incurr'd the worst.
For thee, oppressed king, I am cast down;
Myself could else out-frown false Fortune's frown.
Shall we not see these daughters and these sisters?
Lear. No, no, no, no! Come, let's away to prison;
We two alone will sing like birds i' the cage.

[1] Judge.

When thou dost ask me blessing, I'll kneel down
And ask of thee forgiveness. So we'll live,
And pray, and sing, and tell old tales, and laugh
At gilded butterflies, and hear poor rogues
Talk of court news; and we'll talk with them too,
Who loses and who wins; who's in, who's out;
And take upon 's the mystery of things
As if we were God's spies; and we'll wear out,
In a wall'd prison, packs and sects[2] of great ones,
That ebb and flow by the moon.

Edm. Take them away.

Lear. Upon such sacrifices, my Cordelia,
The gods themselves throw incense. Have I caught thee?
He that parts us shall bring a brand from heaven,
And fire us hence like foxes.[3] Wipe thine eyes;
The good-years[4] shall devour them, flesh and fell,
Ere they shall make us weep. We'll see 'em starv'd first.
Come. *Exeunt* [LEAR *and* CORDELIA, *guarded*].

Edm. Come hither, captain; hark.
Take thou this note [*giving a paper*]; go follow them to prison.
One step I have advanc'd thee; if thou dost
As this instructs thee, thou dost make thy way
To noble fortunes. Know thou this, that men
Are as the time is; to be tender-minded
Does not become a sword. Thy great employment
Will not bear question;[5] either say thou'lt do 't,
Or thrive by other means.

Capt. I'll do 't, my lord.

Edm. About it; and write happy[6] when thou hast done.
Mark, I say, instantly; and carry it so
As I have set it down.

[*Capt.* I cannot draw a cart, nor eat dried oats;
If it be man's work, I'll do 't.] *Exit.*

[2] Factions and parties.
[3] As foxes are driven from their holes, by lighting a fire in them.
[4] Devils, plagues. [5] Discussion. [6] Consider your prosperity assured.

Flourish. Enter ALBANY, GONERIL, REGAN, [*another* Captain] *and* Soldiers

Alb. Sir, you have show'd to-day your valiant strain,[7]
And fortune led you well. You have the captives
Who were the opposites[8] of this day's strife;
I do require them of you, so to use them
As we shall find their merits and our safety
May equally determine.
Edm. Sir, I thought it fit
To send the old and miserable king
To some retention[9] [and appointed guard];
Whose age had charms in it, whose title more,
To pluck the common bosom on his side,
And turn our impress'd lances in our eyes
Which do command them. With him I sent the Queen,
My reason all the same; and they are ready
To-morrow, or at further space, to appear
Where you shall hold your session. [At this time
We sweat and bleed: the friend hath lost his friend;
And the best quarrels, in the heat, are curs'd
By those that feel their sharpness:
The question of Cordelia and her father
Requires a fitter place.]
Alb. Sir, by your patience,
I hold you but a subject of this war,
Not as a brother.
Reg. That's as we list to grace him.
Methinks our pleasure might have been demanded,
Ere you had spoke so far. He led our powers,
Bore the commission of my place and person;
The which immediacy[10] may well stand up,
And call itself your brother.
Gon. Not so hot.
In his own grace he doth exalt himself,
More than in your addition.[11]

[7] Stock. [8] Opponents. [9] Confinement. [10] Close connection. [11] Praises.

Reg. In my rights,
By me invested, he compeers[12] the best.
Gon. That were the most, if he should husband you.
Reg. Jesters do oft prove prophets.
Gon. Holla, holla!
That eye that told you so look'd but a-squint.
Reg. Lady, I am not well; else I should answer
From a full-flowing stomach.[13] General,
Take thou my soldiers, prisoners, patrimony;
Dispose of them, of me; the walls are thine.
Witness the world, that I create thee here
My lord and master.
Gon. Mean you to enjoy him?
Alb. The let-alone[14] lies not in your good will.
Edm. Nor in thine, lord.
Alb. Half-blooded fellow, yes.
Reg. [*To* EDMUND.] Let the drum strike, and prove my title thine.
Alb. Stay yet; hear reason. Edmund, I arrest thee
On capital treason; and, in thy arrest,
This gilded serpent. [*Pointing to* GON.] For your claim, fair sister,
I bar it in the interest of my wife.
'Tis she is sub-contracted to this lord,
And I, her husband, contradict your bans.
If you will marry, make your loves to me,
My lady is bespoke.
Gon. An interlude[15]!
Alb. Thou art armed, Gloucester; let the trumpet sound.
If none appear to prove upon thy person
Thy heinous, manifest, and many treasons,
There is my pledge [*throwing down a glove*]. I'll prove it on thy heart,
Ere I taste bread, thou art in nothing less
Than I have here proclaim'd thee.
Reg. Sick, O sick!
Gon. [*Aside.*] If not, I'll ne'er trust medicine.

[12] Equals. [13] Passionate language. [14] Usually interpreted, hindering. [15] Play.

Edm. There's my exchange [*throwing down a glove*].
What in the world he is
That names me traitor, villain-like he lies.
Call by the trumpet;—he that dares approach,
On him, on you, who not? I will maintain
My truth and honour firmly.
Alb. A herald, ho!
[*Edm.* A herald, ho, a herald!]
Alb. Trust to thy single virtue;[16] for thy soldiers,
All levied in my name, have in my name
Took their discharge.
Reg. My sickness grows upon me.
Alb. She is not well; convey her to my tent. [*Exit* REGAN, *led.*]

Enter a Herald

Come hither, herald,—Let the trumpet sound—
And read out this.
[*Capt.* Sound, trumpet!] *A trumpet sounds.*

Her. (*Reads.*) "If any man of quality or decree within the lists of the army will maintain upon Edmund, supposed Earl of Gloucester, that he is a manifold traitor, let him appear by the third sound of the trumpet. He is bold in his defence."

[*Edm.* Sound!] *First trumpet.*
Her. Again! *Second trumpet.*
Her. Again! *Third trumpet.*
Trumpet answers within.

Enter EDGAR, *at the third sound, armed, with a trumpet*[17] *before him.*

Alb. Ask him his purposes, why he appears
Upon this call o' the trumpet.
Her. What are you?
Your name, your quality? and why you answer
This present summons?
Edg. Know, my name is lost,
By treason's tooth bare-gnawn and canker-bit;[18]

[16] Your unaided strength. [17] Trumpeter. [18] Worm-eaten.

Yet am I noble as the adversary
I come to cope.[19]
Alb. Which is that adversary?
Edg. What's he that speaks for Edmund Earl of Gloucester?
Edm. Himself; what say'st thou to him?
Edg. Draw thy sword,
That, if my speech offend a noble heart,
Thy arm may do thee justice; here is mine.
Behold, it is the privilege of mine honours,
My oath, and my profession. I protest,
Maugre[20] thy strength, place, youth, and eminence,
Despite thy victor-sword and fire-hewn[21] fortune,
Thy valour, and thy heart,[22] thou art a traitor;
False to thy gods, thy brother, and thy father;
Conspirant 'gainst this high illustrious prince;
And, from the extremest upward of thy head
To the descent[23] and dust below thy foot,
A most toad-spotted traitor. Say thou "No,"
This sword, this arm, and my best spirits are bent
To prove upon thy heart, whereto I speak,
Thou liest.
Edm. In wisdom I should ask thy name;
But, since thy outside looks so fair and warlike,
And that thy tongue some 'say[24] of breeding breathes,
What safe and nicely I might well delay,
By rule of knighthood, I disdain and spurn.
Back do I toss these treasons to thy head;
With the hell-hated lie o'erwhelm thy heart;
Which, for they yet glance by and scarcely bruise,
This sword of mine shall give them instant way,
Where they shall rest for ever. Trumpets, speak!
Alarums. They fight. [EDMUND *falls.*]
Alb. Save him, save him!
Gon. This is [mere] practice,[25] Gloucester.
By the law of war thou wast not bound to answer

[19] Encounter. [20] In spite of. [21] Brand-new. [22] Courage. [23] Lowest part.
[24] Taste. [25] Treachery.

An unknown opposite.[26] Thou art not vanquish'd,
But cozen'd[27] and beguil'd.

Alb. Shut your mouth, dame,
Or with this paper shall I stop it. Hold, sir.—
Thou worse than any name, read thine own evil.
No tearing, lady; I perceive you know it.

Gon. Say, if I do, the laws are mine, not thine.
Who can arraign me for 't? [*Exit.*]

Alb. Most monstrous! oh!—
Know'st thou this paper?

Edm. Ask me not what I know.

Alb. Go after her; she's desperate; govern her.

Edm. What you have charg'd me with, that have I done;
And more, much more; the time will bring it out.
'Tis past, and so am I. But what art thou
That hast this fortune on me? If thou 'rt noble,
I do forgive thee.

Edg. Let's exchange charity.
I am no less in blood than thou art, Edmund;
If more, the more thou 'st wrong'd me.
My name is Edgar, and thy father's son.
The gods are just, and of our pleasant vices
Make instruments to plague us.
The dark and vicious place where thee he got
Cost him his eyes.

Edm. Thou 'st spoken right, 'tis true.
The wheel is come full circle; I am here.

Alb. Methought thy very gait did prophesy
A royal nobleness. I must embrace thee.
Let sorrow split my heart, if ever I
Did hate thee or thy father!

Edg. Worthy prince, I know 't.

Alb. Where have you hid yourself?
How have you known the miseries of your father?

Edg. By nursing them, my lord. List a brief tale;
And when 'tis told, oh, that my heart would burst!

[26] Opponent. [27] Cheated.

The bloody proclamation to escape,
That follow'd me so near,—oh, our lives' sweetness!
That we the pain of death would hourly die
Rather than die at once!—taught me to shift
Into a madman's rags, to assume a semblance
That very dogs disdain'd; and in this habit
Met I my father with his bleeding rings,
Their precious stones new lost; became his guide,
Led him, begg'd for him, sav'd him from despair;
Never,—O fault!—reveal'd myself unto him,
Until some half-hour past, when I was arm'd.
Not sure, though hoping, of this good success,
I ask'd his blessing, and from first to last
Told him our pilgrimage; but his flaw'd[28]-heart,
Alack, too weak the conflict to support!
'Twixt two extremes of passion, joy and grief,
Burst smilingly.

Edm. This speech of yours hath mov'd me,
And shall perchance do good. But speak you on;
You look as you had something more to say.

Alb. If there be more, more woeful, hold it in;
For I am almost ready to dissolve,[29]
Hearing of this.

[*Edg.* This would have seem'd a period
To such as love not sorrow; but another,
To amplify too much, would make much more,
And top extremity.[30]
Whilst I was big[31] in clamour came there in a man,
Who, having seen me in my worst estate,
Shunn'd my abhorr'd society; but then, finding
Who 'twas that so endur'd, with his strong arms
He fastened on my neck, and bellowed out
As he'd burst heaven; threw him on my father;
Told the most piteous tale of Lear and him
That ever ear received; which in recounting,
His grief grew puissant, and the strings of life

[28] Cracked. [29] Melt in tears. [30] Surpass everything. [31] Loud.

Began to crack. Twice then the trumpets sounded,
And there I left him tranc'd.
Alb. But who was this?
Edg. Kent, sir, the banish'd Kent; who in disguise
Follow'd his enemy king, and did him service
Improper for a slave.]

Enter a Gentleman *with a bloody knife*

Gent. Help, help, O, help?
Edg. What kind of help?
Alb. Speak, man.
Edg. What means this bloody knife?
Gent. 'Tis hot, it smokes;
It came even from the heart of—O, she's dead!
Alb. Who dead? Speak, man.
Gent. Your lady, sir, your lady; and her sister
By her is poison'd; she confesses it.
Edm. I was contracted to them both. All three
Now marry in an instant.
Edg. Here comes Kent.

Enter KENT

Alb. Produce the bodies, be they alive or dead.
This judgement of the heavens, that makes us tremble,
Touches us not with pity. [*Exit* Gentleman.]
—O, is this he?
The time will not allow the compliment
Which very manners urges.
Kent. I am come
To bid my king and master aye good-night.
Is he not here?
Alb. Great thing of us forgot!
Speak, Edmund, where's the King? and where's Cordelia?
The bodies of GONERIL *and* REGAN *are brought in.*
See'st thou this object,[32] Kent?
Kent. Alack, why thus?

[32] Sight.

Edm. Yet Edmund was belov'd!
The one the other poison'd for my sake,
And after slew herself.

Alb. Even so. Cover their faces.

Edm. I pant for life. Some good I mean to do,
Despite of mine own nature. Quickly send,
Be brief in it, to the castle; for my writ
Is on the life of Lear and on Cordelia.
Nay, send in time.

Alb. Run, run, O, run!

Edg. To who, my lord? Who has the office? Send
Thy token of reprieve.

Edm. Well thought on. Take my sword,
Give it the captain.

Edg. Haste thee, for thy life. [*Exit* Gentleman.]

Edm. He hath commission from thy wife and me
To hang Cordelia in the prison, and
To lay the blame upon her own despair,
That she forbid[33] herself.

Alb. The gods defend her! Bear him hence a while.

[EDMUND *is borne off.*]

Re-enter LEAR *with* CORDELIA *in his arms;* [Gentleman *following*]

Lear. Howl, howl, howl! O, you are men of stones!
Had I your tongues and eyes, I'd use them so
That heaven's vault should crack. She's gone for ever!
I know when one is dead, and when one lives;
She's dead as earth. Lend me a looking-glass;
If that her breath will mist or stain the stone,
Why, then she lives.

Kent. Is this the promis'd end?

Edg. Or image of that horror?[34]

Alb. Fall, and cease!

Lear. This feather stirs; she lives! If it be so,
It is a chance which does redeem all sorrows

[33]Destroyed.

[34]"Is this the state of things foretold as the end of the world? *Edg.* Or only something resembling that fearful day?"—This is the usual interpretation.

That ever I have felt.
Kent. [*Kneeling.*] O my good master!
Lear. Prithee, away.
Edg. 'Tis noble Kent, your friend.
Lear. A plague upon you, murderers, traitors all!
I might have sav'd her; now she's gone for ever!
Cordelia, Cordelia! stay a little. Ha!
What is 't thou say'st? Her voice was ever soft,
Gentle, and low; an excellent thing in woman.
I kill'd the slave that was a-hanging thee.
Gent. 'Tis true, my lords, he did.
Lear. Did I not, fellow?
I have seen the day, with my good biting falchion
I would have made him skip. I am old now,
And these same crosses spoil me. Who are you?
Mine eyes are not o' the best. I'll tell you straight.
Kent. If Fortune brag of two she lov'd and hated,
One of them we behold.
Lear. This is a dull sight. Are you not Kent?
Kent. The same,
Your servant Kent. Where is your servant Caius?
Lear. He's a good fellow, I can tell you that;
He'll strike, and quickly too. He's dead and rotten.
Kent. No, my good lord; I am the very man,—
Lear. I'll see that straight.
Kent. That, from your first of difference and decay,
Have follow'd your sad steps.
Lear. You are welcome hither.
Kent. Nor no man else; all's cheerless, dark, and deadly.
Your eldest daughters have fordone themselves,
And desperately are dead.
Lear. Ay, so I think.
Alb. He knows not what he says; and vain is it
That we present us to him.

Enter a Messenger

Edg. Very bootless.
Mess. Edmund is dead, my lord.

Alb. That's but a trifle here.
You lords and noble friends, know our intent.
What comfort to this great decay[35] may come
Shall be appli'd. For us, we will resign,
During the life of this old majesty,
To him our absolute power; [*to* EDGAR *and* KENT] you, to your rights,
With boot,[36] and such addition as your honours
Have more than merited. All friends shall taste
The wages of their virtue, and all foes
The cup of their deservings. O, see, see!
Lear. And my poor fool is hang'd! No, no, no life!
Why should a dog, a horse, a rat, have life,
And thou no breath at all? Thou'lt come no more,
Never, never, never, never, never!
Pray you, undo this button. Thank you, sir.
Do you see this? Look on her, look, her lips,
Look there, look there! *Dies.*
Edg. He faints! My lord, my lord!
Kent. Break, heart; I prithee, break!
Edg. Look up, my lord.
Kent. Vex not his ghost; O, let him pass! He hates him
That would upon the rack of this tough world
Stretch him out longer.
Edg. He is gone, indeed.
Kent. The wonder is he hath endur'd so long;
He but usurp'd his life.
Alb. Bear them from hence. Our present business
Is general woe. [*To* KENT *and* EDGAR.] Friends of my soul, you twain
Rule in this realm, and the gor'd[37] state sustain.
Kent. I have a journey, sir, shortly to go.
My master calls me; I must not say no.
Edg. The weight of this sad time we must obey;
Speak what we feel, not what we ought to say.
The oldest hath borne most; we that are young
Shall never see so much, nor live so long.
Exeunt, with a dead march.

[35] General disaster (?). Lear (?). [36] Something thrown in to the bargain.
[37] Wounded.

THE TRAGEDY OF MACBETH

BY
WILLIAM SHAKESPEARE

INTRODUCTORY NOTE

Among the tragedies of Shakespeare, "Macbeth" is noted for the exceptional simplicity of the plot and the directness of the action. Here is no underplot to complicate or enrich, hardly more than a glimpse of humor to relieve the dark picture of criminal ambition, only the steady march toward an inevitable catastrophe.

The story belongs to the half-legendary history of Scotland, and was drawn by Shakespeare from the "Chronicles of Holinshed." For the most part, he follows the historian with considerable fidelity, but details such as the drugging of the grooms by Lady Macbeth, the portents described in the fourth scene of the second act, and the voice that called, "Sleep no more!" were suggested by other parts of the "Chronicle" than that dealing with the reigns of Duncan and Macbeth.

Even the witches occur in Holinshed, who says: "The common opinion was that these women were either the weird sisters, that is (as ye would say) the goddesses of destiny, or else some nymphs or fairies, indued with knowledge of prophecy by their necromantical science." While keeping this aspect of these figures as Fates, Shakespeare added details from the witch lore of his time, and made them capable of a symbolical and spiritual signification that brought them into vital relation with the change in the character of Macbeth.

This tragedy illustrates in its close the conventional poetic justice that demands the triumph of the righteous cause and the downfall of the wicked. But there is not lacking that more subtle justice, so impressive in "Lear" because unaccompanied by the temporal reward of the good, which reveals itself in the subduing of character to what it works in. Far more terrible than the defeat and death of Macbeth is the picture of the degradation of his nature, when he appears in the scene before the battle like a beast at bay.

THE TRAGEDY OF MACBETH

[DRAMATIS PERSONÆ

DUNCAN, King of Scotland.
MALCOLM, DONALBAIN, } his sons.
MACBETH, BANQUO, } generals of the King's army.
MACDUFF, LENNOX, ROSS, MENTEITH, ANGUS, CAITHNESS, } noblemen of Scotland.
FLEANCE, son to Banquo.
SIWARD, earl of Northumberland.
Young SIWARD, his son.
SEYTON, an officer attending on Macbeth.

Boy, son to Macduff.
An English Doctor.
A Scotch Doctor.
A Captain.
A Porter.
An Old Man.

LADY MACBETH.
LADY MACDUFF.
Gentlewoman attending on Lady Macbeth.

HECATE.
Three Witches.
Apparitions.

Lords, Gentlemen, Officers, Soldiers, Murderers, Attendants, and Messengers

SCENE: SCOTLAND; ENGLAND]

ACT I

SCENE I. [*A heath*]

Thunder and lightning. Enter three Witches

1. *Witch*

WHEN shall we three meet again
In thunder, lightning, or in rain?
2. *Witch.* When the hurlyburly's done,
When the battle's lost and won.
3. *Witch.* That will be ere the set of sun.
1. *Witch.* Where the place?
2. *Witch.* Upon the heath.
3. *Witch.* There to meet with Macbeth.
1. *Witch.* I come, Graymalkin![1]
[2. *Witch.*] Paddock[2] calls:—Anon!

[1] Cat. [2] Toad. These are the names of the witches' familiars, devils in the form of animals.

All. Fair is foul, and foul is fair;
Hover through the fog and filthy air. *Exeunt.*

SCENE II. [*A camp near Forres*]

Alarum within. Enter DUNCAN, MALCOLM, DONALBAIN, LENNOX, *with* Attendants, *meeting a bleeding* Captain

Dun. What bloody man is that? He can report,
As seemeth by his plight, of the revolt
The newest state.
Mal. This is the sergeant
Who like a good and hardy soldier fought
'Gainst my captivity. Hail, brave friend!
Say to the King the knowledge of the broil
As thou didst leave it.
Cap. Doubtful it stood,
As two spent swimmers that do cling together
And choke their art. The merciless Macdonwald—
Worthy to be a rebel, for to that[1]
The multiplying villainies of nature
Do swarm upon him—from the Western Isles
Of kerns[2] and gallowglasses[3] is suppli'd;
And Fortune, on his damned quarrel smiling,
Show'd like a rebel's whore.[4] But all's too weak;
For brave Macbeth—well he deserves that name—
Disdaining Fortune, with his brandish'd steel,
Which smok'd with bloody execution,
Like Valour's minion[5] carv'd out his passage
Till he fac'd the slave;
Which[6] ne'er shook hands, nor bade farewell to him,
Till he unseam'd him from the nave to the chaps,[7]
And fix'd his head upon our battlements.
Dun. O valiant cousin! worthy gentleman!
Cap. As whence the sun gins his reflection
Shipwrecking storms and direful thunders break,

[1] To that end. [2] Light-armed foot-soldiers. [3] Heavy-armed foot-soldiers.
[4] *I. e.*, fickle. [5] Favorite. [6] *I. e.*, Macbeth.
[7] Ripped him up from navel to jaws.

So from that spring[8] whence comfort seem'd to come
Discomfort swells. Mark, King of Scotland, mark!
No sooner justice had, with valour arm'd,
Compell'd these skipping kerns to trust their heels,
But the Norweyan lord, surveying vantage,[9]
With furbish'd arms and new supplies of men
Began a fresh assault.

Dun. Dismay'd not this
Our captains, Macbeth and Banquo?

Cap. Yes;
As sparrows eagles, or the hare the lion.
If I say sooth, I must report they were
As cannons overcharg'd with double cracks; so they
Doubly redoubled strokes upon the foe.
Except they meant to bathe in reeking wounds,
Or memorize another Golgotha,[10]
I cannot tell.
But I am faint, my gashes cry for help.

Dun. So well thy words become thee as thy wounds;
They smack of honour both. Go get him surgeons.

[*Exit* Captain, *attended.*]

Enter Ross *and* Angus

Who comes here?

Mal. The worthy thane of Ross.

Len. What a haste looks through his eyes! So should he look
That seems to speak things strange.

Ross. God save the King!

Dun. Whence cam'st thou, worthy thane?

Ross. From Fife, great king;
Where the Norweyan banners flout the sky
And fan our people cold. Norway himself,
With terrible numbers,
Assisted by that most disloyal traitor,
The thane of Cawdor, began a dismal conflict;
Till that Bellona's[11] bridegroom, lapp'd in proof,[12]

[8] Source. [9] Noticing a favorable opportunity. [10] Make a scene of slaughter as memorable as Calvary. [11] The goddess of war. [12] Clothed in tested armor.

Confronted him with self-comparisons,[13]
Point against point, rebellious arm 'gainst arm,
Curbing his lavish[14] spirit; and, to conclude,
The victory fell on us;—
Dun. Great happiness!
Ross. That now
Sweno, the Norways' king, craves composition;[15]
Nor would we deign him burial of his men
Till he disbursed at Saint Colme's inch[16]
Ten thousand dollars to our general use.
Dun. No more that thane of Cawdor shall deceive
Our bosom interest.[17] Go pronounce his present death,
And with his former title greet Macbeth.
Ross. I'll see it done.
Dun. What he hath lost, noble Macbeth hath won. *Exeunt.*

SCENE III. [*A heath near Forres*]

Thunder. Enter the three Witches

1. *Witch.* Where hast thou been, sister?
2. *Witch.* Killing swine.
3. *Witch.* Sister, where thou?
1. *Witch.* A sailor's wife had chestnuts in her lap,
And munch'd, and munch'd, and munch'd. "Give me!" quoth I.
"Aroint thee, witch!" the rump-fed ronyon[1] cries.
Her husband's to Aleppo gone, master o' the Tiger;
But in a sieve I'll thither sail,
And, like a rat without a tail,
I'll do, I'll do, and I'll do.
2. *Witch.* I'll give thee a wind.
1. *Witch.* Thou'rt kind.
3. *Witch.* And I another.
1. *Witch.* I myself have all the other,
And the very ports they blow,
All the quarters that they know

[13] Opposed him with a strength equal to his own. [14] Insolent.
[15] Terms of peace. [16] Island. [17] Intimate affection.
[1] A contemptuous term for a woman.

I' the shipman's card.[2]
I'll drain him dry as hay.
Sleep shall neither night nor day
Hang upon his pent-house[3] lid;
He shall live a man forbid.[4]
Weary sevennights nine times nine
Shall he dwindle, peak, and pine.
Though his bark cannot be lost,
Yet it shall be tempest-tost.
Look what I have.

2. *Witch.* Show me, show me.

1. *Witch.* Here I have a pilot's thumb,
Wreck'd as homeward he did come. *Drum within.*

3. *Witch.* A drum, a drum!
Macbeth doth come.

All. The weird sisters, hand in hand,
Posters of the sea and land,
Thus do go about, about;
Thrice to thine, and thrice to mine,
And thrice again, to make up nine.
Peace! the charm's wound up.

Enter MACBETH *and* BANQUO

Macb. So foul and fair a day I have not seen.

Ban. How far is 't call'd to Forres? What are these
So wither'd and so wild in their attire,
That look not like the inhabitants o' the earth,
And yet are on 't? Live you? or are you aught
That man may question? You seem to understand me,
By each at once her choppy finger laying
Upon her skinny lips. You should be women,
And yet your beards forbid me to interpret
That you are so.

Macb. Speak, if you can. What are you?

1. *Witch.* All hail, Macbeth! hail to thee, thane of Glamis!

2. *Witch.* All hail, Macbeth! hail to thee, thane of Cawdor!

[2] Chart, or dial of the compass. [3] Like a lean-to. [4] Accursed.

3. *Witch.* All hail, Macbeth, that shalt be King hereafter!
Ban. Good sir, why do you start, and seem to fear
Things that do sound so fair? [*To the* Witches.] I' the name of truth,
Are ye fantastical,[5] or that indeed
Which outwardly ye show?[6] My noble partner
You greet with present grace and great prediction
Of noble having[7] and of royal hope,
That he seems rapt withal; to me you speak not.
If you can look into the seeds of time,
And say which grain will grow and which will not,
Speak then to me, who neither beg nor fear
Your favours nor your hate.
1. *Witch.* Hail!
2. *Witch.* Hail!
3. *Witch.* Hail!
1. *Witch.* Lesser than Macbeth, and greater.
2. *Witch.* Not so happy, yet much happier.
3. *Witch.* Thou shalt get kings, though thou be none;
So all hail, Macbeth and Banquo!
1. *Witch.* Banquo and Macbeth, all hail!
Macb. Stay, you imperfect speakers, tell me more.
By Sinel's death I know I am thane of Glamis;
But how of Cawdor? The thane of Cawdor lives,
A prosperous gentleman; and to be king
Stands not within the prospect of belief
No more than to be Cawdor. Say from whence
You owe this strange intelligence, or why
Upon this blasted heath you stop our way
With such prophetic greeting. Speak, I charge you.
Witches *vanish.*
Ban. The earth hath bubbles, as the water has,
And these are of them. Whither are they vanish'd?
Macb. Into the air; and what seem'd corporal melted
As breath into the wind. Would they had stay'd!
Ban. Were such things here as we do speak about,

[5] Imaginary. [6] Seem. [7] Present possession.

Or have we eaten on the insane root
That takes the reason prisoner?
Macb. Your children shall be kings.
Ban. You shall be King.
Macb. And thane of Cawdor too; went it not so?
Ban. To the self-same tune and words. Who's here?

Enter Ross *and* Angus

Ross. The King hath happily receiv'd, Macbeth,
The news of thy success; and when he reads
Thy personal venture in the rebels' fight,
His wonders and his praises do contend
Which should be thine or his. Silenc'd with that,
In viewing o'er the rest o' the self-same day,
He finds thee in the stout Norweyan ranks,
Nothing afeard of what thyself didst make,
Strange images of death. As thick as hail
Came post with post; and every one did bear
Thy praises in his kingdom's great defence,
And pour'd them down before him.
Ang. We are sent
To give thee from our royal master thanks;
Only to herald thee into his sight,
Not pay thee.
Ross. And, for an earnest[8] of a greater honour,
He bade me, from him, call thee thane of Cawdor;
In which addition,[9] hail, most worthy thane!
For it is thine.
Ban. [*Aside.*] What, can the devil speak true?
Macb. The thane of Cawdor lives; why do you dress me
In borrowed robes?
Ang. Who was the thane lives yet;
But under heavy judgement bears that life
Which he deserves to lose. Whether he was combin'd
With those of Norway, or did line[10] the rebel

[8] Instalment in advance.
[9] Title. [10] Strengthen.

With hidden help and vantage, or that with both
He labour'd in his country's wreck, I know not;
But treasons capital, confess'd and prov'd,
Have overthrown him.

Macb. [*Aside.*] Glamis, and thane of Cawdor!
The greatest is behind. [*To* Ross *and* Angus.] Thanks for your pains.
[*To* Ban.] Do you not hope your children shall be kings,
When those that gave the thane of Cawdor to me
Promis'd no less to them?

Ban. That trusted home[11]
Might yet enkindle you unto the crown,
Besides the thane of Cawdor. But 'tis strange;
And oftentimes, to win us to our harm,
The instruments of darkness tell us truths,
Win us with honest trifles, to betray 's
In deepest consequence.
Cousins, a word, I pray you.

Macb. [*Aside.*] Two truths are told,
As happy prologues to the swelling act
Of the imperial theme.[12]—I thank you, gentlemen.
[*Aside.*] This supernatural soliciting
Cannot be ill, cannot be good. If ill,
Why hath it given me earnest of success,
Commencing in a truth? I'm thane of Cawdor.
If good, why do I yield to that suggestion[13]
Whose horrid image doth unfix my hair
And make my seated heart knock at my ribs,
Against the use[14] of nature? Present fears
Are less than horrible imaginings.
My thought, whose murder yet is but fantastical,[15]
Shakes so my single state of man[16] that function[17]
Is smother'd in surmise,[18] and nothing is
But what is not.

Ban. Look, how our partner's rapt.

[11] Thoroughly. [12] Drama of kingship. [13] Temptation. [14] Custom. [15] In my imagination. [16] Weak human condition. [17] Power of action. [18] Speculation.

Macb. [*Aside.*] If chance will have me King, why, chance may crown me,
Without my stir.
Ban. New honours come upon him,
Like our strange garments, cleave not to their mould
But with the aid of use.
Macb. [*Aside.*] Come what come may,
Time and the hour runs through the roughest day.[19]
Ban. Worthy Macbeth, we stay upon your leisure.
Macb. Give me your favour;[20] my dull brain was wrought[21]
With things forgotten. Kind gentlemen, your pains
Are regist'red where every day I turn
The leaf to read them. Let us toward the King.
[*To* BAN.] Think upon what hath chanc'd, and, at more time,
The interim having weigh'd it, let us speak
Our free[22] hearts each to other.
Ban. Very gladly.
Macb. Till then, enough. Come, friends. *Exeunt.*

SCENE IV. [*Forres. The palace*]

Flourish. Enter DUNCAN, MALCOLM, DONALBAIN, LENNOX, *and* Attendants

Dun. Is execution done on Cawdor? Are not
Those in commission[1] yet return'd?
Mal. My liege,
They are not yet come back. But I have spoke
With one that saw him die; who did report
That very frankly he confess'd his treasons,
Implor'd your Highness' pardon, and set forth
A deep repentance. Nothing in his life
Became him like the leaving it. He died
As one that had been studied in his death
To throw away the dearest thing he ow'd,
As 'twere a careless trifle.

[19] The thing appointed arrives whatever obstacles seem to lie between.
[20] Pardon. [21] Perplexed. [22] Frank.
[1] Commissioned to carry it out.

Dun. There's no art
To find the mind's construction in the face.
He was a gentleman on whom I built
An absolute trust.

Enter MACBETH, BANQUO, ROSS, *and* ANGUS

O worthiest cousin!
The sin of my ingratitude even now
Was heavy on me. Thou art so far before
That swiftest wing of recompense is slow
To overtake thee. Would thou hadst less deserv'd,
That the proportion both of thanks and payment
Might have been mine! Only I have left to say,
More is thy due than more than all can pay.
Macb. The service and the loyalty I owe,
In doing it, pays itself. Your Highness' part
Is to receive our duties; and our duties
Are to your throne and state children and servants,
Which do but what they should, by doing everything
Safe toward[2] your love and honour.
Dun. Welcome hither!
I have begun to plant thee, and will labour
To make thee full of growing. Noble Banquo,
That hast no less deserv'd, nor must be known
No less to have done so, let me infold thee
And hold thee to my heart.
Ban. There if I grow,
The harvest is your own.
Dun. My plenteous joys,
Wanton[3] in fulness, seek to hide themselves
In drops of sorrow. Sons, kinsmen, thanes,
And you whose places are the nearest, know
We will establish our estate upon
Our eldest, Malcolm, whom we name hereafter
The Prince of Cumberland; which honour must
Not unaccompanied invest him only,

[2] So as to preserve. [3] Unrestrained.

But signs of nobleness, like stars, shall shine
On all deservers. From hence to Inverness,
And bind us further to you.

Macb. The rest is labour, which is not us'd for you.
I'll be myself the harbinger[4] and make joyful
The hearing of my wife with your approach;
So humbly take my leave.

Dun. My worthy Cawdor!

Macb. [*Aside.*] The Prince of Cumberland! That is a step
On which I must fall down, or else o'erleap,
For in my way it lies. Stars, hide your fires;
Let not light see my black and deep desires;
The eye wink[5] at the hand; yet let that be
Which the eye fears, when it is done, to see. *Exit.*

Dun. True, worthy Banquo; he is full so valiant,
And in his commendations I am fed;
It is a banquet to me. Let's after him,
Whose care is gone before to bid us welcome.
It is a peerless kinsman. *Flourish. Exeunt.*

SCENE V. [*Inverness. Macbeth's castle*]

Enter LADY MACBETH, *alone, with a letter*

Lady M. [*Reads.*] "They met me in the day of success; and I have learn'd by the perfect'st report, they have more in them than mortal knowledge. When I burn'd in desire to question them further, they made themselves air, into which they vanish'd. Whiles I stood rapt in the wonder of it, came missives from the King, who all-hail'd me 'Thane of Cawdor;' by which title, before, these weird sisters[1] saluted me, and referr'd me to the coming on of time, with 'Hail, King that shalt be!' This have I thought good to deliver thee, my dearest partner of greatness, that thou mightst not lose the dues of rejoicing, by being ignorant of what greatness is promis'd thee. Lay it to thy heart, and farewell."

Glamis thou art, and Cawdor; and shalt be
What thou art promis'd. Yet do I fear thy nature;

[4] Forerunner. [5] Refuse to see. [1] The three Fates.

It is too full o' the milk of human kindness
To catch the nearest way. Thou wouldst be great,
Art not without ambition, but without
The illness[2] should attend it. What thou wouldst highly,
That wouldst thou holily; wouldst not play false,
And yet wouldst wrongly win. Thou 'dst have, great Glamis,
That which cries, "Thus thou must do, if thou have it;"
And that which rather thou dost fear to do
Than wishest should be undone. Hie thee hither
That I may pour my spirits in thine ear,
And chastise with the valour of my tongue
All that impedes thee from the golden round[3]
Which fate and metaphysical[4] aid doth seem
To have thee crown'd withal.

Enter a Messenger

What is your tidings?

Mess. The King comes here to-night.

Lady M. Thou 'rt mad to say it!
Is not thy master with him? who, were 't so,
Would have inform'd for preparation.

Mess. So please you, it is true; our thane is coming.
One of my fellows had the speed of him,
Who, almost dead for breath, had scarcely more
Than would make up his message.

Lady M. Give him tending;
He brings great news. *Exit* Messenger.
The raven himself is hoarse
That croaks the fatal entrance of Duncan
Under my battlements. Come, you spirits
That tend on mortal[5] thoughts, unsex me here,
And fill me from the crown to the toe top-full
Of direst cruelty! Make thick my blood;
Stop up the access and passage to remorse,[6]
That no compunctious visitings of nature[7]

[2] Wickedness. [3] Crown. [4] Supernatural. [5] Murderous. [6] Pity.
[7] Natural feelings of compunction.

Shake my fell purpose, nor keep peace between
The effect and it! Come to my woman's breasts
And take[8] my milk for gall, you murd'ring ministers,
Wherever in your sightless[9] substances
You wait on nature's mischief! Come, thick night,
And pall[10] thee in the dunnest smoke of hell,
That my keen knife see not the wound it makes,
Nor heaven peep through the blanket of the dark
To cry, "Hold, hold!"

Enter MACBETH

Great Glamis! worthy Cawdor!
Greater than both, by the all-hail hereafter!
Thy letters have transported me beyond
This ignorant present, and I feel now
The future in the instant.

Macb. My dearest love,
Duncan comes here to-night.

Lady M. And when goes hence?

Macb. To-morrow, as he purposes.

Lady M. O, never
Shall sun that morrow see!
Your face, my thane, is as a book where men
May read strange matters. To beguile the time,[11]
Look like the time; bear welcome in your eye,
Your hand, your tongue; look like the innocent flower,
But be the serpent under 't. He that's coming
Must be provided for; and you shall put
This night's great business into my dispatch,
Which shall to all our nights and days to come
Give solely sovereign sway and masterdom.

Macb. We will speak further.

Lady M. Only look up clear;
To alter favour[12] ever is to fear.
Leave all the rest to me. *Exeunt.*

[8] Change. [9] Invisible. [10] Wrap. [11] Deceive onlookers. [12] Countenance

SCENE VI. [*Before Macbeth's castle*]

Hautboys and torches. Enter DUNCAN, MALCOLM, DONALBAIN, BANQUO, LENNOX, MACDUFF, ROSS, ANGUS, *and* Attendants

Dun. This castle hath a pleasant seat; the air
Nimbly and sweetly recommends itself
Unto our gentle[1] senses.
Ban. This guest of summer,
The temple-haunting martlet,[2] does approve,
By his loved masonry, that the heaven's breath
Smells wooingly here; no jutty,[3] frieze,
Buttress, nor coign[4] of vantage, but this bird
Hath made his pendent bed and procreant cradle.
Where they most breed and haunt, I have observ'd
The air is delicate.

Enter LADY MACBETH

Dun. See, see, our honour'd hostess!
The love that follows us sometime is our trouble,
Which still we thank as love. Herein I teach you
How you shall bid God 'eild[5] us for your pains,
And thank us for your trouble.
Lady M. All our service
In every point twice done and then done double
Were poor and single[6] business to contend
Against those honours deep and broad wherewith
Your Majesty loads our house. For those of old,
And the late dignities heap'd up to them,
We rest your hermits.[7]
Dun. Where's the thane of Cawdor?
We cours'd him at the heels, and had a purpose
To be his purveyor;[8] but he rides well,
And his great love, sharp as his spur, hath holp him
To his home before us. Fair and noble hostess,
We are your guest to-night.

[1] Soothed. [2] Martin. [3] Projection. [4] Corner.
[5] Reward. [6] Weak. [7] *I. e.,* We will pray for you. [8] Forerunner.

Lady M. Your servants ever
Have theirs, themselves, and what is theirs, in compt,[9]
To make their audit at your Highness' pleasure,
Still to return your own.
Dun. Give me your hand;
Conduct me to mine host. We love him highly,
And shall continue our graces towards him.
By your leave, hostess. *Exeunt.*

SCENE VII. [*Corridor in Macbeth's castle*]

Hautboys and torches. Enter a Sewer, *and divers* Servants *with dishes and service, over the stage. Then enter* MACBETH

Macb. If it were done when 'tis done, then 'twere well
It were done quickly. If the assassination
Could trammel[1] up the consequence, and catch
With his surcease[2] success; that but this blow
Might be the be-all and the end-all here,
But here, upon this bank and shoal of time,
We'd jump[3] the life to come. But in these cases
We still[4] have judgement here, that we but teach
Bloody instructions, which, being taught, return
To plague the inventor. This even-handed justice
Commends[5] the ingredients of our poison'd chalice
To our own lips. He's here in double trust:
First, as I am his kinsman and his subject,
Strong both against the deed; then, as his host,
Who should against his murderer shut the door,
Not bear the knife myself. Besides, this Duncan
Hath borne his faculties[6] so meek, hath been
So clear[7] in his great office, that his virtues
Will plead like angels, trumpet-tongu'd, against
The deep damnation of his taking-off;
And pity, like a naked new-born babe

[9] Subject to account. [1] Catch, as in a net.
[2] Cessation of the consequence. [3] Risk. [4] Always. [5] Presents.
[6] Official powers. [7] Blameless.

Striding the blast, or heaven's cherubin hors'd
Upon the sightless couriers of the air,
Shall blow the horrid deed in every eye,
That tears shall drown the wind. I have no spur
To prick the sides of my intent, but only
Vaulting ambition, which o'erleaps itself
And falls on the other—

Enter LADY MACBETH

How now! what news?

Lady M. He has almost supp'd. Why have you left the chamber?

Macb. Hath he ask'd for me?

Lady M. Know you not he has?

Macb. We will proceed no further in this business.
He hath honour'd me of late; and I have bought
Golden opinions from all sorts of people,
Which would be worn now in their newest gloss,
Not cast aside so soon.

Lady M. Was the hope drunk
Wherein you dress'd yourself? Hath it slept since?
And wakes it now, to look so green and pale
At what it did so freely? From this time
Such I account thy love. Art thou afeard
To be the same in thine own act and valour
As thou art in desire? Wouldst thou have that
Which thou esteem'st the ornament of life,
And live a coward in thine own esteem,
Letting "I dare not" wait upon "I would,"
Like the poor cat i' the adage?[8]

Macb. Prithee, peace!
I dare do all that may become a man;
Who dares do more is none.

Lady M. What beast was 't, then,
That made you break this enterprise to me?
When you durst do it, then you were a man;
And, to be more than what you were, you would

[8] The proverb runs: "The cat would eat fish, but she will not wet her feet."

Be so much more the man. Nor time nor place
Did then adhere,[9] and yet you would make both.
They have made themselves, and that their fitness now
Does unmake you. I have given suck, and know
How tender 'tis to love the babe that milks me;
I would, while it was smiling in my face,
Have pluck'd my nipple from his boneless gums
And dash'd the brains out, had I so sworn as you
Have done to this.

Macb. If we should fail?

Lady M. We fail!
But screw your courage to the sticking-place,
And we'll not fail. When Duncan is asleep—
Whereto the rather shall his day's hard journey
Soundly invite him—his two chamberlains
Will I with wine and wassail[10] so convince[11]
That memory, the warder of the brain,
Shall be a fume, and the receipt[12] of reason
A limbeck[13] only. When in swinish sleep
Their drenched[14] natures lie as in a death,
What cannot you and I perform upon
The unguarded Duncan? what not put upon
His spongy officers, who shall bear the guilt
Of our great quell?[15]

Macb. Bring forth men-children only;
For thy undaunted mettle should compose
Nothing but males. Will it not be receiv'd,[16]
When we have mark'd with blood those sleepy two
Of his own chamber, and us'd their very daggers,
That they have done 't?

Lady M. Who dares receive it other,
As we shall make our griefs and clamour roar
Upon his death?

Macb. I am settled, and bend up
Each corporal agent to this terrible feat.

[9] Suit. [10] Carousing. [11] Overcome. [12] Receptacle.
[13] Alembic, still. [14] Drowned. [15] Murder. [16] Believed.

Away, and mock the time with fairest show;
False face must hide what the false heart doth know. *Exeunt.*

ACT II

SCENE I. [*Within Macbeth's castle*]

Enter BANQUO, *and* FLEANCE *with a torch before him*

Ban. How goes the night, boy?
Fle. The moon is down; I have not heard the clock.
Ban. And she goes down at twelve.
Fle. I take 't, 'tis later, sir.
Ban. Hold, take my sword. There's husbandry[1] in heaven;
Their candles are all out. Take thee that too.
A heavy summons lies like lead upon me,
And yet I would not sleep. Merciful powers,
Restrain in me the cursed thoughts that nature
Gives way to in repose!

Enter MACBETH, *and a* Servant *with a torch*

Give me my sword.
Who's there?
Macb. A friend.
Ban. What, sir, not yet at rest? The King's a-bed.
He hath been in unusual pleasure, and
Sent forth great largess to your offices.[2]
This diamond he greets your wife withal,
By the name of most kind hostess; and shut up[3]
In measureless content.
Macb. Being unprepar'd,
Our will became the servant to defect;[4]
Which else should free have wrought.
Ban. All's well.
I dreamt last night of the three weird sisters:
To you they have show'd some truth.

[1] Thrift. [2] Servants' rooms. [3] Concluded. [4] Was forced to act as our limitations compelled it.

Macb. I think not of them;
Yet, when we can entreat an hour to serve,
We would spend it in some words upon that business,
If you would grant the time.

Ban. At your kind'st leisure.

Macb. If you shall cleave to my consent,[5] when 'tis,[6]
It shall make honour for you.

Ban. So I lose none
In seeking to augment it, but still keep
My bosom franchis'd[7] and allegiance clear,
I shall be counsell'd.

Macb. Good repose the while!

Ban. Thanks, sir; the like to you!

Exeunt BANQUO [*and* FLEANCE].

Macb. Go bid thy mistress, when my drink[8] is ready,
She strike upon the bell. Get thee to bed. *Exit* [Servant].
Is this a dagger which I see before me,
The handle toward my hand? Come, let me clutch thee.
I have thee not, and yet I see thee still.
Art thou not, fatal[9] vision, sensible
To feeling as to sight? or art thou but
A dagger of the mind, a false creation,
Proceeding from the heat-oppressed brain?
I see thee yet, in form as palpable
As this which now I draw.
Thou marshall'st me the way that I was going,
And such an instrument I was to use.
Mine eyes are made the fools o' the other senses,
Or else worth all the rest.[10] I see thee still,
And on thy blade and dudgeon[11] gouts[12] of blood,
Which was not so before. There's no such thing.
It is the bloody business which informs[13]
Thus to mine eyes. Now o'er the one half-world
Nature seems dead, and wicked dreams abuse[14]
The curtain'd sleep. Witchcraft celebrates

[5] Side with my party. [6] When I have a party. [7] Conscience clear.
[8] The cup drunk before retiring. [9] Sent by fate. [10] As alone trustworthy.
[11] Handle. [12] Drops. [13] Presents forms. [14] Fill with deceptive appearances.

Pale Hecate's offerings, and wither'd murder,
Alarum'd by his sentinel, the wolf,
Whose howl's his watch, thus with his stealthy pace,
With Tarquin's ravishing strides, towards his design
Moves like a ghost. Thou sure and firm set earth,
Hear not my steps, which way they walk, for fear
Thy very stones prate of my whereabout,
And take the present horror[15] from the time,
Which now suits with it. Whiles I threat, he lives:
Words to the heat of deeds too cold breath gives. *A bell rings.*
I go, and it is done; the bell invites me.
Hear it not, Duncan; for it is a knell
That summons thee to heaven or to hell. *Exit.*

Scene II

Enter Lady Macbeth

Lady M. That which hath made them drunk hath made me bold;
What hath quench'd them hath given me fire. Hark! Peace!
It was the owl that shriek'd, the fatal bellman,
Which gives the stern'st good-night. He is about it.
The doors are open; and the surfeited grooms
Do mock their charge with snores. I have drugg'd their possets,[1]
That death and nature do contend about them,
Whether they live or die.

Enter Macbeth

Macb. Who's there? What, ho!
Lady M. Alack, I am afraid they have awak'd,
And 'tis not done. The attempt and not the deed[2]
Confounds us. Hark! I laid their daggers ready;
He could not miss 'em. Had he not resembled
My father as he slept, I had done 't.—My husband!
Macb. I have done the deed. Didst thou not hear a noise?

[15] *I. e.,* silence. [1] A curdled drink containing milk, wine, etc.
[2] *I. e.,* an unsuccessful attempt.

Lady M. I heard the owl scream and the crickets cry.
Did not you speak?
Macb. When?
Lady M. Now.
Macb. As I descended?
Lady M. Ay.
Macb. Hark!
Who lies i' the second chamber?
Lady M. Donalbain.
Macb. This is a sorry sight. [*Looking on his hands.*]
Lady M. A foolish thought, to say a sorry sight.
Macb. There's one did laugh in 's sleep, and one cried "Murder!"
That they did wake each other. I stood and heard them;
But they did say their prayers, and address'd them
Again to sleep.
Lady M. There are two lodg'd together.
Macb. One cried, "God bless us!" and "Amen" the other,
As they had seen me with these hangman's hands.
Listening their fear, I could not say "Amen,"
When they did say, "God bless us!"
Lady M. Consider it not so deeply.
Macb. But wherefore could not I pronounce "Amen"?
I had most need of blessing, and "Amen"
Stuck in my throat.
Lady M. These deeds must not be thought
After these ways; so, it will make us mad.
Macb. Methought I heard a voice cry, "Sleep no more! Macbeth
does murder sleep,"—the innocent sleep,
Sleep that knits up the ravell'd sleave[3] of care,
The death of each day's life, sore labour's bath,
Balm of hurt minds, great nature's second course,
Chief nourisher in life's feast,—
Lady M. What do you mean?
Macb. Still it cried, "Sleep no more!" to all the house;
"Glamis hath murder'd sleep, and therefore Cawdor
Shall sleep no more; Macbeth shall sleep no more."

[3] Tangled raw silk.

Lady M. Who was it that thus cried? Why, worthy thane,
You do unbend your noble strength, to think
So brainsickly of things. Go get some water,
And wash this filthy witness from your hand.
Why did you bring these daggers from the place?
They must lie there. Go carry them; and smear
The sleepy grooms with blood.

Macb. I'll go no more.
I am afraid to think what I have done;
Look on 't again I dare not.

Lady M. Infirm of purpose!
Give me the daggers. The sleeping and the dead
Are but as pictures; 'tis the eye of childhood
That fears a painted devil. If he do bleed,
I'll gild[4] the faces of the grooms withal;
For it must seem their guilt. *Exit. Knocking within.*

Macb. Whence is that knocking?
How is 't with me, when every noise appalls me?
What hands are here? Ha! they pluck out mine eyes.
Will all great Neptune's ocean wash this blood
Clean from my hand? No, this my hand will rather
The multitudinous seas incarnadine,[5]
Making the green one red.

Re-enter LADY MACBETH

Lady M. My hands are of your colour; but I shame
To wear a heart so white. (*Knocking.*) I hear a knocking
At the south entry. Retire we to our chamber.
A little water clears us of this deed;
How easy is it, then! Your constancy
Hath left you unattended. (*Knocking.*) Hark! more knocking.
Get on your nightgown,[6] lest occasion call us
And show us to be watchers. Be not lost
So poorly in your thoughts.

Macb. To know my deed, 't were best not know myself.
Knocking.
Wake Duncan with thy knocking! I would thou couldst! *Exeunt.*

[4] Smear. [5] Make crimson. [6] Dressing-gown.

SCENE III. [*The same*]

Enter a Porter. *Knocking within*

Porter. Here's a knocking indeed! If a man were porter of hell-gate, he should have old turning[1] the key. (*Knocking.*) Knock, knock, knock! Who's there, i' the name of Beelzebub? Here's a farmer, that hang'd himself on the expectation of plenty.[2] Come in time; have napkins enow about you; here you'll sweat for 't. (*Knocking.*) Knock, knock! Who's there, in the other devil's name? Faith, here's an equivocator, that could swear in both the scales against either scale; who committed treason enough for God's sake, yet could not equivocate to heaven. O, come in, equivocator. (*Knocking.*) Knock, knock, knock! Who's there? Faith, here's an English tailor come hither, for stealing[3] out of a French hose. Come in, tailor; here you may roast your goose. (*Knocking.*) Knock, knock; never at quiet! What are you? But this place is too cold for hell. I'll devil-porter it no further. I had thought to have let in some of all professions that go the primrose way to the everlasting bonfire. (*Knocking.*) Anon, anon. I pray you, remember the porter.

[*Opens the gate.*]

Enter MACDUFF *and* LENNOX

Macd. Was it so late, friend, ere you went to bed,
That you do lie so late?

Port. Faith, sir, we were carousing till the second cock; and drink, sir, is a great provoker of three things.

Macd. What three things does drink especially provoke?

Port. Marry, sir, nose-painting, sleep and urine. Lechery, sir, it provokes, and unprovokes; it provokes the desire, but it takes away the performance; therefore, much drink may be said to be an equivocator with lechery: it makes him, and it mars him; it sets him on, and it takes him off; it persuades him, and disheartens him; makes him stand to, and not stand to; in conclusion, equivocates him in a sleep, and, giving him the lie, leaves him.

Macd. I believe drink gave thee the lie last night.

[1] Slang. Plenty of turning. [2] Having hoarded grain.
[3] Stealing part of the cloth supplied.

Port. That it did, sir, i' the very throat on me. But I requited him for his lie; and, I think, being too strong for him, though he took up my legs sometime, yet I made a shift to cast him.

Enter MACBETH

Macd. Is thy master stirring?
Our knocking has awak'd him; here he comes.
Len. Good morrow, noble sir.
Macb. Good morrow, both.
Macd. Is the King stirring, worthy thane?
Macb. Not yet.
Macd. He did command me to call timely[4] on him.
I have almost slipp'd the hour.
Macb. I'll bring you to him.
Macd. I know this is a joyful trouble to you;
But yet 'tis one.
Macb. The labour we delight in physics pain.
This is the door.
Macd. I'll make so bold to call,
For 'tis my limited[5] service. [*Exit.*
Len. Goes the King hence to-day?
Macb. He does;—he did appoint so.
Len. The night has been unruly. Where we lay,
Our chimneys were blown down; and, as they say,
Lamentings heard i' the air; strange screams of death,
And prophesying with accents terrible
Of dire combustion[6] and confus'd events
New hatch'd to the woeful time. The obscure bird
Clamour'd the livelong night; some say, the earth
Was feverous and did shake.
Macb. 'Twas a rough night.
Len. My young remembrance cannot parallel
A fellow to it.

Re-enter MACDUFF

Macd. O horror, horror, horror! Tongue nor heart
Cannot conceive nor name thee!

[4] Early. [5] Appointed. [6] Turmoil.

Macb.
Len. } What's the matter?

Macd. Confusion now hath made his masterpiece!
Most sacrilegious murder hath broke ope
The Lord's anointed temple, and stole thence
The life o' the building!

Macb. What is 't you say? The life?

Len. Mean you his Majesty?

Macd. Approach the chamber, and destroy your sight
With a new Gorgon.[7] Do not bid me speak;
See, and then speak yourselves. *Exeunt* MACBETH *and* LENNOX.
Awake, awake!
Ring the alarum-bell. Murder and treason!
Banquo and Donalbain! Malcolm! awake!
Shake off this downy sleep, death's counterfeit,
And look on death itself! Up, up, and see
The great doom's[8] image! Malcolm! Banquo!
As from your graves rise up, and walk like sprites,
To countenance this horror. Ring the bell. *Bell rings.*

Enter LADY MACBETH

Lady M. What's the business,
That such a hideous trumpet calls to parley
The sleepers of the house? Speak, speak!

Macd. O gentle lady,
'Tis not for you to hear what I can speak;
The repetition in a woman's ear
Would murder as it fell.

Enter BANQUO

O Banquo, Banquo,
Our royal master's murder'd!

Lady M. Woe, alas!
What, in our house?

Ban. Too cruel anywhere.
Dear Duff, I prithee, contradict thyself,
And say it is not so.

[7] Which will turn you to stone, like Medusa's head. [8] Judgment day.

Re-enter MACBETH *and* LENNOX, *with* ROSS

Macb. Had I but died an hour before this chance,
I had liv'd a blessed time; for, from this instant,
There's nothing serious in mortality.[9]
All is but toys;[10] renown and grace is dead;
The wine of life is drawn, and the mere lees
Is left this vault to brag of.

Enter MALCOLM *and* DONALBAIN

Don. What is amiss?
Macb. You are, and do not know 't.
The spring, the head, the fountain of your blood
Is stopp'd; the very source of it is stopp'd.
Macd. Your royal father's murder'd.
Mal. O, by whom?
Len. Those of his chamber, as it seem'd, had done 't.
Their hands and faces were all badg'd[11] with blood;
So were their daggers, which unwip'd we found
Upon their pillows.
They star'd, and were distracted; no man's life
Was to be trusted with them.
Macb. O, yet I do repent me of my fury,
That I did kill them.
Macd. Wherefore did you so?
Macb. Who can be wise, amaz'd, temperate and furious,
Loyal and neutral, in a moment? No man.
The expedition[12] of my violent love
Outrun the pauser, reason. Here lay Duncan,
His silver skin lac'd with his golden blood,
And his gash'd stabs look'd like a breach in nature
For ruin's wasteful entrance; there, the murderers,
Steeped in the colours of their trade, their daggers
Unmannerly breech'd[13] with gore. Who could refrain,
That had a heart to love, and in that heart
Courage to make 's love known?

[9] Human life. [10] Trifles. [11] Marked. [12] Haste. [13] Smeared to the handles.

Lady M. Help me hence, ho!
Macd. Look to the lady.
Mal. [*Aside to* DON.] Why do we hold our tongues,
That most may claim this argument[14] for ours?
Don. [*Aside to* MAL.] What should be spoken here, where our fate,
Hid in an auger-hole, may rush and seize us?
Let's away;
Our tears are not yet brew'd.
Mal. [*Aside to* DON.] Nor our strong sorrow
Upon the foot of motion.[15]
Ban. Look to the lady;
[LADY MACBETH *is carried out.*]
And when we have our naked frailties[16] hid,
That suffer in exposure, let us meet
And question[17] this most bloody piece of work,
To know it further. Fears and scruples shake us.
In the great hand of God I stand, and thence
Against the undivulg'd pretence[18] I fight
Of treasonous malice.
Macd. And so do I.
All. So all.
Macb. Let's briefly put on manly readiness,[19]
And meet i' the hall together.
All. Well contented.
Exeunt [*all but* MALCOLM *and* DONALBAIN].
Mal. What will you do? Let's not consort with them;
To show an unfelt sorrow is an office
Which the false man does easy. I'll to England.
Don. To Ireland, I; our separated fortune
Shall keep us both the safer. Where we are,
There's daggers in men's smiles; the near[20] in blood,
The nearer bloody.
Mal. This murderous shaft that's shot
Hath not yet lighted, and our safest way
Is to avoid the aim. Therefore, to horse;

[14] Subject of discussion. [15] Begun to move. [16] Frail bodies. [17] Discuss.
[18] Undiscovered purpose. [19] Men's clothes. [20] Nearer.

And let us not be dainty of leave-taking,
But shift away. There's warrant in that theft
Which steals itself, when there's no mercy left. [*Exeunt.*

SCENE IV. [*Outside Macbeth's castle*]

Enter ROSS *and an* OLD MAN

Old M. Threescore and ten I can remember well;
Within the volume of which time I have seen
Hours dreadful and things strange; but this sore night
Hath trifled[1] former knowings.
Ross. Ah, good father,
Thou seest the heavens, as troubled with man's act,
Threatens his bloody stage. By the clock 'tis day,
And yet dark night strangles the travelling lamp.[2]
Is 't night's predominance or the day's shame
That darkness does the face of earth entomb,
When living light should kiss it?
Old M. 'Tis unnatural,
Even like the deed that's done. On Tuesday last,
A falcon, tow'ring in her pride of place,
Was by a mousing owl hawk'd at and kill'd.
Ross. And Duncan's horses—a thing most strange and certain—
Beauteous and swift, the minions[3] of their race,
Turn'd wild in nature, broke their stalls, flung out,
Contending 'gainst obedience, as they would make
War with mankind.
Old M. 'Tis said they eat each other.
Ross. They did so, to the amazement of mine eyes
That look'd upon 't.

Enter MACDUFF

Here comes the good Macduff.
How goes the world, sir, now?
Macd. Why, see you not?
Ross. Is 't known who did this more than bloody deed?

[1] Made trifling by comparison. [2] The sun. [3] Favorites.

Macd. Those that Macbeth hath slain.
Ross. Alas, the day!
What good could they pretend?[4]
Macd. They were suborn'd.
Malcolm and Donalbain, the King's two sons,
Are stolen away and fled; which puts upon them
Suspicion of the deed.
Ross. 'Gainst nature still!
Thriftless ambition, that will ravin up[5]
Thine own life's means! Then 'tis most like
The sovereignty will fall upon Macbeth.
Macd. He is already nam'd, and gone to Scone
To be invested.
Ross. Where is Duncan's body?
Macd. Carried to Colmekill,
The sacred storehouse of his predecessors,
And guardian of their bones.
Ross. Will you to Scone?
Macd. No, cousin, I'll to Fife.
Ross. Well, I will thither.
Macd. Well, may you see things well done there,—adieu!—
Lest our old robes sit easier than our new!
Ross. Farewell, father.
Old M. God's benison go with you; and with those
That would make good of bad, and friends of foes! *Exeunt.*

ACT III

Scene I. [*Forres. The palace*]

Enter Banquo

Ban. Thou hast it now: King, Cawdor, Glamis, all,
As the weird women promis'd, and, I fear,
Thou play'dst most foully for 't: yet it was said
It should not stand in thy posterity,
But that myself should be the root and father

[4] Mean. [5] Devour.

Of many kings. If there come truth from them—
As upon thee, Macbeth, their speeches shine[1]—
Why, by the verities on thee made good,
May they not be my oracles as well,
And set me up in hope? But hush! no more.

Sennet sounded. Enter MACBETH, *as King,* LADY [MACBETH, *as Queen*], LENNOX, ROSS, Lords, [Ladies,] *and* Servants

Macb. Here's our chief guest.
Lady M. If he had been forgotten,
It had been as a gap in our great feast,
And all-thing[2] unbecoming.
Macb. To-night we hold a solemn supper, sir,
And I'll request your presence.
Ban. Let your Highness
Command upon me; to the which my duties
Are with a most indissoluble tie
For ever knit.
Macb. Ride you this afternoon?
Ban. Ay, my good lord.
Macb. We should have else desir'd your good advice,
Which still hath been both grave and prosperous,
In this day's council; but we'll take to-morrow.
Is 't far you ride?
Ban. As far, my lord, as will fill up the time
'Twixt this and supper. Go not my horse the better,[3]
I must become a borrower of the night
For a dark hour or twain.
Macb. Fail not our feast.
Ban. My lord, I will not.
Macb. We hear our bloody cousins are bestow'd
In England and in Ireland, not confessing
Their cruel parricide, filling their hearers
With strange invention. But of that to-morrow,
When therewithal we shall have cause of state
Craving us jointly. Hie you to horse; adieu,
Till you return at night. Goes Fleance with you?

[1] Are conspicuously fulfilled. [2] Entirely. [3] Faster.

Ban. Ay, my good lord. Our time does call upon 's.
Macb. I wish your horses swift and sure of foot;
And so I do commend you to their backs.
Farewell. *Exit* BANQUO.
Let every man be master of his time
Till seven at night. To make society
The sweeter welcome, we will keep ourself
Till supper-time alone; while[4] then, God be with you!
Exeunt [*all but* MACBETH, *and a* Servant].
Sirrah, a word with you. Attend those men
Our pleasure?
Serv. They are, my lord, without the palace gate.
Macb. Bring them before us. (*Exit* Servant.)
To be thus is nothing;
But to be safely thus. Our fears in Banquo
Stick deep; and in his royalty of nature
Reigns that which would be fear'd. 'Tis much he dares;
And, to that dauntless temper of his mind,
He hath a wisdom that doth guide his valour
To act in safety. There is none but he
Whose being I do fear; and, under him,
My Genius is rebuk'd, as, it is said,
Mark Antony's was by Cæsar. He chid the sisters
When first they put the name of king upon me,
And bade them speak to him; then prophet-like
They hail'd him father to a line of kings.
Upon my head they plac'd a fruitless crown,
And put a barren sceptre in my gripe,
Thence to be wrench'd with an unlineal hand,
No son of mine succeeding. If 't be so,
For Banquo's issue have I fil'd[5] my mind;
For them the gracious Duncan have I murder'd;
Put rancours in the vessel of my peace
Only for them; and mine eternal jewel[6]
Given to the common enemy of man,
To make them kings, the seed of Banquo kings!
Rather than so, come fate into the list,

[4] Till. [5] Defiled. [6] His soul.

And champion me to the utterance![7] Who's there?

Re-enter Servant, *with two* Murderers

Now go to the door, and stay there till we call. *Exit* Servant.
Was it not yesterday we spoke together?
[1.] *Mur.* It was, so please your Highness.
Macb. Well then, now
Have you consider'd of my speeches? Know
That it was he in the times past which held you
So under fortune, which you thought had been
Our innocent self. This I made good to you
In our last conference, pass'd in probation[8] with you,
How you were borne in hand,[9] how cross'd, the instruments,
Who wrought with them, and all things else that might
To half a soul and to a notion[10] craz'd
Say, "Thus did Banquo."
1. *Mur.* You made it known to us.
Macb. I did so, and went further, which is now
Our point of second meeting. Do you find
Your patience so predominant in your nature
That you can let this go? Are you so gospell'd[11]
To pray for this good man and for his issue,
Whose heavy hand hath bow'd you to the grave
And beggar'd yours for ever?
1. *Mur.* We are men, my liege.
Macb. Ay, in the catalogue ye go for men,
As hounds and greyhounds, mongrels, spaniels, curs,
Shoughs,[12] water-rugs,[13] and demi-wolves, are clept
All by the name of dogs; the valued file[14]
Distinguishes the swift, the slow, the subtle,
The housekeeper, the hunter, every one
According to the gift which bounteous nature
Hath in him clos'd; whereby he does receive
Particular addition,[15] from the bill
That writes them all alike; and so of men.

[7] Challenge me to deadly combat. [8] Proved. [9] Deceived with false hopes. [10] Mind. [11] Christian. [12] A shaggy dog. [13] A poodle. [14] List with values noted. [15] Distinguishing name.

Now, if you have a station in the file,
Not i' the worst rank of manhood, say 't;
And I will put that business in your bosoms,
Whose execution takes your enemy off,
Grapples you to the heart and love of us,
Who wear our health but sickly in his life,
Which in his death were perfect.
2. *Mur.* I am one, my liege,
Whom the vile blows and buffets of the world
Hath so incens'd that I am reckless what
I do to spite the world.
1. *Mur.* And I another
So weary with disasters, tugg'd with fortune,
That I would set my life on any chance,
To mend it, or be rid on 't.
Macb. Both of you
Know Banquo was your enemy.
[*Both*] *Mur.* True, my lord.
Macb. So is he mine; and in such bloody distance,[16]
That every minute of his being thrusts
Against my near'st of life,[17] and though I could
With barefac'd power sweep him from my sight
And bid my will avouch it,[18] yet I must not,
For certain friends that are both his and mine,
Whose loves I may not drop, but wail his fall
Who I myself struck down; and thence it is,
That I to your assistance do make love,
Masking the business from the common eye
For sundry weighty reasons.
2. *Mur.* We shall, my lord,
Perform what you command us.
1. *Mur.* Though our lives—
Macb. Your spirits shine through you. Within this hour at most
I will advise[19] you where to plant yourselves;
Acquaint you with the perfect spy o' the time,
The moment on 't; for 't must be done to-night,

[16] At such dangerously close quarters. [17] My most vital parts.
[18] Take the responsibility. [19] Instruct.

And something from the palace; always thought
That I require a clearness:[20] and with him—
To leave no rubs[21] nor botches[22] in the work—
Fleance his son, that keeps him company,
Whose absence is no less material to me
Than is his father's, must embrace the fate
Of that dark hour. Resolve yourselves apart;
I'll come to you anon.

[*Both*] *Mur.* We are resolv'd, my lord.

Macb. I'll call upon you straight; abide within.

[*Exeunt* Murderers.]

It is concluded. Banquo, thy soul's flight,
If it find heaven, must find it out to-night. *Exit.*

SCENE II. [*The palace*]

Enter LADY MACBETH *and a* Servant

Lady M. Is Banquo gone from court?

Serv. Ay, madam, but returns again to-night.

Lady M. Say to the King, I would attend his leisure
For a few words.

Serv. Madam, I will. *Exit.*

Lady M. Nought's had, all's spent,
Where our desire is got without content.
'Tis safer to be that which we destroy
Than by destruction dwell in doubtful joy.

Enter MACBETH

How now, my lord! why do you keep alone,
Of sorriest fancies your companions making,
Using those thoughts which should indeed have died
With them they think on? Things without all remedy
Should be without regard; what's done is done.

Macb. We have scotch'd[1] the snake, not kill'd it;
She'll close and be herself, whilst our poor malice

[20] It being understood that I must be kept clear of suspicion.
[21] Roughnesses. [22] Patches. [1] Slashed.

Remains in danger of her former tooth.
But let the frame of things disjoint, both the worlds suffer,
Ere we will eat our meal in fear, and sleep
In the affliction of these terrible dreams
That shake us nightly. Better be with the dead
Whom we, to gain our peace, have sent to peace,
Than on the torture of the mind to lie
In restless ecstasy. Duncan is in his grave;
After life's fitful fever he sleeps well.
Treason has done his worst; nor steel, nor poison,
Malice domestic, foreign levy, nothing,
Can touch him further.
  Lady M. Come on,
Gentle my lord, sleek o'er your rugged looks;
Be bright and jovial among your guests to-night.
  Macb. So shall I, love; and so, I pray, be you.
Let your remembrance apply to Banquo;
Present him eminence,[2] both with eye and tongue.
Unsafe the while, that we
Must lave our honours in these flattering streams,
And make our faces vizards to our hearts,
Disguising what they are.
  Lady M. You must leave this.
  Macb. O, full of scorpions is my mind, dear wife!
Thou know'st that Banquo and his Fleance lives.
  Lady M. But in them nature's copy's[3] not eterne.
  Macb. There's comfort yet; they are assailable.
Then be thou jocund; ere the bat hath flown
His cloister'd flight, ere to black Hecate's summons
The shard-borne[4] beetle with his drowsy hums
Hath rung night's yawning peal, there shall be done
A deed of dreadful note.
  Lady M. What's to be done?
  Macb. Be innocent of the knowledge, dearest chuck,
Till thou applaud the deed. Come, seeling[5] night,

[2] Give him distinguished treatment. [3] Copyhold—the tenure of life which nature holds from God. (Manly.) [4] Borne on his wing-cases. [5] Closing the eyelids.

Scarf up the tender eye of pitiful day,
And with thy bloody and invisible hand
Cancel and tear to pieces that great bond
Which keeps me pale! Light thickens, and the crow
Makes wing to the rooky wood;
Good things of day begin to droop and drowse,
Whiles night's black agents to their preys do rouse.
Thou marvell'st at my words, but hold thee still;
Things bad begun make strong themselves by ill.
So, prithee, go with me. *Exeunt.*

SCENE III. [*A park near the palace*]

Enter three Murderers

1. *Mur.* But who did bid thee join with us?
3. *Mur.* Macbeth.
2. *Mur.* He needs not our mistrust, since he delivers[1]
Our offices and what we have to do
To the direction just.
1. *Mur.* Then stand with us;
The west yet glimmers with some streaks of day.
Now spurs the lated traveller apace
To gain the timely inn; and near approaches
The subject of our watch.
3. *Mur.* Hark! I hear horses.
Ban. (*Within.*) Give us a light there, ho!
2. *Mur.* Then 'tis he; the rest
That are within the note of expectation[2]
Already are i' the court.
1. *Mur.* His horses go about.
3. *Mur.* Almost a mile; but he does usually,
So all men do, from hence to the palace gate
Make it their walk.

Enter BANQUO, *and* FLEANCE *with a torch*

2. *Mur.* A light, a light!
3. *Mur.* 'Tis he.

[1] Reports our respective duties. [2] List of those expected.

1. *Mur.* Stand to 't.

Ban. It will be rain to-night.

1. *Mur.* Let it come down.

[*They set upon* BANQUO.]

Ban. O, treachery! Fly, good Fleance, fly, fly, fly!
Thou mayst revenge. O slave! [*Dies.* FLEANCE *escapes.*]

3. *Mur.* Who did strike out the light?

1. *Mur.* Was 't not the way?

3. *Mur.* There's but one down; the son is fled.

2. *Mur.* We have lost
Best half of our affair.

1. *Mur.* Well, let's away, and say how much is done. *Exeunt.*

SCENE IV. [*The same. Hall in the palace*]

A banquet prepar'd. Enter MACBETH, LADY MACBETH, ROSS, LENNOX, Lords, *and* Attendants

Macb. You know your own degrees; sit down. At first
And last, the hearty welcome.

Lords. Thanks to your Majesty.

Macb. Ourself will mingle with society
And play the humble host.
Our hostess keeps her state,[1] but in best time
We will require her welcome.

Lady M. Pronounce it for me, sir, to all our friends,
For my heart speaks they are welcome.

First Murderer [*appears at the door*]

Macb. See, they encounter thee with their hearts' thanks.
Both sides are even; here I'll sit i' the midst.
Be large in mirth; anon we'll drink a measure
The table round. [*Approaching the door.*]
—There's blood upon thy face.

Mur. 'Tis Banquo's then.

Macb. 'Tis better thee without than he within.
Is he dispatch'd?

[1] Throne.

Mur. My lord, his throat is cut; that I did for him.
Macb. Thou art the best o' the cut-throats; yet he's good
That did the like for Fleance. If thou didst it,
Thou art the nonpareil.[2]
Mur. Most royal sir,
Fleance is scap'd.
Macb. Then comes my fit again. I had else been perfect,
Whole as the marble, founded as the rock,
As broad and general as the casing air;
But now I am cabin'd, cribb'd, confin'd, bound in
To saucy doubts and fears. But Banquo's safe?
Mur. Ay, my good lord; safe in a ditch he bides,
With twenty trenched gashes on his head,
The least a death to nature.
Macb. Thanks for that;
There the grown serpent lies. The worm[3] that's fled
Hath nature that in time will venom breed,
No teeth for the present. Get thee gone; to-morrow
We'll hear ourselves again.[4] *Exit* Murderer.
Lady M. My royal lord,
You do not give the cheer. The feast is sold
That is not often vouch'd, while 'tis a-making,
'Tis given with welcome. To feed were best at home;
From thence, the sauce to meat is ceremony;
Meeting were bare without it.

Enter the Ghost *of* BANQUO, *and sits in* MACBETH's *place*

Macb. Sweet remembrancer!
Now, good digestion wait on appetite,
And health on both!
Len. May 't please your Highness sit.
Macb. Here had we now our country's honour roof'd,
Were the grac'd person of our Banquo present,
Who may I rather challenge for unkindness
Than pity for mischance.

[2] The one without equal.
[3] Serpent. [4] Talk together.

Ross. His absence, sir,
Lays blame upon his promise. Please 't your Highness
To grace us with your royal company?
Macb. The table's full.
Len. Here is a place reserv'd, sir.
Macb. Where?
Len. Here, my good lord. What is 't that moves your Highness?
Macb. Which of you have done this?
Lords. What, my good lord?
Macb. Thou canst not say I did it; never shake
Thy gory locks at me.
Ross. Gentlemen, rise: his Highness is not well.
Lady M. Sit, worthy friends; my lord is often thus,
And hath been from his youth. Pray you, keep seat;
The fit is momentary; upon a thought
He will again be well. If much you note him,
You shall offend him and extend his passion.[5]
Feed, and regard him not. [*Aside to* MACBETH.]
Are you a man?
Macb. Ay, and a bold one, that dare look on that
Which might appall the devil.
Lady M. [*Aside to* MACBETH.] O proper[6] stuff!
This is the very painting of your fear;
This is the air-drawn dagger which, you said,
Led you to Duncan. O, these flaws[7] and starts,
Impostors to[8] true fear, would well become
A woman's story at a winter's fire,
Authoriz'd[9] by her grandam. Shame itself!
Why do you make such faces? When all's done,
You look but on a stool.
Macb. Prithee, see there! behold! look! lo! how say you?
Why, what care I? If thou canst nod, speak too.
If charnel-houses and our graves must send
Those that we bury back, our monuments[10]
Shall be the maws of kites. [Ghost *vanishes.*]

[5] Prolong his agitation. [6] Fine. [7] Sudden outbursts.
[8] Compared to. [9] Vouched for. [10] Tombs.

Lady M. [*Aside to* MACBETH.] What, quite unmann'd in folly?
Macb. If I stand here, I saw him.
Lady M. [*Aside to* MACBETH.] Fie, for shame!
Macb. Blood hath been shed ere now, i' the olden time,
Ere humane statute purg'd the gentle weal;[11]
Ay, and since too, murders have been perform'd
Too terrible for the ear. The time has been,
That, when the brains were out, the man would die,
And there an end; but now they rise again,
With twenty mortal murders[12] on their crowns,
And push us from our stools. This is more strange
Than such a murder is.
Lady M. My worthy lord,
Your noble friends do lack you.
Macb. I do forget.
Do not muse at me, my most worthy friends;
I have a strange infirmity, which is nothing
To those that know me. Come, love and health to all;
Then I'll sit down. Give me some wine; fill full.

Re-enter Ghost

I drink to the general joy o' the whole table,
And to our dear friend Banquo, whom we miss;
Would he were here! to all and him we thirst,
And all to all.
Lords. Our duties, and the pledge.
Macb. Avaunt! and quit my sight! let the earth hide thee!
Thy bones are marrowless, thy blood is cold;
Thou hast no speculation[13] in those eyes
Which thou dost glare with!
Lady M. Think of this, good peers,
But as a thing of custom; 'tis no other,
Only it spoils the pleasure of the time.
Macb. What man dare, I dare.
Approach thou like the rugged Russian bear,
The arm'd rhinoceros, or the Hyrcan tiger;

[11] Made the state gentle by purging it. [12] Deadly wounds. [13] Sight.

Take any shape but that, and my firm nerves
Shall never tremble. Or be alive again,
And dare me to the desert with thy sword;
If trembling I inhabit[14] then, protest me
The baby of a girl. Hence, horrible shadow!
Unreal mockery, hence! [Ghost *vanishes.*]
Why, so; being gone,
I am a man again. Pray you, sit still.

Lady M. You have displac'd the mirth, broke the good meeting,
With most admir'd[15] disorder.

Macb. Can such things be,
And overcome[16] us like a summer's cloud,
Without our special wonder? You make me strange[17]
Even to the disposition that I owe,
When now I think you can behold such sights,
And keep the natural ruby of your cheeks,
When mine is blanch'd with fear.

Ross. What sights, my lord?

Lady M. I pray you, speak not; he grows worse and worse;
Question enrages him. At once, good-night.
Stand not upon the order of your going,
But go at once.

Len. Good-night; and better health
Attend his Majesty!

Lady M. A kind good-night to all! *Exeunt* Lords.

Macb. It will have blood, they say; blood will have blood.
Stones have been known to move and trees to speak;
Augures[18] and understood[19] relations have
By maggot-pies and choughs[20] and rooks brought forth
The secret'st man of blood. What is the night?

Lady M. Almost at odds with morning, which is which.

Macb. How say'st thou, that Macduff denies his person
At our great bidding?

Lady M. Did you send to him, sir?

Macb. I hear it by the way; but I will send.

[14] Continue (?). Clothe myself in (?). [15] Producing wonder.
[16] Overshadow. [17] A stranger. [18] Auguries. [19] Secret. [20] Daws.

There's not a one of them but in his house
I keep a servant fee'd. I will to-morrow,
And betimes I will, to the weird sisters.
More shall they speak; for now I am bent to know,
By the worst means, the worst. For mine own good
All causes shall give way. I am in blood
Stepp'd in so far that, should I wade no more,
Returning were as tedious as go o'er.
Strange things I have in head, that will to hand,
Which must be acted ere they may be scann'd.

Lady M. You lack the season[21] of all natures, sleep.

Macb. Come, we'll to sleep. My strange and self-abuse[22]
Is the initiate fear that wants hard use;
We are yet but young in deed. *Exeunt*

SCENE V. [*A heath*][1]

Thunder. Enter the three Witches, *meeting* HECATE

1. *Witch.* Why, how now, Hecate! you look angerly.

Hec. Have I not reason, beldams[2] as you are,
Saucy and overbold? How did you dare
To trade and traffic with Macbeth
In riddles and affairs of death;
And I, the mistress of your charms,
The close[3] contriver of all harms,
Was never call'd to bear my part,
Or show the glory of our art?
And, which is worse, all you have done
Hath been but for a wayward son,
Spiteful and wrathful, who, as others do,
Loves for his own ends, not for you.
But make amends now; get you gone,
And at the pit of Acheron
Meet me i' the morning; thither he
Will come to know his destiny.

[21] Seasoning. [22] Deception.

[1] This scene is probably the interpolation of a later dramatist. [2] Hags.

[3] Secret.

Your vessels and your spells provide,
Your charms and everything beside.
I am for the air; this night I'll spend
Unto a dismal and a fatal end;
Great business must be wrought ere noon.
Upon the corner of the moon
There hangs a vaporous drop profound;
I'll catch it ere it come to ground;
And that distill'd by magic sleights
Shall raise such artificial sprites
As by the strength of their illusion
Shall draw him on to his confusion.
He shall spurn fate, scorn death, and bear
His hopes 'bove wisdom, grace, and fear;
And, you all know, security[4]
Is mortals' chiefest enemy. *Music, and a song*
Hark! I am call'd; my little spirit, see,
Sits in a foggy cloud, and stays for me. [*Exit.*]
(*Sing within:* "Come away, come away," etc.

1. *Witch.* Come, let's make haste; she'll soon be back again.
Exeunt.

Scene VI. [*Forres. The palace*]

Enter Lennox *and another* Lord

Len. My former speeches have but hit your thoughts,
Which can interpret farther; only, I say,
Things have been strangely borne.[1] The gracious Duncan
Was pitied of Macbeth; marry, he was dead:
And the right-valiant Banquo walk'd too late;
Whom, you may say, if 't please you, Fleance kill'd,
For Fleance fled; men must not walk too late.
Who cannot want[2] the thought how monstrous
It was for Malcolm and for Donalbain
To kill their gracious father? Damned fact!
How it did grieve Macbeth! Did he not straight

[4] Over-confidence. [1] Conducted. [2] Can lack.

In pious rage the two delinquents tear,
That were the slaves of drink and thralls of sleep?
Was not that nobly done? Ay, and wisely too;
For 'twould have anger'd any heart alive
To hear the men deny 't. So that, I say,
He has borne all things well; and I do think
That had he Duncan's sons under his key—
As, an 't please Heaven, he shall not—they should find
What 'twere to kill a father; so should Fleance.
But, peace! for from broad[3] words, and 'cause he fail'd
His presence at the tyrant's feast, I hear
Macduff lives in disgrace. Sir, can you tell
Where he bestows himself?

Lord. The son of Duncan,
From whom this tyrant holds the due of birth,
Lives in the English court, and is receiv'd
Of the most pious Edward with such grace
That the malevolence of Fortune nothing
Takes from his high respect. Thither Macduff
Is gone to pray the holy king, upon his aid
To wake Northumberland and warlike Siward;
That, by the help of these—with Him above
To ratify the work—we may again
Give to our tables meat, sleep to our nights,
Free from our feasts and banquets bloody knives,
Do faithful homage and receive free honours;
All which we pine for now: and this report
Hath so exasperate their king that he
Prepares for some attempt of war.

Len. Sent he to Macduff?

Lord. He did; and with[4] an absolute "Sir, not I,"
The cloudy messenger turns me his back,
And hums, as who should say, "You'll rue the time
That clogs me with this answer."

Len. And that well might
Advise him to a caution, to hold what distance

[3] Free. [4] Receiving as answer.

His wisdom can provide. Some holy angel
Fly to the court of England and unfold
His message ere he come, that a swift blessing
May soon return to this our suffering country
Under a hand accurs'd!

Lord. I'll send my prayers with him. *Exeunt.*

ACT IV

SCENE I. [*A cavern. In the middle, a boiling cauldron*]

Thunder. Enter the three Witches

1. *Witch.* Thrice the brinded[1] cat hath mew'd.
2. *Witch.* Thrice, and once the hedge-pig whin'd.
3. *Witch.* Harpier cries; 'tis time, 'tis time.
1. *Witch.* Round about the cauldron go;
In the poison'd entrails throw.
Toad, that under cold stone
Days and nights has thirty-one
Swelt'red[2] venom sleeping got,
Boil thou first i' the charmed pot.

All. Double, double, toil and trouble;
Fire burn and cauldron bubble.

2. *Witch.* Fillet of a fenny[3] snake,
In the cauldron boil and bake;
Eye of newt[4] and toe of frog,
Wool of bat and tongue of dog,
Adder's fork and blind-worm's sting,
Lizard's leg and howlet's wing,
For a charm of powerful trouble,
Like a hell-broth boil and bubble.

All. Double, double, toil and trouble;
Fire burn and cauldron bubble.

3. *Witch.* Scale of dragon, tooth of wolf,
Witches' mummy,[5] maw and gulf[6]

[1] Brindled. [2] Sweated. [3] From the marshes. [4] Water-lizard.
[5] The gum that oozed from embalmed bodies—used as a medicine. [6] Stomach (?).

Of the ravin'd[7] salt-sea shark,
Root of hemlock digg'd i' the dark,
Liver of blaspheming Jew,
Gall of goat, and slips of yew
Sliver'd in the moon's eclipse,
Nose of Turk and Tartar's lips,
Finger of birth-strangled babe
Ditch-deliver'd by a drab,
Make the gruel thick and slab.[8]
Add thereto a tiger's chaudron,[9]
For the ingredients of our cauldron.
All. Double, double, toil and trouble;
Fire burn and cauldron bubble.
2. *Witch.* Cool it with a baboon's blood,
Then the charm is firm and good.

Enter HECATE *to the other three* Witches

Hec. O, well done! I commend your pains;
And every one shall share i' the gains.
And now about the cauldron sing,
Like elves and fairies in a ring,
Enchanting all that you put in.
Music and a song: "Black spirits," etc. [HECATE *retires.*]
2. *Witch.* By the pricking of my thumbs,
Something wicked this way comes.
Open, locks,
Whoever knocks!

Enter MACBETH

Macb. How now, you secret, black, and midnight hags!
What is 't you do?
All. A deed without a name.
Macb. I conjure you, by that which you profess,
Howe'er you come to know it, answer me!
Though you untie the winds and let them fight
Against the churches; though the yesty waves

[7] Ravenous. [8] Glutinous. [9] Entrails.

Confound and swallow navigation up;
Though bladed corn be lodg'd[10] and trees blown down;
Though castles topple on their warders' heads;
Though palaces and pyramids do slope
Their heads to their foundations; though the treasure
Of nature's germens[11] tumble all together,
Even till destruction sicken; answer me
To what I ask you.

1. *Witch.* Speak.

2. *Witch.* Demand.

3. *Witch.* We'll answer.

1. *Witch.* Say, if thou 'dst rather hear it from our mouths,
Or from our master's?

Macb. Call 'em; let me see 'em.

1. *Witch.* Pour in sow's blood, that hath eaten
Her nine farrow;[12] grease that's sweaten
From the murderer's gibbet throw
Into the flame.

All. Come, high or low;
Thyself and office deftly show!

Thunder. First Apparition, *an armed Head*

Macb. Tell me, thou unknown power,—

1. *Witch.* He knows thy thought.
Hear his speech, but say thou nought.

1. *App.* Macbeth! Macbeth! Macbeth! beware Macduff;
Beware the thane of Fife. Dismiss me. Enough. *Descends.*

Macb. Whate'er thou art, for thy good caution, thanks;
Thou hast harp'd my fear aright. But one word more,—

1. *Witch.* He will not be commanded. Here's another,
More potent than the first.

Thunder. Second Apparition, *a bloody Child*

2. *App.* Macbeth! Macbeth! Macbeth!

Macb. Had I three ears, I'd hear thee.

2. *App.* Be bloody, bold, and resolute; laugh to scorn

[10] Let corn not yet in the ear be laid flat. [11] Seeds. [12] Litter of pigs.

The power of man; for none of woman born
Shall harm Macbeth. *Descends.*

Macb. Then live, Macduff: what need I fear of thee?
But yet I'll make assurance double sure,
And take a bond of fate. Thou shalt not live;
That I may tell pale-hearted fear it lies,
And sleep in spite of thunder.

Thunder. Third Apparition, *a Child crowned, with a tree in his hand*

What is this
That rises like the issue of a king,
And wears upon his baby-brow the round
And top of sovereignty?

All. Listen, but speak not to 't.

3. *App.* Be lion-mettled, proud, and take no care
Who chafes, who frets, or where conspirers are.
Macbeth shall never vanquish'd be until
Great Birnam wood to high Dunsinane hill
Shall come against him. *Descends.*

Macb. That will never be.
Who can impress[13] the forest, bid the tree
Unfix his earth-bound root? Sweet bodements![14] good!
Rebellion's head, rise never till the wood
Of Birnam rise, and our high-plac'd Macbeth
Shall live the lease of nature, pay his breath
To time and mortal custom. Yet my heart
Throbs to know one thing: tell me, if your art
Can tell so much, shall Banquo's issue ever
Reign in this kingdom?

All. Seek to know no more.

Macb. I will be satisfied! Deny me this,
And an eternal curse fall on you! Let me know.
Why sinks that cauldron? And what noise is this? *Hautboys.*

1. *Witch.* Show!

2. *Witch.* Show!

[13] Force into service. [14] Predictions.

3. *Witch.* Show!
All. Show his eyes, and grieve his heart;
Come like shadows, so depart!

A show of Eight Kings, *the last with a glass in his hand;* BANQUO's Ghost *following*

Macb. Thou art too like the spirit of Banquo; down!
Thy crown does sear mine eye-balls. And thy hair,
Thou other gold-bound brow, is like the first.
A third is like the former. Filthy hags!
Why do you show me this? A fourth! Start, eyes!
What, will the line stretch out to the crack of doom?
Another yet! A seventh! I'll see no more.
And yet the eighth appears, who bears a glass
Which shows me many more; and some I see
That twofold balls and treble sceptres carry.
Horrible sight! Now, I see, 'tis true;
For the blood-bolter'd[15] Banquo smiles upon me,
And points at them for his. [Apparitions *vanish.*] What, is this so?
1. *Witch.* Ay, sir, all this is so; but why
Stands Macbeth thus amazedly?
Come, sisters, cheer we up his sprites,
And show the best of our delights.
I'll charm the air to give a sound,
While you perform your antic round;
That this great king may kindly say,
Our duties did his welcome pay.

Music. The Witches *dance, and vanish* [*with* HECATE].

Macb. Where are they? Gone? Let this pernicious hour
Stand aye accursed in the calendar!
Come in, without there!

Enter LENNOX

Len. What's your Grace's will?
Macb. Saw you the weird sisters?

[15] With hair clotted with blood.

Len. No, my lord.
Macb. Came they not by you?
Len. No, indeed, my lord.
Macb. Infected be the air whereon they ride;
And damn'd all those that trust them! I did hear
The galloping of horse; who was 't came by?
Len. 'Tis two or three, my lord, that bring you word
Macduff is fled to England.
Macb. Fled to England!
Len. Ay, my good lord.
Macb. Time, thou anticipat'st my dread exploits:
The flighty[16] purpose never is o'ertook
Unless the deed go with it. From this moment
The very firstlings of my heart shall be
The firstlings of my hand. And even now,
To crown my thoughts with acts, be it thought and done.
The castle of Macduff I will surprise;
Seize upon Fife; give to the edge o' the sword
His wife, his babes, and all unfortunate souls
That trace him in his line. No boasting like a fool;
This deed I'll do before this purpose cool.
But no more sights!—Where are these gentlemen?
Come, bring me where they are. *Exeunt.*

SCENE II. [*Fife. Macduff's castle*]

Enter LADY MACDUFF, *her* Son, *and* ROSS

L. Macd. What had he done, to make him fly the land?
Ross. You must have patience, madam.
L. Macd. He had none;
His flight was madness. When our actions do not,
Our fears do make us traitors.
Ross. You know not
Whether it was his wisdom or his fear.
L. Macd. Wisdom! to leave his wife, to leave his babes,
His mansion and his titles,[1] in a place
From whence himself does fly? He loves us not,

[16] Swift. [1] Possessions.

He wants the natural touch; for the poor wren,
The most diminutive of birds, will fight,
Her young ones in her nest, against the owl.
All is the fear and nothing is the love;
As little is the wisdom, where the flight
So runs against all reason.

Ross. My dearest coz,
I pray you, school yourself; but for your husband,
He is noble, wise, judicious, and best knows
The fits[2] o' the season. I dare not speak much further;
But cruel are the times when we are traitors
And do not know ourselves; when we hold rumour
From what we fear, yet know not what we fear,
But float upon a wild and violent sea
Each way and move. I take my leave of you;
Shall not be long but I'll be here again.
Things at the worst will cease, or else climb upward
To what they were before. My pretty cousin,
Blessing upon you!

L. Macd. Father'd he is, and yet he's fatherless.

Ross. I am so much a fool, should I stay longer,
It would be my disgrace and your discomfort.
I take my leave at once. *Exit.*

L. Macd. Sirrah, your father's dead;
And what will you do now? How will you live?

Son. As birds do, mother.

L. Macd. What, with worms and flies?

Son. With what I get, I mean; and so do they.

L. Macd. Poor bird! thou 'dst never fear the net nor lime,
The pitfall nor the gin.

Son. Why should I, mother? Poor birds they are not set for.
My father is not dead, for all your saying.

L. Macd. Yes, he is dead. How wilt thou do for a father?

Son. Nay, how will you do for a husband?

L. Macd. Why, I can buy me twenty at any market.

Son. Then you'll buy 'em to sell again.

L. Macd. Thou speak'st with all thy wit; and yet, i' faith,

[2] Troubles.

With wit enough for thee.

Son. Was my father a traitor, mother?

L. Macd. Ay, that he was.

Son. What is a traitor?

L. Macd. Why, one that swears and lies.

Son. And be all traitors that do so?

L. Macd. Every one that does so is a traitor, and must be hang'd.

Son. And must they all be hang'd that swear and lie?

L. Macd. Every one.

Son. Who must hang them?

L. Macd. Why, the honest men.

Son. Then the liars and swearers are fools; for there are liars and swearers enow to beat the honest men and hang up them.

L. Macd. Now, God help thee, poor monkey!
But how wilt thou do for a father?

Son. If he were dead, you'd weep for him; if you would not, it were a good sign that I should quickly have a new father.

L. Macd. Poor prattler, how thou talk'st!

Enter a Messenger

Mess. Bless you, fair dame! I am not to you known,
Though in your state of honour I am perfect.[3]
I doubt some danger does approach you nearly.
If you will take a homely man's advice,
Be not found here; hence, with your little ones.
To fright you thus, methinks, I am too savage;
To do worse to you were fell cruelty,
Which is too nigh your person. Heaven preserve you!
I dare abide no longer. *Exit.*

L. Macd. Whither should I fly?
I have done no harm. But I remember now
I am in this earthly world, where to do harm
Is often laudable, to do good sometime
Accounted dangerous folly. Why then, alas,
Do I put up that womanly defence,
To say I have done no harm?

[3] I am perfectly familiar with your rank.

Enter Murderers

What are these faces?

[1.] *Mur.* Where is your husband?

L. Macd. I hope, in no place so unsanctified
Where such as thou may'st find him.

[1.] *Mur.* He's a traitor.

Son. Thou liest, thou shag-ear'd villain!

[1.] *Mur.* What, you egg!
[*Stabbing him.*]
Young fry of treachery!

Son. He has kill'd me, mother:
Run away, I pray you! [*Dies.*]

Exit [LADY MACDUFF] *crying* "Murder!" [*Exeunt* Murderers, *following her.*]

SCENE III. [*England. Before the King's palace*]

Enter MALCOLM *and* MACDUFF

Mal. Let us seek out some desolate shade, and there
Weep our sad bosoms empty.

Macd. Let us rather
Hold fast the mortal sword, and like good men
Bestride our down-fallen birthdom.[1] Each new morn
New widows howl, new orphans cry, new sorrows
Strike heaven on the face, that it resounds
As if it felt with Scotland, and yell'd out
Like syllable of dolour.

Mal. What I believe I'll wail,
What know believe, and what I can redress,
As I shall find the time to friend, I will.
What you have spoke, it may be so perchance.
This tyrant, whose sole name blisters our tongues,
Was once thought honest; you have lov'd him well.
He hath not touch'd you yet. I am young; but something
You may deserve of him through me, and wisdom

[1] Native country.

To offer up a weak poor innocent lamb
To appease an angry god.
  Macd. I am not treacherous.
  Mal. But Macbeth is.
A good and virtuous nature may recoil
In an imperial charge.[2] But I shall crave your pardon;
That which you are my thoughts cannot transpose.
Angels are bright still, though the brightest fell.
Though all things foul would wear the brows of grace,
Yet grace must still look so.
  Macd. I have lost my hopes.
  Mal. Perchance even there where I did find my doubts.
Why in that rawness[3] left you wife and child,
Those precious motives, those strong knots of love,
Without leave-taking? I pray you,
Let not my jealousies be your dishonours,
But mine own safeties. You may be rightly just,
Whatever I shall think.
  Macd. Bleed, bleed, poor country!
Great tyranny! lay thou thy basis sure,
For goodness dare not check thee; wear thou thy wrongs;
The title is affeer'd![4] Fare thee well, lord:
I would not be the villain that thou think'st
For the whole space that's in the tyrant's grasp,
And the rich East to boot.
  Mal. Be not offended;
I speak not as in absolute fear of you.
I think our country sinks beneath the yoke;
It weeps, it bleeds; and each new day a gash
Is added to her wounds. I think withal
There would be hands uplifted in my right;
And here from gracious England have I offer
Of goodly thousands. But, for all this,
When I shall tread upon the tyrant's head,
Or wear it on my sword, yet my poor country
Shall have more vices than it had before,

[2] Under a king's orders. [3] Without preparation. [4] Sanctioned.

More suffer and more sundry ways than ever,
By him that shall succeed.
Macd. What should he be?
Mal. It is myself I mean; in whom I know
All the particulars of vice so grafted
That, when they shall be open'd, black Macbeth
Will seem as pure as snow, and the poor state
Esteem him as a lamb, being compar'd
With my confineless[5] harms.
Macd. Not in the legions
Of horrid hell can come a devil more damn'd
In evils to top Macbeth.
Mal. I grant him bloody,
Luxurious,[6] avaricious, false, deceitful,
Sudden,[7] malicious, smacking of every sin
That has a name; but there's no bottom, none,
In my voluptuousness. Your wives, your daughters,
Your matrons, and your maids, could not fill up
The cistern of my lust, and my desire
All continent[8] impediments would o'erbear
That did oppose my will. Better Macbeth
Than such an one to reign.
Macd. Boundless intemperance
In nature is a tyranny; it hath been
The untimely emptying of the happy throne
And fall of many kings. But fear not yet
To take upon you what is yours. You may
Convey[9] your pleasures in a spacious plenty,
And yet seem cold; the time[10] you may so hoodwink.
We have willing dames enough; there cannot be
That vulture in you, to devour so many
As will to greatness dedicate themselves,
Finding it so inclin'd.
Mal. With this there grows
In my most ill-compos'd affection[11] such

[5] Boundless. [6] Lustful. [7] Hasty. [8] Restraining. [9] Carry on. [10] Society.
[11] Badly constituted disposition.

A stanchless[12] avarice that, were I King,
I should cut off the nobles for their lands,
Desire his jewels and this other's house;
And my more-having would be as a sauce
To make me hunger more, that I should forge
Quarrels unjust against the good and loyal,
Destroying them for wealth.

Macd. This avarice
Sticks deeper, grows with more pernicious root
Than summer-seeming[13] lust, and it hath been
The sword of our slain kings. Yet do not fear;
Scotland hath foisons[14] to fill up your will,
Of your mere own. All these are portable,[15]
With other graces weigh'd.[16]

Mal. But I have none. The king-becoming graces,
As justice, verity, temperance, stableness,
Bounty, perseverance, mercy, lowliness,
Devotion, patience, courage, fortitude,
I have no relish[17] of them, but abound
In the division of each several crime,
Acting it many ways. Nay, had I power, I should
Pour the sweet milk of concord into hell,
Uproar the universal peace, confound
All unity on earth.

Macd. O Scotland, Scotland!

Mal. If such an one be fit to govern, speak.
I am as I have spoken.

Macd. Fit to govern!
No, not to live. O nation miserable,
With an untitled[18] tyrant bloody-sceptred,
When shalt thou see thy wholesome days again,
Since that the truest issue of thy throne
By his own interdiction stands accurs'd,
And does blaspheme[19] his breed? Thy royal father
Was a most sainted king; the queen that bore thee,

[12] Insatiable. [13] Belonging to the prime of life. [14] Abundance. [15] Tolerable. [16] Balanced. [17] Flavor. [18] Without just claim. [19] Slander.

Oftener upon her knees than on her feet,
Died every day she liv'd. Fare thee well!
These evils thou repeat'st upon thyself
Hath banish'd me from Scotland. O my breast,
Thy hope ends here!

Mal. Macduff, this noble passion,
Child of integrity, hath from my soul
Wip'd the black scruples, reconcil'd my thoughts
To thy good truth and honour. Devilish Macbeth
By many of these trains[20] hath sought to win me
Into his power, and modest[21] wisdom plucks me
From over-credulous haste. But God above
Deal between thee and me! for even now
I put myself to thy direction, and
Unspeak mine own detraction; here abjure
The taints and blames I laid upon myself,
For strangers to my nature. I am yet
Unknown to woman, never was forsworn,
Scarcely have coveted what was mine own,
At no time broke my faith, would not betray
The devil to his fellow, and delight
No less in truth than life; my first false speaking
Was this upon myself. What I am truly,
Is thine and my poor country's to command;
Whither indeed, before thy here-approach,
Old Siward, with ten thousand warlike men,
Already at a point,[22] was setting forth.
Now we'll together; and the chance of goodness
Be like our warranted quarrel! Why are you silent?

Macd. Such welcome and unwelcome things at once
'Tis hard to reconcile.

Enter a Doctor

Mal. Well; more anon.—Comes the King forth, I pray you?

Doct. Ay, sir; there are a crew of wretched souls
That stay his cure. Their malady convinces[23]

[20] Plots. [21] Discreet. [22] Prepared. [23] Baffles.

The great assay of art;[24] but at his touch—
Such sanctity hath Heaven given his hand—
They presently[25] amend.
Mal. I thank you, doctor. [*Exit* Doctor.
Macd. What's the disease he means?
Mal. 'Tis call'd the evil:
A most miraculous work in this good king;
Which often, since my here-remain in England,
I have seen him do. How he solicits Heaven,
Himself best knows; but strangely-visited[26] people,
All swollen and ulcerous, pitiful to the eye,
The mere despair of surgery, he cures,
Hanging a golden stamp about their necks,
Put on with holy prayers; and 'tis spoken,
To the succeeding royalty he leaves
The healing benediction. With this strange virtue,
He hath a heavenly gift of prophecy,
And sundry blessings hang about his throne,
That speak him full of grace.

Enter Ross

Macd. See, who comes here?
Mal. My countryman; but yet I know him not.
Macd. My ever-gentle cousin, welcome hither.
Mal. I know him now. Good God, betimes[27] remove
The means that makes us strangers!
Ross. Sir, amen.
Macd. Stands Scotland where it did?
Ross. Alas, poor country!
Almost afraid to know itself. It cannot
Be call'd our mother, but our grave; where nothing,
But who knows nothing, is once seen to smile;
Where sighs and groans and shrieks that rend the air
Are made, not mark'd; where violent sorrow seems
A modern ecstasy.[28] The dead man's knell

[24] Attempts of physicians. [25] At once. [26] Afflicted. [27] Soon.
[28] An every-day excitement.

Is there scarce ask'd for who; and good men's lives
Expire before the flowers in their caps,
Dying or ere they sicken.
Macd. O, relation
Too nice,[29] and yet too true!
Mal. What's the newest grief?
Ross. That of an hour's age doth hiss the speaker;[30]
Each minute teems[31] a new one.
Macd. How does my wife?
Ross. Why, well.
Macd. And all my children?
Ross. Well too.
Macd. The tyrant has not batter'd at their peace?
Ross. No; they were well at peace when I did leave 'em.
Macd. Be not a niggard of your speech; how goes 't?
Ross. When I came hither to transport the tidings,
Which I have heavily borne, there ran a rumour
Of many worthy fellows that were out;[32]
Which was to my belief witness'd the rather,
For that I saw the tyrant's power a-foot.
Now is the time of help; your eye in Scotland
Would create soldiers, make our women fight,
To doff their dire distresses.
Mal. Be 't their comfort
We're coming thither. Gracious England hath
Lent us good Siward and ten thousand men;
An older and a better soldier none
That Christendom gives out.
Ross. Would I could answer
This comfort with the like! But I have words
That would be howl'd out in the desert air,
Where hearing should not latch[33] them.
Macd. What concern they?
The general cause? Or is it a fee-grief[34]
Due to some single breast?

[29] Story too fanciful. [30] *I. e.,* as a bringer of stale news.
[31] Produces. [32] In revolt. [33] Catch. [34] Private property in grief.

Ross. No mind that's honest
But in it shares some woe; though the main part
Pertains to you alone.
Macd. If it be mine,
Keep it not from me, quickly let me have it.
Ross. Let not your ears despise my tongue for ever,
Which shall possess them with the heaviest sound
That ever yet they heard.
Macd. Hum! I guess at it.
Ross. Your castle is surpris'd; your wife and babes
Savagely slaughter'd. To relate the manner,
Were, on the quarry[35] of these murder'd deer,
To add the death of you.
Mal. Merciful heaven!
What, man! ne'er pull your hat upon your brows;
Give sorrow words. The grief that does not speak
Whispers the o'er-fraught[36] heart and bids it break.
Macd. My children too?
Ross. Wife, children, servants, all
That could be found.
Macd. And I must be from thence!
My wife kill'd too?
Ross. I have said.
Mal. Be comforted.
Let's make us medicines of our great revenge,
To cure this deadly grief.
Macd. He has no children.—All my pretty ones?
Did you say all? O hell-kite! All?
What, all my pretty chickens and their dam
At one fell swoop?
Mal. Dispute[37] it like a man.
Macd. I shall do so;
But I must also feel it as a man.
I cannot but remember such things were,
That were most precious to me. Did heaven look on,
And would not take their part? Sinful Macduff,

[35] Dead bodies. [36] Over-burdened. [37] Strive against.

They were all struck for thee! Naught[38] that I am,
Not for their own demerits, but for mine,
Fell slaughter on their souls. Heaven rest them now!
Mal. Be this the whetstone of your sword; let grief
Convert to anger; blunt not the heart, enrage it.
Macd. O, I could play the woman with mine eyes
And braggart with my tongue! But, gentle heavens,
Cut short all intermission. Front to front
Bring thou this fiend of Scotland and myself;
Within my sword's length set him; if he scape,
Heaven forgive him too!
Mal. This tune goes manly.
Come, go we to the King; our power is ready;
Our lack is nothing but our leave.[39] Macbeth
Is ripe for shaking, and the powers above
Put on[40] their instruments. Receive what cheer you may;
The night is long that never finds the day. *Exeunt.*

ACT V

Scene I. [*Dunsinane. Ante-room in the castle*]

Enter a Doctor of Physic *and a* Waiting Gentlewoman

Doct. I have two nights watch'd with you, but can perceive no truth in your report. When was it she last walk'd?

Gent. Since his Majesty went into the field, I have seen her rise from her bed, throw her nightgown upon her, unlock her closet, take forth paper, fold it, write upon 't, read it, afterwards seal it, and again return to bed; yet all this while in a most fast sleep.

Doct. A great perturbation in nature, to receive at once the benefit of sleep, and do the effects of watching![1] In this slumb'ry agitation, besides her walking and other actual performances, what, at any time, have you heard her say?

Gent. That, sir, which I will not report after her.

Doct. You may to me: and 'tis most meet you should.

Gent. Neither to you nor any one; having no witness to confirm my speech.

[38] Worthless. [39] Leave-taking. [40] Set to work. [1] Actions of waking.

Enter Lady Macbeth, *with a taper*

Lo you, here she comes! This is her very guise; and, upon my life fast asleep. Observe her; stand close.

Doct. How came she by that light?

Gent. Why, it stood by her. She has light by her continually; 'tis her command.

Doct. You see, her eyes are open.

Gent. Ay, but their sense are shut.

Doct. What is it she does now? Look, how she rubs her hands.

Gent. It is an accustom'd action with her, to seem thus washing her hands. I have known her continue in this a quarter of an hour.

Lady M. Yet here's a spot.

Doct. Hark! she speaks. I will set down what comes from her, to satisfy my remembrance the more strongly.

Lady M. Out, damned spot! out, I say!—One: two: why, then 'tis time to do 't.—Hell is murky!—Fie, my lord, fie! a soldier, and afeard? What need we fear who knows it, when none can call our power to account?—Yet who would have thought the old man to have had so much blood in him?

Doct. Do you mark that?

Lady M. The thane of Fife had a wife; where is she now?—What, will these hands ne'er be clean?—No more o' that, my lord, no more o' that; you mar all with this starting.

Doct. Go to, go to; you have known what you should not.

Gent. She has spoke what she should not, I am sure of that; Heaven knows what she has known.

Lady M. Here's the smell of the blood still; all the perfumes of Arabia will not sweeten this little hand. Oh, oh, oh!

Doct. What a sigh is there! The heart is sorely charg'd.[2]

Gent. I would not have such a heart in my bosom for the dignity of the whole body.

Doct. Well, well, well,—

Gent. Pray God it be, sir.

Doct. This disease is beyond my practice; yet I have known those

[2] Burdened.

which have walk'd in their sleep who have died holily in their beds.

Lady M. Wash your hands, put on your nightgown; look not so pale.—I tell you yet again, Banquo's buried; he cannot come out on 's grave.

Doct. Even so?

Lady M. To bed, to bed! there's knocking at the gate. Come, come, come, come, give me your hand. What's done cannot be undone.—To bed, to bed, to bed! *Exit.*

Doct. Will she go now to bed?

Gent. Directly.

Doct. Foul whisp'rings are abroad; unnatural deeds
Do breed unnatural troubles; infected minds
To their deaf pillows will discharge their secrets.
More needs she the divine than the physician.
God, God, forgive us all! Look after her;
Remove from her the means of all annoyance,[3]
And still keep eyes upon her. So, good-night!
My mind she has mated,[4] and amaz'd my sight.
I think, but dare not speak.

Gent. Good-night, good doctor. *Exeunt.*

Scene II. [*The country near Dunsinane*]

Drum and colours. Enter Menteith, Caithness, Angus, Lennox, *and* Soldiers

Ment. The English power is near, led on by Malcolm,
His uncle Siward, and the good Macduff.
Revenges burn in them; for their dear[5] causes
Would to the bleeding and the grim alarm
Excite the mortified man.[6]

Ang. Near Birnam wood
Shall we well meet them; that way are they coming.

Caith. Who knows if Donalbain be with his brother?

Len. For certain, sir, he is not; I have a file[7]
Of all the gentry. There is Siward's son,

[3] Injury. [4] Paralyzed.
[5] Intimately felt. [6] Hermit (?). Dead man (?). [7] List.

And many unrough[8] youths that even now
Protest[9] their first of manhood.
Ment. What does the tyrant?
Caith. Great Dunsinane he strongly fortifies.
Some say he's mad, others that lesser hate him
Do call it valiant fury; but, for certain,
He cannot buckle his distemper'd cause[10]
Within the belt of rule.
Ang. Now does he feel
His secret murders sticking on his hands;
Now minutely[11] revolts upbraid his faith-breach;
Those he commands move only in command,
Nothing in love. Now does he feel his title
Hang loose about him, like a giant's robe
Upon a dwarfish thief.
Ment. Who then shall blame
His pester'd[12] senses to recoil and start,
When all that is within him does condemn
Itself for being there?
Caith. Well, march we on
To give obedience where 'tis truly ow'd.
Meet we the medicine of the sickly weal,
And with him pour we in our country's purge
Each drop of us.
Len. Or so much as it needs
To dew the sovereign flower and drown the weeds.
Make we our march towards Birnam. *Exeunt, marching.*

SCENE III. [*Dunsinane. A room in the castle*]

Enter MACBETH, Doctor, *and* Attendants

Macb. Bring me no more reports; let them fly all;
Till Birnam wood remove to Dunsinane
I cannot taint with fear. What's the boy Malcolm?
Was he not born of woman? The spirits that know

[8] Beardless. [9] Declare. [10] Cause of his mad behavior.
[11] Occurring every minute. [12] Perturbed.

All mortal[1] consequences have pronounc'd me thus:
"Fear not, Macbeth; no man that's born of woman
Shall e'er have power upon thee." Then fly, false thanes,
And mingle with the English epicures!
The mind I sway by and the heart I bear
Shall never sag with doubt nor shake with fear.

Enter a Servant

The devil damn thee black, thou cream-fac'd loon![2]
Where got'st thou that goose look?
Serv. There is ten thousand—
Macb. Geese, villain?
Serv. Soldiers, sir.
Macb. Go prick thy face, and over-red thy fear,
Thou lily-liver'd boy. What soldiers, patch?[3]
Death of thy soul! those linen cheeks of thine
Are counsellors to fear. What soldiers, whey-face?
Serv. The English force, so please you.
Macb. Take thy face hence. [*Exit* Servant.]
Seyton!—I am sick at heart
When I behold—Seyton, I say!—This push[4]
Will cheer me ever, or disseat me now.
I have liv'd long enough. My way of life
Is fallen into the sear, the yellow leaf;
And that which should accompany old age,
As honour, love, obedience, troops of friends,
I must not look to have; but, in their stead,
Curses, not loud but deep, mouth-honour, breath
Which the poor heart would fain deny, and dare not.
Seyton!

Enter Seyton

Sey. What's your gracious pleasure?
Macb. What news more?
Sey. All is confirm'd, my lord, which was reported.

[1] Affecting men. [2] Fellow, rascal.
[3] Fool. [4] Assault.

Macb. I'll fight till from my bones my flesh be hack'd.
Give me my armour.
Sey. 'Tis not needed yet.
Macb. I'll put it on.
Send out moe[5] horses; skirr[6] the country round;
Hang those that talk of fear. Give me mine armour.
How does your patient, doctor?
Doct. Not so sick, my lord,
As she is troubled with thick-coming fancies,
That keep her from her rest.
Macb. Cure her of that.
Canst thou not minister to a mind diseas'd,
Pluck from the memory a rooted sorrow,
Raze out the written troubles of the brain,
And with some sweet oblivious[7] antidote
Cleanse the stuff'd bosom of that perilous stuff
Which weighs upon the heart?
Doct. Therein the patient
Must minister to himself.
Macb. Throw physic to the dogs; I'll none of it.
Come, put mine armour on; give me my staff.
Seyton, send out. Doctor, the thanes fly from me.
Come, sir, dispatch. If thou couldst, doctor, cast
The water[8] of my land, find her disease,
And purge it to a sound and pristine[9] health,
I would applaud thee to the very echo,
That should applaud again.—Pull 't off, I say.—
What rhubarb, senna, or what purgative drug,
Would scour these English hence? Hear'st thou of them?
Doct. Ay, my good lord; your royal preparation
Makes us hear something.
Macb. Bring it after me.
I will not be afraid of death and bane,[10]
Till Birnam forest come to Dunsinane.

[5] More. [6] Scour. [7] Causing forgetfulness.
[8] Diagnose by inspecting urine. [9] Original. [10] Ruin.

Doct. [*Aside.*] Were I from Dunsinane away and clear,
Profit again should hardly draw me here. *Exeunt.*

SCENE IV. [*Country near Birnam wood*]

Drum and colours. Enter MALCOLM, *old* SIWARD *and his* Son, MACDUFF, MENTEITH, CAITHNESS, ANGUS, [LENNOX, ROSS,] *and* Soldiers, *marching*

Mal. Cousins, I hope the days are near at hand
That chambers will be safe.
Ment. We doubt it nothing.
Siw. What wood is this before us?
Ment. The wood of Birnam.
Mal. Let every soldier hew him down a bough
And bear 't before him; thereby shall we shadow
The numbers of our host and make discovery[1]
Err in report of us.
Soldiers. It shall be done.
Siw. We learn no other but the confident tyrant
Keeps still in Dunsinane, and will endure
Our setting down before[2] 't.
Mal. 'Tis his main hope;
For where there is advantage to be given,
Both more and less[3] have given him the revolt,
And none serve with him but constrained things
Whose hearts are absent too.
Macd. Let our just censures[4]
Attend the true event, and put we on
Industrious soldiership.
Siw. The time approaches
That will with due decision make us know
What we shall say we have and what we owe.
Thoughts speculative their unsure hopes relate,
But certain issue strokes must arbitrate;
Towards which advance the war. *Exeunt, marching.*

[1] The scouts. [2] Besieging. [3] Great and small. [4] Let our opinions await the outcome.

SCENE V. [*Dunsinane. Within the castle*]

Enter MACBETH, SEYTON, *and* Soldiers, *with drum and colours*

Macb. Hang out our banners on the outward walls;
The cry is still, "They come!" Our castle's strength
Will laugh a siege to scorn; here let them lie
Till famine and the ague eat them up.
Were they not forc'd[1] with those that should be ours,
We might have met them dareful, beard to beard,
And beat them backward home. *A cry of women within.*
What is that noise?
Sey. It is the cry of women, my good lord. [*Exit.*]
Macb. I have almost forgot the taste of fears.
The time has been, my senses would have cool'd
To hear a night-shriek, and my fell[2] of hair
Would at a dismal treatise[3] rouse and stir
As life were in 't. I have supp'd full with horrors;
Direness, familiar to my slaughterous thoughts,
Cannot once start me.

[*Re-enter* SEYTON]

Wherefore was that cry?
Sey. The Queen, my lord, is dead.
Macb. She should have died hereafter;
There would have been a time for such a word.
To-morrow, and to-morrow, and to-morrow,
Creeps in this petty pace from day to day
To the last syllable of recorded time;
And all our yesterdays have lighted fools
The way to dusty death. Out, out, brief candle!
Life's but a walking shadow, a poor player
That struts and frets his hour upon the stage
And then is heard no more. It is a tale
Told by an idiot, full of sound and fury,
Signifying nothing.

[1] Reinforced. [2] Covering of hair. [3] Story.

Enter a Messenger

Thou com'st to use thy tongue; thy story quickly.
Mess. Gracious my lord,
I should report that which I say I saw,
But know not how to do it.
Macb. Well, say, sir.
Mess. As I did stand my watch upon the hill,
I look'd toward Birnam, and anon, methought,
The wood began to move.
Macb. Liar and slave!
Mess. Let me endure your wrath, if 't be not so.
Within this three mile may you see it coming;
I say, a moving grove.
Macb. If thou speak'st false,
Upon the next tree shall thou hang alive,
Till famine cling[4] thee; if thy speech be sooth,
I care not if thou dost for me as much.
I pull in resolution, and begin
To doubt the equivocation of the fiend
That lies like truth. "Fear not, till Birnam wood
Do come to Dunsinane;" and now a wood
Comes toward Dunsinane. Arm, arm, and out!
If this which he avouches does appear,
There is nor flying hence nor tarrying here.
I gin to be aweary of the sun,
And wish the estate o' the world were now undone.
Ring the alarum-bell! Blow, wind! come, wrack!
At least we'll die with harness on our back. *Exeunt.*

SCENE VI. [*Dunsinane. Before the castle*]

Drum and colours. Enter MALCOLM, *old* SIWARD, MACDUFF, *and their* Army, *with boughs*

Mal. Now near enough; your leavy screens throw down,
And show like those you are. You, worthy uncle,
Shall, with my cousin, your right noble son,

[4] Shrivel.

Lead our first battle.[1] Worthy Macduff and we
Shall take upon 's what else remains to do,
According to our order.

Siw. Fare you well.
Do we but find the tyrant's power to-night,
Let us be beaten, if we cannot fight.

Macd. Make all our trumpets speak; give them all breath,
Those clamorous harbingers[2] of blood and death.

Exeunt. Alarums continued.

SCENE VII. [*The same*]

Enter MACBETH

Macb. They have tied me to a stake; I cannot fly,
But, bear-like, I must fight the course.[3] What's he
That was not born of woman? Such a one
Am I to fear, or none.

Enter young SIWARD

Y. Siw. What is thy name?

Macb. Thou'lt be afraid to hear it.

Y. Siw. No; though thou call'st thyself a hotter name
Than any is in hell.

Macb. My name's Macbeth.

Y. Siw. The devil himself could not pronounce a title
More hateful to mine ear.

Macb. No, nor more fearful.

Y. Siw. Thou liest, abhorred tyrant; with my sword
I'll prove the lie thou speak'st.

They fight and young SIWARD *is slain.*

Macb. Thou wast born of woman.
But swords I smile at, weapons laugh to scorn,
Brandish'd by man that's of a woman born. *Exit.*

Alarums. Enter MACDUFF

Macd. That way the noise is. Tyrant, show thy face!
If thou be'st slain and with no stroke of mine,

[1] Battalion. [2] Forerunners, announcers. [3] The attack of the dogs.

My wife and children's ghosts will haunt me still.
I cannot strike at wretched kerns,[4] whose arms
Are hir'd to bear their staves; either thou, Macbeth,
Or else my sword with an unbattered edge
I sheathe again undeeded. There thou shouldst be;
By this great clatter, one of greatest note
Seems bruited.[5] Let me find him, Fortune!
And more I beg not. *Exit. Alarums.*

Enter MALCOLM *and old* SIWARD

Siw. This way, my lord; the castle's gently rend'red:[6]
The tyrant's people on both sides do fight;
The noble thanes do bravely in the war;
The day almost itself professes yours,
And little is to do.
Mal. We have met with foes
That strike beside us.[7]
Siw. Enter, sir, the castle. [*Exeunt. Alarums.*

SCENE VIII. [*The same*]

Enter MACBETH

Macb. Why should I play the Roman fool, and die
On mine own sword? Whiles I see lives, the gashes
Do better upon them.

Enter MACDUFF

Macd. Turn, hell-hound, turn!
Macb. Of all men else I have avoided thee.
But get thee back; my soul is too much charg'd
With blood of thine already.
Macd. I have no words,
My voice is in my sword, thou bloodier villain
Than terms[1] can give thee out! *They fight. Alarum.*

[4] Light-armed foot-soldiers. [5] Announced. [6] Peaceably surrendered.
[7] On our side, or, so as not to wound us. [1] Words.

Macb. Thou losest labour.
As easy mayst thou the intrenchant[2] air
With thy keen sword impress as make me bleed.
Let fall thy blade on vulnerable crests;
I bear a charmed life, which must not yield
To one of woman born.
Macd. Despair thy charm;
And let the angel whom thou still hast serv'd
Tell thee, Macduff was from his mother's womb
Untimely ripp'd.
Macb. Accursed be that tongue that tells me so,
For it hath cow'd my better part of man!
And be these juggling fiends no more believ'd
That palter with us in a double sense,
That keep the word of promise to our ear,
And break it to our hope. I'll not fight with thee.
Macd. Then yield thee, coward,
And live to be the show and gaze o' the time.
We'll have thee, as our rarer monsters are,
Painted upon a pole,[3] and underwrit,
"Here may you see the tyrant."
Macb. I will not yield,
To kiss the ground before young Malcolm's feet
And to be baited with the rabble's curse.
Though Birnam wood be come to Dunsinane,
And thou oppos'd, being of no woman born,
Yet I will try the last. Before my body
I throw my warlike shield. Lay on, Macduff,
And damn'd be him that first cries, "Hold, enough!"
Exeunt, fighting. Alarums.

Retreat. Flourish. Enter, with drum and colours, MALCOLM, *old* SIWARD, ROSS, *the other* Thanes, *and* Soldiers

Mal. I would the friends we miss were safe arriv'd.
Siw. Some must go off;[4] and yet, by these I see,

[2] Not to be injured by cutting. [3] A cloth hanging from a pole. [4] Die

So great a day as this is cheaply bought.

Mal. Macduff is missing, and your noble son.

Ross. Your son, my lord, has paid a soldier's debt.
He only liv'd but till he was a man;
The which no sooner had his prowess confirm'd
In the unshrinking station where he fought,
But like a man he died.

Siw. Then he is dead?

Ross. Ay, and brought off the field. Your cause of sorrow
Must not be measur'd by his worth, for then
It hath no end.

Siw. Had he his hurts before?

Ross. Ay, on the front.

Siw. Why then, God's soldier be he!
Had I as many sons as I have hairs,
I would not wish them to a fairer death.
And so, his knell is knoll'd.

Mal. He's worth more sorrow,
And that I'll spend for him.

Siw. He's worth no more.
They say he parted well, and paid his score;
And so, God be with him! Here comes newer comfort.

Re-enter MACDUFF, *with* MACBETH's *head*

Macd. Hail, king! for so thou art. Behold, where stands
The usurper's cursed head. The time is free.
I see thee compass'd with thy kingdom's pearl,
That speak my salutation in their minds;
Whose voices I desire aloud with mine:
Hail, King of Scotland!

All. Hail, King of Scotland! *Flourish.*

Mal. We shall not spend a large expense of time
Before we reckon with your several loves,
And make us even with you. My thanes and kinsmen,
Henceforth be earls, the first that ever Scotland
In such an honour nam'd. What's more to do,
Which would be planted newly with the time,

As calling home our exil'd friends abroad
That fled the snares of watchful tyranny;
Producing forth the cruel ministers
Of this dead butcher and his fiend-like queen,
Who, as 'tis thought, by self and violent hands
Took off her life; this, and what needful else
That calls upon us, by the grace of Grace,
We will perform in measure, time, and place.
So, thanks to all at once and to each one,
Whom we invite to see us crown'd at Scone. *Flourish. Exeunt.*

THE TEMPEST

BY

WILLIAM SHAKESPEARE

INTRODUCTORY NOTE

It is entirely probable that the date of "The Tempest" is 1611, and that this was the last play completed by Shakespeare before he retired from active connection with the theater to spend the remainder of his life in leisure in his native town of Stratford-on-Avon.

The main thread of the plot of the drama seems to have been some folk-tale of a magician and his daughter, which, in the precise form in which Shakespeare knew it, has not been recovered. The storm and the island were, it is believed, suggested by the wreck on the Bermudas in 1609 of one of the English expeditions to Virginia. Traces are found, too, of the author's reading in contemporary books of travel.

But the plot itself is of less importance than usual. Supernatural elements are introduced with great freedom, and the dramatist's interest was clearly not in the reproduction of lifelike events. The presentation of character and the attractive picturing of the beauty of magnanimity and forgiveness are the things which, along with its delightful poetry, make the charm of this play. It is not to be wondered at that readers have frequently been led to find in the figure of the great magician, laying aside his robes and wonder-working rod in a spirit of love and peace toward all men, a symbol of the dramatist himself at the close of his great career; and it is surely legitimate to play with this idea without assuming that Shakespeare consciously embodied it. One can hardly conceive a more fitting epilogue to the volume which is the crown of the world's dramatic literature than the romance of "The Tempest."

THE TEMPEST

[DRAMATIS PERSONÆ]

ALONSO, king of Naples.
SEBASTIAN, his brother.
PROSPERO, the right duke of Milan.
ANTONIO, his brother, the usurping duke of Milan.
FERDINAND, son to the king of Naples.
GONZALO, an honest old Counsellor.
ADRIAN, FRANCISCO, Lords.
CALIBAN, a savage and deformed Slave.
TRINCULO, a Jester.
STEPHANO, a drunken Butler.

Master of a Ship.
Boatswain.
Mariners.

MIRANDA, daughter to Prospero.

ARIEL, an airy Spirit.
IRIS, CERES, JUNO, Nymphs, Reapers, Spirits.

[Other Spirits attending on Prospero]

SCENE: [A SHIP AT SEA;] AN UNINHABITED ISLAND

ACT I

SCENE I. [*On a ship at sea:*] *a tempestuous noise of thunder and lightning heard*

Enter a Ship-Master *and a* Boatswain

Master

BOATSWAIN!

Boats. Here, master; what cheer?

Mast. Good; speak to the mariners. Fall to 't, yarely,[1] or we run ourselves aground. Bestir, bestir. *Exit.*

Enter Mariners

Boats. Heigh, my hearts! cheerly, cheerly, my hearts! yare,[1] yare! Take in the topsail. Tend to the master's whistle.—Blow till thou burst thy wind, if room enough!

[1] Smartly.

Enter ALONSO, SEBASTIAN, ANTONIO, FERDINAND, GONZALO, *and others*

Alon. Good boatswain, have care. Where's the master? Play the men.

Boats. I pray now, keep below.

Ant. Where is the master, boatswain?

Boats. Do you not hear him? You mar our labour. Keep your cabins; you do assist the storm.

Gon. Nay, good, be patient.

Boats. When the sea is. Hence! What cares these roarers for the name of king? To cabin! silence! trouble us not.

Gon. Good, yet remember whom thou hast aboard.

Boats. None that I more love than myself. You are a counsellor; if you can command these elements to silence, and work the peace of the present, we will not hand a rope more; use your authority. If you cannot, give thanks you have liv'd so long, and make yourself ready in your cabin for the mischance of the hour, if it so hap.—Cheerly, good hearts!—Out of our way, I say. *Exit.*

Gon. I have great comfort from this fellow. Methinks he hath no drowning mark upon him; his complexion is perfect gallows. Stand fast, good Fate, to his hanging; make the rope of his destiny our cable, for our own doth little advantage. If he be not born to be hang'd, our case is miserable. *Exeunt.*

Re-enter Boatswain

Boats. Down with the topmast! yare! lower, lower! Bring her to try[2] wi' the main-course. A plague *A cry within.*

Enter SEBASTIAN, ANTONIO, *and* GONZALO

upon this howling! They are louder than the weather or our office. —Yet again! What do you here? Shall we give o'er and drown? Have you a mind to sink?

Seb. A pox o' your throat, you bawling, blasphemous, incharitable dog!

Boats. Work you, then.

[2] Close to the wind.

Ant. Hang, cur! hang, you whoreson, insolent noisemaker! We are less afraid to be drown'd than thou art.

Gon. I'll warrant him for drowning though the ship were no stronger than a nut-shell and as leaky as an unstanched wench.

Boats. Lay her a-hold,[3] a-hold! Set her two courses[4] off to sea again! Lay her off.

Enter Mariners *wet*

Mariners. All lost! To prayers, to prayers! All lost!

Boats. What, must our mouths be cold?

Gon. The King and Prince at prayers! Let's assist them,
For our case is as theirs.

Seb. I'm out of patience.

Ant. We are merely[5] cheated of our lives by drunkards.
This wide-chapp'd rascal—would thou mightst lie drowning
The washing of ten tides!

Gon. He'll be hang'd yet,
Though every drop of water swear against it
And gape at wid'st to glut him. *A confused noise within.*
Mercy on us!
We split, we split! Farewell, my wife and children!
Farewell, brother! We split, we split, we split!

Ant. Let's all sink wi' the King.

Seb. Let's take leave of him. *Exit.*

Gon. Now would I give a thousand furlongs of sea for an acre of barren ground, long heath, brown furze, anything. The wills above be done! but I would fain die a dry death. *Exeunt.*

Scene II. [*The island. Before Prospero's cell*]

Enter Prospero *and* Miranda

Mir. If by your art, my dearest father, you have
Put the wild waters in this roar, allay them.
The sky, it seems, would pour down stinking pitch,
But that the sea, mounting to the welkin's cheek,
Dashes the fire out. O, I have suffered

[3] Bring her close to the wind. [4] The mainsail and foresail. [5] Absolutely.

With those that I saw suffer! A brave vessel,
Who had, no doubt, some noble creature in her,
Dash'd all to pieces! O, the cry did knock
Against my very heart. Poor souls, they perish'd.
Had I been any god of power, I would
Have sunk the sea within the earth or ere
It should the good ship so have swallow'd and
The fraughting[1] souls within her.

Pros. Be collected;
No more amazement. Tell your piteous heart
There's no harm done.

Mir. O, woe the day!

Pros. No harm.
I have done nothing but in care of thee,
Of thee, my dear one, thee, my daughter, who
Art ignorant of what thou art, nought knowing
Of whence I am, nor that I am more better
Than Prospero, master of a full poor cell,
And thy no greater father.

Mir. More to know
Did never meddle with my thoughts.

Pros. 'Tis time
I should inform thee farther. Lend thy hand,
And pluck my magic garment from me. So,
[*Lays down his mantle.*]
Lie there, my art. Wipe thou thine eyes; have comfort.
The direful spectacle of the wreck, which touch'd
The very virtue of compassion in thee,
I have with such provision in mine art
So safely ordered that there is no soul—
No, not so much perdition as an hair
Betid to any creature in the vessel
Which thou heard'st cry, which thou saw'st sink. Sit down;
For thou must now know farther.

Mir. You have often
Begun to tell me what I am, but stopp'd

[1] Composing the freight.

And left me to a bootless inquisition,
Concluding, "Stay, not yet."
Pros. The hour's now come;
The very minute bids thee ope thine ear.
Obey and be attentive. Canst thou remember
A time before we came unto this cell?
I do not think thou canst, for then thou wast not
Out three years old.
Mir. Certainly, sir, I can.
Pros. By what? By any other house or person?
Of anything the image tell me, that
Hath kept with thy remembrance.
Mir. 'Tis far off
And rather like a dream than an assurance
That my remembrance warrants. Had I not
Four or five women once that tended me?
Pros. Thou hadst, and more, Miranda. But how is it
That this lives in thy mind? What seest thou else
In the dark backward and abysm[2] of time?
If thou rememb'rest aught ere thou cam'st here,
How thou cam'st here thou may'st.
Mir. But that I do not.
Pros. Twelve year since, Miranda, twelve year since,
Thy father was the Duke of Milan and
A prince of power.
Mir. Sir, are not you my father?
Pros. Thy mother was a piece of virtue, and
She said thou wast my daughter; and thy father
Was Duke of Milan, and his only heir
And princess no worse issued.
Mir. O the heavens!
What foul play had we, that we came from thence?
Or blessed was 't we did?
Pros. Both, both, my girl.
By foul play, as thou say'st, were we heav'd thence,
But blessedly holp hither.

[2] Depth.

Mir. O, my heart bleeds
To think o' the teen[3] that I have turn'd you to,
Which is from my remembrance! Please you, farther.
Pros. My brother and thy uncle, call'd Antonio—
I pray thee, mark me—that a brother should
Be so perfidious!—he whom next thyself
Of all the world I lov'd, and to him put
The manage[4] of my state; as at that time
Through all the signories[5] it was the first,
And Prospero the prime duke, being so reputed
In dignity, and for the liberal arts
Without a parallel; those being all my study,
The government I cast upon my brother
And to my state grew stranger, being transported
And rapt in secret studies. Thy false uncle—
Dost thou attend me?
Mir. Sir, most heedfully.
Pros. Being once perfected how to grant suits,
How to deny them, who to advance and who
To trash for overtopping,[6] new created
The creatures that were mine, I say, or chang'd 'em,
Or else new form'd 'em; having both the key
Of officer and office, set all hearts i' the state
To what tune pleas'd his ear; that now he was
The ivy which had hid my princely trunk,
And suck'd my verdure out on 't. Thou attend'st not.
Mir. O, good sir, I do.
Pros. I pray thee, mark me.
I, thus neglecting worldly ends, all dedicated
To closeness[7] and the bettering of my mind
With that which, but by being so retir'd,
O'er-priz'd all popular rate,[8] in my false brother
Awak'd an evil nature; and my trust,
Like a good parent, did beget of him
A falsehood, in its contrary as great

[3] Trouble. [4] Management. [5] Lordships. [6] To check for excessive ambition.
[7] Seclusion. [8] Was more valuable than popularity.

As my trust was; which had indeed no limit,
A confidence sans[9] bound. He being thus lorded,
Not only with what my revenue yielded,
But what my power might else exact,—like one
Who having into truth, by telling of it,
Made such a sinner of his memory
To credit his own lie,—he did believe
He was indeed the Duke. Out o' the substitution,[10]
And executing the outward face of royalty,
With all prerogative, hence his ambition growing—
Dost thou hear?

Mir. Your tale, sir, would cure deafness.

Pros. To have no screen between this part he play'd
And him he play'd it for, he needs will be
Absolute Milan. Me, poor man!—my library
Was dukedom large enough—of temporal royalties
He thinks me now incapable; confederates—
So dry[11] he was for sway—wi' the King of Naples
To give him annual tribute, do him homage,
Subject his coronet to his crown, and bend
The dukedom yet unbow'd—alas, poor Milan!—
To most ignoble stooping.

Mir. O the heavens!

Pros. Mark his condition and the event, then tell me
If this might be a brother.

Mir. I should sin
To think but nobly of my grandmother.
Good wombs have borne bad sons.

Pros. Now the condition.
This King of Naples, being an enemy
To me inveterate, hearkens my brother's suit;
Which was, that he, in lieu o' the premises[12]
Of homage and I know not how much tribute,
Should presently extirpate me and mine
Out of the dukedom, and confer fair Milan

[9] Without. [10] From being deputy.
[11] Thirsty. [12] In return for the conditions.

With all the honours on my brother; whereon,
A treacherous army levied, one midnight
Fated to the purpose did Antonio open
The gates of Milan; and, i' the dead of darkness,
The ministers for the purpose hurried thence
Me and thy crying self.
Mir. Alack, for pity!
I, not rememb'ring how I cried out then,
Will cry it o'er again. It is a hint[13]
That wrings mine eyes to 't.
Pros. Hear a little further,
And then I'll bring thee to the present business
Which now's upon 's, without the which this story
Were most impertinent.[14]
Mir. Wherefore did they not
That hour destroy us?
Pros. Well demanded, wench;
My tale provokes that question. Dear, they durst not
(So dear the love my people bore me) set
A mark so bloody on the business; but
With colours fairer painted their foul ends.
In few, they hurried us aboard a bark,
Bore us some leagues to sea; where they prepared
A rotten carcass of a butt,[15] not rigg'd,
Nor tackle, sail, nor mast; the very rats
Instinctively have quit it. There they hoist us,
To cry to the sea that roar'd to us, to sigh
To the winds whose pity, sighing back again,
Did us but loving wrong.
Mir. Alack, what trouble
Was I then to you!
Pros. O, a cherubin
Thou wast that did preserve me. Thou didst smile,
Infused with a fortitude from heaven,
When I have deck'd the sea with drops full salt,
Under my burden groan'd; which rais'd in me

[13] Occasion, suggestion. [14] Not to the purpose. [15] Old tub, hulk.

An undergoing[16] stomach, to bear up
Against what should ensue.
Mir. How came we ashore?
Pros. By Providence divine.
Some food we had and some fresh water that
A noble Neapolitan, Gonzalo,
Out of his charity, who being then appointed
Master of this design, did give us, with
Rich garments, linens, stuffs, and necessaries,
Which since have steaded much;[17] so, of his gentleness,
Knowing I lov'd my books, he furnish'd me
From mine own library with volumes that
I prize above my dukedom.
Mir. Would I might
But ever see that man!
Pros. Now I arise. [*Puts on his robe.*]
Sit still, and hear the last of our sea-sorrow.
Here in this island we arriv'd; and here
Have I, thy schoolmaster, made thee more profit
Than other princess can that have more time
For vainer hours, and tutors not so careful.
Mir. Heavens thank you for 't! And now, I pray you, sir,
For still 'tis beating in my mind, your reason
For raising this sea-storm?
Pros. Know thus far forth.
By accident most strange, bountiful Fortune,
Now my dear lady, hath mine enemies
Brought to this shore; and by my prescience
I find my zenith[18] doth depend upon
A most auspicious star, whose influence
If now I court not but omit, my fortunes
Will ever after droop. Here cease more questions.
Thou art inclin'd to sleep; 'tis a good dulness,
And give it way. I know thou canst not choose. [MIRANDA *sleeps.*]
Come away, servant, come; I am ready now.
Approach, my Ariel; come.

16 Enduring. 17 Stood in good stead. 18 The highest point in my fortunes.

Enter ARIEL

Ari. All hail, great master! grave sir, hail! I come
To answer thy best pleasure, be 't to fly,
To swim, to dive into the fire, to ride
On the curl'd clouds. To thy strong bidding task
Ariel and all his quality.[19]

Pros. Hast thou, spirit,
Perform'd to point[20] the tempest that I bade thee?

Ari. To every article.
I boarded the king's ship; now on the beak,
Now in the waist, the deck, in every cabin,
I flam'd amazement. Sometime I'd divide,
And burn in many places. On the topmast,
The yards and bowsprit, would I flame distinctly,
Then meet and join. Jove's lightnings, the precursors
O' the dreadful thunder-claps, more momentary
And sight-outrunning were not; the fire and cracks
Of sulphurous roaring the most mighty Neptune
Seem to besiege, and make his bold waves tremble,
Yea, his dread trident shake.

Pros. My brave spirit!
Who was so firm, so constant, that this coil[21]
Would not infect his reason?

Ari. Not a soul
But felt a fever of the mad, and play'd
Some tricks of desperation. All but mariners
Plung'd in the foaming brine and quit the vessel,
Then all afire with me. The King's son, Ferdinand,
With hair up-staring,—then like reeds, not hair,—
Was the first man that leap'd; cried, "Hell is empty,
And all the devils are here."

Pros. Why, that's my spirit!
But was not this nigh shore?

Ari. Close by, my master.

[19] Power. [20] Exactly.
[21] Turmoil.

Pros. But are they, Ariel, safe?
Ari. Not a hair perish'd;
On their sustaining garments not a blemish,
But fresher than before; and, as thou bad'st me,
In troops I have dispers'd them 'bout the isle.
The King's son have I landed by himself,
Whom I left cooling of the air with sighs
In an odd angle of the isle, and sitting,
His arms in this sad knot.
Pros. Of the King's ship
The mariners say how thou hast dispos'd,
And all the rest o' the fleet.
Ari. Safely in harbour
Is the King's ship; in the deep nook, where once
Thou call'dst me up at midnight to fetch dew
From the still-vex'd Bermoothes, there she's hid;
The mariners all under hatches stow'd,
Who, with a charm join'd to their suff'red labour,
I have left asleep; and for the rest o' the fleet,
Which I dispers'd, they all have met again,
And are upon the Mediterranean float[22]
Bound sadly home for Naples,
Supposing that they saw the King's ship wreck'd
And his great person perish.
Pros. Ariel, thy charge
Exactly is perform'd; but there's more work.
What is the time o' the day?
Ari. Past the mid season.
Pros. At least two glasses. The time 'twixt six and now
Must by us both be spent most preciously.
Ari. Is there more toil? Since thou dost give me pains,
Let me remember thee what thou hast promis'd,
Which is not yet perform'd me.
Pros. How now? moody?
What is 't thou canst demand?
Ari. My liberty.

[22] Sea.

Pros. Before the time be out? No more!
Ari. I prithee,
Remember I have done thee worthy service,
Told thee no lies, made thee no mistakings, serv'd
Without or grudge or grumblings. Thou did promise
To bate[23] me a full year.
Pros. Dost thou forget
From what a torment I did free thee?
Ari. No.
Pros. Thou dost, and think'st it much to tread the ooze
Of the salt deep,
To run upon the sharp wind of the north,
To do me business in the veins o' the earth
When it is bak'd with frost.
Ari. I do not, sir.
Pros. Thou liest, malignant thing! Hast thou forgot
The foul witch Sycorax, who with age and envy
Was grown into a hoop? Hast thou forgot her?
Ari. No, sir.
Pros. Thou hast. Where was she born? Speak; tell me.
Ari. Sir, in Argier.[24]
Pros. O, was she so? I must
Once in a month recount what thou hast been,
Which thou forget'st. This damn'd witch Sycorax,
For mischiefs manifold and sorceries terrible
To enter human hearing, from Argier,
Thou know'st, was banish'd; for one thing she did
They would not take her life. Is not this true?
Ari. Ay, sir.
Pros. This blue-ey'd hag was hither brought with child,
And here was left by the sailors. Thou, my slave,
As thou report'st thyself, was then her servant;
And, for thou wast a spirit too delicate
To act her earthy and abhorr'd commands,
Refusing her grand hests,[25] she did confine thee,
By help of her more potent ministers

[23] Reduce my service. [24] Algiers. [25] Commands.

And in her most unmitigable rage,
Into a cloven pine; within which rift
Imprison'd thou didst painfully remain
A dozen years; within which space she died
And left thee there, where thou didst vent thy groans
As fast as mill-wheels strike. Then was this island—
Save for the son that she did litter here,
A freckl'd whelp, hag-born,—not honour'd with
A human shape.

Ari. Yes, Caliban her son.

Pros. Dull thing, I say so; he, that Caliban
Whom now I keep in service. Thou best know'st
What torment I did find thee in; thy groans
Did make wolves howl, and penetrate the breasts
Of ever angry bears. It was a torment
To lay upon the damn'd, which Sycorax
Could not again undo. It was mine art,
When I arriv'd and heard thee, that made gape
The pine, and let thee out.

Ari. I thank thee, master.

Pros. If thou more murmur'st, I will rend an oak
And peg thee in his knotty entrails till
Thou hast howl'd away twelve winters.

Ari. Pardon, master;
I will be correspondent[26] to command
And do my spiriting gently.

Pros. Do so, and after two days
I will discharge thee.

Ari. That's my noble master!
What shall I do? say what. What shall I do?

Pros. Go make thyself like a nymph o' the sea; be subject
To no sight but thine and mine, invisible
To every eyeball else. Go take this shape
And hither come in 't. Go, hence with diligence! *Exit* ARIEL.
Awake, dear heart, awake! Thou hast slept well;
Awake!

[26] Responsive.

Mir. The strangeness of your story put
Heaviness in me.
Pros. Shake it off. Come on,
We'll visit Caliban my slave, who never
Yields us kind answer.
Mir. 'Tis a villain, sir,
I do not love to look on.
Pros. But, as 'tis,
We cannot miss him. He does make our fire,
Fetch in our wood, and serves in offices
That profit us. What, ho! slave! Caliban!
Thou earth, thou! speak.
Cal. (*Within.*) There's wood enough within.
Pros. Come forth, I say! there's other business for thee.
Come, thou tortoise! when?

Re-enter Ariel *like a water-nymph*

Fine apparition! My quaint Ariel,
Hark in thine ear.
Ari. My lord, it shall be done. *Exit.*
Pros. Thou poisonous slave, got by the devil himself
Upon thy wicked dam, come forth!

Enter Caliban

Cal. As wicked dew as e'er my mother brush'd
With raven's feather from unwholesome fen
Drop on you both! A south-west blow on ye
And blister you all o'er!
Pros. For this, be sure, to-night thou shalt have cramps,
Side-stitches that shall pen thy breath up; urchins[27]
Shall, for that vast[28] of night that they may work,
All exercise on thee; thou shalt be pinch'd
As thick as honeycomb, each pinch more stinging
Than bees that made 'em.

[27] Elves in the form of hedgehogs. [28] Empty stretch.

Cal. I must eat my dinner.
This island's mine, by Sycorax my mother,
Which thou tak'st from me. When thou cam'st first
Thou strok'dst me and made much of me, wouldst give me
Water with berries in 't, and teach me how
To name the bigger light, and how the less,
That burn by day and night; and then I lov'd thee
And show'd thee all the qualities o' the isle,
The fresh springs, brine-pits, barren place and fertile.
Curs'd be I that did so! All the charms
Of Sycorax, toads, beetles, bats, light on you!
For I am all the subjects that you have,
Which first was mine own king; and here you sty me
In this hard rock, whiles you do keep from me
The rest o' the island.

Pros. Thou most lying slave,
Whom stripes may move, not kindness! I have us'd thee,
Filth as thou art, with human care, and lodg'd thee
In mine own cell, till thou didst seek to violate
The honour of my child.

Cal. O ho, O ho! would 't had been done!
Thou didst prevent me; I had peopl'd else
This isle with Calibans.

[*Pros.*] Abhorred slave,
Which any print of goodness wilt not take,
Being capable of all ill! I pitied thee,
Took pains to make thee speak, taught thee each hour
One thing or other. When thou didst not, savage,
Know thine own meaning, but wouldst gabble like
A thing most brutish, I endow'd thy purposes
With words that made them known. But thy vile race,
Though thou didst learn, had that in 't which good natures
Could not abide to be with; therefore wast thou
Deservedly confin'd into this rock,
Who hadst deserv'd more than a prison.

Cal. You taught me language; and my profit on 't

Is, I know how to curse. The red plague rid you
For learning me your language!
Pros. Hag-seed, hence!
Fetch us in fuel; and be quick, thou 'rt best,
To answer other business. Shrug'st thou, malice?
If thou neglect'st or dost unwillingly
What I command, I'll rack thee with old cramps,
Fill all thy bones with aches, make thee roar
That beasts shall tremble at thy din.
Cal. No, pray thee.
[*Aside.*] I must obey. His art is of such power
It would control my dam's god, Setebos,
And make a vassal of him.
Pros. So, slave; hence! *Exit* CALIBAN

Re-enter ARIEL, *invisible, playing and singing;* FERDINAND [*following*]

ARIEL'S SONG

Come unto these yellow sands,
And then take hands.
Curtsied when you have, and kiss'd
The wild waves whist,[29]
Foot it featly[30] here and there,
And, sweet sprites, the burden bear.
Burden (*dispersedly*). Hark, hark!
Bow-wow.
The watch-dogs bark!
Bow-wow.
Ari. Hark, hark! I hear
The strain of strutting chanticleer
Cry, "Cock-a-diddle-dow."

Fer. Where should this music be? I' the air or the earth?
It sounds no more; and, sure, it waits upon
Some god o' the island. Sitting on a bank,

[29] Silent. [30] Nimbly.

Weeping again the King my father's wreck,
This music crept by me upon the waters,
Allaying both their fury and my passion
With its sweet air; thence I have follow'd it,
Or it hath drawn me rather. But 'tis gone.
No, it begins again.

ARIEL'S SONG

Full fathom five thy father lies;
Of his bones are coral made;
Those are pearls that were his eyes:
Nothing of him that doth fade
But doth suffer a sea-change
Into something rich and strange.
Sea-nymphs hourly ring his knell:
Burden. Ding-dong.
[*Ari.*] Hark! now I hear them,—ding-dong, bell.

Fer. The ditty does remember my drown'd father.
This is no mortal business, nor no sound
That the earth owes. I hear it now above me.
Pros. The fringed curtains of thine eye advance
And say what thou seest yond.
Mir. What is 't? A spirit?
Lord, how it looks about! Believe me, sir,
It carries a brave form. But 'tis a spirit.
Pros. No, wench; it eats and sleeps and hath such senses
As we have, such. This gallant which thou seest
Was in the wreck; and, but he's something stain'd
With grief, that's beauty's canker, thou mightst call him
A goodly person. He hath lost his fellows
And strays about to find 'em.
Mir. I might call him
A thing divine; for nothing natural
I ever saw so noble.
Pros. [*Aside.*] It goes on, I see,
As my soul prompts it. Spirit, fine spirit! I'll free thee
Within two days for this.

Fer. Most sure, the goddess
On whom these airs attend! Vouchsafe my prayer
May know if you remain upon this island,
And that you will some good instruction give
How I may bear me here. My prime request,
Which I do last pronounce, is, O you wonder!
If you be maid or no?
Mir. No wonder, sir,
But certainly a maid.
Fer. My language! heavens!
I am the best of them that speak this speech,
Were I but where 'tis spoken.
Pros. How? the best?
What wert thou, if the King of Naples heard thee?
Fer. A single thing, as I am now, that wonders
To hear thee speak of Naples. He does hear me;
And that he does I weep. Myself am Naples,
Who with mine eyes, never since at ebb, beheld
The King my father wreck'd.
Mir. Alack, for mercy!
Fer. Yes, faith, and all his lords; the Duke of Milan
And his brave son being twain.
Pros. [*Aside.*] The Duke of Milan
And his more braver daughter could control thee,
If now 'twere fit to do 't. At the first sight
They have chang'd eyes. Delicate Ariel,
I'll set thee free for this. [*To* FER.] A word, good sir;
I fear you have done yourself some wrong; a word.
Mir. Why speaks my father so ungently? This
Is the third man that e'er I saw, the first
That e'er I sigh'd for. Pity move my father
To be inclin'd my way!
Fer. O, if a virgin,
And your affection not gone forth, I'll make you
The Queen of Naples.
Pros. Soft, sir! one word more.
[*Aside.*] They are both in either's powers; but this swift business

I must uneasy make, lest too light winning
Make the prize light. [*To* FER.] One word more; I charge thee
That thou attend me. Thou dost here usurp
The name thou ow'st not; and hast put thyself
Upon this island as a spy, to win it
From me, the lord on 't.
Fer. No, as I am a man.
Mir. There's nothing ill can dwell in such a temple.
If the ill spirit have so fair a house,
Good things will strive to dwell with 't.
Pros. Follow me.
Speak not you for him; he's a traitor. Come,
I'll manacle thy neck and feet together.
Sea-water shalt thou drink; thy food shall be
The fresh-brook mussels, wither'd roots and husks
Wherein the acorn cradled. Follow.
Fer. No;
I will resist such entertainment till
Mine enemy has more power.
He draws, and is charmed from moving.
Mir. O dear father,
Make not too rash a trial of him, for
He's gentle and not fearful.[31]
Pros. What! I say;
My foot my tutor? Put thy sword up, traitor,
Who mak'st a show but dar'st not strike, thy conscience
Is so possess'd with guilt. Come from thy ward,
For I can here disarm thee with this stick
And make thy weapon drop.
Mir. Beseech you, father.
Pros. Hence! hang not on my garments.
Mir. Sir, have pity.
I'll be his surety.
Pros. Silence! one word more
Shall make me chide thee, if not hate thee. What!
An advocate for an impostor! hush!

[31] Nobly-born and no coward.

Thou think'st there is no more such shapes as he,
Having seen but him and Caliban. Foolish wench!
To the most of men this is a Caliban,
And they to him are angels.
Mir. My affections
Are then most humble; I have no ambition
To see a goodlier man.
Pros. Come on; obey.
Thy nerves[32] are in their infancy again
And have no vigour in them.
Fer. So they are.
My spirits, as in a dream, are all bound up.
My father's loss, the weakness which I feel,
The wreck of all my friends, nor this man's threats,
To whom I am subdu'd, are but light to me,
Might I but through my prison once a day
Behold this maid. All corners else o' the earth
Let liberty make use of; space enough
Have I in such a prison.
Pros. [*Aside.*] It works. [*To* FER.] Come on.
—Thou hast done well, fine Ariel! [*To* FER.] Follow me.
[*To* ARI.] Hark what thou else shalt do me.
Mir. Be of comfort;
My father's of a better nature, sir,
Than he appears by speech. This is unwonted
Which now came from him.
Pros. [*To* ARI.] Thou shalt be as free
As mountain winds; but then exactly do
All points of my command.
Ari. To the syllable.
Pros. [*To* MIR. *and* FER.] Come, follow. Speak not for him.
Exeunt.

[32] Sinews.

ACT II

Scene I. [*Another part of the island*]

Enter Alonso, Sebastian, Antonio, Gonzalo, Adrian, Francisco, *and others*

Gon. Beseech you sir, be merry; you have cause,
So have we all, of joy; for our escape
Is much beyond our loss. Our hint[1] of woe
Is common; every day some sailor's wife,
The masters of some merchant, and the merchant
Have just our theme of woe; but for the miracle,
I mean our preservation, few in millions
Can speak like us. Then wisely, good sir, weigh
Our sorrow with our comfort.

Alon. Prithee, peace.

Seb. He receives comfort like cold porridge.

Ant. The visitor will not give him o'er so.

Seb. Look, he's winding up the watch of his wit; by and by it will strike.

Gon. Sir,—

Seb. One. Tell.[2]

Gon. When every grief is entertain'd that's offer'd,
Comes to the entertainer—

Seb. A dollar.

Gon. Dolour comes to him, indeed; you have spoken truer than you purpos'd.

Seb. You have taken it wiselier than I meant you should.

Gon. Therefore, my lord,—

Ant. Fie, what a spendthrift is he of his tongue!

Alon. I prithee, spare.

Gon. Well, I have done. But yet,—

Seb. He will be talking.

Ant. Which, of he or Adrian, for a good wager, first begins to crow?

Seb. The old cock.

[1] Occasion. [2] Count.

Ant. The cockerel.

Seb. Done. The wager?

Ant. A laughter.

Seb. A match!

Adr. Though this island seem to be desert,—

Seb. Ha, ha, ha! Antonio! So you're paid.

Adr. Uninhabitable and almost inaccessible,—

Seb. Yet,—

Adr. Yet,—

Ant. He could not miss 't.

Adr. It must needs be of subtle, tender, and delicate temperance.[3]

Ant. Temperance was a delicate wench.

Seb. Ay, and a subtle; as he most learnedly deliver'd.

Adr. The air breathes upon us here most sweetly.

Seb. As if it had lungs and rotten ones.

Ant. Or as 'twere perfum'd by a fen.

Gon. Here is everything advantageous to life.

Ant. True; save means to live.

Seb. Of that there's none, or little.

Gon. How lush[4] and lusty the grass looks! How green!

Ant. The ground indeed is tawny.

Seb. With an eye of green in 't.

Ant. He misses not much.

Seb. No; he doth but mistake the truth totally.

Gon. But the rarity of it is,—which is indeed almost beyond credit,—

Seb. As many vouch'd rarities are.

Gon. That our garments, being, as they were, drench'd in the sea, hold notwithstanding their freshness and glosses, being rather new-dy'd than stain'd with salt water.

Ant. If but one of his pockets could speak, would it not say he lies?

Seb. Ay, or very falsely pocket up his report.

Gon. Methinks our garments are now as fresh as when we put them on first in Afric, at the marriage of the King's fair daughter Claribel to the King of Tunis.

[3] Temperature. [4] Luxuriant.

Seb. 'Twas a sweet marriage, and we prosper well in our return.

Adr. Tunis was never grac'd before with such a paragon to their queen.

Gon. Not since widow Dido's time.

Ant. Widow! a pox o' that! How came that widow in? Widow Dido!

Seb. What if he had said "widower Æneas" too? Good Lord, how you take it!

Adr. "Widow Dido" said you? You make me study of that. She was of Carthage, not of Tunis.

Gon. This Tunis, sir, was Carthage.

Adr. Carthage?

Gon. I assure you, Carthage.

Ant. His word is more than the miraculous harp.

Seb. He hath rais'd the wall and houses too.

Ant. What impossible matter will he make easy next?

Seb. I think he will carry this island home in his pocket and give it his son for an apple.

Ant. And, sowing the kernels of it in the sea, bring forth more islands.

Gon. Ay.

Ant. Why, in good time.

Gon. Sir, we were talking that our garments seem now as fresh as when we were at Tunis at the marriage of your daughter, who is now Queen.

Ant. And the rarest that e'er came there.

Seb. Bate,[5] I beseech you, widow Dido.

Ant. O, widow Dido! ay, widow Dido.

Gon. Is not, sir, my doublet as fresh as the first day I wore it? I mean, in a sort.

Ant. That sort was well fish'd for.

Gon. When I wore it at your daughter's marriage?

Alon. You cram these words into mine ears against
The stomach of my sense.[6] Would I had never
Married my daughter there! for, coming thence,
My son is lost and, in my rate,[7] she too,

[5] Except. [6] My inclination to hear. [7] Opinion.

Who is so far from Italy removed
I ne'er again shall see her. O thou mine heir
Of Naples and of Milan, what strange fish
Hath made his meal on thee?
Fran. Sir, he may live.
I saw him beat the surges under him,
And ride upon their backs. He trod the water,
Whose enmity he flung aside, and breasted
The surge most swoln that met him. His bold head
'Bove the contentious waves he kept, and oared
Himself with his good arms in lusty stroke
To the shore, that o'er his wave-worn basis bowed,
As stooping to relieve him. I not doubt
He came alive to land.
Alon. No, no, he's gone.
Seb. Sir, you may thank yourself for this great loss,
That would not bless our Europe with your daughter,
But rather lose her to an African;
Where she at least is banish'd from your eye,
Who hath cause to wet the grief on 't.
Alon. Prithee, peace.
Seb. You were kneel'd to and importun'd otherwise
By all of us, and the fair soul herself
Weigh'd between loathness and obedience, at
Which end o' the beam should bow. We have lost your son,
I fear, for ever. Milan and Naples have
Moe[8] widows in them of this business' making
Than we bring men to comfort them.
The fault's your own.
Alon. So is the dear'st o' the loss.
Gon. My lord Sebastian,
The truth you speak doth lack some gentleness
And time to speak it in. You rub the sore,
When you should bring the plaster.
Seb. Very well.
Ant. And most chirurgeonly.[9]

[8] More. [9] Like a surgeon.

Gon. It is foul weather in us all, good sir,
When you are cloudy.
Seb. Foul weather?
Ant. Very foul.
Gon. Had I plantation[10] of this isle, my lord,—
Ant. He'd sow 't with nettle-seed.
Seb. Or docks, or mallows.
Gon. And were the king on 't, what would I do?
Seb. Scape being drunk for want of wine.
Gon. I' the commonwealth I would by contraries
Execute all things; for no kind of traffic
Would I admit; no name of magistrate;
Letters should not be known; riches, poverty,
And use of service, none; contract, succession,
Bourn,[11] bound of land, tilth, vineyard, none;
No use of metal, corn, or wine, or oil;
No occupation; all men idle, all;
And women too, but innocent and pure;
No sovereignty;—
Seb. Yet he would be king on 't.
Ant. The latter end of his commonwealth forgets the beginning.
Gon. All things in common nature should produce
Without sweat or endeavour: treason, felony,
Sword, pike, knife, gun, or need of any engine,[12]
Would I not have; but nature should bring forth,
Of it own kind, all foison,[13] all abundance,
To feed my innocent people.
Seb. No marrying 'mong his subjects?
Ant. None, man; all idle; whores and knaves.
Gon. I would with such perfection govern, sir,
To excel the golden age.
Seb. Save his Majesty!
Ant. Long live Gonzalo!
Gon. And,—do you mark me, sir?
Alon. Prithee, no more; thou dost talk nothing to me.
Gon. I do well believe your Highness; and did it to minister occa-

[10] Colonization. [11] Boundary. [12] Implement. [13] Plenty.

sion to these gentlemen, who are of such sensible and nimble lungs that they always use to laugh at nothing.

Ant. 'Twas you we laugh'd at.

Gon. Who in this kind of merry fooling am nothing to you. So you may continue and laugh at nothing still.

Ant. What a blow was there given!

Seb. An it had not fallen flatlong.[14]

Gon. You are gentlemen of brave mettle; you would lift the moon out of her sphere, if she would continue in it five weeks without changing.

Enter ARIEL [*invisible*], *playing solemn music*

Seb. We would so, and then go a bat-fowling.

Ant. Nay, good my lord, be not angry.

Gon. No, I warrant you; I will not adventure my discretion so weakly. Will you laugh me asleep, for I am very heavy?

Ant. Go sleep, and hear us.

[*All sleep except* ALON., SEB., *and* ANT.]

Alon. What, all so soon asleep! I wish mine eyes
Would, with themselves, shut up my thoughts. I find
They are inclin'd to do so.

Seb. Please you, sir,
Do not omit the heavy offer of it.
It seldom visits sorrow; when it doth,
It is a comforter.

Ant. We two, my lord,
Will guard your person while you take your rest,
And watch your safety.

Alon. Thank you. Wondrous heavy.

[ALONSO *sleeps. Exit* ARIEL.]

Seb. What a strange drowsiness possesses them!

Ant. It is the quality o' the climate.

Seb. Why
Doth it not then our eyelids sink? I find not
Myself dispos'd to sleep.

Ant. Nor I; my spirits are nimble.

[14] On the flat side.

They fell together all, as by consent;
They dropp'd, as by a thunder-stroke. What might,
Worthy Sebastian, O, what might—? No more:—
And yet methinks I see it in thy face,
What thou shouldst be. The occasion speaks thee, and
My strong imagination sees a crown
Dropping upon thy head.

Seb. What, art thou waking?

Ant. Do you not hear me speak?

Seb. I do; and surely
It is a sleepy language, and thou speak'st
Out of thy sleep. What is it thou didst say?
This is a strange repose, to be asleep
With eyes wide open; standing, speaking, moving,
And yet so fast asleep.

Ant. Noble Sebastian,
Thou let'st thy fortune sleep—die, rather; wink'st
Whiles thou art waking.

Seb. Thou dost snore distinctly;
There's meaning in thy snores.

Ant. I am more serious than my custom; you
Must be so too, if heed me; which to do
Trebles thee o'er.

Seb. Well, I am standing water.[15]

Ant. I'll teach you how to flow.

Seb. Do so. To ebb
Hereditary sloth instructs me.

Ant. O,
If you but knew how you the purpose cherish
Whiles thus you mock it! how, in stripping it,
You more invest it! Ebbing men, indeed,
Most often do so near the bottom run
By their own fear or sloth.

Seb. Prithee, say on.
The setting[16] of thine eye and cheek proclaim
A matter from thee, and a birth indeed

[15] *I. e.*, in an indifferent attitude. [16] Fixed expression.

Which throes thee much to yield.
Ant. Thus, sir:
Although this lord of weak remembrance, this,
Who shall be of as little memory[17]
When he is earth'd, hath here almost persuaded—
For he's a spirit of persuasion, only
Professes to persuade—the King his son's alive,
'Tis as impossible that he's undrown'd
As he that sleeps here swims.
Seb. I have no hope
That he's undrown'd.
Ant. O, out of that no hope
What great hope have you! No hope that way is
Another way so high a hope that even
Ambition cannot pierce a wink beyond,
But doubt discovery there.[18] Will you grant with me
That Ferdinand is drown'd?
Seb. He's gone.
Ant. Then, tell me,
Who's the next heir of Naples?
Seb. Claribel.
Ant. She that is Queen of Tunis; she that dwells
Ten leagues beyond man's life; she that from Naples
Can have no note, unless the sun were post—
The man i' the moon's too slow—till new-born chins
Be rough and razorable; she that—from whom
We all were sea-swallow'd, though some cast again,
And by that destiny to perform an act
Whereof what's past is prologue, what to come
In yours and my discharge.
Seb. What stuff is this! How say you?
'Tis true, my brother's daughter's Queen of Tunis;
So is she heir of Naples; 'twixt which regions
There is some space.
Ant. A space whose every cubit
Seems to cry out, "How shall that Claribel

[17] As little remembered. [18] Whether there is anything higher to be seen.

Measure us back to Naples? Keep in Tunis,
And let Sebastian wake." Say, this were death
That now hath seiz'd them; why, they were no worse
Than now they are. There be that can rule Naples
As well as he that sleeps; lords that can prate
As amply and unnecessarily
As this Gonzalo; I myself could make
A chough of as deep chat.[19] O, that you bore
The mind that I do! what a sleep were this
For your advancement! Do you understand me?
Seb. Methinks I do.
Ant. And how does your content[20]
Tender[21] your own good fortune?
Seb. I remember
You did supplant your brother Prospero.
Ant. True.
And look how well my garments sit upon me;
Much feater[22] than before. My brother's servants
Were then my fellows; now they are my men.
Seb. But, for your conscience?
Ant. Ay, sir, where lies that? If 'twere a kibe,[23]
'Twould put me to my slipper; but I feel not
This deity in my bosom. Twenty consciences,
That stand 'twixt me and Milan, candied be they
And melt ere they molest! Here lies your brother,
No better than the earth he lies upon
If he were that which now he's like, that's dead;
Whom I, with this obedient steel, three inches of it,
Can lay to bed for ever; whiles you, doing thus,
To the perpetual wink for aye might put
This ancient morsel, this Sir Prudence, who
Should not upbraid our course. For all the rest,
They'll take suggestion as a cat laps milk;
They'll tell the clock to any business that
We say befits the hour.

[19] A jackdaw that could talk as profoundly. [20] Inclination. [21] Regard.
[22] Better fitting. [23] Chilblain.

Seb. Thy case, dear friend,
Shall be my precedent; as thou got'st Milan,
I'll come by Naples. Draw thy sword. One stroke
Shall free thee from the tribute which thou payest,
And I the King shall love thee.
Ant. Draw together;
And when I rear my hand, do you the like,
To fall it on Gonzalo.
Seb. O, but one word. [*They talk apart.*]

Re-enter ARIEL [*invisible*], *with music and song*

Ari. My master through his art foresees the danger
That you, his friend, are in; and sends me forth—
For else his project dies—to keep them living.
Sings in GONZALO's *ear.*

While you here do snoring lie,
Open-ey'd Conspiracy
His time doth take.
If of life you keep a care,
Shake off slumber, and beware;
Awake, awake!

Ant. Then let us both be sudden.
Gon. Now, good angels
Preserve the King. [*Wakes* ALON.]
Alon. Why, how now? Ho, awake! Why are you drawn?
Wherefore this ghastly looking?
Gon. What's the matter?
Seb. Whiles we stood here securing your repose,
Even now, we heard a hollow burst of bellowing
Like bulls, or rather lions. Did 't not wake you?
It struck mine ear most terribly.
Alon. I heard nothing.
Ant. O, 'twas a din to fright a monster's ear,
To make an earthquake! Sure, it was the roar
Of a whole herd of lions.
Alon. Heard you this, Gonzalo?

Gon. Upon mine honour, sir, I heard a humming,
And that a strange one too, which did awake me.
I shak'd you, sir, and cried. As mine eyes open'd,
I saw their weapons drawn. There was a noise,
That's verily. 'Tis best we stand upon our guard,
Or that we quit this place. Let's draw our weapons.
Alon. Lead off this ground; and let's make further search
For my poor son.
Gon. Heavens keep him from these beasts!
For he is, sure, i' the island.
Alon. Lead away.
Ari. Prospero my lord shall know what I have done.
So, King, go safely on to seek thy son. [*Exeunt.*

SCENE II. [*Another part of the island*]

Enter CALIBAN *with a burden of wood. A noise of thunder heard*

Cal. All the infections that the sun sucks up
From bogs, fens, flats, on Prosper fall and make him
By inch-meal[1] a disease! His spirits hear me
And yet I needs must curse. But they'll nor pinch,
Fright me with urchin-shows,[2] pitch me i' the mire,
Nor lead me, like a firebrand, in the dark
Out of my way, unless he bid 'em; but
For every trifle are they set upon me,
Sometime like apes that mow[3] and chatter at me
And after bite me, then like hedgehogs which
Lie tumbling in my barefoot way and mount
Their pricks at my footfall; sometime am I
All wound with adders who with cloven tongues
Do hiss me into madness.

Enter TRINCULO

Lo, now, lo!
Here comes a spirit of his, and to torment me
For bringing wood in slowly. I'll fall flat;
Perchance he will not mind me.

[1] Inch by inch. [2] Goblin apparitions. [3] Grimace.

Trin. Here's neither bush nor shrub, to bear off any weather at all, and another storm brewing; I hear it sing i' the wind. Yond same black cloud, yond huge one, looks like a foul bombard[4] that would shed his liquor. If it should thunder as it did before, I know not where to hide my head; yond same cloud cannot choose but fall by pailfuls. What have we here? A man or a fish? Dead or alive? A fish; he smells like a fish; a very ancient and fish-like smell; a kind of not-of-the-newest Poor-John.[5] A strange fish! Were I in England now, as once I was, and had but this fish painted, not a holiday fool there but would give a piece of silver. There would this monster make a man; any strange beast there makes a man. When they will not give a doit[6] to relieve a lame beggar, they will lay out ten to see a dead Indian. Legg'd like a man! and his fins like arms! Warm, o' my troth! I do now let loose my opinion, hold it no longer: this is no fish, but an islander, that hath lately suffered by a thunderbolt. [*Thunder.*] Alas, the storm is come again! My best way is to creep under his gaberdine;[7] there is no other shelter hereabout. Misery acquaints a man with strange bedfellows. I will here shroud till the dregs of the storm be past.

Enter STEPHANO, *singing* [*: a bottle in his hand*].

Ste. "I shall no more to sea, to sea,
Here shall I die ashore—"

This is a very scurvy tune to sing at a man's funeral. Well, here's my comfort. *Drinks.*

(*Sings.*) "The master, the swabber,[8] the boatswain, and I,
The gunner and his mate
Lov'd Moll, Meg, and Marian, and Margery,
But none of us car'd for Kate;
For she had a tongue with a tang,
Would cry to a sailor, Go hang!
She lov'd not the savour of tar nor of pitch,
Yet a tailor might scratch her where'er she did itch;
Then to sea, boys, and let her go hang!"

[4] A leathern vessel for liquor. [5] Salted hake. [6] Small Dutch coin.
[7] Long cloak. [8] Cleaner of the decks.

This is a scurvy tune too; but here's my comfort. *Drinks.*

Cal. Do not torment me! Oh!

Ste. What's the matter? Have we devils here? Do you put tricks upon 's with savages and men of Ind, ha? I have not scap'd drowning to be afeard now of your four legs; for it hath been said, "As proper[9] a man as ever went on four legs[10] cannot make him give ground"; and it shall be said so again while Stephano breathes at nostrils.

Cal. The spirit torments me! Oh!

Ste. This is some monster of the isle with four legs, who hath got, as I take it, an ague. Where the devil should he learn our language? I will give him some relief, if it be but for that. If I can recover him and keep him tame and get to Naples with him, he's a present for any emperor that ever trod on neat's leather.[11]

Cal. Do not torment me, prithee; I'll bring my wood home faster.

Ste. He's in his fit now and does not talk after the wisest. He shall taste of my bottle; if he have never drunk wine afore, it will go near to remove his fit. If I can recover him and keep him tame, I will not take too much for him; he shall pay for him that hath him, and that soundly.

Cal. Thou dost me yet but little hurt; thou wilt anon, I know it by thy trembling. Now Prosper works upon thee.

Ste. Come on your ways. Open your mouth; here is that which will give language to you, cat. Open your mouth; this will shake your shaking, I can tell you, and that soundly. You cannot tell who's your friend. Open your chaps again.

Trin. I should know that voice; it should be—but he is drown'd; and these are devils. O defend me!

Ste. Four legs and two voices; a most delicate monster! His forward voice now is to speak well of his friend; his backward voice is to utter foul speeches and to detract. If all the wine in my bottle will recover him, I will help his ague. Come. Amen! I will pour some in thy other mouth.

Trin. Stephano!

Ste. Doth thy other mouth call me? Mercy, mercy! This is a devil, and no monster. I will leave him; I have no long spoon.

[9] Fine. [10] *I. e.,* on crutches. [11] Cow-hide.

Trin. Stephano! If thou beest Stephano, touch me and speak to me; for I am Trinculo,—be not afeard—thy good friend Trinculo.

Ste. If thou beest Trinculo, come forth. I'll pull thee by the lesser legs. If any be Trinculo's legs, these are they. Thou art very Trinculo indeed! How cam'st thou to be the siege[12] of this moon-calf? Can he vent Trinculos?

Trin. I took him to be kill'd with a thunderstroke. But art thou not drown'd, Stephano? I hope now thou art not drown'd. Is the storm over-blown? I hid me under the dead moon-calf's[13] gaberdine for fear of the storm. And art thou living, Stephano? O Stephano, two Neapolitans scap'd!

Ste. Prithee, do not turn me about; my stomach is not constant.

Cal. [*Aside.*] These be fine things, and if they be not sprites.
That's a brave god and bears celestial liquor.
I will kneel to him.

Ste. How didst thou scape? How cam'st thou hither? Swear by this bottle how thou cam'st hither,—I escap'd upon a butt of sack which the sailors heaved o'erboard—by this bottle, which I made of the bark of a tree with mine own hands since I was cast ashore.

Cal. I'll swear upon that bottle to be thy true subject; for the liquor is not earthly.

Ste. Here; swear then how thou escap'dst.

Trin. Swam ashore, man, like a duck. I can swim like a duck, I'll be sworn.

Ste. Here, kiss the book. Though thou canst swim like a duck, thou art made like a goose.

Trin. O Stephano, hast any more of this?

Ste. The whole butt, man. My cellar is in a rock by the seaside where my wine is hid. How now, moon-calf! how does thine ague?

Cal. Hast thou not dropp'd from heaven?

Ste. Out o' the moon, I do assure thee. I was the man i' the moon when time was.

Cal. I have seen thee in her and I do adore thee.
My mistress show'd me thee and thy dog and thy bush.

Ste. Come, swear to that; kiss the book. I will furnish it anon with new contents. Swear.

[12] Stool. [13] Monstrosity.

Trin. By this good light, this is a very shallow monster! I afeard of him! A very weak monster! The man i' the moon! A most poor credulous monster! Well drawn,[14] monster, in good sooth!

Cal. I'll show thee every fertile inch o' the island;
And I will kiss thy foot. I prithee, be my god.

Trin. By this light, a most perfidious and drunken monster! When 's god's asleep, he'll rob his bottle.

Cal. I'll kiss thy foot. I'll swear myself thy subject.

Ste. Come on then; down, and swear.

Trin. I shall laugh myself to death at this puppy-headed monster. A most scurvy monster! I could find in my heart to beat him—

Ste. Come, kiss.

Trin. But that the poor monster's in drink.
An abominable monster!

Cal. I'll show thee the best springs; I'll pluck thee berries;
I'll fish for thee and get thee wood enough.
A plague upon the tyrant that I serve!
I'll bear him no more sticks, but follow thee,
Thou wondrous man.

Trin. A most ridiculous monster, to make a wonder of a poor drunkard!

Cal. I prithee, let me bring thee where crabs grow;
And I with my long nails will dig thee pig-nuts;
Show thee a jay's nest and instruct thee how
To snare the nimble marmoset.[15] I'll bring thee
To clust'ring filberts and sometimes I'll get thee
Young scamels[16] from the rock. Wilt thou go with me?

Ste. I prithee now, lead the way without any more talking. Trinculo, the King and all our company else being drown'd, we will inherit here. Here! bear my bottle. Fellow Trinculo, we'll fill him by and by again.

Cal.. (*Sings drunkenly.*)
Farewell, master; farewell, farewell!

Trin. A howling monster; a drunken monster!

Cal. No more dams I'll make for fish;
Nor fetch in firing

[14] Drunk. [15] A kind of monkey. [16] Perhaps, seamews.

At requiring;
Nor scrape trenchering, nor wash dish.
'Ban, 'Ban, Cacaliban
Has a new master, get a new man.
Freedom, hey-day! hey-day, freedom! freedom, hey-day, freedom!
Ste. O brave monster! Lead the way. *Exeunt.*

ACT III

SCENE I. [*Before Prospero's cell*]

Enter FERDINAND, *bearing a log*

Fer. There be some sports are painful, and their labour
Delight in them sets off; some kinds of baseness
Are nobly undergone, and most poor matters
Point to rich ends. This my mean task
Would be as heavy to me as odious, but
The mistress which I serve quickens what's dead
And makes my labours pleasures. O, she is
Ten times more gentle than her father's crabbed,
And he's compos'd of harshness. I must remove
Some thousands of these logs and pile them up,
Upon a sore injunction.[1] My sweet mistress
Weeps when she sees me work, and says such baseness
Had never like executor.[2] I forget;
But these sweet thoughts do even refresh my labours,
Most busy least, when I do it.

Enter MIRANDA; *and* PROSPERO [*at a distance, unseen*]

Mir. Alas, now, pray you,
Work not so hard. I would the lightning had
Burnt up those logs that you are enjoin'd to pile!
Pray, set it down and rest you. When this burns,
'Twill weep for having wearied you. My father
Is hard at study; pray now, rest yourself;
He's safe for these three hours.

[1] Pain of severe punishment. [2] Performer.

Fer. O most dear mistress,
The sun will set before I shall discharge
What I must strive to do.
Mir. If you'll sit down,
I'll bear your logs the while. Pray, give me that;
I'll carry it to the pile.
Fer. No, precious creature;
I had rather crack my sinews, break my back,
Than you should such dishonour undergo,
While I sit lazy by.
Mir. It would become me
As well as it does you; and I should do it
With much more ease, for my good will is to it,
And yours it is against.
Pros. Poor worm, thou art infected![3]
This visitation[4] shows it.
Mir. You look wearily.
Fer. No, noble mistress; 'tis fresh morning with me
When you are by at night. I do beseech you—
Chiefly that I might set it in my prayers—
What is your name?
Mir. Miranda.—O my father,
I have broke your hest to say so!
Fer. Admir'd Miranda!
Indeed the top of admiration! worth
What's dearest to the world! Full many a lady
I have ey'd with best regard, and many a time
The harmony of their tongues hath into bondage
Brought my too diligent ear; for several virtues
Have I lik'd several women, never any
With so full soul, but some defect in her
Did quarrel with the noblest grace she ow'd[5]
And put it to the foil;[6] but you, O you,
So perfect and so peerless, are created
Of every creature's best!

[3] Smitten (with love). [4] Visit.
[5] Owned. [6] Marred it.

Mir. I do not know
One of my sex; no woman's face remember,
Save, from my glass, mine own; nor have I seen
More that I may call men than you, good friend,
And my dear father. How features are abroad,
I am skilless[7] of; but, by my modesty,
The jewel in my dower, I would not wish
Any companion in the world but you,
Nor can imagination form a shape,
Besides yourself, to like of. But I prattle
Something too wildly, and my father's precepts
I therein do forget.
Fer. I am in my condition
A prince, Miranda; I do think, a king;
I would, not so!—and would no more endure
This wooden[8] slavery than to suffer
The flesh-fly blow my mouth. Hear my soul speak.
The very instant that I saw you, did
My heart fly to your service; there resides,
To make me slave to it; and for your sake
Am I this patient log-man.
Mir. Do you love me?
Fer. O heaven, O earth, bear witness to this sound,
And crown what I profess with kind event
If I speak true! if hollowly, invert
What best is boded me to mischief! I
Beyond all limit of what else i' the world
Do love, prize, honour you.
Mir. I am a fool
To weep at what I am glad of.
Pros. Fair encounter
Of two most rare affections! Heavens rain grace
On that which breeds between 'em!
Fer. Wherefore weep you?
Mir. At mine unworthiness, that dare not offer
What I desire to give, and much less take

[7] Ignorant. [8] Of carrying wood.

What I shall die to want. But this is trifling;
And all the more it seeks to hide itself,
The bigger bulk it shows. Hence, bashful cunning!
And prompt me, plain and holy innocence!
I am your wife, if you will marry me;
If not, I'll die your maid. To be your fellow
You may deny me; but I'll be your servant,
Whether you will or no.
Fer. My mistress, dearest;
And I thus humble ever.
Mir. My husband, then?
Fer. Ay, with a heart as willing
As bondage e'er of freedom. Here's my hand.
Mir. And mine, with my heart in 't. And now farewell
Till half an hour hence.
Fer. A thousand thousand!

Exeunt [FER. *and* MIR. *severally*].

Pros. So glad of this as they I cannot be,
Who are surpris'd withal; but my rejoicing
At nothing can be more. I'll to my book,
For yet ere supper-time must I perform
Much business appertaining. *Exit.*

SCENE II. [*Another part of the island*]

Enter CALIBAN, STEPHANO, *and* TRINCULO

Ste. Tell not me. When the butt is out, we will drink water; not a drop before; therefore bear up, and board[1] 'em. Servant-monster, drink to me.

Trin. Servant-monster! the folly of this island! They say there's but five upon this isle: we are three of them; if the other two be brain'd like us, the state totters.

Ste. Drink, servant-monster, when I bid thee. Thy eyes are almost set in thy head.

Trin. Where should they be set else? He were a brave monster indeed, if they were set in his tail.

[1] Attack (the bottle). The figure is from naval warfare.

Ste. My man-monster hath drown'd his tongue in sack. For my part, the sea cannot drown me; I swam, ere I could recover the shore, five and thirty leagues off and on. By this light, thou shalt be my lieutenant, monster, or my standard.[2]

Trin. Your lieutenant, if you list; he's no standard.

Ste. We'll not run, Monsieur Monster.

Trin. Nor go neither; but you'll lie like dogs and yet say nothing neither.

Ste. Moon-calf, speak once in thy life, if thou beest a good moon-calf.

Cal. How does thy honour? Let me lick thy shoe.
I'll not serve him; he's not valiant.

Trin. Thou liest, most ignorant monster! I am in case to justle a constable. Why, thou debosh'd[3] fish, thou, was there ever man a coward that hath drunk so much sack as I to-day? Wilt thou tell a monstrous lie, being but half a fish and half a monster?

Cal. Lo, how he mocks me! Wilt thou let him, my lord?

Trin. "Lord" quoth he! That a monster should be such a natural!

Cal. Lo, lo, again! Bite him to death, I prithee.

Ste. Trinculo, keep a good tongue in your head. If you prove a mutineer,—the next tree! The poor monster's my subject and he shall not suffer indignity.

Cal. I thank my noble lord. Wilt thou be pleas'd to hearken once again to the suit I made to thee?

Ste. Marry, will I; kneel and repeat it. I will stand, and so shall Trinculo.

Enter ARIEL, *invisible*

Cal. As I told thee before, I am subject to a tyrant a sorcerer, that by his cunning hath cheated me of the island.

Ari. Thou liest.

Cal. Thou liest, thou jesting monkey, thou. I would my valiant master would destroy thee! I do not lie.

Ste. Trinculo, if you trouble him any more in 's tale, by this hand, I will supplant some of your teeth.

[2] Standard-bearer. [3] Debauched.

Trin. Why, I said nothing.
Ste. Mum, then, and no more. Proceed.
Cal. I say, by sorcery he got this isle;
From me he got it. If thy greatness will
Revenge it on him,—for I know thou dar'st,
But this thing dare not,—
Ste. That's most certain.
Cal. Thou shalt be lord of it and I'll serve thee.

Ste. How now shall this be compass'd? Canst thou bring me to the party?

Cal. Yea, yea, my lord. I'll yield him thee asleep,
Where thou mayst knock a nail into his head.
Ari. Thou liest; thou canst not.
Cal. What a pied ninny's[4] this! Thou scurvy patch![5]
I do beseech thy greatness, give him blows
And take his bottle from him. When that's gone
He shall drink nought but brine; for I'll not show him
Where the quick freshes[6] are.

Ste. Trinculo, run into no further danger. Interrupt the monster one word further, and, by this hand, I'll turn my mercy out o' doors and make a stock-fish[7] of thee.

Trin. Why, what did I? I did nothing. I'll go farther off.
Ste. Didst thou not say he lied?
Ari. Thou liest.
Ste. Do I so? Take thou that. [*Beats* TRIN.]
As you like this, give me the lie another time.

Trin. I did not give the lie. Out o' your wits and hearing too? A pox o' your bottle! this can sack and drinking do. A murrain[8] on your monster, and the devil take your fingers!

Cal. Ha, ha, ha!
Ste. Now, forward with your tale. Prithee, stand farther off.
Cal. Beat him enough. After a little time
I'll beat him too.
Ste. Stand farther. Come, proceed.
Cal. Why, as I told thee, 'tis a custom with him,
I' the afternoon to sleep. There thou mayst brain him,

[4] Motley fool. [5] Fool. [6] Fresh-water streams. [7] Dried cod. [8] Plague.

Having first seiz'd his books, or with a log
Batter his skull, or paunch him[9] with a stake,
Or cut his wezand[10] with thy knife. Remember
First to possess his books; for without them
He's but a sot, as I am, nor hath not
One spirit to command. They all do hate him
As rootedly as I. Burn but his books.
He has brave utensils,—for so he calls them,—
Which, when he has a house, he'll deck withal.
And that most deeply to consider is
The beauty of his daughter. He himself
Calls her a nonpareil. I never saw a woman
But only Sycorax my dam and she;
But she as far surpasseth Sycorax
As greatest does least.

Ste. Is it so brave a lass?

Cal. Ay, lord; she will become thy bed, I warrant,
And bring thee forth brave brood.

Ste. Monster, I will kill this man. His daughter and I will be king and queen,—save our Graces!—and Trinculo and thyself shall be viceroys. Dost thou like the plot, Trinculo?

Trin. Excellent.

Ste. Give me thy hand. I am sorry I beat thee; but, while thou liv'st, keep a good tongue in thy head.

Cal. Within this half hour will he be asleep.
Wilt thou destroy him then?

Ste. Ay, on mine honour.

Ari. This will I tell my master.

Cal. Thou mak'st me merry; I am full of pleasure.
Let us be jocund. Will you troll the catch[11]
You taught me but while-ere?

Ste. At thy request, monster, I will do reason, any reason. Come on, Trinculo, let us sing. *Sings.*

Flout 'em and scout 'em
And scout 'em and flout 'em;
Thought is free.

[9] Rip up his belly. [10] Windpipe. [11] Part-song.

Cal. That's not the tune. ARIEL *plays the tune on a tabor and pipe.*

Ste. What is this same?

Trin. This is the tune of our catch, played by the picture of Nobody.

Ste. If thou beest a man, show thyself in thy likeness. If thou be'st a devil, take 't as thou list.

Trin. O, forgive me my sins!

Ste. He that dies pays all debts. I defy thee. Mercy upon us!

Cal. Art thou afeard?

Ste. No, monster, not I.

Cal. Be not afeard. The isle is full of noises,
Sounds and sweet airs, that give delight and hurt not.
Sometimes a thousand twangling instruments
Will hum about mine ears, and sometime voices
That, if I then had wak'd after long sleep,
Will make me sleep again; and then, in dreaming,
The clouds methought would open and show riches
Ready to drop upon me, that, when I wak'd,
I cried to dream again.

Ste. This will prove a brave kingdom to me, where I shall have my music for nothing.

Cal. When Prospero is destroy'd.

Ste. That shall be by and by. I remember the story.

Trin. The sound is going away. Let's follow it, and after do our work.

Ste. Lead, monster; we'll follow. I would I could see this taborer; he lays it on.

Trin. Wilt come? I'll follow Stephano. *Exeunt.*

SCENE III. [*Another part of the island*]

Enter ALONZO, SEBASTIAN, ANTONIO, GONZALO, ADRIAN, FRANCISCO, *etc.*

Gon. By 'r lakin,[1] I can go no further, sir;
My old bones ache. Here's a maze trod indeed
Through forth-rights and meanders![2] By your patience,
I needs must rest me.

[1] Little lady (the Virgin). [2] Straight and winding paths.

Alon. Old lord, I cannot blame thee,
Who am myself attach'd[3] with weariness
To the dulling of my spirits. Sit down, and rest.
Even here I will put off my hope and keep it
No longer for my flatterer. He is drown'd
Whom thus we stray to find, and the sea mocks
Our frustrate search on land. Well, let him go.

Ant. [*Aside to* SEB.] I am right glad that he's so out of hope.
Do not, for one repulse, forego the purpose
That you resolv'd to effect.

Seb. [*Aside to* ANT.] The next advantage
Will we take throughly.

Ant. [*Aside to* SEB.] Let it be to-night;
For, now they are oppress'd with travel, they
Will not, nor cannot, use such vigilance
As when they are fresh.

Solemn and strange music; and PROSPERO *on the top invisible. Enter several strange shapes, bringing in a banquet; and dance about it with gentle actions of salutation; and, inviting the King, etc., to eat, they depart.*

Seb. [*Aside to* ANT.] I say, to-night. No more.

Alon. What harmony is this? My good friends, hark!

Gon. Marvellous sweet music!

Alon. Give us kind keepers, heavens! What were these?

Seb. A living drollery.[4] Now I will believe
That there are unicorns, that in Arabia
There is one tree, the phœnix' throne, one phœnix
At this hour reigning there.

Ant. I'll believe both;
And what does else want credit, come to me,
And I'll be sworn 'tis true. Travellers ne'er did lie,
Though fools at home condemn 'em.

Gon. If in Naples
I should report this now, would they believe me?
If I should say, I saw such islanders—

[3] Seized. [4] Puppet-show.

For, certes, these are people of the island—
Who, though they are of monstrous shape, yet, note,
Their manners are more gentle, kind, than of
Our human generation you shall find
Many, nay, almost any.

Pros. [*Aside.*] Honest lord,
Thou hast said well; for some of you there present
Are worse than devils.

Alon. I cannot too much muse[5]
Such shapes, such gesture, and such sound, expressing,
Although they want the use of tongue, a kind
Of excellent dumb discourse.

Pros. [*Aside.*] Praise in departing.

Fran. They vanish'd strangely.

Seb. No matter, since
They have left their viands behind, for we have stomachs.
Will 't please you taste of what is here?

Alon. Not I.

Gon. Faith, sir, you need not fear. When we were boys,
Who would believe that there were mountaineers
Dew-lapp'd like bulls,[6] whose throats had hanging at 'em
Wallets of flesh? or that there were such men
Whose heads stood in their breasts? which now we find
Each putter-out of five for one[7] will bring us
Good warrant of.

Alon. I will stand to and feed,
Although my last. No matter, since I feel
The best is past. Brother, my lord the Duke,
Stand to and do as we.

Thunder and lightning. Enter Ariel, *like a harpy; claps his wings upon the table; and, with a quaint device,*[8] *the banquet vanishes.*

Ari. You are three men of sin, whom Destiny,
That hath to instrument[9] this lower world
And what is in 't, the never-surfeited sea

[5] Wonder at. [6] *I. e.*, with the goitre. [7] Traveler who insured himself at the rate of five for one. [8] Ingenious contrivance. [9] In its control.

Hath caus'd to belch up you; and on this island
Where man doth not inhabit; you 'mongst men
Being most unfit to live. I have made you mad;
And even with such-like valour men hang and drown
Their proper selves. [ALON., SEB., *etc., draw their swords.*]
You fools! I and my fellows
Are ministers of Fate. The elements,[10]
Of whom your swords are temper'd,[11] may as well
Wound the loud winds, or with bemock'd-at stabs
Kill the still-closing waters, as diminish
One dowle[12] that's in my plume. My fellow-ministers
Are like invulnerable. If you could hurt,
Your swords are now too massy for your strengths
And will not be uplifted. But remember—
For that's my business to you—that you three
From Milan did supplant good Prospero;
Expos'd unto the sea, which hath requit it,
Him and his innocent child; for which foul deed
The powers, delaying, not forgetting, have
Incens'd the seas and shores, yea, all the creatures,
Against your peace. Thee of thy son, Alonso,
They have bereft; and do pronounce by me
Ling'ring perdition, worse than any death
Can be at once, shall step by step attend
You and your ways; whose wraths to guard you from—
Which here, in this most desolate isle, else falls
Upon your heads—is nothing but heart's sorrow
And a clear life ensuing.

He vanishes in thunder; then, to soft music, enter the shapes again, and dance with mocks and mows, and carrying out the table

Pros. Bravely the figure of this harpy hast thou
Perform'd, my Ariel; a grace it had, devouring.
Of my instruction hast thou nothing bated[13]
In what thou hadst to say; so, with good life[14]

[10] Materials. [11] Composed. [12] Downy feather. [13] Omitted. [14] Lifelikeness.

And observation[15] strange, my meaner ministers
Their several kinds have done. My high charms work,
And these mine enemies are all knit up
In their distractions. They now are in my power;
And in these fits I leave them, while I visit
Young Ferdinand, whom they suppose is drown'd,
And his and mine lov'd darling. [*Exit above.*]

Gon. I' the name of something holy, sir, why stand you
In this strange stare?

Alon. O, it is monstrous, monstrous!
Methought the billows spoke and told me of it;
The winds did sing it to me, and the thunder,
That deep and dreadful organ-pipe, pronounc'd
The name of Prosper; it did bass[16] my trespass.
Therefore my son i' the ooze is bedded, and
I'll seek him deeper than e'er plummet sounded
And with him there lie mudded. [*Exit.*]

Seb. But one fiend at a time,
I'll fight their legions o'er.

Ant. I'll be thy second.

Exeunt [SEB. *and* ANT.]

Gon. All three of them are desperate: their great guilt,
Like poison given to work a great time after,
Now gins to bite the spirits. I do beseech you
That are of suppler joints, follow them swiftly
And hinder them from what this ecstasy[17]
May now provoke them to.

Adr. Follow, I pray you. *Exeunt.*

ACT IV

SCENE I. [*Before Prospero's cell*]

Enter PROSPERO, FERDINAND, *and* MIRANDA

Pros. If I have too austerely punish'd you,
Your compensation makes amends, for I

[15] Attention. [16] Pronounce in deep tones. [17] Excitement.

Have given you here a third of mine own life,
Or that for which I live; who once again
I tender[1] to thy hand. All thy vexations
Were but my trials of thy love, and thou
Hast strangely stood the test. Here, afore Heaven,
I ratify this my rich gift. O Ferdinand,
Do not smile at me that I boast her off,
For thou shalt find she will outstrip all praise
And make it halt behind her.

Fer. I do believe it
Against an oracle.

Pros. Then, as my gift and thine own acquisition
Worthily purchas'd, take my daughter. But
If thou dost break her virgin-knot before
All sanctimonious ceremonies may
With full and holy rite be minist'red,
No sweet aspersion[2] shall the heavens let fall
To make this contract grow; but barren Hate,
Sour-eyed Disdain and Discord shall bestrew
The union of your bed with weeds so loathly
That you shall hate it both. Therefore take heed,
As Hymen's lamps shall light you.

Fer. As I hope
For quiet days, fair issue, and long life,
With such love as 'tis now, the murkiest den,
The most opportune place, the strong'st suggestion[3]
Our worser genius can, shall never melt
Mine honour into lust, to take away
The edge of that day's celebration
When I shall think or Phœbus' steeds are founder'd
Or Night kept chain'd below.

Pros. Fairly spoke.
Sit then and talk with her; she is thine own.
What, Ariel! my industrious servant, Ariel!

[1] Offer. [2] Sprinkling. [3] Temptation.

Enter Ariel

Ari. What would my potent master? Here I am.
Pros. Thou and thy meaner fellows your last service
Did worthily perform; and I must use you
In such another trick. Go bring the rabble,
O'er whom I give thee power, here to this place.
Incite them to quick motion; for I must
Bestow upon the eyes of this young couple
Some vanity of mine art. It is my promise,
And they expect it from me.
Ari. Presently?
Pros. Ay, with a twink.
Ari. Before you can say "come" and "go,"
And breathe twice and cry "so, so,"
Each one, tripping on his toe,
Will be here with mop[4] and mow.
Do you love me, master? No?
Pros. Dearly, my delicate Ariel. Do not approach
Till thou dost hear me call.
Ari. Well, I conceive.[5] *Exit.*
Pros. Look thou be true; do not give dalliance
Too much the rein. The strongest oaths are straw
To the fire i' the blood. Be more abstemious,
Or else, good night your vow!
Fer. I warrant you, sir;
The white cold virgin snow upon my heart
Abates the ardour of my liver.[6]
Pros. Well.
Now come, my Ariel! bring a corollary,[7]
Rather than want a spirit. Appear, and pertly!
No tongue! all eyes! Be silent. *Soft music.*

Enter Iris

Iris. Ceres, most bounteous lady, thy rich leas
Of wheat, rye, barley, vetches, oats, and pease;

[4] Grimace. [5] Understand. [6] Supposed to be the seat of passion. [7] Overplus.

Thy turfy mountains, where live nibbling sheep,
And flat meads thatch'd with stover,[8] them to keep;
Thy banks with pioned[9] and twilled[10] brims,
Which spongy April at thy hest betrims
To make cold nymphs chaste crowns; and thy brown groves,
Whose shadow the dismissed bachelor loves,
Being lass-lorn; thy pole-clipp'd[11] vineyard;
And thy sea-marge, sterile and rocky-hard,
Where thou thyself dost air;—the queen o' the sky,
Whose watery arch and messenger am I,
Bids thee leave these, and with her sovereign grace,

JUNO *descends.*

Here on this grass-plot, in this very place,
To come and sport; here peacocks fly amain.
Approach, rich Ceres, her to entertain.

Enter CERES

Cer. Hail, many-coloured messenger, that ne'er
Dost disobey the wife of Jupiter;
Who with thy saffron wings upon my flowers
Diffusest honey-drops, refreshing showers,
And with each end of thy blue bow dost crown
My bosky[12] acres and my unshrubb'd down,
Rich scarf to my proud earth; why hath thy queen
Summon'd me hither, to this short-grass'd green?
Iris. A contract of true love to celebrate;
And some donation freely to estate[13]
On the blest lovers.
Cer. Tell me, heavenly bow,
If Venus or her son, as thou dost know,
Do now attend the Queen? Since they did plot
The means that dusky Dis my daughter got,
Her and her blind boy's scandal'd[14] company
I have forsworn.

[8] Hay. [9] Overgrown with peony (?). [10] Reedy (?).
[11] The poles embraced by the vines.
[12] Covered with bushes. [13] Bestow. [14] Scandalous.

Iris. Of her society
Be not afraid. I met her deity
Cutting the clouds towards Paphos, and her son
Dove-drawn with her. Here thought they to have done
Some wanton charm upon this man and maid,
Whose vows are, that no bed-right shall be paid
Till Hymen's torch be lighted; but in vain.
Mars's hot minion[15] is return'd again;
Her waspish-headed son has broke his arrows,
Swears he will shoot no more, but play with sparrows
And be a boy right out.
Cer. Highest queen of state,
Great Juno, comes; I know her by her gait.

[*Enter* JUNO]

Juno. How does my bounteous sister? Go with me
To bless this twain, that they may prosperous be
And honour'd in their issue. *They sing.*
Juno. Honour, riches, marriage-blessing,
Long continuance, and increasing,
Hourly joys be still upon you!
Juno sings her blessings on you.
[*Cer.*] Earth's increase, foison[16] plenty,
Barns and garners never empty,
Vines with clustering bunches growing,
Plants with goodly burden bowing.
Spring come to you at the farthest
In the very end of harvest!
Scarcity and want shall shun you;
Ceres' blessing so is on you.
Fer. This is a most majestic vision, and
Harmonious charmingly. May I be bold
To think these spirits?
Pros. Spirits, which by mine art
I have from their confines call'd to enact
My present fancies.

[15] *I. e.,* Venus. [16] Abundance.

Fer. Let me live here ever;
So rare a wond'red[17] father and a wise
Makes this place Paradise.

Pros. Sweet, now, silence!
Juno and Ceres whisper seriously.
There's something else to do; hush, and be mute,
Or else our spell is marr'd.

JUNO *and* CERES *whisper, and send* IRIS *on employment.*

Iris. You nymphs, call'd Naiads, of the winding brooks,
With your sedg'd crowns and ever-harmless looks,
Leave your crisp channels, and on this green land
Answer your summons; Juno does command.
Come, temperate nymphs, and help to celebrate
A contract of true love; be not too late.

Enter certain Nymphs

You sunburnt sicklemen, of August weary,
Come hither from the furrow and be merry.
Make holiday; your rye-straw hats put on
And these fresh nymphs encounter every one
In country footing.

Enter certain Reapers, *properly habited: they join with the Nymphs in a graceful dance; towards the end whereof* PROSPERO *starts suddenly, and speaks; after which, to a strange, hollow, and confused noise, they heavily vanish*

Pros. [*Aside.*] I had forgot that foul conspiracy
Of the beast Caliban and his confederates
Against my life. The minute of their plot
Is almost come. [*To the* Spirits.] Well done! avoid. No more!

Fer. This is strange. Your father's in some passion[18]
That works him strongly.

Mir. Never till this day
Saw I him touch'd with anger, so distemper'd.[19]

Pros. You do look, my son, in a mov'd sort,
As if you were dismay'd. Be cheerful, sir,

[17] Wonder-working. [18] Emotion. [19] Perturbed.

Our revels now are ended. These our actors,
As I foretold you, were all spirits, and
Are melted into air, into thin air;
And, like the baseless fabric of this vision,
The cloud-capp'd towers, the gorgeous palaces,
The solemn temples, the great globe itself,
Yea, all which it inherit, shall dissolve
And, like this insubstantial pageant faded,
Leave not a rack[20] behind. We are such stuff
As dreams are made on, and our little life
Is rounded with a sleep. Sir, I am vex'd,—
Bear with my weakness—my old brain is troubled.
Be not disturb'd with my infirmity.
If you be pleas'd, retire into my cell
And there repose. A turn or two I'll walk,
To still my beating mind.

Fer. Mir. We wish your peace. *Exeunt.*

Pros. Come with a thought. I thank thee, Ariel; come.

Enter ARIEL

Ari. Thy thoughts I cleave to. What's thy pleasure?

Pros. Spirit,
We must prepare to meet with Caliban.

Ari. Ay, my commander. When I presented Ceres,
I thought to have told thee of it, but I fear'd
Lest I might anger thee.

Pros. Say again, where didst thou leave these varlets?

Ari. I told you, sir, they were red-hot with drinking;
So full of valour that they smote the air
For breathing in their faces; beat the ground
For kissing of their feet; yet always bending
Towards their project. Then I beat my tabor;
At which, like unback'd colts, they prick'd their ears,
Advanc'd their eyelids, lifted up their noses
As they smelt music. So I charm'd their ears
That calf-like they my lowing follow'd through

[20] Shred of cloud.

Tooth'd briers, sharp furzes, pricking gorse, and thorns,
Which ent'red their frail shins. At last I left them
I' the filthy-mantled pool beyond your cell,
There dancing up to the chins, that the foul lake
O'erstunk their feet.

Pros. This was well done, my bird.
Thy shape invisible retain thou still.
The trumpery in my house, go bring it hither,
For stale[21] to catch these thieves.

Ari. I go, I go. *Exit.*

Pros. A devil, a born devil, on whose nature
Nurture can never stick; on whom my pains,
Humanely taken, all, all lost, quite lost;
And as with age his body uglier grows,
So his mind cankers. I will plague them all,
Even to roaring.

Re-enter ARIEL, *loaden with glittering apparel, etc.*

Come, hang them on this line.[22]

[PROSPERO *and* ARIEL *remain, invisible.*] *Enter* CALIBAN, STEPHANO, *and* TRINCULO, *all wet*

Cal. Pray you, tread softly, that the blind mole may not
Hear a foot fall; we now are near his cell.

Ste. Monster, your fairy, which you say is a harmless fairy, has done little better than play'd the Jack[23] with us.

Trin. Monster, I do smell all horse-piss, at which my nose is in great indignation.

Ste. So is mine. Do you hear, monster? If I should take a displeasure against you, look you,—

Trin. Thou wert but a lost monster.

Cal. Good my lord, give me thy favour still.
Be patient, for the prize I'll bring thee to
Shall hoodwink[24] this mischance; therefore speak softly.
All's hush'd as midnight yet.

Trin. Ay, but to lose our bottles in the pool,—

[21] Lure. [22] Probably, lime-tree. [23] Knave. [24] Make you forget.

Ste. There is not only disgrace and dishonour in that, monster, but an infinite loss.

Trin. That's more to me than my wetting; yet this is your harmless fairy, monster!

Ste. I will fetch off my bottle, though I be o'er ears for my labour.

Cal. Prithee, my king, be quiet. See'st thou here,
This is the mouth o' the cell. No noise, and enter.
Do that good mischief which may make this island
Thine own for ever, and I, thy Caliban,
For aye thy foot-licker.

Ste. Give me thy hand. I do begin to have bloody thoughts.

Trin. O King Stephano! O peer! O worthy Stephano! look what a wardrobe here is for thee!

Cal. Let it alone, thou fool; it is but trash.

Trin. O, ho, monster! we know what belongs to a frippery.[25] O King Stephano!

Ste. Put off that gown, Trinculo; by this hand, I'll have that gown.

Trin. Thy grace shall have it.

Cal. The dropsy drown this fool! what do you mean
To dote thus on such luggage? Let's alone
And do the murder first. If he awake,
From toe to crown he'll fill our skins with pinches,
Make us strange stuff.

Ste. Be you quiet, monster. Mistress line, is not this my jerkin? Now is the jerkin under the line.[26] Now, jerkin, you are like to lose your hair and prove a bald jerkin.

Trin. Do, do; we steal by line and level, an 't like your Grace.

Ste. I thank thee for that jest; here's a garment for 't. Wit shall not go unrewarded while I am king of this country. "Steal by line and level" is an excellent pass of pate;[27] there's another garment for 't.

Trin. Monster, come, put some lime upon your fingers, and away with the rest.

Cal. I will have none on 't. We shall lose our time,
And all be turn'd to barnacles, or to apes
With foreheads villainous low.

[25] Old-clothes shop. [26] Punning on line = lime-tree, and line = equinoctial line.
[27] Sally to wit.

Ste. Monster, lay-to your fingers. Help to bear this away where my hogshead of wine is, or I'll turn you out of my kingdom. Go to, carry this.

Trin. And this.

Ste. Ay, and this.

A noise of hunters heard. Enter divers Spirits, *in shape of dogs and hounds, hunting them about,* Prospero *and* Ariel *setting them on*

Pros. Hey, Mountain, hey!
Ari. Silver! there it goes, Silver!
Pros. Fury, Fury! there, Tyrant, there! hark! hark!
[Cal., Ste., *and* Trin. *are driven out.*]
Go charge my goblins that they grind their joints
With dry convulsions, shorten up their sinews
With aged cramps, and more pinch-spotted make them
Than pard or cat o' mountain.[28]
Ari. Hark, they roar!
Pros. Let them be hunted soundly. At this hour
Lies at my mercy all mine enemies.
Shortly shall all my labours end, and thou
Shalt have the air of freedom. For a little
Follow, and do me service. *Exeunt.*

[ACT V]

Scene I. [*Before Prospero's cell*]

Enter Prospero *in his magic robes, and* Ariel

Pros. Now does my project gather to a head.
My charms crack[1] not; my spirits obey; and Time
Goes upright with his carriage.[2] How's the day?
Ari. On the sixth hour; at which time, my lord,
You said our work should cease.
Pros. I did say so,
When first I rais'd the tempest. Say, my spirit,
How fares the King and 's followers?

[28] Wild-cat. [1] Fail. [2] Burden.

Ari. Confin'd together
In the same fashion as you gave in charge,
Just as you left them; all prisoners, sir,
In the line-grove which weather-fends[3] your cell;
They cannot budge till your release. The King,
His brother, and yours, abide all three distracted,
And the remainder mourning over them,
Brimful of sorrow and dismay; but chiefly
Him that you term'd, sir, "The good old lord, Gonzalo,"
His tears run down his beard, like winter's drops
From eaves of reeds. Your charm so strongly works 'em
That if you now beheld them, your affections
Would become tender.

Pros. Dost thou think so, spirit?

Ari. Mine would, sir, were I human.

Pros. And mine shall.
Hast thou, which art but air, a touch, a feeling
Of their afflictions, and shall not myself,
One of their kind, that relish all as sharply
Passion[4] as they, be kindlier mov'd than thou art?
Though with their high wrongs I am struck to the quick.
Yet with my nobler reason 'gainst my fury
Do I take part. The rarer action is
In virtue than in vengeance. They being penitent,
The sole drift of my purpose doth extend
Not a frown further. Go release them, Ariel.
My charms I'll break, their senses I'll restore,
And they shall be themselves.

Ari. I'll fetch them, sir. *Exit.*

Pros. Ye elves of hills, brooks, standing lakes, and groves,
And ye that on the sands with printless foot
Do chase the ebbing Neptune, and do fly him
When he comes back; you demi-puppets[5] that
By moonshine do the green sour ringlets make,
Whereof the ewe not bites; and you whose pastime
Is to make midnight mushrooms, that rejoice

[3] Protects from the weather. [4] Feel emotion as keenly.
[5] Beings half as big as puppets.

To hear the solemn curfew; by whose aid,
Weak masters though ye be, I have bedimm'd
The noontide sun, call'd forth the mutinous winds
And 'twixt the green sea and the azur'd vault
Set roaring war; to the dread rattling thunder
Have I given fire, and rifted Jove's stout oak
With his own bolt; the strong-bas'd promontory
Have I made shake, and by the spurs pluck'd up
The pine and cedar; graves at my command
Have wak'd their sleepers, op'd, and let 'em forth
By my so potent art. But this rough magic
I here abjure, and, when I have requir'd
Some heavenly music, which even now I do,
To work mine end upon their senses that
This airy charm is for, I'll break my staff,
Bury it certain fathoms in the earth,
And deeper than did ever plummet sound
I'll drown my book. *Solemn music.*

Here enters Ariel *before: then* Alonzo, *with a frantic gesture, attended by* Gonzalo; Sebastian *and* Antonio *in like manner, attended by* Adrian *and* Francisco. *They all enter the circle which* Prospero *had made, and there stand charmed; which* Prospero *observing, speaks*

A solemn air and the best comforter
To an unsettled fancy cure thy brains,
Now useless, boil'd within thy skull! There stand,
For you are spell-stopp'd.
Holy Gonzalo, honourable man,
Mine eyes, even sociable[6] to the shew of thine,
Fall fellowly drops. The charm dissolves apace,
And as the morning steals upon the night,
Melting the darkness, so their rising senses
Begin to chase the ignorant fumes that mantle
Their clearer reason. O good Gonzalo,
My true preserver, and a loyal sir
To him thou follow'st! I will pay thy graces

[6] Sympathetic.

Home[7] both in word and deed. Most cruelly
Didst thou, Alonso, use me and my daughter.
Thy brother was a furtherer in the act.
Thou art pinch'd for 't now, Sebastian. Flesh and blood,
You, brother mine, that entertain'd ambition,
Expell'd remorse and nature,[8] whom, with Sebastian,
Whose inward pinches therefore are most strong,
Would here have kill'd your king, I do forgive thee,
Unnatural though thou art. Their understanding
Begins to swell, and the approaching tide
Will shortly fill the reasonable shore[9]
That now lies foul and muddy. Not one of them
That yet looks on me, or would know me! Ariel,
Fetch me the hat and rapier in my cell;
I will discase[10] me, and myself present
As I was sometime Milan. Quickly, spirit;
Thou shalt ere long be free.

ARIEL *sings and helps to attire him*

Ari. "Where the bee sucks, there suck I.
In a cowslip's bell I lie;
There I couch when owls do cry.
On the bat's back I do fly
After summer merrily.
Merrily, merrily shall I live now
Under the blossom that hangs on the bough."

Pros. Why, that's my dainty Ariel! I shall miss thee;
But yet thou shalt have freedom. So, so, so.
To the King's ship, invisible as thou art;
There shalt thou find the mariners asleep
Under the hatches. The master and the boatswain
Being awake, enforce them to this place,
And presently, I prithee.
Ari. I drink the air before me, and return
Or ere your pulse twice beat. *Exit.*
Gon. All torment, trouble, wonder, and amazement

[7] Utterly. [8] Natural pity. [9] Shore of reason. [10] Take off my magician's robes.

Inhabits here. Some heavenly power guide us
Out of this fearful country!
Pros. Behold, sir King,
The wronged Duke of Milan, Prospero.
For more assurance that a living prince
Does now speak to thee, I embrace thy body;
And to thee and thy company I bid
A hearty welcome.
Alon. Whe'er thou be'st he or no,
Or some enchanted trifle to abuse[11] me,
As late I have been, I not know. Thy pulse
Beats as of flesh and blood; and, since I saw thee,
The affliction of my mind amends, with which
I fear, a madness held me. This must crave,
An if this be at all, a most strange story,
Thy dukedom I resign and do entreat
Thou pardon me my wrongs. But how should Prospero
Be living and be here?
Pros. First, noble friend,
Let me embrace thine age, whose honour cannot
Be measur'd or confin'd.
Gon. Whether this be
Or be not, I'll not swear.
Pros. You do yet taste
Some subtleties o' the isle, that will not let you
Believe things certain. Welcome, my friends all!
[*Aside to* SEB. *and* ANT.] But you, my brace of lords, were I so minded,
I here could pluck his Highness' frown upon you
And justify you traitors. At this time
I will tell no tales.
Seb. [*Aside.*] The devil speaks in him.
Pros. No.
For you, most wicked sir, whom to call brother
Would even infect my mouth, I do forgive
Thy rankest fault; all of them; and require

[11] Deceive.

My dukedom of thee, which perforce, I know,
Thou must restore.

Alon. If thou be'st Prospero,
Give us particulars of thy preservation,
How thou hast met us here, whom three hours since
Were wreck'd upon this shore, where I have lost —
How sharp the point of this remembrance is!—
My dear son Ferdinand.

Pros. I am woe for 't, sir.

Alon. Irreparable is the loss, and Patience
Says it is past her cure.

Pros. I rather think
You have not sought her help, of whose soft grace
For the like loss I have her sovereign aid
And rest myself content.

Alon. You the like loss!

Pros. As great to me as late; and, supportable
To make the dear loss, have I means much weaker
Than you may call to comfort you, for I
Have lost my daughter.

Alon. A daughter?
O heavens, that they were living both in Naples,
The King and Queen there! That they were, I wish
Myself were mudded in that oozy bed
Where my son lies. When did you lose your daughter?

Pros. In this last tempest. I perceive, these lords
At this encounter do so much admire[12]
That they devour their reason and scarce think
Their eyes do offices of truth, their words
Are natural breath; but, howsoe'er you have
Been justled from your senses, know for certain
That I am Prospero and that very duke
Which was thrust forth of Milan, who most strangely
Upon this shore, where you were wreck'd, was landed,
To be the lord on 't. No more yet of this;
For 'tis a chronicle of day by day,

[12] Wonder.

Not a relation for a breakfast nor
Befitting this first meeting. Welcome, sir;
This cell's my court. Here have I few attendants,
And subjects none abroad. Pray you, look in.
My dukedom since you have given me again,
I will requite you with as good a thing;
At least bring forth a wonder, to content ye
As much as me my dukedom.

Here PROSPERO *discovers* FERDINAND *and* MIRANDA *playing at chess*

Mir. Sweet lord, you play me false.
Fer. No, my dearest love,
I would not for the world.
Mir. Yes, for a score of kingdoms you should wrangle,
And I would call it fair play.
Alon. If this prove
A vision of the island, one dear son
Shall I twice lose.
Seb. A most high miracle!
Fer. Though the seas threaten, they are merciful;
I have curs'd them without cause. [*Kneels.*]
Alon. Now all the blessings
Of a glad father compass thee about!
Arise, and say how thou cam'st here.
Mir. O, wonder!
How many goodly creatures are there here!
How beauteous mankind is! O brave new world,
That has such people in 't!
Pros. 'Tis new to thee.
Alon. What is this maid with whom thou wast at play?
Your eld'st acquaintance cannot be three hours.
Is she the goddess that hath sever'd us,
And brought us thus together?
Fer. Sir, she is mortal,
But by immortal Providence she's mine.
I chose her when I could not ask my father
For his advice, nor thought I had one. She

Is daughter to this famous Duke of Milan,
Of whom so often I have heard renown,
But never saw before; of whom I have
Receiv'd a second life; and second father
This lady makes him to me.

Alon. I am hers,
But, O, how oddly will it sound that I
Must ask my child forgiveness!

Pros. There, sir, stop.
Let us not burden our remembrances with
A heaviness that's gone.

Gon. I have inly wept,
Or should have spoke ere this. Look down, you gods,
And on this couple drop a blessed crown!
For it is you that have chalk'd forth the way
Which brought us hither.

Alon. I say, Amen, Gonzalo!

Gon. Was Milan thrust from Milan, that his issue
Should become Kings of Naples? O, rejoice
Beyond a common joy, and set it down
With gold on lasting pillars: in one voyage
Did Claribel her husband find a Tunis,
And Ferdinand, her brother, found a wife
Where he himself was lost, Prospero his dukedom
In a poor isle, and all of us ourselves
When no man was his own.

Alon. [*To* Fer. *and* Mir.] Give me your hands.
Let grief and sorrow still embrace his heart
That doth not wish you joy!

Gon. Be it so! Amen!

Re-enter Ariel, *with the* Master *and* Boatswain *amazedly following*

O, look, sir, look, sir! here is more of us.
I prophesi'd, if a gallows were on land,
This fellow could not drown. Now, blasphemy,
That swear'st grace o'erboard, not an oath on shore?
Hast thou no mouth by land? What is the news?

Boats. The best news is, that we have safely found
Our king and company; the next, our ship—
Which, but three glasses[13] since, we gave out split—
Is tight and yare[14] and bravely rigg'd as when
We first put out to sea.

Ari. [*Aside to* PROS.] Sir, all this service
Have I done since I went.

Pros. [*Aside to* ARI.] My tricksy spirit!

Alon. These are not natural events; they strengthen
From strange to stranger. Say, how came you hither?

Boats. If I did think, sir, I were well awake,
I'd strive to tell you. We were dead of sleep,
And—how we know not—all clapp'd under hatches;
Where but even now with strange and several noises
Of roaring, shrieking, howling, jingling chains.
And moe diversity of sounds, all horrible,
We were awak'd; straightway, at liberty;
Where we, in all her trim, freshly beheld
Our royal, good, and gallant ship, our master
Cap'ring to eye[15] her. On a trice, so please you,
Even in a dream, were we divided from them
And were brought moping[16] hither.

Ari. [*Aside to* PROS.] Was 't well done?

Pros. [*Aside to* ARI.] Bravely, my diligence. Thou shalt be free.

Alon. This is as strange a maze as e'er men trod;
And there is in this business more than nature
Was ever conduct of. Some oracle
Must rectify our knowledge.

Pros. Sir, my liege,
Do not infest[17] your mind with beating on
The strangeness of this business. At pick'd leisure,
Which shall be shortly, single[18] I'll resolve you,
Which to you shall seem probable, of every
These happen'd accidents; till when, be cheerful
And think of each thing well. [*Aside to* ARI.] Come hither, spirit.
Set Caliban and his companions free;

[13] Hour-glasses. [14] Ready. [15] See. [16] Dazed. [17] Trouble. [18] Alone.

Untie the spell. [*Exit* ARIEL.] How fares my gracious sir?
There are yet missing of your company
Some few odd lads that you remember not.

Re-enter ARIEL, *driving in* CALIBAN, STEPHANO *and* TRINCULO, *in their stolen apparel*

Ste. Every man shift for all the rest, and let no man take care for himself; for all is but fortune. Coragio, bully-monster, coragio!

Trin. If these be true spies which I wear in my head, here's a goodly sight.

Cal. O Setebos, these be brave spirits indeed!
How fine my master is! I am afraid
He will chastise me.

Seb. Ha, ha!
What things are these, my lord Antonio?
Will money buy 'em?

Ant. Very like; one of them
Is a plain fish, and, no doubt, marketable.

Pros. Mark but the badges[19] of these men, my lords,
Then say if they be true. This mis-shapen knave,
His mother was a witch, and one so strong
That could control the moon, make flows and ebbs,
And deal in her command without[20] her power.
These three have robb'd me; and this demi-devil—
For he's a bastard one—had plotted with them
To take my life. Two of these fellows you
Must know and own; this thing of darkness I
Acknowledge mine.

Cal. I shall be pinch'd to death.

Alon. Is not this Stephano, my drunken butler?

Seb. He is drunk now. Where had he wine?

Alon. And Trinculo is reeling ripe. Where should they
Find this grand liquor that hath gilded[21] 'em?
How cam'st thou in this pickle?

Trin. I have been in such a pickle since I saw you last that, I fear me, will never out of my bones. I shall not fear fly-blowing.

[19] Showing they were Alonso's servants. [20] Beyond. [21] Made drunk.

Seb. Why, how now, Stephano!

Ste. O, touch me not; I am not Stephano, but a cramp.

Pros. You'd be King o' the isle, sirrah?

Ste. I should have been a sore one then.

Alon. This is a strange thing as e'er I look'd on.

Pointing to CALIBAN.

Pros. He is disproportion'd in his manners
As in his shape. Go, sirrah, to my cell;
Take with you your companions. As you look
To have my pardon, trim it handsomely.

Cal. Ay, that I will; and I'll be wise hereafter
And seek for grace. What a thrice-double ass
Was I, to take this drunkard for a god
And worship this dull fool!

Pros. Go to; away!

Alon. Hence, and bestow your luggage where you found it.

Seb. Or stole it, rather. [*Exeunt* CAL., STE., *and* TRIN.]

Pros. Sir, I invite your Highness and your train
To my poor cell, where you shall take your rest
For this one night; which, part of it, I'll waste
With such discourse as, I not doubt, shall make it
Go quick away,—the story of my life
And the particular accidents gone by
Since I came to this isle. An in the morn
I'll bring you to your ship and so to Naples,
Where I have hope to see the nuptial
Of these our dear-belov'd solemnized;
And thence retire me to my Milan, where
Every third thought shall be my grave.

Alon. I long
To hear the story of your life, which must
Take the ear strangely.

Pros. I'll deliver all;
And promise you calm seas, auspicious gales,
And sail so expeditious that shall catch
Your royal fleet far off. [*Aside to* ARI.] My Ariel, chick,

That is thy charge. Then to the elements
Be free, and fare thou well! Please you, draw near.

Exeunt omnes.

EPILOGUE

Spoken by Prospero

Now my charms are all o'erthrown,
And what strength I have's mine own,
Which is most faint. Now, 'tis true,
I must be here confin'd by you,
Or sent to Naples. Let me not,
Since I have my dukedom got
And pardon'd the deceiver, dwell
In this bare island by your spell;
But release me from my bands
With the help of your good hands.
Gentle breath of yours my sails
Must fill, or else my project fails,
Which was to please. Now I want
Spirits to enforce, art to enchant,
And my ending is despair,
Unless I be reliev'd by prayer,
Which pierces so that it assaults
Mercy itself and frees all faults.
As you from crimes would pardon'd be,
Let your indulgence set me free. *Exit.*